CAMBRIDGE

International History, 1870–1939

for Cambridge International AS Level History

COURSEBOOK

John Etty & Patrick Walsh-Atkins

Third edition with Digital access

CAMBRIDGE
UNIVERSITY PRESS & ASSESSMENT

Shaftesbury Road, Cambridge CB2 8EA, United Kingdom

One Liberty Plaza, 20th Floor, New York, NY 10006, USA

477 Williamstown Road, Port Melbourne, VIC 3207, Australia

314–321, 3rd Floor, Plot 3, Splendor Forum, Jasola District Centre, New Delhi – 110025, India

103 Penang Road, #05–06/07, Visioncrest Commercial, Singapore 238467

Cambridge University Press & Assessment is a department of the University of Cambridge.

We share the University's mission to contribute to society through the pursuit of education, learning and research at the highest international levels of excellence.

www.cambridge.org
Information on this title: www.cambridge.org/9781009556323

First published 2013
Second edition 2019
Third edition 2025

20 19 18 17 16 15 14 13 12 11 10 9 8 7 6 5 4 3 2 1

Printed in Poland by Opolgraf

A catalogue record for this publication is available from the British Library

ISBN 978-1-00-955632-3 Paperback with Digital Access
ISBN 978-1-00-955630-9 Digital Coursebook
ISBN 978-1-00-955629-3 Coursebook eBook

Additional resources for this publication at www.cambridge.org/9781009556323

Endorsement statement

Endorsement indicates that a resource has passed Cambridge International Education's rigorous quality-assurance process and is suitable to support the delivery of their syllabus. However, endorsed resources are not the only suitable materials available to support teaching and learning, and are not essential to achieve the qualification. For the full list of endorsed resources to support this syllabus, visit www.cambridgeinternational.org/endorsed-resources

Any example answers to questions taken from past question papers, practice questions, accompanying marks and mark schemes included in this resource have been written by the authors and are for guidance only. They do not replicate examination papers. In examinations the way marks are awarded may be different. Any references to assessment and/or assessment preparation are the publisher's interpretation of the syllabus requirements. Examiners will not use endorsed resources as a source of material for any assessment set by Cambridge International Education.

While the publishers have made every attempt to ensure that advice on the qualification and its assessment is accurate, the official syllabus, specimen assessment materials and any associated assessment guidance materials produced by the awarding body are the only authoritative source of information and should always be referred to for definitive guidance.

Our approach is to provide teachers with access to a wide range of high-quality resources that suit different styles and types of teaching and learning.

For more information about the endorsement process, please visit www.cambridgeinternational.org/endorsed-resources

Third-party websites and resources referred to in this publication are not endorsed.

Contents

How to use this series

This suite of resources supports learners and teachers following the Cambridge International AS Level History syllabuses (9489/9981/9982). The components in the series are designed to work together and help learners develop the necessary knowledge and skills for studying History.

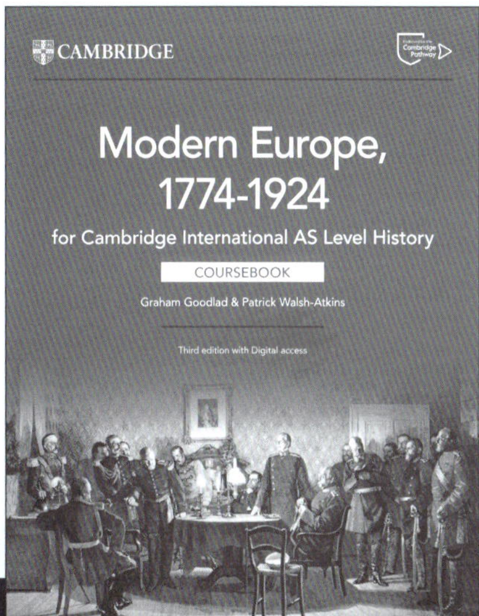

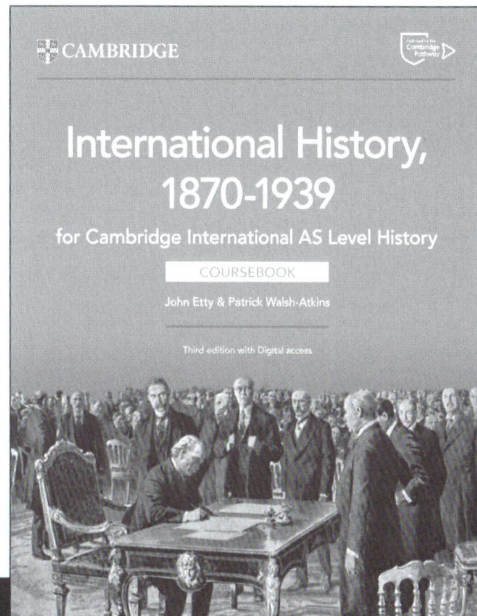

The Coursebooks are designed for learners to use in class with guidance from the teacher. One of the Coursebooks offers coverage of European option: Modern Europe, 1774–1924 and the other offers coverage of International option: International history, 1870–1939 of the Cambridge International AS Level History syllabus. Each chapter contains in-depth explanations, definitions and a variety of activities and questions to engage learners and develop their historical skills.

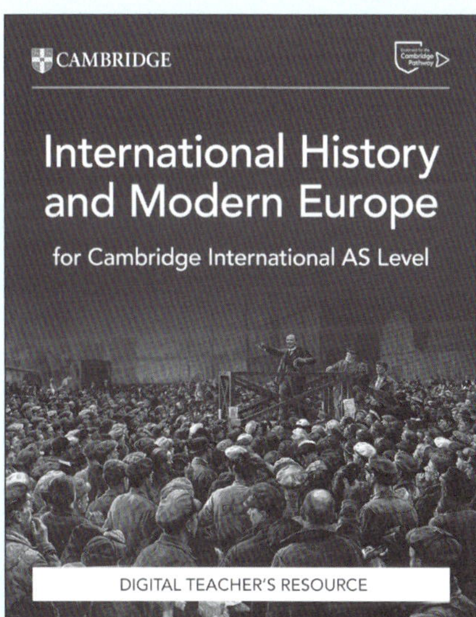

The Teacher's Resource is the foundation of this series. It offers inspiring ideas about how to teach this course including teaching notes, how to avoid common misconceptions, suggestions for differentiation, formative assessment and language support, answers and extra materials such as worksheets and historical sources.

How to use this book

This book contains a number of features to help you in your study.

KEY QUESTIONS

Each chapter begins with Key questions that briefly set out the topics you should understand once you have completed the chapter.

Timeline

The timeline at the start of each chapter provides a visual guide to the key events which happened during the years covered by the topic.

GETTING STARTED

Getting started activities will help you think about what you already know about the topic of the chapter.

ACTIVITY

Activities are a mixture of individual, pair and group tasks to help you develop your skills and practise applying your understanding of a topic. Some activities use sources to help you practise your skills in analysis. Please note, some sources have been abridged or adapted.

KEY CONCEPT

Key concept boxes contain questions that help you develop a conceptual understanding of History, start to make judgements based on your knowledge and understanding, and think about how the different topics you study are connected.

KEY TERM

Key terms are important terms in the topic you are learning. They are highlighted in bold where they first appear in the text, and definitions are given in the Key terms boxes. All of the key terms are included in the glossary at the end of the book.

KEY FIGURE

Key figure boxes highlight important historical figures that you need to remember, and briefly explain what makes them a key figure.

Reflection

Reflection boxes give you the opportunity to think about how you approach certain activities, and how you might improve this in the future.

Practice questions

These questions, written by the authors, help you prepare for assessment by writing longer answers.

Improve this answer

These sample answers to some of the practice questions are accompanied by notes on what works well and how they could be improved. After reading the comments, you are challenged to write a better answer to the question.

The answers and the commentary are written by the authors.

TIP

Tips are included in the Preparing for assessment chapter. These give advice on important things to remember and what to avoid doing when revising.

SELF-EVALUATION CHECKLIST

Each chapter ends with a checklist of the main points covered in that topic, and gives you space to think about how confident you are with these points. Take time to fully reflect on your current level of understanding before you select an option. If you select 'Needs more work' or 'Almost there' for any of the points, revisit the relevant content and make a clear action plan for increasing your confidence in that area. It is worth revisiting the checklists when preparing for assessment.

You should be able to:	Needs more work	Almost there	Ready to move on

Please be aware that this book contains some historical texts and images that may distress the reader. This material reflects the language and attitudes of the period in which they were created, but not does not align with the current values and practices of Cambridge University Press & Assessment. Teacher support is advised.

The maps included in this book are historical and are not intended to represent current border and country agreements. They are provided for educational and illustrative purposes only.

Getting started with Cambridge International AS Level History

Introduction

Congratulations on choosing to study Cambridge International AS Level History – a subject that is highly regarded by universities and employers. AS Level History helps students to understand why the modern world is the way it is and how it has changed over time.

Aside from studying fascinating information about extremely important events that have had an impact on the way many people live today, students of History also get lots of practice at analysing large amounts of information, prioritising and extracting the most relevant information, synthesising and comparing different information, and constructing and assessing arguments. These skills are essential in careers such as law, administration, politics and government, TV research and journalism.

History students spend time enquiring and searching for information, learning where to look and what questions to ask. These skills are essential in careers such as policing, investigative reporting and market research.

Historians communicate their ideas in an organised, structured and logical fashion. History requires extended, logical, reasoned debate in writing. These skills are essential in careers that require writing reports, including academia, the civil service and journalism.

History teaches you to understand individuals and groups – their feelings, attitudes, prejudices and motivations. These skills are essential in careers such as personnel, law, teaching and social work.

AS Level History introduces you to historical skills such as explaining cause and consequence, change and continuity, which are essential in any career that requires analysis and strategy, such as the armed forces, teaching, advertising, medicine, banking and accountancy.

History helps you to develop skills of problem solving and evaluating solutions, information handling, communicating ideas, flexibility and tolerance – skills that are essential in problem solving in industry, and in research and development teams in science and engineering.

While studying AS Level History, you will work independently and participate in discussion, which is essential for developing your own ideas and judgement. Your teacher cannot tell you what to think or what opinions to have, although they can help you learn how to think and how to form opinions. To be successful in this course, you will have to put forward your own views on a subject and explain your reasons for coming to those views.

History is not a series of universally accepted facts which once learned, will provide you with a detailed and accurate understanding of the past. Just as historical events were perceived in many different (and often contradictory) ways by people who experienced them at the time, so they have been interpreted in many different (and often contradictory) ways by historians who have studied them subsequently. Historical debates rage all the time, which makes it very clear that historians often disagree fundamentally about the reasons for, or the significance of, certain key events.

You need to understand, for example, that there is no right answer to why countries expanded the areas under their control and created empires in the 19th and early 20th centuries. Many historians have researched this topic in depth and have come to very different conclusions. You will need to learn to reflect on those conclusions and to reach your own judgement. This process of reflection will also give you an insight into the methods historians use to put across their ideas; you will be able to adapt these methods for your own use when answering historical questions.

You will be asked for your opinion or judgement on an issue like this, and will have to make up your own mind. You need to study the evidence, reflect on what kind of evidence it is and then analyse what it proves. This will allow you to form an opinion. When asked for an opinion or judgement, you will need to back up what you offer with reasons and evidence. In this way, historians are like lawyers in court. You are making a case and then proving it.

Sometimes your fellow learners and teachers might disagree with your opinion and be able to provide compelling evidence to demonstrate why. Sometimes they might convince you to change your mind. Sometimes you will be able to convince them to change or refine their opinions. Sometimes you might just agree to differ. It is this ability to see things in different ways, and to have the confidence to use your own knowledge and understanding to make judgements, form opinions and develop arguments, that makes studying history so interesting and challenging.

The information in this section is based on the Cambridge International Education syllabus. You should always refer to the appropriate syllabus document for the year of examination to confirm the details and for more information. The syllabus document is available on the website: www.cambridgeinternational.org.

How does Cambridge International AS Level History differ from Cambridge IGCSE™ History?

If you have studied Cambridge IGCSE or O Level History, it is likely that you will have encountered some parts of your AS Level topics before, but you will also encounter interesting new topics. The topics you will study are covered in more depth at AS Level than at Cambridge IGCSE and O Level.

When studying Cambridge IGCSE History, students consider how attitudes to events differed, but the differences are often quite obvious. At AS Level, you will continue to investigate how historical events were perceived in many different (and often contradictory) ways by people who experienced them at the time, but you will consider in more depth why these differences arose. Study at AS Level requires you to engage much more carefully with the sometimes subtle differences of opinion, to think really deeply about the different attitudes that underpinned people's positions, and to explain the complex relationships between different ideas that motivated people in the past.

The skills you will develop at AS Level are the same as those required at Cambridge IGCSE History. You will need to recall, select and use historical knowledge appropriately and effectively. At AS Level, however, you will need a much greater depth of knowledge, a much higher level of sophistication in the responses you write, and a much bigger emphasis on:

- analysis and substantiated judgements (judgements backed up evidence) about causation, changes and continuities, consequences and significance, and the relationships between key features and characteristics of the periods studied
- analysis and interpretation of a range of source materials
- evaluation of source materials.

What are the Key concepts?

The syllabus identifies key concepts for AS and A Level History. Considering these concepts and keeping them in mind as you work through the course will help you see patterns, make connections, develop a deeper understanding and gain new perspectives. You will also come across Key concept boxes as you work through this book where we draw your attention to particular links, patterns and ideas. The key concepts for this course are as follows.

Cause and consequence

Causation (the study of causes) relates to the major events you will study. Its focus is not on the events themselves, but on:

- the circumstances and conditions that shaped the events
- the things that led directly or indirectly to the events
- the actions people took (and the beliefs that motivated them) to bring about the events.

Consequences are the effects, results and outcomes of events. They can be direct or indirect.

Change and continuity

When you study the history of a given period and/or place, you will almost always investigate how and why things changed. These changes may be big or small, and they may have profound or relatively trivial impacts. Just as history involves the study of these patterns and processes of change, it can also involve analysis of how some other things remained the same. Continuities can be just as important for historians as changes.

Similarity and difference

Despite living in different periods and places, people can have quite similar experiences. Despite having similar causes, comparable events can have remarkably different outcomes. Despite experiencing the same circumstances and having access to the same information, people can adopt profoundly different attitudes and form totally different opinions on certain issues. History involves study of the similarities and the differences in each case.

Significance

History is not a set of facts that everyone accepts. Some aspects of the past are considered more important by some people than others. People make judgements about significance at the time, and historians continue to make these judgements as time goes by. Studying history involves understanding that people think that different things are significant depending on their own context, values, interests and concerns.

Interpretations

The work of historians involves researching, reconstructing and explaining events in the past. There is no single correct way to do this work, so historians go about their work in different ways. One consequence of these different approaches is that historians present different interpretations of the past, and historians can disagree with each other. Especially at A Level and beyond, study of history involves investigation of historical interpretations and the methods that created them. This key concept is not assessed at AS Level.

What topics will I study?

You may be studying Cambridge International AS Level History (9489). In this syllabus, there are three content options. You are studying the International option: International history, 1870–1939.

Alternatively you may be studying Cambridge International AS Level International history (9982). Both syllabuses have the same content and assessment structure.

The period 1870–1939 saw major events that made the modern world. Countries that now exert a significant influence on world affairs rose to prominence in this period. Understandings and agreements that shaped the relationships between these countries were formed, and disrupted, by the events of these years. Conflicts and rivalries created crises and led to war, and were overcome, at this time. Indeed, the attempts to maintain peace and the efforts to maintain military and diplomatic supremacy in the period 1870–1939 shaped the 20th century.

This course investigates the relationships between countries, as well as developments in places in Europe, Africa, the Americas and Asia.

You will study three topics. These topics match the content chapters in this coursebook:

1 Imperialism and the emergence of world powers, c.1870–1918

   This chapter investigates why and how European countries embarked on imperial projects, built empires in different forms that altered millions of people's lives, and came into conflict over their imperial possessions. It explores the increasing significance of the United States of America, Japan and Germany, and the effects of their emergence.

2 International relations, 1919–29: conflict and cooperation

   This chapter considers the challenges of peacemaking after the First World War, including the widespread dissatisfaction that was felt about the peace settlements of 1919–20, and the tensions that remained, despite the work of the League of Nations. It also asks how and why international relations still improved in the 1920s.

3 International history, 1929–39: the rise of extremism and the road to war

   This chapter looks at the rise of extremism, and its effects on international relations. It examines the efforts that were made to keep the peace in the 1930s, by international organisations and conferences, and by individuals and nations, and analyses why (despite all of the efforts to avoid it) the biggest war of all broke out at the end of the period.

You must study all three topics. Each topic is divided into four Key questions and each Key question contains different historical content. For instance, the first Key question you will look at is 'Why was imperialism a significant force in Africa from 1870?'.

You could be assessed on any of the content that is specified under the Key questions, so make sure you have studied it all. This coursebook covers all of the Key questions and syllabus content for the International option.

How will I be assessed?

Assessment for Cambridge International AS Level History is via two papers, often known as Historical Sources (Paper 1) and Outline Study (Paper 2).

Historical Sources (Paper 1)

In this paper you will answer one question which is based on historical sources. This question will always have part **a** and part **b**, and you must answer both parts.

Paper 1 will examine one of the three topics, but

- you cannot choose which topics you write about on Paper 1
- the topics will rotate from year to year
- no topic will appear on both Paper 1 and Paper 2 at the same time.

Outline Study (Paper 2)

Whichever topics were **not** assessed on Paper 1 will be examined on Paper 2. The examination paper will contain two essay-based questions: one on each of the remaining two topics. These questions will always have part a and part b, and you must answer both parts of both questions.

Your teacher will confirm which topics will be assessed on which paper. The information is also included in the syllabus. Make sure you know the allocation for your year of examination.

What types of questions will test my skills?

As discussed in the paper descriptions, there are two broad types of question: source-based questions and essay-based questions. You will look at these in more detail in the Preparing for assessment chapter at the end of the book.

There are certain key words that appear in many AS Level History questions. These 'command words' are the instructions that specify what you need to do. They make it clear what is expected from a response in terms of skills, knowledge and understanding.

The guidance and suggested approach that appear in Table 0.1 have been written by the authors.

Command word	Meaning	Guidance	How to approach these questions
Compare	Identify/comment on similarities and/or differences.	You should identify at least one point where the sources differ in relation to the prompt and at least one where they agree, as well as providing good evidence from the sources to explain those similarities and differences. You should also comment on the sources' provenance (the term used for a source's background) using contextual knowledge.	Ensure that you fully demonstrate your grasp of the sources. Don't just describe the contents – make sure you use the information in the sources to compare them. Also demonstrate that you have carefully evaluated the sources.
Explain	Set out purposes or reasons / make the relationships between things clear / say why and/or how and support with relevant evidence.	You should give about three clear points explaining why something happened. Each point should be backed up by a relevant and accurate detail.	Try and prioritise those points making it evident why you thought one of those points was more important that the others.
To what extent ... ? How far do you agree ... ? How far was ... successful? How far was ... unsuccessful? How far was ... the key factor? How far was ... the main reason? How important was ... ? How successful was ... ?		You should develop a clear case both for and against the view stated, demonstrating not only your knowledge and understanding of the topic but also your ability to analyse the question and come to a reasoned conclusion.	You should make a firm judgement on the issue of extent.

Table 0.1: Syllabus command words and meanings with additional guidance from the authors.

Working with sources

Source-based questions are testing your ability to read, contrast, evaluate and judge a range of sources.

In order to make judgements about past events, historians usually gather a lot of information and evidence. They can use a wide variety of sources for this, including written extracts, speeches, photographs, cartoons, posters, film footage, oral records and archaeological finds.

Often, the evidence contains conflicting views and even contradictory or incomplete information. This does not necessarily mean that the historian cannot use the information. In fact, historians have to use this kind of evidence, because no source is perfectly complete, trustworthy and useful for any purpose. Historians just have to use what they can find, and make wise decisions about how to use the different pieces of evidence they have available.

Writing history involves careful analysis of the evidence, while considering the limitations of the sources from which the evidence derives. Sometimes the limitations come from the people who created the records in the first place. All sources reflect the perspectives and opinions of the people who produced them, but some sources are so one-sided or narrow in their viewpoint that they have to be used with great caution.

A note on bias

The word 'bias' is often misused in history essays. A dictionary definition of bias is 'the action of supporting a particular person or thing in an unfair way by allowing personal opinions to influence your judgement'. Bias can be explicit and conscious, for example, politicians seeking election will naturally emphasise the good points about their record, and emphasise the bad points about their opponent's. Bias can also be implicit and unconscious.

Take the example of a photograph: you can easily imagine how a photographer can choose what to include in an image and what to leave out. The photograph can turn out quite differently, depending on what the photographer wanted to capture. Written documents are the same.

Historians must remember that any source of evidence can be created (or altered later) by those wishing to present a particular picture. Historians, therefore, need to analyse their sources very carefully in order to form their own opinions and judgements about the past while avoiding a one-sided or very biased study of an event or person. Learning how to reflect on and evaluate information before you make up your own mind on a subject – whether this is who you might vote for or which mobile phone you might buy – is an important skill to acquire.

You will meet a variety of different historical sources during your course. You will need to be able to analyse those sources in the light of your own subject knowledge. The key word here is *analyse*. This means going far beyond just a basic *comprehension* of what a source is saying or showing. A mistake to avoid in answering source-based questions is just describing or summarising the source. You need to ask yourself questions about how reliable the source is and why it appears to contradict what some other sources seem to suggest.

Primary sources

A primary source is one that was written, spoken, drawn or photographed at, or very near, the time. It could also be a recollection some years later of an event or person. It was usually produced by someone who was directly involved in the event, or who was an eyewitness to it.

Different types of primary source you might be asked to use include:

- a speech
- a private letter
- a diary
- an official document, such as an Act of Parliament, an order from a minister to a civil servant, a report from an ambassador to their foreign secretary, a secret memorandum by an official, a legal judgement
- an autobiography
- a cartoon

- a photograph
- a newspaper report
- an interview.

Primary sources often reflect the customs and beliefs of their creator as well as the time and place in which they are created, which is called their historical context. You must remember that primary sources must be studied and understood within the context in which they were written. You should not disregard the usefulness of a primary source just because it does not reflect your own values. For example, opinions about human rights today are very different from those held by many people 150 years ago.

A primary source has many advantages to a historian:

- It provides a first-hand, contemporary account.
- It can offer an insight into the author's perceptions and emotions at the time.
- A source created by someone directly involved in an event might give detailed 'inside information' that other people could not know.

A primary source is not necessarily a better source of information, however. Disadvantages of a primary source might be:

- The source only gives the reader the opinions of the person who created it. These opinions might not be typical of opinions at the time.
- A source created by someone directly involved might contain bias – for example, in trying to convince an audience to agree with a particular line of argument.
- Eyewitnesses might not always be completely reliable. They might not have access to the full details of an event, and they might be reporting an incomplete or an inaccurate version of events.
- The source might be based on the memory of an event or meeting which happened many years before, or it could be over-reliant on the recollections of another person.

A note on hindsight

Hindsight is the ability to look back at an event some time after it has occurred, with a fuller appreciation of the facts, consequences and effects. With hindsight, it is easier to understand the reasons why an event took place, its significance and the impact it had. Historians are fortunate to have hindsight, but it is vital to remember that people living at the time of the event did not have the advantage of hindsight! Although many Europeans felt at the time that the colonisation of Africa was something positive, for example, it is clear with hindsight that there were a great many significant negative consequences.

Assessing the reliability of sources

It should now be clear that historians have to be extremely careful when using sources. They cannot just accept that everything a source tells them is completely reliable or true. People exaggerate. People tell lies. People might not have seen everything there was to see. People have opinions that others do not share. People simply make mistakes.

Imagine you are out walking, lost in your own thoughts, when you hear a screeching of brakes and a thud behind you. As you turn in the direction of the sounds, you see a pedestrian fall to the ground, clearly having been hit by a car, that you see driving quickly away.

You are the only person around. Your first priority is to try to assist the pedestrian and call the emergency services. The police, when they arrive, see you as a vital eyewitness to the accident, and they want to take a statement from you.

But were you really an eyewitness? Did you see the accident, or just hear it and see the result? You saw the car drive quickly away, but does that mean the driver was speeding or driving dangerously at the time? How might your sense of pity for the pedestrian affect your idea of what actually happened? Could you be certain the pedestrian was not to blame for the accident? Could the pedestrian have stumbled into the path of the car? Deliberately jumped? Could you describe the car in detail, or the driver? How far might your own shock influence your recollection of the event? How and why might the statements of the car driver and the pedestrian differ from your own?

So, as historians, what can we do to minimise the risk of drawing inaccurate conclusions from sources? There are several questions that might be asked in order to determine how reliable a source is and to evaluate its provenance. Although there is no "right" way to structure a response to a source-based question, you can use these as "thinking tools" to help your analysis and evaluation. These questions apply to all types of sources, not just written ones:

- Who wrote/spoke/produced the source?
- When was it written/produced?
- What does the source actually say? What is its message?
- What is the context?
- Who was the intended audience?
- Why was it written/produced? What was the author's motive?
- How does it compare with other sources?
- How reliable is it likely to be?

Suppose, for example, that the driver of the car involved in the accident later gave this statement to the police:

> I was driving carefully along the road well within the speed limit. Suddenly and without warning, a pedestrian jumped out in front of me from behind a parked vehicle. I did not see him until it was far too late, and it was impossible for me to stop in time and avoid hitting the pedestrian. In a state of panic, I did not stop. I drove away, in shock, but within minutes I calmed down and realised that I had to go and report the issue to the police. I had my children in the car, so once I had taken them home, I reported the incident to the police.

Who wrote the source?

The driver of the car involved in the accident. If the driver was anxious not to be blamed for the accident, they might have a very good reason for being less than honest.

When was it written?

Later on the same day as the accident. By this time, the driver would have recovered from the initial shock and understood that there was probably no option but to report the incident to the police. However, there would have been time for the driver to reflect on the incident and develop a version of events so that the responsibility for the incident could be placed on the pedestrian. Considering how quickly the event took place, the shock caused by what happened and what might have happened since, can we be sure that the driver's memory is completely accurate? Some details might accurate, but not others – how can we tell which bits to believe?

What does it actually say?

The driver claims not to have been driving too fast or dangerously. The driver says that the accident was entirely the pedestrian's fault for jumping out suddenly into the road from behind a vehicle, without checking for traffic. The driver admits to leaving the scene of the accident out of panic.

What is the context?

The driver reporting to the police to admit involvement in the accident. The police would take this statement if the case went to court. Does the seriousness of the context make people more or less likely to be completely truthful?

Who was the intended audience?

Initially the police, but also possibly a lawyer who might have to decide whether or not to take the driver to court, and therefore, a judge and a jury.

Why was it written? What was the author's motive?

The statement had to be written as it was the law. It is possible that the driver accepted the need to report their involvement in the accident. It is also possible that the driver realised that the police would probably catch up with them, and so was anxious to report the incident to clear their name by blaming the pedestrian.

How might it compare with other sources?

The police are in a difficult position here.

- The driver might well be telling the whole truth and giving a perfectly accurate description.
- The driver might also have made up the entire story if they were driving too fast or using their phone.
- Other witnesses might be able to comment on how fast the car was going at the time.
- There might be some CCTV footage of the accident (though the quality of the footage might not be good).
- Mobile phone records can be checked.
- Marks on the road can be assessed.
- The driver mentions 'children' in the car. Would they be able to give a version of events? But, if so, would they just support their parent?
- If the parked vehicle that hid the pedestrian from view was no longer there, can an accurate picture of the whole event be made?
- The pedestrian might be concussed and not have an accurate recollection of events.
- If the police discover that the pedestrian suffered from depression, might that make it more likely that he had 'jumped out' as the driver's statement alleges?

How reliable is it likely to be?

This source is not reliable on its own. It is somewhat reliable if we were studying the perspective of the driver, but we must consider their possible purposes for their statements in the source. The driver would not want to be blamed for the accident, as previously mentioned, which reduces the reliability of this source. We must also consider when the source was written when thinking about its reliability. This source was written after the driver had time to think about what they would say to the police, rather than on the scene of the accident. This also makes the contents of the source questionable. We would need to look at a variety of other sources to find out what actually happened in the accident.

Finding the truth can be a very challenging task. Your analysis skills will develop as you work through the source-based activities and questions in this coursebook.

Essay-writing skills

Essay-based questions test your knowledge, understanding and skills of analysis. The activities and practice questions in this coursebook will help you to develop your essay-writing skills. To write a strong answer, you should:

Plan your answer

You do not need to write a plan to impress anyone else – your plan only has to be useful for you, so it does not have to go into the same level of detail as your essay. You should include just enough information about your ideas to help you structure your answer and to ensure that you do not forget key points and that you focus on the specific question set.

One of the best ways to understand how to approach essay-writing is to write some detailed plans. The other chapters in this book provide practice questions and there are several examples in the Preparing for assessment chapter at the end of the book. You should work through as many as you can, to ensure that you fully understand what essay-based questions require.

Stay focused on the question

Take time to make sure you understand the question and what is required. It is important to keep a clear and fixed focus on this question alone. Make sure that you are not just trying to repeat a question that looks similar to one that you may have answered before but that is, in fact, very different.

Be clear and precise in your writing

Use words you understand and select key words carefully in order to convey the meaning you want to communicate. History essays are generally written in formal, academic language, so:

- Write impersonally: in other words, do not use 'I' or 'we' in your essays. This applies particularly when you are asked to reach a judgement or a conclusion.
- Take care with sentences and punctuation: in general, try to write in short sentences. Stick to the point and use words you fully understand.
- Write one idea in each paragraph and fully develop it. Begin the paragraph by clearly stating the point that you are making; the detail that follows should directly support this point.

- Support the statements you make: provide developed arguments and support your ideas with evidence. Do not miss out stages in your logic. For example, do not just write that something was a consequence of a person's beliefs – explain the connection fully and include evidence of it.
- When you are asked to reach a judgement on an issue, you must make sure that your judgement is based on analysis you have provided in your essay. It is always worth emphasising what you feel is the most important factor in reaching your judgement.

How can I be successful in this course?

To achieve to the best of your abilities when studying Cambridge International AS Level History, you can focus on:

Acquiring in-depth subject knowledge

Acquire the required knowledge and learn it as you go along. Do not wait until the end of the course before you attempt to learn the content, because your ability to analyse the content during the course depends on what you can recall. Space out your study sessions so that you have short breaks between sessions, revisit previously learned material so that you remind yourself of the content, and ask your teacher for help if you get confused. When you study, use a combination of quizzing, self-testing, reading and noting, listening, writing answers to questions and discussing your ideas.

The notes you make during the course are very important, and it is essential that you present your notes effectively. Copying lists of facts from a book can be a pointless exercise. You need to think about what you are writing, understand it and learn to analyse it. Make your notes in such a way that you are answering a simple question. For example: 'Why was there so much imperial expansion in Africa after 1870?' Don't just write a list of the causes. Prioritise them with reasons. This will prompt you to study the reasons why various nations expanded into Africa. You will think about which issues were the most important and why. Once you have identified the key points, make sure there are two or three relevant factors which show that you understand why they were key points. Doing this will then help you deal with a variety of questions on imperial expansion and the motives for it. Good notes will help you to revise effectively later.

Selecting and using that knowledge effectively

Once you have acquired the appropriate subject knowledge, you must practise using it effectively. If you are asked a question on why the Japanese allowed American influence in Japan to grow in the 19th century, you should not write about American influence in other regions or Japanese relations with China.

Developing independent thinking skills

You must learn how to think for yourself and be able to challenge ideas. You will be asked for your view on a subject – for example whether it was German U-boat tactics or affinity with the Allied Powers that led the USA to join the First World War in 1917. Think carefully about both sides of the argument implied by the question, and about whether there is actually a third possibility that could overlap with both of the opposing points of view. Consider whether they might both have been true at different points in time, or whether it was the interplay of both factors that was critical. You will have to consider both sides of the argument and come to a judgement.

Handling and evaluating different sources

You need to look at different sources and assess how accurate they are, how much you can trust them as evidence, how valuable they might be for a historian, and what they contribute to your own knowledge and understanding of a topic. For example, you may need to put yourself in the position of a historian who is writing about the League of Nations. Some contemporary sources are very optimistic about the League's prospects for success; others can be strongly critical of it. Some are obviously from writers or cartoonists with a strong bias; others may have been produced by people who are more balanced in their views. Which is the most reliable and useful? Why? This is the sort of skill that might be useful in the present day – for example, if you are deciding which way to vote in an election after you have been presented with arguments from all sides.

Analysing and making judgements

This combination is an essential skill. You might be asked for a judgement on, for example, whether the British and French policy of appeasement in the 1930s was successful – or not. First, you will have to work out for yourself what the criteria for 'success' are in this context. Then you will need to consider the grounds on which historians might see appeasement as a success – you may like to imagine yourself as the defence lawyer in a trial. Next, you should consider the grounds on which historians might not see appeasement as a success. Finally, in the most difficult part, you will have to weigh up the two sides and come to a conclusion. You must reach a clear judgement on which factor was most important, and be prepared to give clear reasons to defend your decision.

Explaining

You will need to explain quite complex issues clearly. For example, you could be asked to explain why Hitler's foreign policy was important to the outbreak of world war in 1939, and have ten minutes in which to do it. You will have to briefly explain how Hitler's foreign policy contributed to the outbreak of the Second World War, then in three or four sentences explain why his actions were important. Try to identify what you think was the most important reason and explain why. Always stress what you feel is the most important point and provide factual evidence to back this up. Suggest also what other factors are less important and why – but always make sure you keep the links between them clear. The key is to show that you have really thought about it.

You are now ready to start the course! While it may be challenging at points, we are confident that you will also find it interesting and enjoyable. We hope you find the course as rewarding as we found writing this book for you.

John Etty and Patrick Walsh-Atkins

> Chapter 1

Imperialism and the emergence of world powers, c.1870–1918

KEY QUESTIONS

This chapter will help you to answer these questions:

- Why was imperialism a significant force in Africa from 1870?
- What was the impact of imperial expansion on international relations?
- Why did Japan emerge as a world power and what was the impact on international relations?
- Why did the USA emerge as a world power and what was the impact on international relations?

Timeline

Nov 1869
Opening of the Suez Canal

Nov 1884–Feb 1885
Berlin Conference

Feb 1885
Berlin Treaty

Jul 1894–Apr 1895
First China-Japan War

Apr 1895
Shimonoseki Treaty

Dec 1895–Jan 1896
Jameson Raid

Jan 1896
Kruger Telegram

Apr–Aug 1898
Spanish-American War

Sep 1898
Fashoda Incident

Oct 1899–May 1902
Boer War

Jan 1902
Anglo-Japanese Alliance

Feb 1904–Sep 1905
Russo-Japanese War

Sep 1905
Treaty of Portsmouth

Jan–Apr 1906
Algeciras Conference

Jul 1914
Outbreak of First World War

Aug 1914
Opening of Panama Canal

Apr 1917
USA enters First World War

Jan 1918
President Wilson's 14 Points Speech

GETTING STARTED

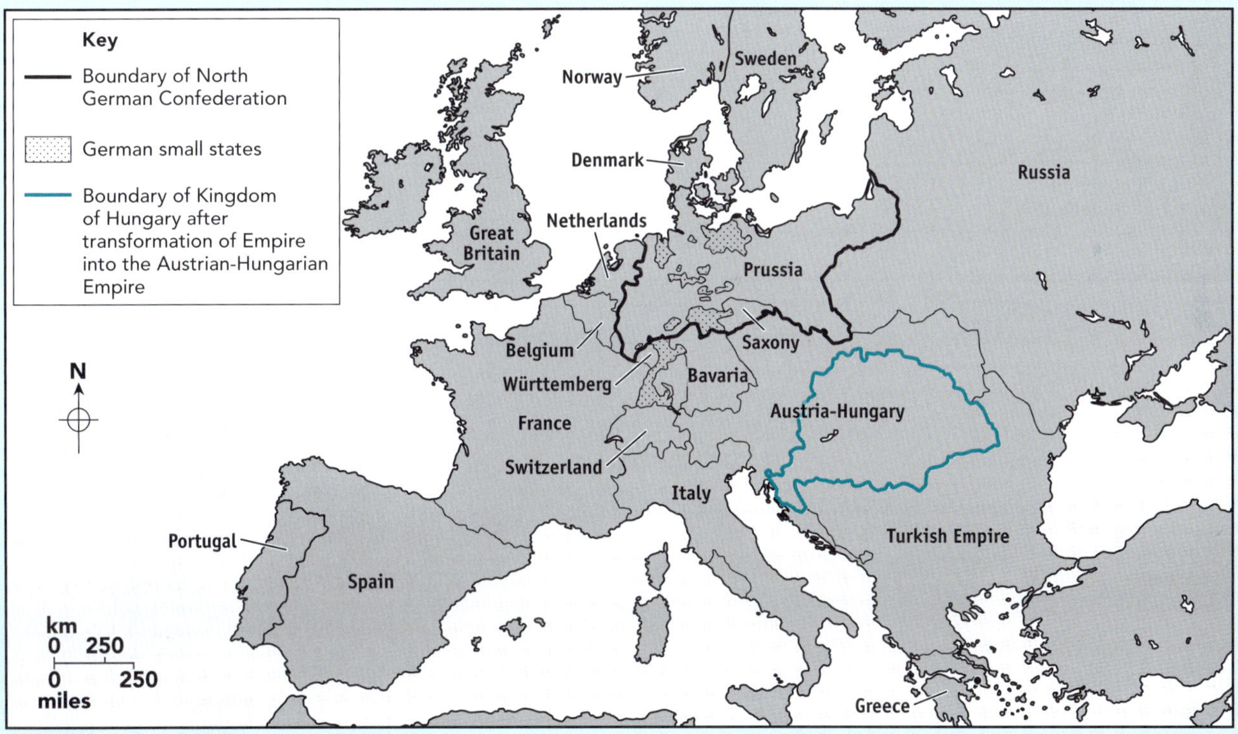

Figure 1.1: Europe in 1870.

CONTINUED

Figure 1.2: Europe in 1914.

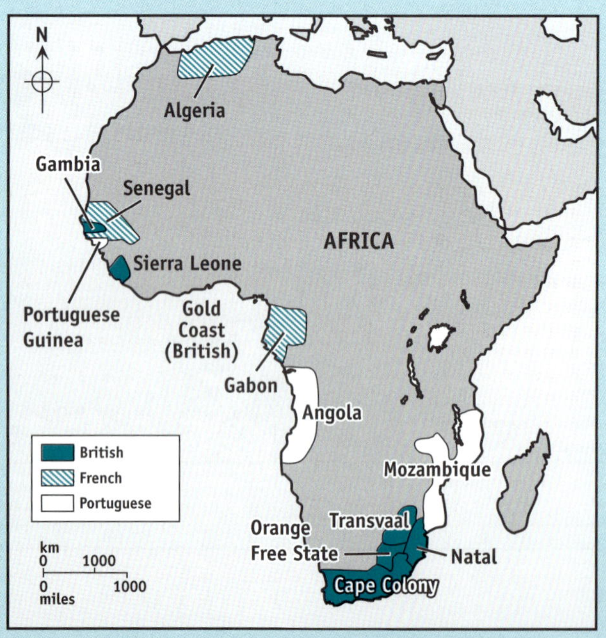

Figure 1.3: Africa in 1870.

Figure 1.4: Africa in 1914.

CONTINUED

Look carefully at Figures 1.1–1.4, maps showing Europe and Africa in 1870 and 1914. Working in pairs, answer the following questions:

a i Describe the changes you notice in Europe between 1870 and 1914.
  ii Describe the changes you notice in Africa over the same period.

b Which countries appear to have gained the most control in Africa during this period?

c Based on what you can tell from the maps, which countries might have come into conflict in Europe between 1870 and 1914?

d Again, using the maps, which European countries might come into conflict with each other in Africa between 1870 and 1914?

Introduction

Some European countries had **colonies** as early as the 16th century. Powerful European nations attempted to increase their wealth through overseas trade and their main motivation was to find and exploit new trading opportunities. Governments established firm control over all aspects of overseas trade, and private traders, who were driven by a belief in **mercantilism**, tried to buy up valuable raw materials such as gold and silver, and valuable products such as spices and silks.

European governments understood that gaining overseas territory (sometimes called '**possessions**') provided a cheap source of these valuable goods, which were not available in Europe, and provided a guaranteed market for European goods. Governments, therefore, encouraged European businessmen and private companies and supported them if they got into conflict. This support acknowledged that acquiring and protecting colonies could have an impact on **international relations**.

Many traders became extremely wealthy by exploiting this trading situation. The most obvious example of this exploitation is the trade in enslaved people (sometimes known as the 'slave trade'). From the 16th century, European ships sailed to the coast of Africa, where European traders would acquire enslaved people, either by bartering (exchanging goods without money) with local chieftains or by capturing local people. They then shipped the enslaved people across the Atlantic Ocean, and the people were sold to plantation owners in North America and the Caribbean islands to work in enslavement picking cotton or harvesting tobacco or sugar. The traders would buy these goods and sell them for large profits when they returned to Europe.

As trade prospered and European influence grew in Africa and other parts of the world, many European countries gradually increased their control over resources and territory, often claiming these for themselves as colonies. By this method, European countries gradually built up large empires.

KEY TERMS

Colonies: Areas under the direct or indirect control of another country, acquired by colonisation processes.

Mercantilism: An economic policy based on the belief that there was only a limited amount of wealth in the world. European nations aimed to increase their share of that wealth at the expense of their rivals. This situation encouraged the acquisition of colonies and led to frequent wars.

Possessions: In the context of imperialism, areas under the control of another country, acquired by any means, including colonisation, conquest, purchase or lease (an agreement by which a land is given, for a specific time, in return for payment).

International relations: The relationships between countries.

- **The Spanish and Portuguese empires:** The Spanish and Portuguese were the first to build global empires. Explorers from Spain and Portugal established naval bases, forts and trading posts in South America, Africa and East Asia in the 15th and 16th centuries, and the Spanish Empire grew to include huge spaces in North, Central and South America, the Mediterranean, North Africa and islands in the Atlantic, East Asia and the Pacific. The power of these empires was declining by the 1800s, however, and once Brazil declared full independence from Portugal in 1825 very little remained of the **Latin American** empires of either Spain or Portugal.
- **The Dutch Empire:** The Dutch were also early empire builders. They set up forts, factories and trading bases along coastlines in North and South America, Africa, the Middle East, and East Asia. The Dutch were more interested in trading relationships rather than control of territory.
- **The Austro-Hungarian Empire:** Austria-Hungary was created by a diplomatic alliance between Austria and Hungary in 1867. It was the second-largest country in Europe, and one of Europe's five '**great powers**'. It was known as an empire because its boundaries contained multiple diverse cultures, languages and **ethnic** groups, although it controlled no territory outside Europe.
- **The Turkish Empire:** The Turkish (or Ottoman) Empire dated back to the 13th century. By the late 19th century it controlled territory in the Middle East, North Africa and south-eastern Europe. Ottoman power was declining by the late 19th century, and Tsar Nicholas I of Russia described the Turkish Empire as 'the sick man of Europe'.
- **The Russian Empire:** Russia had expanded its land empire since the 15th century. It took over huge amounts of territory from eastern Europe, and expanded into the Arctic Circle in the north, Central Asia in the south, and as far as the Pacific coast to the east. In the 1800s, Russia even controlled Alaska, until it was purchased by the USA in 1867. Russia was the largest country in Europe, the second-largest empire in the world and one of the great powers before 1914.
- **The Italian Empire:** The Roman Empire and age of Italian Renaissance exploration made many people see Italy as an imperial power, but it controlled very little territory overseas before 1914. Once Italy was unified as a nation-state in 1870, some Italians had ambitions to gain territory in Africa and the Mediterranean. Although some people saw Italy as a great power in Europe, it was much weaker than the other powers.
- **The Belgian Empire:** King Leopold II of Belgium (see Section 1.1) wanted to increase his country's prestige, and he personally pursued a colonial policy, establishing the Congo Free State under his control in 1885. Belgium also acquired other territories in Africa and in China.
- **The French Empire:** France had established colonies in North America, the Caribbean and India, but it had lost almost all of them before 1800. The French took part in the '**Scramble for Africa**', and built a new overseas empire in the second half of the 19th century, mainly in Africa, Indochina, and the islands of the South Pacific. France was one of Europe's great powers.
- **The British Empire:** Britain's empire developed from the late 16th century. In the second half of the 18th century, Britain fought expensive wars to maintain its control in North America. While Britain was able to retain Canada, it lost control over its 13 colonies in North America following the American War of Independence (1775–83). Despite this, the British Empire was at its peak in the 1800s, when it covered 24% of the world's land surface area and contained around the same percentage of the world's population. Although its army was small by European standards, Britain had the world's largest and most powerful navy at this time. It used its navy to connect and control territory from New Zealand in the South Pacific to Canada in the North Atlantic. In the Scramble for Africa, Britain acquired more territory than any other country.
- **The German Empire:** Germany was unified in 1871, and it quickly became one of Europe's wealthiest and most industrialised powers. Germany built a powerful navy that rivalled Britain's by 1914. Under Chancellor Otto von Bismarck (see Section 1.2), Germany did not acquire territory abroad until 1884. After this, it joined in the Scramble for Africa and acquired some islands in the South Pacific. By 1914, only France and Britain had larger overseas empires.

KEY TERMS

Latin America: The parts of North, South, and Central America south of the United States, where Spanish, Portuguese or French are spoken by many people.

Great power: The term 'great power' was first used in the early 1800s to describe the five most powerful countries in Europe: the Austrian Empire, France, Great Britain, Prussia and Russia.

Ethnic: Relating to a group of people who share a common history and culture.

Scramble for Africa: The phrase 'Scramble for Africa' was first used in the British newspaper *The Times*, in 1884. Since then, it has been used by historians to describe the way European powers competed to gain control of territory in Africa, between approximately 1870 and 1914.

Figure 1.5: Soldiers from British colonial regiments in London before Queen Victoria's Diamond Jubilee celebrations, June 1897.

1.1 Why was imperialism a significant force in Africa from 1870?

In the mid-19th century, it seemed to many people in Europe that the costs of overseas colonies outweighed the benefits. Belief in mercantilism had begun to decline during the 18th century. Maintaining control over overseas possessions and protecting vital trade routes from rival nations was expensive and could lead to wars.

New economic theories suggested that a nation's wealth should be judged not by the amount of gold and silver it possessed, but by its ability to produce goods and services. The most influential of these theories was put forward by the Scottish economist Adam Smith in *An Inquiry into the Nature and Causes of the Wealth of Nations*, published in 1776. Smith suggested that, in many respects, **imperialism** was far from profitable. Smith was writing at a time when Britain was beginning to undergo its industrial revolution. He argued that a nation's ability to increase its production of goods and services depended on investment in new methods. Government control over a nation's economy, he concluded, was neither necessary nor desirable. Wealthy individuals would be more likely to invest if they could get financial rewards without government interference.

In line with these new economic theories, the motivation for government-sponsored imperial **expansionism** declined. The end of the trade in enslaved people led to changing attitudes towards British involvement in Africa, and in 1852, the Chancellor of the Exchequer and future Prime Minister, Benjamin Disraeli, described Britain's colonies as 'a millstone round our necks'.

KEY TERMS

Imperialism: The policy of extending a nation's power by gaining political and economic control over more territory. This is sometimes referred to as colonialism and the territories taken under control are known as colonies.

Expansionism: The policy of expanding the size of the territories under a country's control.

Adding territory to an empire was costly and likely to lead to conflict, but it still brought prestige, power, wealth and strategic advantages. As their interests in the Americas declined, European nations began to look elsewhere, such as Africa and Asia. This led to a new wave of imperialism in the period from 1871 to 1914.

As Figure 1.3 shows, in 1870 only 10% of the continent of Africa was controlled by European powers. Those areas were coastal, since expeditions inland were too dangerous for Europeans to attempt because of disease and a lack of transport. By 1900, only two African nations (Liberia and Abyssinia) were not colonised by European countries, which equates to around 10% of the continent. The British and French empires each increased in size by over 13 million square km, and several other European nations acquired colonial possessions.

Motives for the 'Scramble for Africa'

The motivation for this new wave of imperialism was complex: different groups of people acted for different reasons, and the motives for imperial conquest in Africa changed over time. This complexity means that, although there is **consensus** on the main reasons, historians do not agree on all aspects of the causes of the Scramble for Africa.

> **KEY TERM**
>
> **Consensus:** General agreement between people.

Economic motives

In 1902, the British economist John A. Hobson argued that imperial expansion was driven by the search for new markets and opportunities for investment. Others also saw economics as the central motivation for imperialism. Vladimir Illyich Lenin, leader of the Russian Bolshevik Party (see Section 1.3), similarly argued that imperialism arose from the financial interests of weapon manufacturers, banks and big business.

The search for new sources of raw materials

Beginning in Britain, the industrial revolution made mass production possible. The new scale and speed of industrial production meant that industry needed new sources of raw materials, such as cotton, copper, rubber and tin. Large quantities of these materials could be found in Africa and Asia. For example, raw cotton was sourced in Mozambique and India, copper in southern Africa, rubber in the Congo and tin in British Malaya (modern Malaysia). At the same time, Africa and Asia offered other products that were highly valued in Europe – tea and silk (China), gold and diamonds (the Transvaal), and palm oil (West Africa). In 1867, a young girl picked up a stone beside the Orange River in southern Africa which turned out to be a 21-carat diamond. Within four years, 5000 miners from all over the world had arrived in the region. The desire to control the territories from which such raw materials could be extracted motivated European governments. Even after 1870, however, European manufacturers relied on the same raw materials, getting them largely from the same local sources as before, and continued to make large quantities of the same kinds of goods as before. In other words, imperialism in Africa did not revolutionise industrial production in Europe.

The search for new investment opportunities

The people who benefited most from **industrialisation** in Europe believed in **capitalism**. These people had made rapid profits from industrial development at home in Europe, and now sought new places in which to invest their wealth. According to Hobson and Lenin, this investment was usually in the form of direct investments or loans to foreign governments. Britain invested between 4% and 7% of the nation's income in overseas colonies after 1860, with the result that British capitalists owned 55% of the world's foreign investments in the final decade before the First World War. Modern research suggests that foreign investment was not especially profitable, but that does not mean that it was not a motivating factor for some.

> **KEY TERMS**
>
> **Industrialisation:** The process of economic change a country undergoes as agriculture becomes less important and manufacturing industries become larger and more important.
>
> **Capitalism:** An economic and political system in which individuals, rather than the state, own businesses to make a profit.

The search for new markets to which to sell European goods

Britain benefited from being the first country to undergo an industrial revolution in the first half of the 19th century, being able to produce goods more quickly and more cheaply than any other country. Britain became known as 'The Workshop of the World' as steam-powered machinery revolutionised textiles production, new techniques made the production of iron and steel more efficient and railways and steamships enabled Britain to transport its products further and faster than ever before.

After 1850, Britain's economic advantages disappeared, as industrialisation revolutionised the economies of Germany, the USA and other nations. The development of railways and the formation of a customs union (the Zollverein) enabled greater trade between German states. The increase in trade reduced demand for British goods and introduced a powerful new industrial competitor.

In the period 1873 to 1896 the production of goods was greater than demand, and as a consequence there was a 'Long Depression', a period of price **deflation**. Businessmen and industrialists were forced to lower their prices, which led to declining wages and job losses. To protect and promote their nations' economies and not fall behind, European powers needed to find new places to sell their products. France strengthened its trading interests in Senegal and Algeria and established naval bases in the Indian Ocean (in the Seychelles) and Indo-China (Cambodia and Vietnam) to enhance and protect French trade with Asia.

KEY TERM

Deflation: Falling prices caused by a drop in demand. This leads to falling wages and unemployment, which, in turn, further reduces demand as fewer people can afford to buy goods.

Religious and cultural motives: 'the civilising mission'

Most European people knew nothing about Africa before 1870. It was known by many as the 'Dark Continent', which conveyed their lack of knowledge of the place, but also their attitudes towards the people who lived there. What many Europeans did know about Africa was related to the trade in enslaved people, which had been banned for decades in most European countries but remained common in Africa. This led many Europeans to believe that they had a moral duty to put an end to this practice and led some Europeans to make judgements about the morality of all Africans. Europeans' assumptions about Africa were based on very limited information, and their judgements were therefore fundamentally flawed.

While it was more common to believe that all people were descended from a single couple (Adam and Eve) it was still widely believed that Europe had produced Christian societies that were scientifically, technologically, economically and socially superior to anything to be found in Africa. This belief motivated many Europeans who saw it as their duty to bring civilisation (or 'light') to the people of Africa. They popularised this idea in Europe by publicising their work to raise money for their missions. Many missionary societies in Europe were very influential forces driving imperialism. The British, Germans and French used Christianity to extend their political influence in Africa, Asia and the Pacific. French missionary leaders in Indo-China (Bishops Lefèbvre, Pellerin and Puginier) actively assisted French military forces in taking over parts of Vietnam.

The French economist, Paul Leroy Beaulieu, writing in 1891, suggested that:

> The great part of the world is inhabited by barbarian tribes or savages who participate in wars without end and brutal customs. They do not know how to work, invent, or exploit their land and its natural resources. The civilised people of the west have a duty to spread knowledge of medicine, law and Christian religion.
>
> **From Paul Leroy-Beaulieu, *On the Desirability of Imperialism* (1891).**

The idea that European nations were gaining overseas possessions to improve the lives of local people was a convenient justification for actions that in reality were motivated by self-interest and characterised by exploitation and **racism**.

KEY TERM

Racism: A belief in the superiority of one race over another, based on prejudice and leading to discrimination.

ACTIVITY 1.1

Figure 1.6: 'Modern Apostles' by a German cartoonist, published in the German satirical magazine *Simplicissimus* in 1904, a German satire of imperialism.

Study the cartoon in Figure 1.6.

a Who do you think the large figures are meant to represent? How do you know?

b Who are the small figures in the bottom right of the image? What are they doing?

c Who are the small figures in the bottom left of the image? What are they doing?

d Is there a connection between the large figures and the small figures? What is it?

e What is happening in the background? What do you think might have caused this?

f Cartoons often criticise a person, an action or an idea. Sometimes there are several critical messages in a cartoon. Discuss all of the criticisms you can find in this image with a partner. Compare notes.

g Which criticisms seem to be the most important? Do both you and your partner agree? How are the most important criticisms drawn into this cartoon?

National and strategic rivalry

Political concerns such as developing a sense of national pride within a nation, and rivalry and power struggles between the nations of Europe also drove imperial expansion.

Nationalism

Imperial expansion was one way that European nations could increase their power and status, without coming into direct conflict with each other. By 1871, Germany and Italy had declared themselves unified nations, and the map of Europe's national boundaries was established. It would not change significantly until 1918. Governments and peoples in these new nation-states became more conscious of what it meant to be a member of these nations just as European nations began to look beyond their boundaries for opportunities to expand further. **Nationalism** became connected with acquiring colonies in songs, plays and newspapers (sometimes described, collectively, as 'popular culture').

Imperialism was seen as evidence of the strength of a nation, but also as a way to strengthen a nation further. Charles Darwin published his book *On the Origin of Species* in 1859. Some applied Darwin's theory of evolution by natural selection to the way nations interact with each other. This idea (known as 'social Darwinism') suggested that nations were constantly in struggles with each other, and that only the strongest or 'fittest' would survive. Imperial conquest came to be seen as the forum where these international struggles would play out, and **nationalist** newspapers, songs, cartoons and politicians all joined in to support imperialism.

KEY TERMS

Nationalism: A sense of belonging to a nation and supporting its interests above those of other nations. Also the belief that your country is superior ethnically, culturally, politically and historically to all other countries.

Nationalist: Someone who strongly identifies with their nation and supports its interests, even where this may harm the interests of other nations.

Imperialism was a unifying theme which helped politicians to distract people from everyday concerns. Industrialisation had led to the emergence of a large and increasingly organised working class, which demanded social, economic and political reform. The wealthy landowners, businessmen and entrepreneurs who made up most of the ruling classes were concerned that their political control was under threat. They, therefore, used imperialism as a way of diverting popular attention away from social, economic and political inequalities. Describing overseas expansion as beneficial to everyone, senior politicians, such as the long-serving French prime minister Jules Ferry and Britain's Joseph Chamberlain, argued that imperialism would provide their countries with the finance required to pay for social reform, and improve the condition of the working classes by ensuring steady employment. Governments, therefore, used imperialism as a way of uniting their peoples, regardless of wealth or class, behind a common aim – the development of the economic and political power of their country through overseas expansion.

Strategic rivalry

In 1889, Britain passed the Naval Defence Act, and formally adopted the 'two power standard'. This aimed to ensure that the British navy remained at least as powerful as the combined strength of the next two largest navies (French and Russian at the time). This commitment was important for maintaining the kind of navy that could support a global empire, but it also reflected the belief that military strength, imperial power and national security were all signs of a healthy nation.

Addressing the British **parliament** in February 1870, for example, the Earl of Carnarvon said:

> We have an Empire such as no other people ever possessed. Spain had a great empire, but it has almost disappeared. France had considerable possessions across the seas, but it has seen them gradually absorbed by other nations. Britain alone has built up a vast Empire. It is an Empire of which we have reason to be proud.
>
> **From a parliamentary speech by the Earl of Carnarvon, 14 February 1870.**

KEY TERM

Parliament: The organisation within a government that makes laws.

French governments, determined to recover from France's humiliating defeat in the Franco-Prussian War (1870–71), argued that it was France's destiny to be superior to other nations and to spread its language, culture and beliefs to other parts of the world through overseas expansion. The French politician Paul Doumer argued: 'Just as Rome civilised the barbarians beyond its borders, we too have a duty to extend French culture and religion to the backwards people of the world.'

ACTIVITY 1.2

SOURCE A

The policy of imperial expansion is a political and economic system. In the area of economics, there is a need, felt more and more urgently by the industrialised population of Europe, and especially the people of our rich and hard-working country of France – the need for outlets for exports. What our major industries lack more and more are outlets. Germany and the USA are setting up trade barriers. Not only are these great markets becoming more and more difficult to access, but these great states are beginning to pour into our own markets. Our navy needs safe harbours and supply centres on the high seas. That is why we need imperial expansion. If we do not expand into Africa and the Far East, in less time than you think, France will sink from the first rank of nations to the third or fourth.

From Jules François Camille Ferry's speech before the French Chamber of Deputies, 28 March 1884.

SOURCE B

Should Germany begin on the road to imperialism? I believe we should. We are an industrial nation. In order to maintain our factories and produce our goods we need access to natural resources which can be found in Africa and Asia. Obtaining overseas possessions will open up new markets to trade our goods, and provide our bankers with new projects to invest money in. Imperialism will strengthen our military and defend our nation. By engaging in imperialism we can limit the power of our competitors, Britain and France. We can prevent territory falling into their hands. Taking part in imperialism would increase national pride in Germany. We will show the world that we are a strong nation. We can restore Germany's position as the most prestigious, important and influential nation in Europe.

From Friedrich Fabri, *Does Germany Need Colonies?* (1879).

CONTINUED

Working in pairs, compare the arguments used by Ferry and Fabri to justify imperial expansion by their respective countries. Use the following prompts to help you answer and take detailed notes:

a What economic factors encouraged European nations to seek overseas possessions in the late 19th century?

b How do Ferry and Fabri use economic justifications? What are the similarities and differences?

c Are there any economic factors they don't mention? Why might that be?

d What political factors encouraged European nations to seek overseas possessions in the late 19th century?

e How important are the political factors for Ferry and Fabri?

f Look at the countries Ferry and Fabri refer to when they discuss their countries' rivals. What do you notice about these countries? Why do you think these countries are mentioned in this way?

ACTIVITY 1.3

Construct a mind map of all the factors that led to European colonialism in Africa. Show how the factors were interconnected.

Process of colonisation of Africa

The wave of colonialism seen in the period from 1871 to 1914, which is referred to by some as 'New Imperialism', differed from previous waves of imperialism. It centred on Africa and Asia, whereas colonial acquisitions had previously been in North and South America. The process began with European exploration and interest, which led to informal influence being established, and was followed by more formal extensions of control by the imperial power. It was a 'scramble' in the sense that it was largely uncoordinated. It was a rush from the coasts into the interior of Africa, and it combined military engagements with more diplomatic agreements which led to territorial border lines being drawn on maps and formal political control being established. Rivalries developed as European nations acquired new overseas possessions, but there were genuine attempts to ensure that these rivalries did not lead to warfare. The Treaty of Berlin of 1885, for example, set out the principles that would govern the way European nations would acquire new territories (see Section 1.2). On the ground, however, a number of developments made this 'New Imperialism' possible.

Influence of the advance of technology and science

There were a number of significant advances in science and technology that made it easier for Europeans to capture and control territories in Africa.

Steam power

Before 1870, European exploration of Africa was restricted to coastal regions, since wooden sailing ships needed strong wind and deep water and, therefore, could not travel far up rivers. The development of small steam-driven ships with iron hulls enabled European explorers to navigate through rapids and up rivers such as the Congo, the Zambezi and the Niger much more easily. Large steam ships transported cargo across oceans, to and from colonies distant from Europe. Steam locomotives carried raw materials and goods such as palm oil across Africa. African cacao farmers in the British Gold Coast benefited from the booming (rapidly growing) cocoa trade, while in Congo, steam power speeded up the exploitation of rubber vines.

Quinine

In the late 18th century, Africa was known as 'the white man's grave' because of the dangers of diseases such as malaria. As many as eight in every ten Europeans who travelled to tropical Africa in the 18th century died from the disease. French scientists found a way to make quinine from tree bark in 1820 and by the 1850s it had become a commonly used medicine for treating malaria. Fears of dying from diseases gradually faded as treatments became more effective, and the African interior and the jungles of Asia became more accessible to Europeans.

The Maxim Gun and modern weapons

From the 1860s, European weapons manufacturers had been making breech-loading rifles, which could be fired much more rapidly, and in 1884, Hiram Maxim invented the first fully automatic machine gun. Some African societies had traded guns with European merchants since long before the colonial period, and guns were often exchanged for enslaved people during the era of

Figure 1.7: The steam launch Ma Robert, built for the British explorer David Livingstone's exploration of the Zambezi River.

trade in enslaved people. However, by the 19th century the new Maxim gun and fast-firing rifles were decisive in battles where Europeans could cut down African armies before they could get close. Although outnumbered in the Matabele War of 1893, for example, troops from the British South Africa Company armed with machine guns rapidly won victory. With such devastating weapons, European armies could capture territory using force that overpowered resistance from local people.

Communications

It became far easier for imperial nations to administer and control their overseas possessions as global communications systems improved. From the mid-19th century, the telegraph was the fastest way to communicate over long distances. A network of communications wires was established which meant that telegraph messages (electronic messages) could be sent and received almost instantly. By 1891 its cables reached from London to North and South America, India and New Zealand.

ACTIVITY 1.4

a Consider the question 'Why did technological advances make the process of colonisation easier for Europeans?' Write a detailed essay plan in answer to this question. Identify three technological advances and think carefully about how each one contributed to the colonisation process. For each one, find at least one specific example.

b Compare your plan with a partner's plan for the same question. How much do you agree with the other approach? Is there anything you would change about your own plan?

Activities of European explorers

As Europeans became aware that Africa contained a rich supply of valuable minerals and other raw materials including rubber and tin, interest in exploring the continent grew. The enthusiasm for exploring for commercial gain was often combined with a spirit of scientific enquiry, as organisations such as the Royal Geographical Society in London financed expeditions of discovery, and/or missionary activity. European explorers used modern technologies to navigate and chart Africa's major rivers in the 19th century, gathering information about raw materials, peoples, settlements and trade networks as they went. Missionaries travelled into areas new to Europeans to preach to people whom they saw as 'uncivilised'. These expeditions led to commercial gains for the explorers themselves, and for those who funded them, and were often followed by the extension of government control. Before the 1880s, missionaries and explorers sometimes found themselves in dangerous situations and they were occasionally met with hostility, but they were mostly treated with a mixture of amusement and mild contempt. The impact of missionaries on African history would be profound (deep and far-reaching).

Barth, Livingstone and Stanley

Heinrich Barth was a German scholar and explorer. Funded by the British government, Barth was part of an expedition across the Sahara Desert to Sudan and then south into Central and West Africa. He investigated the histories and languages of the places he visited and sent accounts of his experiences back to Europe, where they were published.

David Livingstone was a Scottish doctor, missionary and one of the pioneers of British exploration. He crossed the African continent in the 1850s, traced the course of the Zambezi and Shire rivers by the mid-1860s and spent the rest of his life charting the tributaries of the Congo River. He died in modern-day Zambia in 1873.

Henry Morton Stanley was a Welsh-American journalist and soldier who continued Livingstone's exploration work. He set out in the 1870s to chart the course of the Lualaba and Congo Rivers. Upon completion of this expedition, he was hired by Leopold II, King of Belgium, to secure treaties with local chieftains along the course of the Congo River. In a letter to the *Daily Telegraph* in 1875 he called for Christian missionaries to travel to what is now Uganda. Many missionaries acted on his request.

ACTIVITY 1.5

You might like to do some further research into the activities of Barth, Livingstone and Stanley. Work in small groups: each group could research one of these explorers (or another 19th-century explorer of your choice) and prepare a presentation for the class.

Expansion and government of colonies

After the 'scramble' for control of Africa, European nations found different ways to control the regions they now possessed. These methods were often used in combination, and each region had unique arrangements.

Indirect methods

Early in the period 1870–1914, the British, French, Belgians and Germans relied on indirect methods of control. Although European powers frequently won and held onto colonial possessions through military force, either through swift conquests or through long and difficult campaigns, afterwards their government of colonies often rested on cultural and political methods of control.

European colonisers sometimes used local African rulers within the colonial governments, with these rulers generally being given subordinate roles. Powerful local individuals would continue to exercise their traditional powers (and even enjoy increased power, prestige and territorial control in some cases) and would be included in the institutions of government brought by Europeans. In West Africa, the British High Commissioner, Frederick Lugard, allied with the traditional elites in African society, and created a system in which only military control, taxation and foreign relations were operated by the British, while all other aspects of governance remained in local hands. In 1894, Uganda became a British **protectorate**, and Nigeria followed in 1900.

Lugard attempted to justify his system as follows:

> It was the task of civilisation to put an end to slavery, to establish Courts of Law, to inculcate in the natives a sense of individual responsibility, of liberty, and of justice ... above all, to see to it that the system of education should be such as to produce happiness and progress. I am confident that the verdict of history will award high praise to the efforts and the achievements of Great Britain in the discharge of these great responsibilities. For, in my belief, under no other rule ... does the African enjoy such a measure of freedom and of impartial justice, or a more sympathetic treatment, and for that reason I am a profound believer in the British Empire and its mission in Africa.
>
> **From Frederick Lugard, *The Dual Mandate in British Tropical Africa*, 1923.**

Indirect government was also often achieved by granting **charters** to private companies. These chartered companies took responsibility for controlling the colonies on behalf of the countries. For example, the British East Africa Company was established in 1888, and it signed treaties with local peoples promising protection in return for giving the company **sovereignty** over the region. In this way, it colonised Kenya on behalf of Britain, and governed it as a protectorate until 1893.

The British South Africa Company was another example. It was founded in 1887. Led by John Cecil Rhodes, it forcibly colonised Nyasaland (now Malawi), Northern Rhodesia (now Zambia), and Southern Rhodesia (now Zimbabwe) and governed them for Britain until 1923, when more direct forms of control came into force.

KEY TERMS

Protectorate: A territory under indirect rule, that is, under the protection but not direct control of another country. Local rulers retained control over internal affairs and the colonial power controlled defence and foreign relations.

Charter: A written grant by a superior power, by which a body such as a company is founded and/or has its rights defined.

Sovereignty: The right to supreme power or authority.

Direct methods

When European countries established direct control, they did so by imposing administrative and military authority over a territory. They often set out to weaken local rulers and institutions They replaced them with colonial governors without negotiation and introduced legal controls to facilitate **assimilation** of local populations and transform them into African reflections of their European colonisers.

This approach was taken by the French and Belgians in their African colonies. The systems of government, taxation, labour, resources, and even the rules that governed newspaper publishing, came under colonial control. Direct control sometimes meant that decisions affecting daily life in French colonies in West Africa were taken by officials in Paris. In other cases, French officials were appointed to positions based in African colonies, and they ruled on behalf of French authorities.

KEY TERM

Assimilation: The process of becoming similar to others by taking in and using their customs and culture.

Development of the Suez Canal

Before 1869, ships travelling between Europe and India or East Asia had to sail around the southern tip of Africa. To make this journey easier Britain established a port and supply station, called Cape Colony, in southern Africa. The only alternative to this long and dangerous voyage was to sail to Alexandria in Egypt, travel overland across Egypt, and then take another sailboat in Suez. This was not suitable for all types of cargo, and winds in the Red Sea were unpredictable, but it was the fastest communication route until a canal was completed.

A canal through Egypt, linking the Mediterranean Sea and the Red Sea, had been imagined for centuries. Even when modern engineering made it possible, the British government had been strongly opposed to the plan. The journey to India was long and dangerous, but British control of the seas meant that British ships were better able to manage the voyage than anyone else. A canal would make access easier for everyone in peacetime and could be captured and closed by an enemy in wartime. Between 1859 and 1869, the Suez Canal Company, financed largely by French entrepreneurs, constructed a canal. A French diplomat, Ferdinand de Lesseps, and Egyptian labourers built the canal. This enabled European ships to travel to and from India and East Asia more quickly and more cost-effectively. Within a decade, shipping tonnage passing through the canal was around half a million tons annually, and by 1882 it was over 5 million tons a year.

Foreign interest in Egypt increased, loans flowed in for major investments and Egypt's economy seemed to be booming. By 1875, however, it was clear that the Egyptian government was in financial difficulties. The instability of the Egyptian government became a concern to the British. The ruler of Egypt held 45% of the shares in the Suez Canal Company but was so heavily in debt that he considered selling them to French investors. To protect their strategic interests, the British government bought the shares.

In 1876, the Egyptian government asked for more financial assistance. British and French bankers and government officials were appointed to take charge of managing Egypt's finances, but by 1879 Egyptian army officers (who received encouragement from Germany) rebelled against European control. Britain initially sought French and Italian support for joint action, but then acted alone in 1882. Britain defeated the Egyptian army and captured the Suez Canal, subsequently taking over the administration of Egypt. The British intervention, initially framed as facilitating commercial activity, evolved into a form of financial and military imperialism. The strategic takeover of Egypt and subsequent moves toward Sudan were driven by geopolitical and economic interests, with the primary aim of securing control over a crucial shipping route and preventing rival powers from gaining influence in the region. Many historians believe that it was the establishment of British power in Egypt that triggered moves by other European nations to acquire territory elsewhere in Africa.

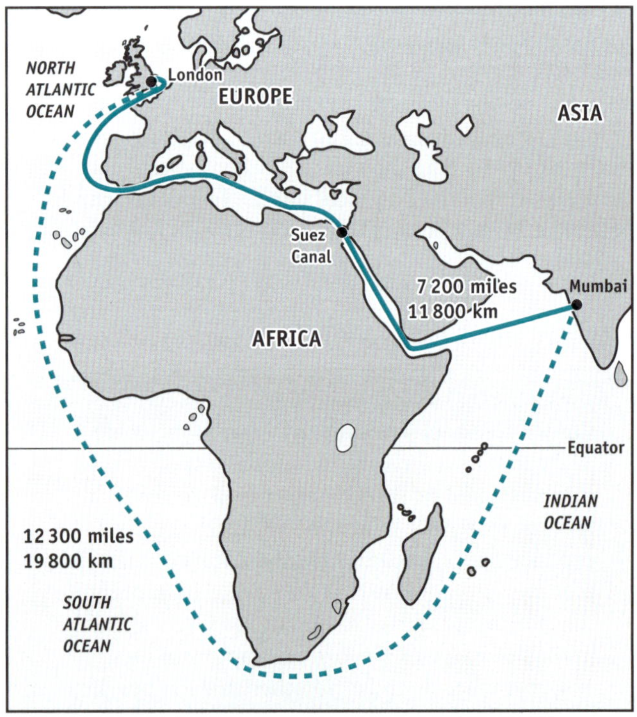

Figure 1.8: The opening of the Suez Canal greatly shortened the journey from Europe to India and East Asia.

ACTIVITY 1.6

It is well to realise that it is for our advantage – and not alone at the dictates of duty – that we have undertaken responsibilities in East Africa. It is in order to foster [encourage] the growth of the trade of this country, and to find an outlet for our manufactures that our far-seeing statesmen and our commercial men **advocate** colonial expansion ... There are some who say we have no right in Africa at all, that it 'belongs to the native'. I hold that our right is the necessity that is upon us to provide for our ever-growing population and to stimulate trade by finding new markets, since we know what misery trade depression brings at home. While thus serving our own interest as a nation, we may bring at the same time many advantages to Africa.

From F. D. Lugard, *The Rise of Our East African Empire* (1893).

a Answer the following questions and then discuss your answers in pairs or small groups.

i In your own words, explain why the opening of the Suez Canal was so important to European nations.

ii What did Lord Lugard say were the reasons for British imperialism in the late 19th century?

iii How did European nations attempt to justify their takeover of African territory in the late 19th century? List the three most important factors.

iv Put into an order of significance the various reasons why European countries began to seek territory in Africa during the late 19th century. Put what you consider to be the most important factor at the top, and the least important at the bottom.

v Hold a group discussion on the reasons. Each student should make the case for their most important factor. Remember you must provide evidence for your reason.

CONTINUED

b Look back over the previous section, and the work you have done on it.

i Construct a summary chart to visualise the different methods that were used in the process of colonization.

ii Present your summary chart to a small group and ask for feedback.

iii Revise your chart.

iv Which method do you think was most important? How did you reach your judgement?

KEY TERM

Advocate: To argue strongly for something; an advocate is someone who argues strongly for something.

Impact of colonialism on Africa

European colonialism in the years before 1914 had profound impacts on all aspects of life in Africa. The European imperialists might point to benefits they had brought to the African people during the period of colonisation as a whole. They might have argued that their intervention led to the development of modern states with administrative and governmental systems; communications, transport, water and sanitation systems; more efficient methods of farming and new, more productive crops, such as maize, pear, cassava, cotton, sisal and plantain.

However, it is clear that these benefits came at a devastating cost to the people of Africa.

Imposition of arbitrary national boundaries

Before 1885, there were few political borders in Africa. Many regions in Africa had low population densities, and there were few natural or agreed boundaries. There were frontiers, or dividing lines, between different groups of people, but these were not drawn on maps, and they were not static. Colonial boundaries were drawn on maps mainly in the 30 years after the 1884–85 Berlin Conference, at which European countries discussed how they would go about establishing colonies in Africa (see Section 1.2).

The borders drawn by Europeans were **arbitrary** (apparently at random, and without reference to the actual situation on the ground), and began from short lines, drawn roughly at right angles to the coastline, to define different European **spheres of influence**.

KEY TERMS

Arbitrary: Not based on a system (this means that if something is seen as arbitrary it is often believed to be unfair).

Sphere of influence: An area in which a country has the power to affect events and developments, despite it being outside the country's direct control.

Those who drew the lines used physical features when they knew about them, but because the continent was not fully mapped at the time, many boundaries followed lines of longitude or latitude. Sometimes, boundaries were redrawn once physical features became known, for example between the Congo (Zaire), Uganda and the Sudan after the Nile and Congo Rivers had been explored. Although some Europeans did attempt to draw their boundaries to reflect local cultures, ethnicities, traditions and wishes, this was rare. Ethnic groups, and groups of people who shared beliefs, behaviours and practices, were split across borders. People who needed to travel, for example for trade, continued to do so, and sometimes got into trouble with imperial authorities for not following immigration, tax or import rules.

Indeed, it was common for boundaries not to coincide with tribal areas, and in fact every national boundary in Africa divides tribal or cultural areas at least once. The boundaries of Burkina Faso divide 21 cultural areas. These divisions fuelled existing tensions, created new rivalries and led to problems that persist to this day.

As the British prime minister, Lord Salisbury, admitted:

> We have been engaged in drawing lines upon maps where no white man's feet have ever trod; we have been giving away mountains and rivers and lakes to each other, only hindered by the small impediment that we never knew exactly where the mountains and rivers and lakes were.
>
> **Lord Salisbury, reported in *The Times*, 7 August 1890.**

Human exploitation and abuse: the Belgian Congo

Imperialism was characterised by exploitation and abuse of resources and people in all parts of Africa, but one particularly cruel example was in the Belgian Congo. By the 1860s, Belgium was a modern power, but its size and newness meant it was not a significant power. This frustrated **King Leopold II**, so he looked abroad for opportunities to increase his country's status. Henry Morton Stanley's expeditions in the Congo attracted his attention.

Leopold sponsored geographic conferences and international organisations to encourage the exploration of the region. In 1879 he hired Henry Morton Stanley to act as an agent for the International Association of the Congo (IAC) to build a road to bypass the Congo River rapids that made river travel difficult, to establish trading posts, and to agree treaties with local leaders, many of whom could not read the documents they were signing, to establish the IAC's sovereignty over their areas. King Leopold attempted to win international support at the 1884–85 Berlin Conference (see Section 1.2). Leopold emphasised humanitarian (concerned with promoting human welfare) aims such as ending the trade in enslaved people in the area and the economic goal of ensuring free trade along the river, when he presented the treaties Stanley had signed. He engaged in skilful diplomacy, persuading the conference to recognise the legitimacy of IAC sovereignty over the region. This recognition effectively made the region the private property of King Leopold. Within months of the end of the conference, Leopold had declared that a 2.5 million square km territory and the population of almost 30 million people who lived in it would be renamed the Congo Free State.

The Belgian government had little interest in an empire, and the Belgian parliament had no power over Leopold's government of the colony. Leopold was not limited by a **constitution** in Congo, so he exploited the region to make money from its ivory and rubber, and he did so in a manner that became notable for its cruelty. Leopold strengthened his control, using a small European military force and a much larger number of African soldiers, a network of traders in enslaved people who saw allegiance with Leopold and his agents as being in their interests, Christian missionaries and Stanley's ability to negotiate treaties. He used his control over the region to make a personal profit from it, by trading ivory (in demand for piano keys, jewellery and false teeth, among other things) and rubber (used for making tyres and for protecting communications cables, for example).

Leopold's government built 240 miles of railway between the port of Matadi and Leopoldville (now Kinshasa), and regulated trade along the Congo, imposing trade and taxes.

KEY FIGURE

King Leopold II of Belgium (1835–1909)

Leopold was king of Belgium from 1865 to 1909. Belgium was recognised as an independent **constitutional monarchy** (a system of government where the king or queen has limited power) in the 1839 Treaty of London. Leopold financed the colonisation of the Congo Free State (now the Democratic Republic of the Congo), which he exploited to make money from ivory and rubber. Leopold's regime in Africa was characterised by brutality towards the native inhabitants, and he was eventually forced to hand control of the Congo to the Belgian government in 1908.

KEY TERMS

Constitution: The set of rules according to which a country or organisation is run.

Constitutional monarchy: A system in which a country is ruled by a king or queen; however the ruler's powers are limited by a set of rules known as a constitution, and most power lies with democratically elected ministers who are accountable to an elected parliament.

The rubber trade became Leopold's main concern. Rubber vines grew high into the top of the tree canopy in the tropical forests, so rubber collectors had to climb dangerously high, cut the stems open with a knife to tap the vines, and then collect the sap that flowed out. The indigenous population were forced to work in the rubber trade. They were paid virtually nothing, set quotas for their work and punished harshly if they failed to collect enough. Pressure to produce more rubber meant that quotas were increased, but as the vines were tapped out they died, so villagers had to travel deeper into the forests and give more of their time to collecting rubber. In the rubber-producing regions, all other economic activity stopped, food became scarce, and people began to suffer from hunger and disease. Punishments for not meeting quotas became more severe, as hostages were taken, beaten, had their hands cut off, and were brutally murdered when rubber collectors did not collect enough rubber.

Leopold never visited the Congo and little of his money was spent on developing his colony, but the rubber trade made him a vast fortune, which he spent on lavish projects in Belgium. Leopold kept information about the Congo Free State closely under control, until 1890, when an African American politician called George Washington Williams published an open letter to King Leopold following his travels through the area. In it, he outlined the multiple ways that the government of the Congo Free State did not match Leopold's professed ideals and reputation. Williams' letter encouraged more people to publish their observations, and over the next 15 years the evidence of humanitarian abuses increased.

Leopold attempted to counter the accusations at every public opportunity and commissioned a public Commission of Inquiry to investigate and report on the administration of the Congo Free State. Leopold did not manage to control the process or the results of the investigation, and the final report was so damaging that he was forced to hand control of the Congo to the Belgian government in 1908.

The missionary John Hobbis Harris was so shocked by what he saw in the Congo that he wrote to Leopold's representative in the area:

> I have just returned from a journey inland to the village of Insongo Mboyo ... The abject misery and utter abandon is positively indescribable ... I was so moved, Your Excellency, by the people's stories that I took the liberty of promising them ... that in future you will only kill them for crimes they commit.
>
> **From John Harris, quoted in Congo Reform Association, *Evidence laid before the Congo Commission of Inquiry* (1905).**

ACTIVITY 1.7

SOURCE A

Figure 1.9: A cartoon from the British magazine *Punch*, 1906, shows an African man caught in King Leopold's coils. The image text reads: 'In the Rubber Coils. Scene–The Congo "Free" State.'

SOURCE B

The task which Belgian agents have to accomplish in the Congo is noble. We have to carry on the work of civilisation in Africa. The aim is to improve races whose misfortune is hard to realise. This is already lessening, little by little, through our intervention. Each step forward by our people should mark an improvement in the condition of the natives. In those huge regions of land, mostly uncultivated and unproductive, where the natives hardly knew how to get their own daily food, European experience, knowledge, resources and enterprise have brought to life unimaginable wealth. Exploration of new lands goes on, communications are established, highways are opened and trade is established.

From a public letter by King Leopold II of Belgium, June 1897.

Study the cartoon in Figure 1.9 (Source A).

a Why does the snake have a human head with a crown on it? Who is the head supposed to represent? Does the snake represent only one person, or might it represent something larger? Discuss your ideas with a partner.

b What do the coils suggest about the snake? What is the snake doing to the man in the image? What message do you think the snake's actions are meant to suggest?

c Look at the man in the image. Who do you think he is meant to represent? Do you think that the man represents all of Africa's population? If not, which part of Africa do you think he represents?

d How is the man drawn? How is he responding to the snake? What message do you think the cartoonist wants to convey about the man?

e Look at what is happening in the background. Why do you think the cartoonist has chosen to include this detail? How do you think it is intended to influence your views on what is going on in Africa?

f Remember that cartoonists often intend to convey a criticism of something in a cartoon. Who or what is being criticised in this image? How do you know?

g Discuss this interpretation in small groups: the cartoonist is criticising all European colonialism in this image. Would you agree? Why, or why not?

Comparing sources

Look carefully at King Leopold II's public letter of 1897 (Source B).

h In what ways did he claim that Belgian occupation of the Congo was benefiting the native people? List the main points.

i In what ways does the cartoon in Source A contradict King Leopold's public letter? Note down the main points next to your list from the answer to question h.

j Compare the letter from John Hobbis Harris. In what ways does this letter contradict King Leopold's letter? Note down the main points again, so that you can compare the lists.

CONTINUED

k What does the weight of the evidence suggest about the treatment of native people in the Congo?

l Imagine that you are part of the Public Commission of Inquiry and you are considering evidence on the treatment of the people of the Belgian Congo. Of the three sources, which one persuades you most, and why? Which of the three do you think is least valuable as evidence? Explain your answer to a partner and compare your ideas with theirs.

Conversion to Christianity

In the north, west and east of Africa, Islam and **indigenous** African religions dominated, but pre-European missionaries helped to spread Christianity. Indeed, some of the first kingdoms to adopt Christianity were in Africa.

KEY TERM

Indigenous: Relating to the people who lived in a place long before the arrival of colonists.

In the 19th century, around 40 000 Catholic and 20 000 Protestant missionaries tried to bring Christianity to Africa. This 'civilising mission' made little impact on the beliefs of African people, and many of the missionaries died of disease, or were killed. Most missionaries stayed in coastal regions until the 1880s, when travel further into the African interior became easier.

Christian missionaries contributed to the sense of racial and cultural superiority that was common among Europeans at this time. They communicated an image of Africa as uncivilised and ready to be converted to Christianity. When Henry Morgan Stanley's letter to *The Daily Telegraph* from Uganda was published in 1875,

Figure 1.10: Mary Slessor (1848–1915) was a Scottish Protestant missionary who travelled to what is now Nigeria. She learned the languages of the people who lived there and developed an interest in working with children. She adopted several children and was appointed to an official position in the courts system in her later life.

Protestant and Catholic missionaries were encouraged to go to Uganda to join him. They enjoyed some success and the elites in the kingdom began to send their children and staff to church schools.

French Catholic missionaries led the way in France's imperial expansion in coastal West Africa in the 1860s and 1870s, and German missionaries created a missionary society to accompany their expeditions in East Africa in the 1880s. British arguments for 'Christianity and commerce' helped to strengthen missionary activities in modern-day Malawi in the 1880s, and humanitarian arguments that rested on Christian missionary work were often used to justify the extension of British control in new regions. Missionary activity accompanied explorers and the extension of military and economic control, as European imperial territories expanded.

Christian missions began to attract thousands of new believers. In southern Africa in the 1880s and 1890s the 'Abyssinian Church' movement, as Christianity was known, became very popular. Converting to Christianity was advantageous for African elites too, since missionaries often brought political and economic opportunities, as well as literacy and access to alliances and trade. Most mission schools provided only basic education, because their aim was to ensure that people learned 'proper' Christian principles, but missionaries also set up churches, hospitals, shops, and plantations. The missionaries began to exercise a strong moral influence over the lives of their converts, banning polygamy (the custom of having more than one husband or wife at the same time), indigenous forms of singing, dancing, ancestor-worship and a lot of other customs.

Missionary settlements disrupted traditional society, creating new elites often distinguished by clothing, education and Christian values. The adoption of Christianity also meant acceptance of Western ideas, customs, lifestyles and technology, which fundamentally altered African societies. Africans did not passively accept all aspects of **Westernisation,** however, and they rejected or adapted some Western influences.

KEY TERM

Westernisation: The process of becoming more like a country in the so-called Western world (usually including the countries in western Europe, North America and Australasia).

Missionary settlements were, therefore, instrumental in the creation of a new kind of culture. The African Christian clergymen took some of the content at face value, for example, and preached that the 'second coming' of Christ meant salvation from colonial oppression. Christianity thus contributed to the beginnings of anti-colonialism, nationalism and independence movements in Africa.

Healthcare

Bringing healthcare and education to African populations was always a purported aim (an aim that was stated, but not necessarily believed in) of European colonial powers. So European systems were recreated in Africa, a large amount of development funding went towards medical projects instead of social care, and in many colonial states most of those working in the technical services were medical personnel. Even so, there were only four or five colonial medical personnel per 100 000 people in Ghana in 1897, and only 11 colonial healthcare facilities (including seven hospitals) in the whole country in 1905, all of which were in the south, where most Europeans lived. Medical training schools were set up, and Africans were trained and employed as 'assistant doctors' in some regions, including Ivory Coast for example, but Africans faced discrimination when training and working in colonial health systems. Differences between traditional medicine and Western treatments meant that many Africans were unwilling to be treated in colonial health facilities, but numbers did increase in the years before 1914.

The other effects of colonialism impacted on the health of African people, however, and the colonial health systems were not well equipped to cope. Since colonial health systems were funded by local taxation, facilities and equipment were limited. The process of colonisation was aggressive and had hugely disruptive effects, including changes to the environment that brought people into closer contact with disease-carrying creatures such as tsetse flies. A rampant, terrifying epidemic of 'sleeping sickness', caused by tsetse flies, led to the deaths of hundreds of thousands of people, and Belgian, German, French, and British officials in affected locations did not have the resources to control the outbreak. Africans who found work in the new schemes in mining, infrastructure or agriculture usually had no protection from the hazards of the work and were injured or fell ill as a result. For example, there were increases in tuberculosis rates in the mining areas of Southern Africa and the Belgian Congo.

Education

Education was usually a family or a community activity in pre-colonial Africa, and education did not normally take place in formal school systems. When Europeans arrived in Africa, their attitudes to education in Africa differed significantly. Colonial powers such as Spain, Portugal, Belgium and France generally introduced only very limited systems of education. In French West Africa, for example, only 70 schools had been established by 1900, but in areas under British control there were generally more schools. French schools were controlled by the state, and, therefore, education in these schools was secular (unconnected to religion) and in French, since it was aimed at producing people capable to taking on administrative work in the colonial state. British colonial schools were largely run by missionary associations at first, and so the education they provided was Christian. They generally taught in local languages, although in some areas teaching was done in English.

ACTIVITY 1.8

Figure 1.11: A photograph (published as a postcard) supposedly showing children being taught by a French colonial teacher in Brazzaville, French Congo, around 1900.

Look at the photograph in Figure 1.11.

a How does the colonial teacher appear in this image?

b How do the children appear in the image?

c What message do you think the publisher wanted to convey here?

The first Europeans to translate African languages were Portuguese and Spanish. One African man, an enslaved man renamed Juan Latino, worked for a Spanish general from 1530, and became a professor of Latin at the University of Granada. In the 1880s, some British Christian missionaries worked to translate local languages, and to transcribe works of African literature, with the aim of increasing literacy rates and spreading Christianity. Literacy rates increased before 1900, although they are estimated to have remained below 10% of the total population. The number of numerate people also increased towards the end of the 19th century and at the beginning of the 20th century. So colonial efforts appear to have improved education, by Western standards. The education offered was designed by Europeans, however, and so indigenous knowledge was not taught in most schools.

Infrastructure development

Pre-colonial Africa had complex, extensive long-distance trading networks, served by thousands of people who made a living as porters, travelling in groups (known as caravans) carrying goods. These caravans travelled along footpaths, and by river in other places, and were supplied by the settlements that sprang up along them.

There were very few motorised vehicles in Africa in the 19th century, but roads were built for ox-drawn carts in modern-day Tanzania in the 1870s. Only a few kilometres were built, and they were so little used that they were overgrown with vegetation again by the 1890s. Colonial officials soon learned that the caravan routes were used by local armies to attack them, so broad, open highways were built along the lines of traditional footpaths. Nonetheless, travel along the caravan routes remained dangerous and difficult before 1914.

Elsewhere, in places such as modern-day Malawi, small road networks were built in the 1890s, to serve the colonial administration and the army. By 1914, road and railway construction projects had been completed across the continent.

Railways were the most modern transport technology of the time, and they offered faster and safer means of travel than roads. Railways made transport faster, cheaper, and easier. It facilitated the movement of large numbers of people (especially soldiers), the transport of administrators and military supplies, and the extraction of raw materials. The first railway in Africa was started in Alexandria, Egypt, in 1852. Although it remained incomplete, the Cape to Cairo railway was a major British infrastructure project, as was the French Senegal to Djibouti plan. Other major railways were built in the years before 1914, and in some places there were railway lines hundreds of kilometres long by that time. In German South West Africa (now Namibia) the rail network of 2100 km formed the backbone of the colony's economy and infrastructure.

Financial, logistical and practical problems meant that infrastructure development in Africa did not achieve the aspirations of the colonists who designed them before 1914, but the infrastructure development that European colonists did achieve was crucial in accelerating the progress of imperialism.

ACTIVITY 1.9

a Using any resources available to you, research the history of rail, road or other infrastructure development in a country in Africa. How much of the country's infrastructure was already built, or was under construction, by 1914?

b Present your findings to the class.

ACTIVITY 1.10

SOURCE A

Figure 1.12: Imperialist, explorer and businessman Cecil Rhodes as a colossus bestriding Africa. The caption reads: 'The Rhodes Colossus Striding from Cape Town to Cairo.' From the British satirical magazine *Punch* in 1892.

CONTINUED

SOURCE B

Figure 1.13: An American cartoonist's view of Britain's relationship with Africa. The caption below reads: 'Don't bite off more than you can chew, John'. Published in an American newspaper, *The Tribune*, in 1900.

a Study the British cartoon depicting Cecil Rhodes in Figure 1.12 (Source A). Discuss this image in pairs or small groups.

  i Where is he standing (both feet)?

  ii What kind of cable do you think he is holding, and what does this represent?

  iii Why is he carrying a gun?

  iv How would you describe his facial expression?

  v Why is he drawn at this size and with this stance?

b What do you think is the cartoonist's message?

c Study the American cartoon depicting John Bull in Figure 1.13 (Source B). In what ways does it give a contrasting impression of Britain's activities in Africa?

d What does this suggest about the American attitude towards imperialism?

Causes and impact of African resistance

European colonists regularly came into conflict with Africans who resisted their attempts to expand and strengthen their control. In many cases, although they were still important, the attempts at resistance were small scale, isolated, and limited in their impact, and therefore they have not been recorded by history. In the 1870s and 1880s, however, there was a series of African defensive resistance attempts, aimed at maintaining sovereignty and holding back European expansion. On some famous occasions in the 1890s and 1900s, Africans went on the offensive with military force in areas where the European colonial rule was already established.

The Anglo-Zulu War, 1879

Following the discovery of diamonds in the region, in 1877, Sir Henry Frere, a British colonial administrator, was sent to Cape Town to create a **federation** under British control. The region contained British colonies, regions under African control and republics of **Boer** settlers.

Frere realised that British control would be impossible if the African kingdoms in the region were not crushed, so British forces set about defeating the armies of the African rulers in the area. In December 1878, Frere and the British governor of Natal and the Transvaal sent the Zulu king **Cetshwayo** an **ultimatum** demanding, among other things, that he disband his army. Knowing that Cetshwayo would never accept these terms, Frere had been preparing for war. Despite being armed with inferior weaponry, Cetshwayo's army fought bravely and almost defeated the British.

KEY TERMS

Federation: A group of states which have independence over their own internal affairs but are organised and controlled by a single central government.

Boer: People of southern Africa who trace their ancestry back to Dutch, German and French settlers who moved to the area in the late 17th century. The Boers' present-day descendants are the Afrikaners.

Ultimatum: A final demand that, if rejected, will lead to serious consequences such as war.

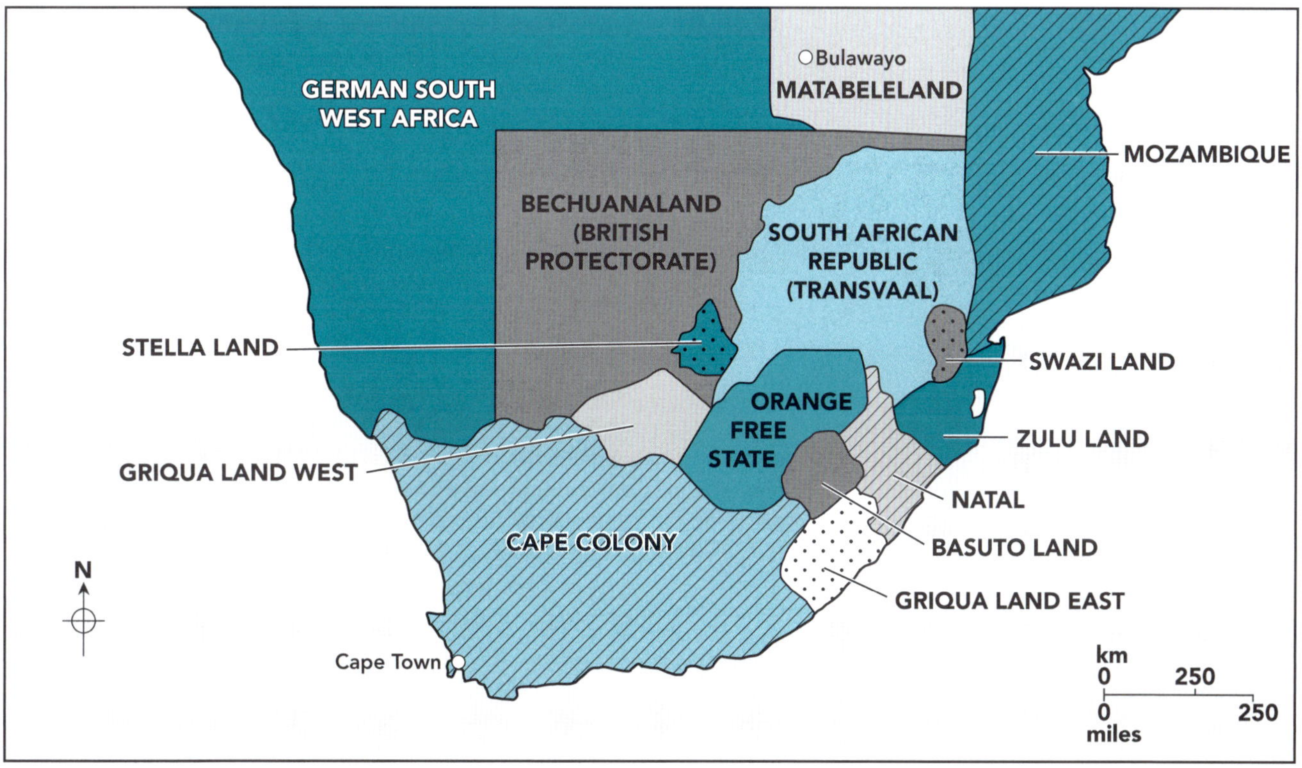

Figure 1.14: Map showing southern Africa in 1877.

In January 1879, a Zulu force of around 25 000 warriors took the British by surprise and won the Battle of Isandlwana. In the months that followed, British troops were besieged at their fort at Eshowe (January–April) and defeated at the Battles of Intombe and Hlobane (March). The British forces were only able to defeat the Zulu after they received reinforcements sent from England. After the Battle of Ulundi in July and the capture of King Cetshwayo in August 1879, the Anglo-Zulu War was over.

Following the war, the British dismantled the Zulu monarchy and partitioned Zululand. Cetshwayo was dispossessed of his lands and exiled first to Cape Town and then to London. A period of internal conflict ensued. In 1883, the British attempted to stabilize the region by reinstating Cetshwayo to his throne, but he died the following year. By 1887, Zululand had been formally incorporated into British colonial territory.

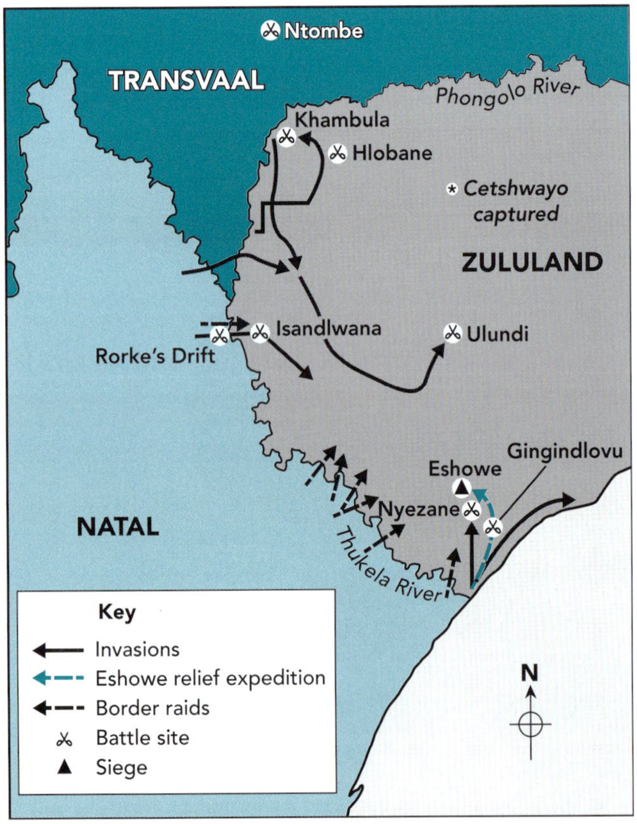

Figure 1.15: Map showing some of the major battles in the Anglo-Zulu War.

KEY FIGURE

King Cetshwayo (1826–84)

Cetshwayo was the last king of the independent Zulu nation from 1872 to 1879. His strong leadership, personal authority and political skill made him a respected ruler. He led an army of 40 000 Zulu warriors who fought the British imperial forces on numerous occasions.

The Ndebele rebellion (also known as the Matabele Wars), 1896

In 1889, the British government granted a charter to the British South Africa Company to administer the area between the Limpopo River and the Zambezi River. Cecil Rhodes sent settlers and soldiers into the region to found new forts, establish control over the land, and search for gold. Their aggressive behaviour and their attempts to take cattle belonging to the Ndebele people aroused hatred. There were skirmishes (small fights) and disputes between European settlers and the Ndebele from 1893, including the British capture of Bulawayo, the capital of King Lobengula. Even after the death of King Lobengula, the fighting continued, until the British had control of the whole region. They declared Rhodesia their capital in 1895, encouraged the arrival of large numbers of gold prospectors, and connected with Cape Town by building a railway to Bulawayo by 1897. The Ndebele appeared to have been defeated.

In March 1896 a more significant Ndebele uprising against the British began. A spiritual leader, the Mlimo, convinced the Ndebele and the neighbouring Shona people that the white settlers were responsible for locust plagues, the drought and the cattle disease rinderpest that was badly affecting the country at the time. The Mlimo planned to take Bulawayo by surprise, and to drive all the settlers out of the city and kill them.

The uprising was not well organised, but hundreds of settlers were attacked and killed. Settlers fortified themselves inside the city of Bulawayo and sent patrols out to rescue anyone stuck outside. 10 000 Ndebele warriors besieged the city, unwilling to engage against the firepower of British weaponry, but they did not block the roads to the south, nor did they cut the telegraph lines that linked the city to British forces in South Africa. Reinforcements were thus sent, and the warriors were dispersed. Settlers and British troops pursued the Ndebele, found and killed the Mlimo, and regained control over the region.

ACTIVITY 1.11

SOURCE A

Figure 1.16: An illustration from an Italian magazine, entitled 'Abyssinian forces attacking the Italian Brigadier', published 29 May 1896.

SOURCE B

Figure 1.17: An Abyssinian painting of the Battle of Adwa, by an unknown artist, from 1940.

Study the images in Figure 1.16 (Source A) and Figure 1.17 (Source B). Discuss the images with a partner or in a small group. Use the following prompts to help you:

- **a** How are the Abyssinians depicted in the Italian magazine?
- **b** Why are there so few Italians in the Italian illustration?
- **c** How does the Abyssinian painting in Figure 1.17 depict the two armies?
- **d** Why do you think the Abyssinian painting includes a saint at the top of the image?
- **e** Overall, how valuable are these two sources as evidence about the colonial wars in Abyssinia in the 1890s?

The Battle of Adwa, 1896

From the mid-19th century, Abyssinia (known now as Ethiopia) was ruled by an emperor, but when the emperor died in 1889 there was a power struggle among his would-be successors. Among them was the king of Shewa, who had received Italian money, modern weaponry and ammunition. He used this backing to incorporate smaller Abyssinian kingdoms under his rule and to secure his claim to the title of emperor, taking the name Menilek II. The Italians had occupied the Red Sea port of Massawa in 1885, and after this they established the colony of Eritrea and captured much of present-day Somalia. They backed Menilek for the throne of Abyssinia because they wanted to reach agreement with him and absorb his kingdom into their East African colony. A disputed 1889 treaty was at the heart of the growing conflict. Two versions of the treaty existed. The Italians argued that the correct version was the one that made Abyssinia an Italian protectorate, and that Menilek had knowingly signed it. Emperor Menilek II argued that no such wording existed in the version written in Amharic (the language used by Menilek), which was the correct treaty.

In December 1894, a rebellion in Italian-controlled Eritrea led to the Italian occupation of the regional capital, Adwa. In 1895, the Italians advanced into Abyssinian territory, but Menelik gathered his forces and defeated the Italians at the battle of Amba Alage in December 1895. An offensive was hurriedly organised, and the Italians ferried thousands of troops to the area, but they were still outnumbered by an estimated five to one. The Italians were poorly organised, equipped with old weaponry, and supplied with inaccurate maps. The Italian army was overwhelmed because of a series of mistakes by Italian commanders, and because they were unable to cope with the terrain.

As many as 6000 Italians were killed and many others were captured. As a direct consequence of the defeat, Italy signed the Treaty of Addis Ababa in October 1896, recognising Abyssinia as an independent state. Abyssinia and Liberia remained the only independent African nations up to 1914.

The Herero War, 1904–08

The colony of German South West Africa (modern day Namibia) was created in 1884, when German Chancellor Otto von Bismarck (see Section 1.2) granted permission for land to be bought from a local tribe and placed under the protection of Germany. German claims on the land were confirmed at the Berlin Conference of 1884–85 (see Section 1.2). German government of the region was unpopular with Africans, and relations between the locals and the growing number of German settlers worsened over the years. In particular, relations with the Herero people in the region suffered. The Herero suffered at the hands of the German colonial government in a number of ways. German colonists were encouraged to seize land and cattle from the indigenous Herero and to use them as labourers. The traditional Herero way of life as cattle herders and farmers was disrupted by German attempts to control rinderpest by restricting population and livestock movement in 1896. Resentment grew over the loss of property, freedom and status as more German rancher settlers arrived, and increased further when the Germans sent colonial troops to the region to pacify it.

In 1903, the Herero learned of plans to build a railway through their lands and discovered that the Germans intended to move them into **reservations** that would concentrate their population into a much smaller area. A railway line would have brought new waves of Europeans into the area. Also, a change to the policy on debt collection in the area led many traders and money lenders to seize Herero cattle if they feared they would not get their money back.

The Herero revolted in 1904, attacking remote settler farms and violently killing around 150 German settlers. The Herero surrounded German settler towns and destroyed a railway bridge. The Germans called in 14 000 troops from Germany and crushed the rebellion in the Battle of Waterberg in August 1904. The Germans pursued the survivors, killing every Herero man, woman and child they caught. They drove the Herero into the desert, guarded and poisoned wells and water holes, and put captives into **concentration camps** where cruelty and mistreatment were common. An estimated 80% of the Herero population were killed between 1904 and 1908. In 1985, the United Nations described these events as a **genocide**, and in 2015 the German government also formally acknowledged that these acts of brutal repression represented genocide.

KEY TERMS

Reservations: Areas of land set aside for members of an indigenous group.

Concentration camps: Places where prisoners or members of persecuted minorities are imprisoned in a small area, and with inadequate facilities.

Genocide: The deliberate and systematic destruction of an ethnic, racial, religious or national group.

ACTIVITY 1.12

SOURCE A

Figure 1.18: A German postcard shows an imperialist version of events in German South West Africa. The postcard caption reads: 'The uprising in German South-West Africa: The pillaging of Herrn Gamisch's farm'.

SOURCE B

Figure 1.19: A photograph of Herero survivors, frail and emaciated.

a Would you describe the postcard in Figure 1.18 (Source A) as showing a fair representation of life for African people under colonial rule?

b Discuss with a partner how the photograph in Figure 1.19 (Source B) might be used in different contexts.

  i How might it be used in a German publication on empire in the 1900s?

  ii How might it be used in a British publication after the First World War?

c What do you think the photographer's intentions were in taking the photograph?

Reflection

Look back at the answers you gave to the questions in the Getting started activity at the beginning of this chapter. How would you amend those answers in the light of your subsequent reading?

KEY CONCEPT 1.1

Similarity and difference

The changes brought about by European imperialism in Africa were profound, but the impacts varied according to the local circumstances. Look back over this section and the work you have completed on it. Work with a partner.

- One person should write a generalisation about the impact of colonialism in Africa that would be broadly true for all regions of the continent – a comment about the similarities – and look for some examples to support the judgement.
- The other person should write a generalisation about one of the major differences in the ways Africa was affected by colonialism. This difference might relate to geographical variations, the imperial power concerned, the date when colonial control was established, or the methods used by the colonial power.

1.2 What was the impact of imperial expansion on international relations?

As European nations competed to control overseas territory, there was always the risk that war might break out between them. European statesmen understood this and did everything possible to avoid conflict over colonies. At the same time, they also wanted to limit the growth of others' empires and expand their own.

The Belgian King Leopold had been extending his plans for his colony in the Congo, and he wanted to win international support so that no-one would stand in his way. He was a skilled diplomat and began attempting to persuade other European leaders. When France, Britain, Portugal and Germany became aware of the implications of King Leopold's plans for a colony in the Congo, they became concerned, and agreed to attend a major international conference in Berlin in 1884.

The Berlin Conference, 1884–85

In 1884, Germany was Europe's youngest major power. The **unification** of the various German states had taken place during the 1860s through the leadership of the state of Prussia, and the German Empire had been created following the defeat of France in 1871.

Germany's Chancellor, **Otto von Bismarck**, was perhaps Europe's leading statesman. He was highly skilled at international diplomacy, but he had previously shown no interest in acquiring colonies. In 1881, for example, he encouraged France to **annex** Tunis (now Tunisia) because he hoped it would distract France from its desire for revenge against Germany after 1871, and create a lasting rivalry with Italy, who also wanted control of Tunis.

The Italians were so angry with France that they signed the Triple Alliance with Germany and Austria-Hungary in 1882. This alliance became a key part of Bismarck's **alliance system**, which he used to maintain Germany's security.

By the mid-1880s, however, German businessmen and industrialists were putting pressure on the government, and Bismarck was becoming increasingly aware that a colonial policy could be beneficial. So the government changed its previous policy of resistance to gaining territory in Africa.

KEY TERMS

Unification: A process of becoming unified or made whole. In the case of Germany, the process by which the various German states were formed into the country of Germany during the 19th century.

Annex: To take possession of a territory, usually by force or without permission.

Alliance system: A formal agreement between two or more states for mutual support in case of war.

ACTIVITY 1.13

Figure 1.20: A drawing showing European statesmen at the negotiating table at the Berlin Conference.

Study the drawing in Figure 1.20. Discuss your impressions of this image with a partner. How would you describe the Berlin Conference, based on this depiction?

KEY FIGURE

Otto von Bismarck (1815–98)

Otto von Bismarck was a Prussian statesman and diplomat. He unified the German states into one country between the 1860s and 1871, and then served as the first chancellor of the German Empire until 1890. During that time, he dominated European international affairs. Germany was located in the centre of Europe, surrounded by potential enemies. This location led Bismarck to concentrate on national security by forming alliances and avoiding unnecessary rivalry with other countries. He managed rivalries between other European countries expertly to maintain Germany's security. When Wilhelm II became Kaiser (emperor) of Germany, Bismarck fell out of favour, and he was dismissed in 1890. He retired to write his memoirs.

Purpose of the conference

In 1884 Bismarck called on 13 European nations and the USA to take part in a major conference. The purpose of the conference was to agree a common policy towards establishing colonies in Africa. The conference took place between November 1884 and February 1885. There were no representatives from Africa, and only two of the delegates had even travelled to Africa. Of course, the process of imperial conquest was well underway at this time, but the general aim was to agree the international laws that would govern the behaviour of European colonial policy.

Pressures on Bismarck

Bismarck was still mainly interested in Africa because it could divide other European countries and assist him with domestic politics. However, in 1884 he judged that it was in Germany's interests to join in the competition for possessions in Africa.

Bismarck gave charters and formal support for German claims in South West Africa, Togoland (modern day Togo and part of Ghana), the Cameroons (modern day Cameroon), and East Africa (modern day Burundi, Rwanda, Tanzania and part of Mozambique). These moves were only intended to encourage German traders, but this was an unexpected change in the situation in Africa, and it raised the prospect of conflict with Britain.

Bismarck did not find such a conflict unwelcome. He wanted to encourage friendlier relations with France, and the prospect of a disagreement over colonies with Britain offered the possibility of common ground with the French, who were still angry with Britain over their annexation of Egypt in 1882.

Involvement in colonial affairs also offered Bismarck some domestic political opportunities. The heir to the throne, Crown Prince Frederick, was married to the daughter of England's Queen Victoria, was pro-British and was surrounded by pro-British advisers. Bismarck knew that if the aging Kaiser Wilhelm I died, he would have much more difficulty in pursuing an independent foreign policy unless he acted to make the pro-British elements in the monarchy more cautious. He thus appears to have decided that a colonial policy that could bring Germany into conflict with Britain at any moment was politically convenient.

Bismarck also began to realise that colonialism and the nationalist sentiments it stirred would be politically helpful in the German Reichstag (parliament) election campaign of 1884, when he wanted to turn the public away from the growing Social Democratic Party (SPD). There was increasing pressure from German businessmen and industrialists to pursue a colonial policy that might benefit them economically and distract the working classes from the appeals of **socialism**.

Colonisation was genuinely popular in Germany, as it was elsewhere in Europe at this time. The German Colonial Society had been formed in 1882. It received much support from industry, nationalist organisations including the Pan-German League, and several influential members of the German Reichstag. The public supported it and it became politically influential.

Intentions of different powers

Several developments contributed to a sense that European countries needed to reach agreement on colonial matters. There was a desire to regulate trade in Africa, as well as general agreement that the principles underpinning colonial expansion ought to be discussed. Not all the countries attending the conference had direct involvement in Africa. Russia, Austria, Denmark, the USA and Sweden, for example, had little interest in the continent. Other countries, meanwhile, had little previous involvement, but did not want to be left out. The Turkish Empire, for example, protested that its interests in Africa would be affected if it was not invited.

Other nations had very specific intentions:

- King Leopold wanted confirmation that the International Association of the Congo had **legitimate** ownership of the regions agreed by Stanley's treaties. Leopold had emphasised the IAC's humanitarian aims such as ending the trade in enslaved people in the area and the economic goal of ensuring free trade along the river. All of the powers represented at the conference agreed with these aims.
- Portugal wanted recognition of its claim to the area between its colonies in Angola and Mozambique. This large area (much of modern-day Zimbabwe, Zambia and Malawi) was claimed by Portugal. Britain disputed Portugal's claim.

KEY TERMS

Socialism: An economic and political philosophy that pursues social ownership of the means of production (for example, factories), as opposed to private ownership.

Legitimate: Allowed or accepted by laws or rules.

ACTIVITY 1.14

a Why did Germany enter the race for African territory later than other European nations?

b Why did German industrialists and businessmen want Germany to seek territorial possessions in Africa? Write a plan for a short essay in answer to this question. You should include at least three main reasons and decide which was the most important of the factors.

c In pairs, discuss why European nations became involved in the Scramble for Africa. Copy and complete the table. In the left column, list evidence which suggests that national pride was the main reason. In the right column, write other factors that encouraged European nations to seek possessions in Africa. How do the two lists balance?

Evidence for national pride	Evidence for other factors

- France claimed land in north, west and central Africa, and also had interests in northern Congo. The French were concerned that increasing British and Belgian territories threatened their plans for expansion. They were also angry about Britain's annexation of Egypt in 1882 and were willing to work with Germany to prevent their rivals from increasing their power.
- The British wished to be included in European decision-making on African colonisation and wanted to protect their existing colonial possessions. Britain had plans for imperial expansion as well and would not allow a rival power to advance a claim that would endanger those goals.
- Italy had begun to build its Italian possessions in modern-day Eritrea in 1880 and wanted to acquire Abyssinia. Emperor Menelik was not invited to attend, but he wrote to the Berlin Conference attendees and expressed his concern that the European powers were planning to divide up Africa between them. He also signalled that he intended to try to enlarge his country's territory in future. Italy was determined to advance its territorial ambitions in eastern Africa.

Outcomes

Negotiations resulted in the Treaty of Berlin (1885). The main articles of the treaty included the following.

The principle of 'effective occupation'

Perhaps the most significant outcome of the conference was agreement on the principle that, to take possession of an African territory, a European nation had to already have 'effective occupation'. If the European power had treaties with local leaders, flew its flag there, established a government and a police force to keep order there and was making use of the colony economically, it had the right to inform the other powers and, in this way, get rights of ownership.

This was intended to prevent a country claiming an area over which it had no real control simply to prevent rival countries attempting to gain it. In fact it encouraged European nations to rush to 'effectively occupy' African territory because they saw this as a way to avoid the risk of fighting over it. Article XII of the treaty specified that any disputes regarding colonial control should be settled by negotiation rather than war. In this way, the Berlin Conference added impetus to the 'Scramble for Africa'.

Recognising King Leopold's Congo claim

King Leopold's territorial claims in the Congo were recognised and accepted formally by the conference. Although Leopold had to make promises about how he would treat the people of Congo (he was required to improve their welfare) and the existence of free trade zones slightly restricted his absolute freedom to govern, the conference endorsed his rule without imposing significant checks or oversight from other major powers. The conference used the name 'International Congo Society' to describe the owners of the territories in the Congo, and it named the region the Congo Free State. This appeared to confirm what Leopold had promised, and to keep the country open to investment from any European country. In practice, however, the conference made the territory of what is now the Democratic Republic of the Congo the property of Leopold II. He gained exclusive rights to the vast economic resources of the Congo, including rubber and ivory, which he exploited for personal and Belgian profit.

The end of slavery

The conference agreed that slavery should be abolished by African and Islamic powers throughout the African continent. This was included in the treaty to satisfy those who had doubts about the right of European countries simply to take land in Africa. Those at the conference felt that abolishing slavery provided a suitable justification for imperialism in Africa.

Free trade and navigation

The conference also agreed some measures which guaranteed rights of free trade and navigation in Africa. There was definition of regions in which each European power had the right to pursue exclusive ownership. The conference confirmed free navigation for all ships on the Niger and Congo rivers, both of which provided access to the African interior. The conference also confirmed free trade throughout the Congo basin, around Lake Malawi and other areas.

ACTIVITY 1.15

Consider the statement 'Leopold got everything he wanted from the Berlin Conference, and more.' How far would you agree with this view?

a Do you think it is true to say that he got everything he wanted?

b Do you think it is going too far to say that he got even more than he had originally thought possible?

c Write an essay plan which covers both sides of the argument.

Rivalries between colonial powers

European imperialism provoked conflict with African peoples. In addition, despite the efforts of the representatives at the Berlin Conference, it increased the rivalries between European nations. Although there were carefully laid plans to avoid armed conflict between rival imperial nations, tensions inevitably remained.

Rivalries between Britain and Germany

The tensions between Britain and Germany intensified when Germany entered the race for African possessions. Bismarck had feared that when Friedrich became Kaiser (emperor) he would introduce a pro-British direction to German foreign affairs, but Friedrich died shortly after becoming Kaiser in 1888. When Wilhelm II became Kaiser later that year, it became clear that German foreign policy would take a different turn. Wilhelm and Bismarck disagreed on numerous issues, and Bismarck was forced to resign in 1890.

In 1890, Anglo-German relations were relatively good. In that year, Britain and Germany signed an agreement: Germany gained Heligoland in the North Sea, in return for giving up claims to Zanzibar and East Africa. However, relations between Germany and Britain deteriorated gradually and reached several low points in the following decade. For example, in March 1899, British and American ships shelled the Samoan capital Apia and damaged the German consulate there during a dispute over the succession to the Samoan throne.

Weltpolitik and naval rivalry

Wilhelm embarked on a policy of Weltpolitik (World Policy). Weltpolitik was designed chiefly by von Bülow, a foreign policy expert and later chancellor, and von Tirpitz, a naval commander. It was an ambitious policy, which ultimately aimed to make Germany a major world power. Weltpolitik involved actively seeking overseas possessions, or, as Kaiser Wilhelm termed it, 'a place in the sun'. By 1914, Germany had taken possession of four colonies in Africa:

- Kamerun (an area now divided between Cameroon and a part of Nigeria)
- German East Africa (an area now divided between Rwanda, Burundi and most of Tanzania)
- German South-West Africa (now Namibia)
- Togoland (an area now divided between Togo and part of Ghana).

Germany had also taken possession of numerous scattered islands in the Pacific, including:

- part of New Guinea
- the Bismarck Archipelago
- the western half of Samoa
- the northern half of the Solomon Islands
- Nauru
- the Mariana, Caroline and Marshall Islands.

By the time that Germany entered the race for African possessions, most of the profitable areas had already been taken by other nations. This meant that Germany's colonies in East Africa cost Germany much more than they were worth. Also Germany's late entry into the race for African possessions added to the existing tensions. Britain, in particular, saw German acquisitions in Africa as a threat to its own strategic and commercial interests.

Germany's programme of naval expansion concerned the British even more. Britain had possessed the largest and most powerful navy in the world for over a hundred years. Most people in Britain saw the navy as an essential sign of British power, and vital to maintaining the empire. In the 1889 Naval Defence Act, the British government formally adopted the 'two power standard'. This standard was committed to ensuring that the British navy remained at least as powerful as the combined strength of the next two largest navies. (At the time, this meant the French and Russian navies.) Germany's Navy Laws put the British government under pressure to meet this commitment. In 1906, the British launched HMS Dreadnought, a battleship that was dramatically superior to previous warships in every way. This new battleship gave the Royal Navy a huge, but short-lived advantage.

Five German Navy Laws were passed between 1898 and 1912, and Germany's navy quickly set about building battleships to rival HMS Dreadnought. Germany's navy became the second-largest in the world, and by 1914 the German fleet included 15 Dreadnoughts and seven powerful battle cruisers. Without an extensive overseas empire, and with only a northern coastline and no obvious threat from the seas, Germany did not appear to depend upon a strong navy in the way the British felt they did. In addition, the British navy was spread all over the world, protecting its empire. As Germany had few overseas possessions, it would be able to concentrate its navy in the North Sea, which could be seen as a threat to Britain. Many people in Britain felt that Germany's naval expansion was, therefore, an aggressive move intended to challenge them. This feeling was strengthened as Britain's government and public were unsettled by Kaiser Wilhelm's repeated complaints about British madness and disrespect towards his country.

Kaiser Wilhelm explained the reasons for Germany's naval expansion in an interview with a British journalist in 1908:

> Germany is a young and growing empire. It has a world-wide commerce which is rapidly expanding and to which the legitimate ambition of patriotic Germans refuses to assign any bounds. Germany must have a powerful fleet to protect that commerce and its many interests in even the most distant seas. Germany expects those interests to go on growing, and it must be able to champion them manfully in any quarter of the globe. Germany's horizons stretch far away, and it must be prepared for any eventualities. Only those powers that have great navies will be listened to with respect and, if for that reason only, Germany must have a powerful fleet.
>
> **From an interview with Kaiser Wilhelm published in *The Daily Telegraph*, 28 October 1908.**

The British government expanded the Royal Navy's building programme to maintain Britain's advantage, and a **naval race** began. In both countries, public opinion, encouraged by newspapers, popular writers and naval pressure groups, demanded more battleships. From 1906 to 1914 the British built 29 Dreadnoughts, and the Germans built 15. The British can, therefore, be said to have 'won' the naval race.

KEY TERM

Naval race: An arms race in which two or more countries build warships to maintain an advantage over their rivals.

British public finances were stretched to crisis point in order to stay ahead in the naval race. Meanwhile the British government became increasingly concerned with Germany's foreign policies (see following section on tensions in South Africa). In 1912, the government despatched a diplomat, Lord Haldane, to Berlin to try to reduce tensions.

ACTIVITY 1.16

a Study the extract from Kaiser Wilhelm's letter to *The Daily Telegraph* in 1908. In pairs, discuss and make notes on the following questions:

  i What reasons did Kaiser Wilhelm II give to explain his decision to expand the German navy?

  ii Why would the expansion of the German navy cause concern in Britain?

b Using any resources available to you, do some research on the impact of the naval rivalries in Britain and Germany.

  i You might like to look for some information relating to the way politics was affected, the way ordinary people felt about the expansion of their navies, and the ways governments tried to raise money to pay for the ships.

  ii You might also like to investigate how countries in the British Empire contributed to the effort to win the naval race.

c Present your findings on a poster or a digital presentation.

d Work with a partner. One person should consider why Britain went to such lengths to avoid defeat in the naval race. The other person should think about why Germany wanted to win the naval race so badly. Work together to create a chart to demonstrate the similarities and differences in their motives. Were their motives always the same, or do you think that their reasons changed as time went by?

Figure 1.21: An illustration titled 'The "Dreadnought" Fever'. It shows the global growth of Dreadnoughts from one in 1905 to approximately 150 in 1913.

Tension over South Africa

As well as the African kingdoms of the region, in the 19th century southern Africa contained four states populated by non-African colonist settlers. The British had the colonies of Cape Colony and Natal, and there were two independent Boer republics – the Orange Free State and the South African Republic, commonly referred to as the Transvaal.

Britain saw its territorial possessions in South Africa as critical economic and strategic parts of its empire in the 1870 and 1880s. The Cape at the southernmost tip of Africa had always been a vital supply station for British shipping, but the situation in South Africa was transformed by the discovery of gold in the Transvaal in 1886. German involvement in Africa changed the international situation, after Bismarck decided to defend the interests of a German trading company by asserting a claim in South West Africa. Bismarck saw the opportunity to bargain with Britain by supporting French claims in Egypt, and he exploited the 'Egyptian Lever' to try to get German control in Zanzibar and German East Africa in 1885. Two agreements were signed in 1886 and 1890 that kept relations peaceful for a short time.

Southern Africa continued to cause problems between Britain and Germany in the 1890s, however. Britain was determined to prevent other European countries, particularly France and Germany, from effectively occupying the potentially mineral-rich areas for themselves. Britain, therefore, moved quickly to secure its control of the region. British administrators, including Cecil Rhodes, who became prime minister of Cape Colony in 1890, began to dominate the region. As more English-speaking gold and diamond prospectors flooded into the area, concerns rose in the Boer republics about a potential British takeover.

Cecil Rhodes, the British prime minister of Cape Colony, came up with a plan to create a federation of South African states under British control. Believing that an uprising of 'uitlanders' (outsiders, most of whom were British gold miners) against the Transvaal government was imminent, in December 1895 Rhodes used a dispute between the governments of Cape Colony and the Transvaal, over taxes and access for goods transported through Transvaal territory, as the excuse for a plan to 'restore order' in Transvaal. A force of 600 men under the command of Leander Starr Jameson was assembled to cross the border into Transvaal, but the plan was chaotic and poorly executed. The Jameson Raid failed, and the raiders were captured. The plan immediately became an embarrassment to the British, but the intervention of Kaiser Wilhelm II turned the public mood.

In January 1896 the Kaiser sent a telegram to **President Kruger** of the Transvaal, congratulating him on defeating the Jameson Raid, 'without the help of friendly powers'. This implied that Germany would have assisted the Boers and caused an anti-German reaction among the British public.

The Kaiser's telegram to President Kruger read:

> I express to you my sincere congratulations that you and your people, without appealing to the help of friendly powers, have succeeded, by your own energetic action against the armed bands which invaded your country as disturbers of the peace, in restoring peace and in maintaining the independence of the country against attack from without.
>
> **From a telegram from Wilhelm II to Paul Kruger, 3 January 1896.**

KEY FIGURE

Paul Kruger (1825–1904)

Kruger was president of the South African Republic (Transvaal) 1883–1900. Kruger played a role in strengthening self-government in the region in the 1880s. He later led the Boers in their struggle against Britain during the Boer War, 1899–1902.

The Boers began arming themselves, importing thousands of modern rifles and artillery from Germany between 1895 and 1899. The Boer War, between Britain and the Boer republics, began in 1899 and lasted until 1902. When this war broke out, volunteers from Germany joined the Boers, and the German press was strongly anti-British in its coverage.

After three years of fighting, the Boers surrendered. Britain's victory was confirmed by the Treaty of Vereeniging in 1902. This treaty placed Orange Free State and Transvaal firmly under British control, but damage was done to the relationship between Britain and Germany. Germany condemned British actions in the war, in particular the use of **'scorched earth'** tactics to destroy property and crops and concentration camps for prisoners. German criticisms left Britain feeling isolated and offended.

KEY TERM

'Scorched earth': A battle tactic in which an army deliberately burns crops and property in an area to deny the enemy food and shelter.

Emily Hobhouse was a British woman who opposed the Boer Wars and was concerned about the suffering of South African women and children. After visiting a concentration camp in Bloemfontein in January 1901, she wrote a report which she shared with Sir Henry Campbell-Bannerman, who was leader of the Liberal Party in Britain, on her return to England:

> When the eight, ten or twelve people who lived in the bell tent were squeezed into it to find shelter against the heat of the sun, the dust or the rain, there was no room to stir and the air in the tent was beyond description. Soap was an article that was not dispensed. The water supply was inadequate. No bedsteads or mattresses were available. The rations were extremely poor and when, as I frequently experienced, the actual quantity dispensed fell short of the amount prescribed, it simply meant famine.
>
> **From Emily Hobhouse's 'Report on Bloemfontein Concentration Camp', January 1901.**

KEY FIGURE

Emily Hobhouse (1860–1926)

Emily Hobhouse was a campaigner for workers' welfare and a pacifist (opponent of war). She is remembered for her criticisms of British treatment of South African women and children in 'concentration camps' during the Boer War. Her letters about the camps, which were published in British newspapers, raised awareness. She raised money in Britain to fund education for women and girls in South Africa after the war.

ACTIVITY 1.17

Consider the following questions. Prepare notes on the key points. Do some research using the sources of information available to you to add more detail if necessary.

a What factors might explain why Britain found it so difficult to defeat a relatively small number of Boer farmers?

b Did the British find it difficult to defeat African forces such as the Ndebele for the same reasons?

c Why did other European countries object to the methods that Britain used in order to defeat the Boers?

d What were the implications of the Boer War for British foreign policy?

e Discuss with a partner the problems which Britain faced in defeating the Boers and the implications of the Boer War for British foreign policy between 1901 and 1914. If you were responsible for British foreign policy after 1902, would you have regarded the Boer War as a minor issue or a major embarrassment?

Rivalries between France and Britain

The Berlin Conference had encouraged European nations to occupy areas of Africa that were not already under their control. Britain and France had a colonial rivalry that dated back over a hundred years and included territories from Canada to India.

By the 1880s, both Britain and France wanted to create transcontinental colonial territories. France resented the way the British had annexed Egypt in 1882, and the British were determined to protect their strategic and trading interests from French competition.

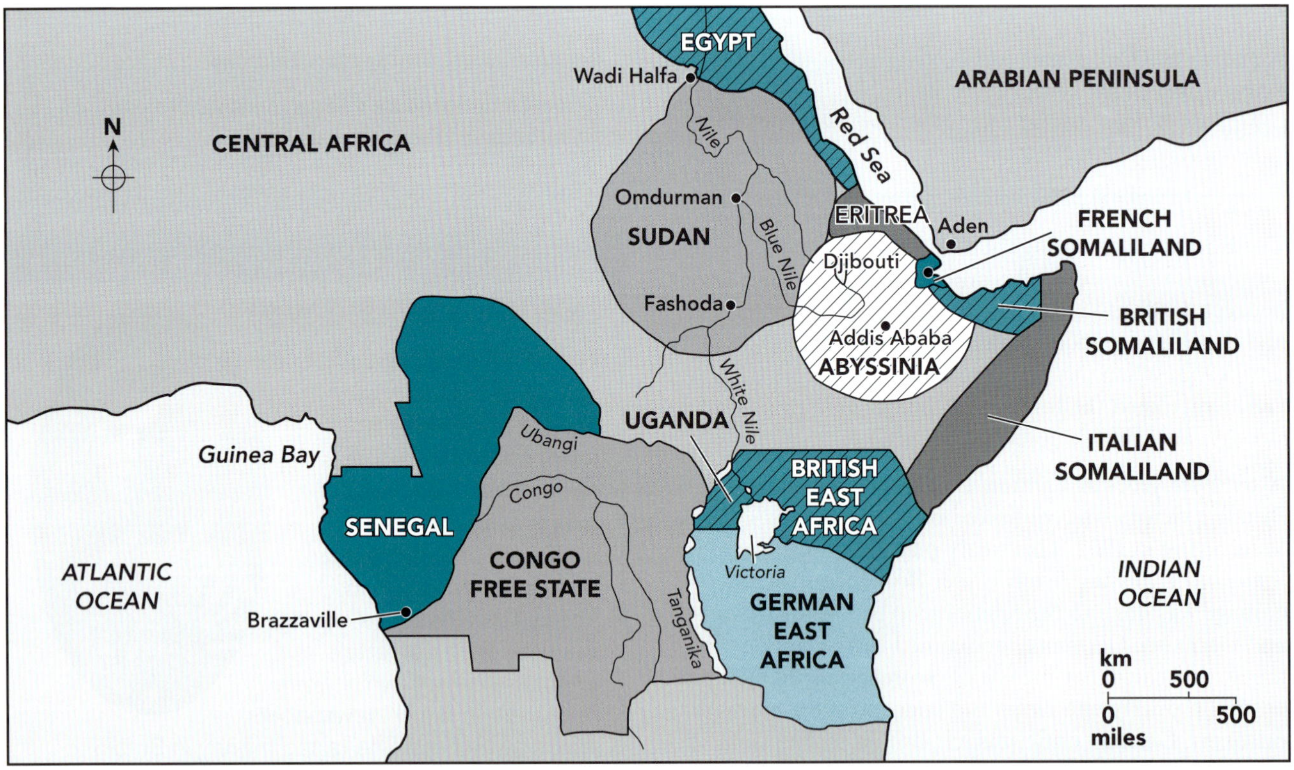

Figure 1.22: The political situation in eastern and central Africa in 1898.

The Sudan

Sudan had been under Egyptian control since the early 19th century. During the 1870s, when Egypt was weakened by economic insecurity and British involvement in Egypt had increased, Sudan had also come under British influence. Britain aimed to connect its territories in Egypt and South Africa with an uninterrupted north–south corridor, and, since Sudan bordered on Egypt to the south, it was critical to these plans. By the early 1890s, however, local armies had defeated Egyptian and British forces, and Italy had begun to expand into the region. After the Italian defeat at Adwa in 1896, the British decided to reassert their control in Sudan.

France wanted a continuous link between Senegal and French Somaliland. Expansion from the west progressed through the 1870s and 1880s, and by the 1890s control of Sudan had become critical to the completion of the French plan. French and British colonial ambitions ran into conflict with each other in Sudan, at Fashoda.

The Fashoda Incident

Fashoda was an abandoned military base and trading post built by the Egyptians in 1855, and it offered the ability to control the Upper Nile valley. The French could see its strategic advantage, and they sent Major Jean-Baptiste Marchand, a French officer, to occupy the area around Fashoda. Marchand and his men had arrived at Fashoda in July 1898 after a 24-month journey on foot and by boat from the Congo River and they begun to rebuild the fort. They were expecting reinforcements, but they were not anticipating contact with other Europeans.

In September 1898, a British expedition from Egypt, led by Herbert Kitchener, defeated the Sudanese at the Battle of Omdurman. As Kitchener's men pursued the surviving Sudanese retreat, they encountered Major Marchand and his men at Fashoda. The British hugely outnumbered Marchand's men.

Both sides insisted that they had the right to control Fashoda, but Kitchener and Marchand were diplomatic, and the meeting was polite. They compromised and agreed to fly the Egyptian flag over the fort, but a stand-off ensued. There was a period of intense diplomatic exchanges between London and Paris and public opinion on both sides (encouraged by the press) favoured war to settle the matter. A domestic political crisis in France, as well as Russia's refusal to back France in the event of war with Britain, convinced the French to back down. The French government ordered the French forces to leave in November, and Marchand returned to Paris. Britain's position in east Africa was strengthened, and Anglo-French relations remained bitter for a number of years after 1898.

Rivalries between France and Germany

As a consequence of defeat in the Franco-Prussian War in 1871, France had handed control of the regions of Alsace and Lorraine to Germany and been forced to submit to a humiliating peace. The desire for revenge in France was strong for a generation, and under Bismarck Germany had played a careful game of keeping France isolated without provoking further conflict. Under Wilhelm II, however, that policy of balancing European power came under threat, and Morocco was the location of an important diplomatic crisis.

Morocco

By 1900, businessmen from several European countries had begun to trade in Morocco. France controlled neighbouring Algeria and, disappointed in Egypt and Sudan, aimed to extend its empire in North Africa. An 1880 international agreement signed in Madrid had granted European powers equal access in Morocco, but in the 1904 Anglo-French **entente** known as the Entente Cordiale, Britain had recognised French interests there. France had begun secret negotiations with Spain and Italy over a future French occupation of Morocco.

While on a Mediterranean cruise, the Kaiser landed at Tangier in March 1905. Through his public statements, he challenged the existing Anglo-French diplomatic arrangements regarding Morocco's political status and appeared to affirm the Sultan of Morocco's sovereign position. Wilhelm formally demanded that Morocco's status should be referred to an international conference. His actions suggested an attempt to assert Germany's diplomatic significance in international negotiations, emphasizing the country's desire to be consulted on major global issues. He possibly also wanted to force France to back down and thereby weaken its credibility as an ally in the eyes of Great Britain and Russia. He may have wanted to test Britain's commitment to backing France. Some in the French government tried to force a confrontation with Germany over Wilhelm's behaviour, but it was impossible to reject Wilhelm's calls for an international conference. The conference took place at Algeciras in Spain In January–March 1906.

KEY TERM

Entente: Less formal than a treaty, an entente is a friendly understanding or informal agreement between states.

ACTIVITY 1.18

With a partner, discuss and make notes on the following questions:

a Both the Fashoda Incident and Kaiser Wilhelm's actions in Morocco threatened to lead to war between major European countries. In both cases, war was avoided. How might this be explained?

b Britain and France had been traditional enemies and their rival imperial ambitions had almost led to war between them. However, by the end of the 19th century, relations between Britain and France were becoming more friendly. What do you consider were the two main reasons for this?

c Was a formal alliance between Britain and France likely by 1900, do you think? What factors might have prevented such an alliance?

Attempts to resolve tensions between imperial nations after 1900

Although they were rivals for control in Africa, imperial nations felt that tensions in Africa were not important enough to fight over, so they did their best to avoid war.

The end of Britain's 'splendid isolation' and the Anglo-French Entente

At times, countries may find themselves isolated, without military or diplomatic alliances or lacking trading partnerships. In some cases this is not a deliberate choice, but sometimes countries will opt for a policy of **isolationism**. Britain's prime minister and foreign secretary between 1886 and 1891 was Lord Salisbury, and he firmly believed that Britain should avoid 'entangling alliances'. He wanted to avoid formal alliances that might commit Britain to unreliable allies or unnecessary military interventions.

Germany, Austria-Hungary, Russia, Italy and France all signed binding treaties with each other in the last 30 years of the 19th century. However, with only a couple of exceptions (the 1887 Mediterranean Agreements with Italy, and the 1890 Heligoland–Zanzibar Agreement with Germany) Britain remained deliberately isolated from other European countries. This policy was known as 'splendid isolation'.

By the beginning of the 20th century, it became clear that Britain needed to abandon this policy. There were a number of reasons for this:

- It was becoming increasingly difficult for Britain to protect and maintain control over its vast empire.
- The Boer War had exposed fundamental weaknesses in Britain's military capabilities.
- The negative reaction of the other European powers to Britain's involvement in the Boer War left Britain feeling isolated and vulnerable.
- Germany had adopted a more aggressive foreign policy under Kaiser Wilhelm II – German acquisitions in Africa posed a threat to British possessions on the continent; more significantly, Germany's naval development programme threatened to undermine the supremacy of the British navy.
- Russian expansion in East Asia was now posing a significant threat to Britain's commercial interests in China.

By 1907, Britain had signed three alliances with some new allies:

The Anglo-Japanese Treaty (1902)

The agreement outlined the following key provisions: both parties acknowledged the sovereignty of China and Korea; specific zones of influence in China were delineated; Britain acknowledged Japan's strategic interests in Korea; Japan committed to naval protection of British interests in East Asia; the parties established mutual **neutrality** protocols, with provisions for military support under specific conflict scenarios involving third powers.

KEY TERMS

Isolationism: The policy of keeping one's country separate from the affairs of other nations, by avoiding alliances and international commitments.

Neutrality: Staying out of a conflict; not supporting either side in a war. Countries which do this are known as neutral countries.

The signing of the Anglo-Japanese Treaty was greeted favourably in both Britain and Japan. The British felt that their strategic and economic interests in East Asia were now adequately protected against Russian expansion. To the Japanese, the alliance was a major triumph. Japan could now count on British support in a war against Russia if any other country, such as France or Germany, sided with the Russians. Also, the signing of the alliance marked the first time that Japan had been recognised as an equal by one of the major European powers. Some historians have argued that the alliance established Japan's emergence as a world power in its own right.

You will read more about the Anglo-Japanese Treaty of 1902 in Section 1.3.

ACTIVITY 1.19

Figure 1.23: A British cartoon, published in 1905. The caption reads: '"Oh, East is East, and West is West ... But there is neither East nor West, Border, nor Breed, nor Birth, When two strong men stand face to face, tho' they come from the ends of the earth!" –Rudyard Kipling.'

a Working in pairs:

- i One person should write down the reasons why Britain formed the 1902 alliance with Japan. Write each reason on a separate piece of paper.
- ii The other person should write down the reasons why Japan formed the 1902 alliance with Britain. Make sure you write each reason on a separate piece of paper.
- iii Compare reasons and arrange them into three piles: one pile for Britain's motives, one pile for Japan's motives, and one pile for motives shared by both Britain and Japan.
- iv Discuss together: how similar were the motives of both powers?
- v Which side had more to gain from the alliance? How did you reach that judgement?

b

- i Look carefully at the cartoon in Figure 1.23. How does this cartoon represent Britain? How is the figure drawn? What message about Britain do you think you are meant to see here?
- ii What message are we meant to see about Japan, from the way the Japanese character is drawn?
- iii Do you think that the cartoonist sees the two countries as equals? Explain your judgement, referring to the details in the cartoon to support your points.
- iv What is the point of the text from Rudyard Kipling, do you think?
- v What can historians learn from this cartoon about attitudes to the Anglo-Japanese Alliance in Britain?

The Anglo-French Entente, 1904

This alliance was made up of three agreements:

- **The agreement respecting Egypt and Morocco:** France accepted British control in Egypt. Britain accepted French influence in Morocco. The declaration was not aimed against another power, no joint action was planned and there was no military aspect to the agreement. The declaration guaranteed free passage for all ships from any country through the Suez Canal and banned the building of fortifications on part of the Moroccan coast.
- **The agreement relating to Newfoundland and portions of West and Central Africa:** The agreement respecting Newfoundland and portions of West and Central Africa: In return for giving up its rights to part of Newfoundland's western coast, France was given the Iles de Los (located in present-day Guinea) and a settlement near the current border of The Gambia and Senegal. Britain and France also reached agreement on territorial disputes over areas around the Niger River, in what are now Niger and Nigeria.
- **The agreement respecting Siam (now Thailand), Madagascar and the New Hebrides (now Vanuatu):** France and Britain agreed that France had influence over Siam, but that neither country would attempt to take over there. Although Britain had objected to it before, France was now allowed to introduce a **tariff** in Madagascar. Both countries agreed not to allow disagreements over the New Hebrides to lead to war.

> **KEY TERM**
>
> **Tariff:** A tax imposed on specific goods imported from specific countries, usually used to make those goods more expensive than the locally produced alternatives.

The Anglo-French agreement was known as the 'Entente Cordiale'. The agreement resolved a number of longstanding colonial disputes and established a friendlier kind of diplomatic understanding between the two countries than had existed previously. However, it stopped short of binding either country to any military undertaking in support of the other. France was keen to establish an ally in case of possible German aggression and signed the entente hoping to establish a more formal alliance.

Britain was also keen to cooperate, because of increasing German naval strength. The entente, therefore, included an agreement that the French navy would cover the Mediterranean, if the Royal Navy would concentrate its forces in the North Sea.

The German Kaiser believed that the new friendship between Britain and France posed a threat to Germany's international prestige and influence. He viewed French claims over Morocco as an opportunity to weaken the improved relationship between Britain and France. This may have inspired the 1905 Moroccan Crisis.

The Anglo-Russian Entente, 1907

The terms of this agreement covered three disputed regions:

- **Persia:** Persia was divided into three zones – a large northern Russian zone, a southern British zone and a neutral zone in between.
- **Tibet:** Britain and Russia acknowledged Chinese sovereignty over Tibet and agreed to keep out of the region.
- **Afghanistan:** Afghanistan was acknowledged as a British preserve, although it was not to be annexed.

The Anglo-Russian Entente did not entirely stop Britain and France from competing against each other with their policies in Persia. However, it did mean that from 1907 the two countries worked better together. This helped to consolidate the **Triple Entente** that would go to war in 1914.

> **KEY TERM**
>
> **Triple Entente:** The name given to Britain, France and the Russian Empire – the countries that signed ententes in 1904 and 1907.

The Algeciras conference

Following the crisis over French involvement in Morocco begun by Kaiser Wilhelm's 1905 speech, a conference was called at Algeciras in Spain (January–March 1906). Germany hoped to isolate Britain and expected that the conference would expose the weaknesses in the Entente Cordiale, signed in 1904. Germany expected that, once the French realised that the British were unwilling to support them if the crisis became serious, friendlier relations between Germany and France might become possible. Germany also hoped that Russia would be open to cooperation, after the embarrassment of defeat to the Japanese in the 1904–05 Russo-Japanese War (see Section 1.3).

Such hopes were unrealistic, because Kaiser Wilhelm's behaviour before the conference made the French very mistrustful of him. It was clear to both Britain and France that they needed to cooperate with each other when dealing with Germany.

The outcome of the conference was very different from what Wilhelm had expected. Only Morocco and Austria-Hungary backed Germany's position; Spain, Italy, Russia, Great Britain and the USA all supported French rights in Morocco. The British and French held special meetings while at the conference. These meetings actually strengthened the Entente Cordiale, as did the public display of support for the French position by the British Foreign Secretary, Sir Edward Grey. The Russians also supported France strongly, partly because they hoped to agree a large loan.

The Moroccans were hampered at the conference because the information provided to them, and the translations of the discussions, were inadequate.

At the end of the conference, in April 1906,

- the independence of the sultan of Morocco was confirmed
- the economic equality of all the powers with respect to trade with Morocco was confirmed
- regulations concerning the repression of weapons-smuggling were agreed
- a new State Bank of Morocco was set up, and loans from the European powers were agreed
- the Moroccan police force remained under the sultan of Morocco's control, but French and Spanish police would be responsible for training Moroccan police officers
- the French and Spanish would police the ports in Morocco
- a Swiss inspector would oversee the work of the Spanish and French police and report to the Sultan of Morocco.

Germany had failed to end French influence in Morocco. The Anglo-French Entente Cordiale held firm, and Germany was embarrassed.

The convention of November 1911 that ended the Agadir crisis

On occasions in 1908 and 1909, when the issue of French control in Morocco might have created conflict between France and Germany, Wilhelm accepted French interests and avoided further disputes. In 1909, for example, France and Germany agreed that France would have political influence in Morocco, but Germany would be allowed to retain economic interests in Morocco.

In 1911, however, a rebellion broke out in Morocco and the French despatched a large force to the capital, Fez, to assert their authority. They also forced the sultan to sign a new treaty in which he promised not to sign any other treaties without French approval. This promise appeared to break previous agreements. Germany did not protest about French military deployment but saw an opportunity and demanded the whole of French Congo as territorial compensation.

The German gunboat Panther was sent to the Moroccan port of Agadir. The excuse for this was that the gunboat was protecting German trade interests, but the threat was clear. Britain and France reacted immediately. Politicians and senior military officials on both sides began discussions and talked of preparing for war. Franco-German discussions were held in Paris, while the British prime minister, David Lloyd George, made a key speech in which he emphasised British support for the French.

A financial crisis and the influence of more moderate (less aggressive) ministers in Berlin led the Germans to de-escalate the crisis. Secret negotiations began, and in November 1911 the Franco-German Accord was signed. Germany accepted France's position in Morocco, as well as a small area in modern-day Chad, in return for 275 000 square km of territory in Congo (now the Republic of the Congo).

For politicians in France and Germany the crisis ended with embarrassment, but the Agadir Crisis (also known as the second Moroccan Crisis) confirmed the strength of the Entente Cordiale.

The situation in 1914

By 1914, European colonial empires dominated the globe.

The extent of European empires

The British Empire covered more than 30 million square kilometres and contained at least 400 million people. The French Empire covered over 10 million square kilometres and ruled over 60 million people. Germany's empire was much smaller (around 2.6 million square kilometres), but Germany's pursuit of imperial possessions had far-reaching effects. Without Germany's involvement in the Scramble for Africa and the race for colonies elsewhere, Britain and France might not have been so fearful in the years before 1914.

Not counting those men and women who served in non-combat roles in the First World War of 1914–18, the empires of European countries would still contribute huge numbers of people to the fighting. Fighting on the side of the British alone, for example, were 1.4 million men from India, 458 000 Canadians, 8000 Newfoundlanders, 332 000 Australians, 112 000 New Zealanders, 136 000 South Africans, 16 000 West Indians, 34 000 East Africans, and 25 000 West Africans. France was also served by over 500 000 colonial troops.

The influence of imperial expansion on European alliances

In many ways, the expansion of European empires provided a way to relieve diplomatic and economic pressures without any of the powers doing each other harm in the years before 1914. Since rivalries and disputes did not involve their own territories, European countries could behave aggressively or back down without fear of provoking a war or losing face. The legacy created by the rivalries between these imperial powers was significant, however. Rivalries and conflicts were increased, affecting the opinions of politicians and public alike.

In the years before 1914, many Germans had believed that their legitimate colonial expansion was repeatedly blocked by the French and British. This belief increased German resentment and frustration and led to nationalistic sentiment. By 1914, German colonial policy had harmed relations with other powers. In addition, it had failed to provide an overseas empire to rival Britain's, and this led to a sense of frustration. Germans felt insecure, encircled and concerned that Germany's prestige did not mirror its economic power. However, these were European concerns, and Germany's alliances reflected them.

Britain's alliances – like its empire – were global. Agreements with Japan, France and Russia were signed partly with European concerns in mind, but largely because of their potential to make Britain's empire more secure. Britain's view of Germany was shaped by the way German policy threatened Britain's imperial power. Likewise, Britain's involvement in European affairs in the years after 1900 was driven by the desire to maintain Britain's empire. Britain's relations with France, which were crucial to the formation of the major alliances that fought the First World War, were influenced, for good and bad, by how much they could cooperate on colonial questions.

Nevertheless, it is important to remember that Russia, Austria-Hungary and Serbia – the countries that were central to the crisis that began the war – were most concerned about problems relating to continental (rather than overseas) empires. Events in Africa, Asia and the Pacific held little interest for them.

Contemporary views and verdicts

When war approached in 1914, in Germany, many people reacted to news of the approaching crisis with a sense that war was inevitable. Many Germans felt that Britain and France were preventing Germany's legitimate plan for expansion. They also believed that threats to Germany from Russia justified declaring war.

Russians and Austrians were concerned about problems relating to continental empire. Pro-war sentiment in Russia was often anti-German, but since many Russians sympathised with the plight of all peoples in central and eastern Europe who speak Slavic languages (known collectively as **Slavs**) and saw their duty as protector of all the Slavs, pro-war attitudes can also be described as Pan-Slav. Austrians saw the assassination of Archduke Franz Ferdinand as a national insult and wanted revenge against Serbia.

However, the problems of colonial possessions abroad did not motivate most people. There were **pacifist** demonstrations across Europe, rather than pro-empire calls to arms. At the end of July 1914, the French press was more concerned with the trial of the wife of a leading politician, who had shot and killed a newspaper editor. In Britain, political problems relating to Ireland were a more urgent problem than overseas colonies.

The British Foreign Secretary, Sir Edward Grey, was convinced that Britain should not get drawn into military commitment to European problems. Later, a journalist asked British troops on the Western Front whether they were fighting for the Empire and one soldier said 'yes'. His comrades asked him what he meant. He answered that he was fighting for the Empire Music Hall in Hackney, a **working-class** area in London.

Empire contributed to tensions between European powers before 1914 and was one of the factors that created the conditions in which war could break out. However, empire was not in itself a major cause of the war.

KEY TERMS

Slav: A member of a group of peoples in central and eastern Europe speaking Slavic languages.

Pacifist: Someone who opposes war or violence as a means of settling disputes.

Working-class: Belonging to the working class, a group in society consisting of people who work, often in jobs involving physical labour, and who earn or possess little money compared to other social classes.

ACTIVITY 1.20

a Look back over the information in this section, and the work you have done on it. Work in a small group to construct a timeline showing the major events from this section that led to increased tensions between the European powers. You could put this timeline together on a wall display.

b Look back over all the events on your timeline. Use some coloured sticky notes, or some similar method, to indicate which events were directly related to colonial territories.

c Consider the argument: 'The tensions that created the First World War were colonial tensions.' How far does the evidence from your timeline support this view? Discuss with your partners and be ready to support your viewpoint with evidence from your timeline.

ACTIVITY 1.21

Look back at the information in this chapter so far. In small groups, do some research on whether the economic benefits of empires outweighed the costs for European nations. Make sure that one group investigates the costs and benefits of empire for Britain, Germany, France, and Belgium. Prepare a presentation for the rest of the class. In each case, present your findings on:

- How important were economic motivations for colonisers?
- Were economic motivations equally important for all colonial actors (individuals and states, for example) and were they always important?
- How many non-economic motives were there at play, and how did they overlap with economic factors?
- Do you think that people at the time had such clear-cut ideas about their motives?

Reflection

Discuss your ideas about these questions with a partner or a small group. Why do debates like this matter to historians? Think about how two historians – one with an economics focus, and the other with a religious focus – might approach the topic of the Scramble for Africa differently from each other.

KEY CONCEPT 1.2

Interpretations

Although he disagreed with them, British economist John Hobson outlined the reasons for imperial expansion in the last quarter of the 19th century as entirely related to economics. His ideas were supported by V. I. Lenin, leader of the Bolsheviks in Russia (see Section 1.3), and for a long time, the economic explanation for imperialism was accepted.

> Imperialists argue that we must have new markets for our growing manufactures and new outlets for the investment of our surplus capital. Imperial expansion is a necessity for a nation with our great and growing powers of production. An ever larger share of our population is devoted to manufacturing and commerce, and is therefore dependent for life and work upon food and raw materials from foreign lands. In order to buy and pay for these things, we must sell our goods abroad.
>
> **From John A. Hobson, 'The Economic Taproot of Imperialism' in *Imperialism: A Study* (1902).**

At the time, European supporters of colonial policies certainly used economic arguments to justify their actions, but they also used what they considered to be moral and religious arguments:

> Beyond doubt I think the most useful missions are the medical and the industrial, in the initial stages of savage development. A combination of the two is, in my opinion, an ideal mission. As the skill of the European in medicine asserts its superiority over the crude methods of the medicine man, so does he in proportion gain an influence in his teaching of the great truths of Christianity. He teaches the savage where knowledge and art cease, how far natural remedies produce their effects, independent of charms or supernatural agencies, and where divine power overrules all human efforts. Such demonstration from a medicine man, whose skill they cannot fail to recognize as superior to their own, has naturally more weight than any mere preaching.
>
> **From Capt. F. D. Lugard, *The Rise of Our East African Empire*, 1893.**

> Gentlemen, we must speak more loudly and more honestly! We must say openly that indeed the higher races have a right over the lower races. ... I repeat, that the superior races have a right because they have a duty. They have the duty to civilize the inferior races. ... In the history of earlier centuries these duties, gentlemen, have often been misunderstood, and certainly when the Spanish soldiers and explorers introduced slavery into Central America, they did not fulfil their duty as men of a higher race.
>
> **From Jules Ferry's speech before the French Chamber of Deputies, 28 March 1884.**

By the 1960s and 1970s, historians began to re-evaluate the economic motives for colonialism. As one historian put it, in the British government 'decisions to annex or not to annex were made usually on the basis of political or geopolitical considerations'. In fact, this historian went on, more recent studies tended 'to shift the emphasis from the economic motive to a plurality of motives'.

Look back on the information in this section. Work with a partner and think about the reasons why European powers became colonial powers.

- How much evidence do you find in support of Hobson and Lenin's views?
- How persuasive do you find this evidence, compared with the evidence in support of other arguments?

1.3 Why did Japan emerge as a world power and what was the impact on international relations?

The first half of the 19th century was a period known as the Tokugawa shogunate (after the shogun, or military **dictator**, Tokugawa Ieyasu). For most of the previous 800 years, Japan had been dominated by the samurai, a small class of hereditary nobility. Japan was peaceful, politically stable and wealthy, and it was also isolated from the rest of the world. Japan followed a policy of self-enforced isolation through a series of policies called 'sakoku' meaning 'closed country'.

These policies ensured that:

- Christianity was banned
- Japanese people were prohibited from making or returning from trips overseas
- trade with various foreign countries was not allowed
- foreign powers were almost entirely banned from any diplomatic relations with Japan.

KEY TERM

Dictator: A leader of a country who has no limits to their power.

ACTIVITY 1.22

Use the resources available to you. Do some research on the samurai system in Japan in the 1800s. Construct a one-page summary of the key information you find.

In the latter half of the 19th century, however, Japan's relations with Western powers changed, as Japan began to seek overseas possessions of its own in an effort to acquire the raw materials that it needed to modernise and develop. By 1914 Japan had emerged as a world power.

Japanese relations with Western powers in the 19th century

Japanese shoguns believed that influences from abroad would destabilise the country. They allowed trade with the Chinese, and also with Dutch ships. The Dutch were allowed only limited access, however: Dutch ships could land at just one port (Dejima) and merchants were subject to strict rules and were not allowed out of the port to interact with Japanese traders.

Japan did not experience an industrial revolution like the ones in Europe and the USA, and by the mid-19th century, when **Western powers** were exploring new markets and territories for colonial expansion, Japan had fallen behind. In 1844, the Dutch king sent a letter warning Japan that foreign intervention would come by force if the Japanese did not end their isolation.

KEY TERM

Western powers: A term used to refer to the European countries with the most powerful economies, armies and navies, and the USA.

In fact, the Americans had been sending ships into Japanese waters for some years by this time. In the 1830s, several American missions had been sent to Japan, but they had all been turned away because they did not have permission to land there. American whaling fleets had requested access to Japanese ports in order to take on vital supplies, especially coal, but these requests had been denied. In the 1840s, American naval officers made official requests for trade agreements, but these were rejected. In 1849, the USA sent a warship, USS *Preble,* to Japan to rescue American sailors who had been shipwrecked off the Japanese coast. The Japanese did not allow the *Preble* to enter the port until the Americans threatened to use force. The USA was angered by the harsh treatment its sailors had received from the Japanese.

In 1851, President Millard Fillmore signed a letter to the Japanese offering a trading arrangement as part of the return of shipwrecked Japanese sailors. Responsibility for pursuing this plan was given to Commodore Matthew Perry.

Commodore Perry's mission

Commodore Perry was a senior navy officer with combat experience (for example in the Mexican–American War), and some experience in diplomacy. He gathered a small squadron of two steamers and two sailing vessels in preparation for his mission. Then, in July 1853, Perry and his ships sailed to Edo Bay, Tokyo. The Japanese met them with a hostile response and ordered them to leave. Perry then turned his guns towards the town of Uraga. Perry's ships fired blank shots. Officials boarded Perry's ship and repeated the message that the Americans should leave. Perry refused to discuss the matter and sent the message that unless a more senior Japanese representative agreed to receive him, he would land American troops on shore. Perry continued to threaten the Japanese with the use of force. After several days, with no guns or cannons to use in their defence, the Japanese allowed Perry to land so that he could deliver his letter from President Fillmore. Perry promised to return to collect the reply, and his ships departed.

Figure 1.24: This painting shows a Japanese artist's impression of the visit of Commodore Perry's ship to Tokyo in 1853. What can you learn from this image about the impact of Perry's mission?

ACTIVITY 1.23

I have no other object in sending Commodore Perry to Japan but to propose that the United States and Japan should live in friendship and have commercial intercourse [relations] with each other. I am desirous that our two countries should trade with each other, for the benefit both of Japan and the United States.

Many of our ships pass every year from California to China, and a great number of our people pursue whale fishery near the shores of Japan. It sometimes happens, in stormy weather, that one of our ships is wrecked on Japan's shores. In all such cases, we ask and expect that our unfortunate people should be treated with kindness until we can send a vessel and bring them away.

Our steamships, in crossing the great ocean, burn a great deal of coal, and it is not convenient to bring it all the way from America. We wish that our steamships and other vessels should be allowed to stop in Japan and supply themselves with coal, provisions and water. They will pay for them in money, or anything else you may prefer.

These are the only reasons I have sent Commodore Perry, with a powerful squadron of ships, to Japan.

From a letter from the President of the United States of America to the Emperor of Japan, 13 November 1852.

CONTINUED

Look carefully at the extracts from President Fillmore's letter to the Japanese.

a How would you describe the tone of the letter? Note down the phrases you would use as examples in your answer.

b What requests did it make?

c Why do you think it mentions that Commodore Perry had 'a powerful squadron of ships'?

Russia, Britain, France and the Netherlands all followed Perry's mission with visits of their own to request trade agreements with Japan, so Perry travelled back to Japan early in 1854. This time Perry was accompanied by eight ships and 1600 men. He again threatened the Japanese and exchanged gifts in prolonged negotiations. The Treaty of Kanagawa was signed in March 1854. By the terms of this treaty, Japan would protect stranded American sailors, open two ports (Shimoda and Hakodate) to American ships and allow American **consuls** to live in these ports. The treaty also included a clause that guaranteed that if Japan signed any future trade deals with another country, the same rights would also be granted to the USA. This treaty created the basis for future American contact and trade with Japan.

KEY TERM

Consul: An official appointed by a state to live in a foreign country to protect the state's citizens' interests there.

The unequal treaties with Japan

The first American consul to arrive in Shimoda was Townsend Harris. He spent much of the first two years there warning the Japanese that if they did not sign formal trading agreements with the Americans, the British would make their own demands, and that they would do so in a much more aggressive manner. These warnings resulted in the Harris Treaty of July 1858. The treaty opened up five new ports for American trade, stated that American citizens were exempt from Japanese law and were guaranteed religious freedom while in Japan, and prevented the Japanese from imposing tariffs on imported goods under a policy of **protectionism**.

KEY TERM

Protectionism: The placing of high tariffs on imports to protect domestic industries from foreign competition. Protectionism is the opposite of free trade.

The Americans took advantage of the Japanese and as a result, the Japanese signed the first 'unequal treaty'. Unequal treaties are agreements which have very one-sided terms, requiring the weaker country to give up much more than the other party. (They are often signed after a military defeat.) Within a year, the Japanese had signed a series of similar agreements with Britain, Russia, the Netherlands and France. These agreements were known as the Ansei Treaties of 1858. They extended the same rights negotiated by Harris to each of the other nations. Without fully understanding what would happen next, the Japanese had opened their country to foreign exploitation.

Reasons for rapid modernisation and military development

Japan lacked natural resources, and its mountains meant that only a fifth of the country was suitable for agriculture. Japan had been ruled by a small group of aristocratic warriors and isolated from the rest of the world for hundreds of years, so it did not have a modern state or society by Western standards at the time. In 1850, a transformation was unthinkable, but by 1914 Japan had become a major power.

The Meiji Restoration

Japan had always had an emperor, but since the 1600s a military government led by the shogun had dominated. The opening of Japan to the West and the shock induced by the unequal treaties of 1858 led to a reform movement in Japan. As one Japanese lord said, 'if we take the initiative, we can dominate; if we do not, we will be dominated'.

With military backing, foreign merchants had already seized control of large areas of China, imposing their own laws and destroying local culture. There was an obvious risk that Japan would face the same fate and be divided up between competing foreign powers. In the mid-1860s, therefore, reformers joined forces and challenged the Tokugawa shogunate. In 1868, the Tokugawa shogunate came to an end. The shogun lost his power, and the emperor was restored to the position of supreme ruler. This event was known as the Meiji Restoration, after the new Emperor Meiji. The Meiji Restoration stimulated Japan's modernisation.

Under Emperor Meiji, a range of reforms to Japan's government, transport and communications systems, society, military and economy were introduced. Meiji was advised by a group of young, capable men from the lower ranks of the samurai. These men swiftly dismantled the power of the higher-ranking samurai families. By 1871 they had abolished the domain (or land ownership) system upon which the aristocratic social system depended. They created a central state, uniting all the previously independent regions of Japan under one government in one capital city. They established a dominant national dialect to standardise the Japanese language, wrote a constitution, based on the German model, that established an elected parliament, and designed a highly centralised, **bureaucratic** government.

KEY TERM

Bureaucratic: Describes the way a government runs using state officials, systems and rules to make important decisions, rather than based on decisions by elected representatives.

Industrialisation

From 1869 to 1871, the new Meiji government attempted to abolish **feudalism** and develop a modern industrial economy.

KEY TERM

Feudalism: The main form of social, political and economic organisation in the medieval and early modern world. Land and power was distributed to the nobility by the monarch, and taxes and military service were provided to the monarch by the lower classes in society.

Industrialisation and modernisation had begun in the 1850s in response to Western interest in Japan. However, progress had not been swift. From the 1860s, several developments contributed to the modernisation of the economy:

- the development of a capitalist economy
- the growth of cotton and silk workshops on an increasingly large scale

- the development of mines, iron and steel works, and shipbuilding. Some of these were established by the government and then handed over to **private enterprise**. Others were built by samurai, such as Iwasaki Yataro, who founded the Mitsubishi shipyards.
- currency reform and (in 1882) the creation of a national bank
- the construction of a modern railway network, using loans from Britain
- the building of telegraph and telephone systems
- the development of consumer industries (sugar, glass, textiles, cement, and chemicals, for example).

KEY TERM

Private enterprise: Businesses owned and managed by individuals, free of government restrictions.

To cover the costs of this rapid modernisation, Japan concentrated on promoting its export trade, especially in textiles. In 1868, Japan produced around 1000 tons of silk per year; by 1914 this had increased to well over 12000 tons annually.

In the 1870s, Japan produced less than 1 million tons of coal per year, but as the capacity of Japanese industry and demand for steam power increased, over 20 million tons of coal were delivered. Japan had just 30 kilometres of rail and 30 steamships in the early 1870s; by the outbreak of the First World War it had over 11500 kilometres of track and over 1500 steamships by the outbreak of the First World War.

One-third of the national budget was spent on the army and navy. Military service became compulsory for all adult males, and by 1894, Japan possessed 28 modern warships.

Adoption of Western technology

In order to bring about this rapid modernisation, Japan relied heavily on foreign experts. Thousands of engineers, medical specialists, mathematicians and experts in military and naval technology, civil engineering and railway construction were brought to Japan, usually on two- or three-year contracts. They assisted with the introduction of Western technology and trained Japanese people to operate it.

Japan also imported Western technology, but Japanese engineers quickly learned from the foreign technology they worked with and adapted it.

- To create a national telephone network, Ministry of Communications engineers researched widely, visited Britain, the USA and Germany, and bought the advanced equipment they could not make themselves. Japanese engineers and workers built the rest of the equipment, created the network of telegraph lines and introduced the systems they needed.
- The Japanese navy purchased battleships from Britain, and sent engineers to observe them as they were being built and prepared for delivery. The engineers returned to Japan, ready to implement what they had learned in local Japanese shipyards. The Japanese navy continued to buy ships from foreign builders, but they also began to purchase them from companies such as Mitsubishi and Kawasaki, which bought equipment from abroad and used it to develop their own methods for building steel-hulled ships.
- To build a textile industry, the government set up ten factories, each equipped with cotton-spinning machines from Britain. Government engineers supervised, while young Japanese graduate engineers ran the factories. Within a few years, Japanese university-educated engineers were travelling to Britain to purchase machinery to set up the next generation of Japanese factories.

Education

The Meiji leadership established a national public education system to help Japan modernise. Japanese experts travelled abroad to learn about the education systems of leading Western nations and returned to design a system. The new schools taught students reading, writing and mathematics, as well as 'moral training', which taught students about their duty to the emperor and the Japanese state. Elementary schooling was made compulsory in 1872, and between then and 1900 enrolment in elementary schools increased from around 30% to around 90% of the school-age population. Further reforms extended the school and university systems in the 1880s.

ACTIVITY 1.24

a Construct a mind map of the main factors which made the rapid modernisation of Japan possible. Which do you feel was the most important and why? Put the reasons next to your notes.

b Think about the question 'Why was Japan able to modernise by 1914?' Compile an essay plan for an answer to this question.

International recognition of Japan as a world power

By 1914, Japan had maintained its independence and modernised effectively. In fact, it became an imperial power, defeated a great power in war, signed an alliance with another great power, and emerged as a world power in its own right.

Japanese foreign policy objectives: relations with Korea

The Japanese leadership looked for opportunities to protect the country against threats from abroad.

War with China, 1894–95

The First China–Japan War in 1894–95 showed that Japan had become a major world power. This war arose from a conflict with the Qing Dynasty of China over influence in East Asia and control of Korea in particular. Korea had been in China's sphere of influence for a long time; but as Japan became increasingly powerful it became more interested in Korea's coal and iron ore.

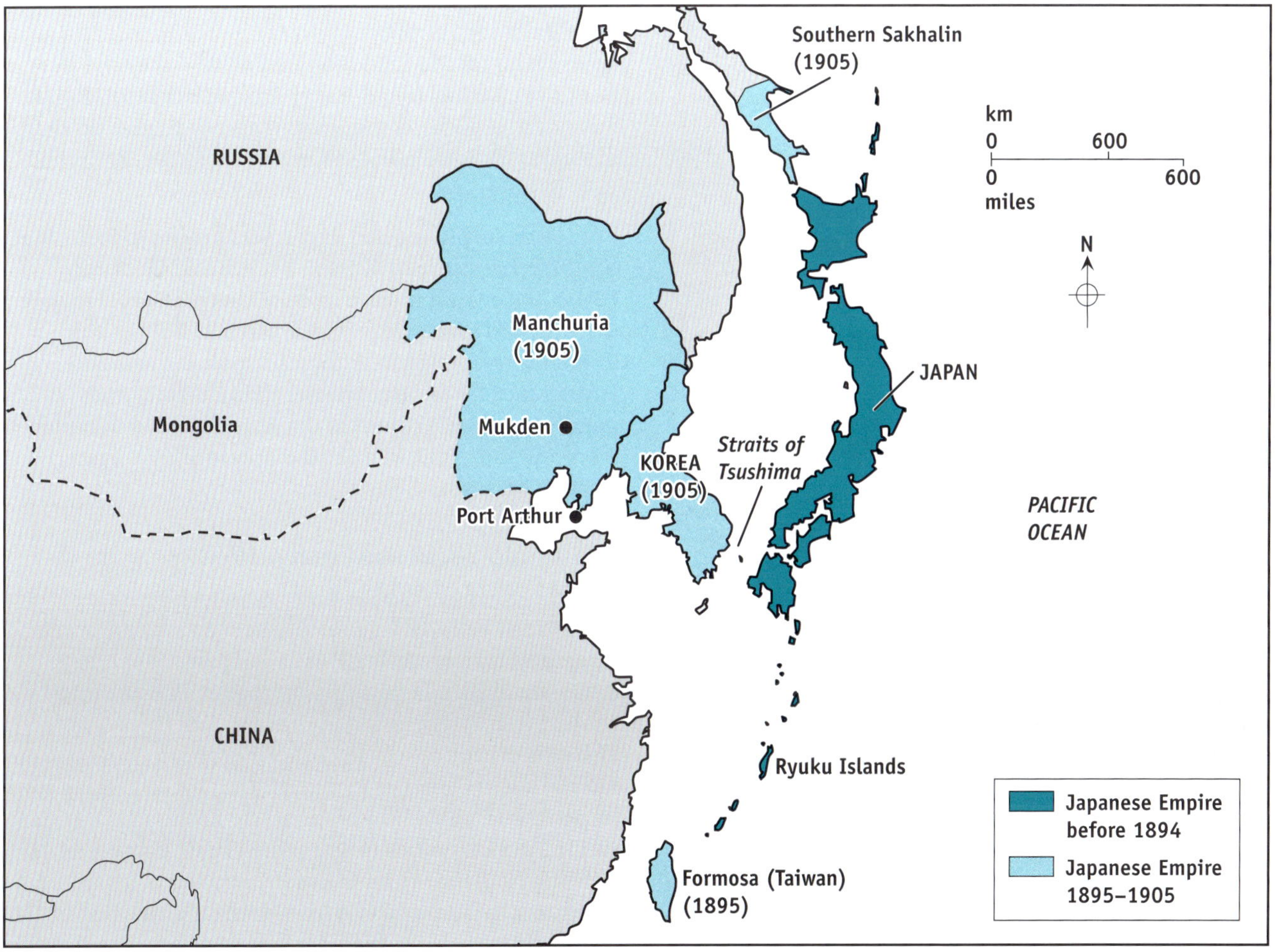

Figure 1.25: Japanese expansion, 1894-1905.

Japan relied upon imported raw materials and, like the European powers who expanded into Africa, looked overseas for economic opportunities. In 1875, Japan forced Korea to open itself up to foreign trade and to declare independence from China, but China sought to maintain its influence over the peninsula. Both China and Japan saw control of Korea as key to dominating the region, and both countries attempted to influence Korean opinion.

In 1894, a pro-Japanese Korean reformer was murdered in Shanghai and his body was displayed in Korea as a warning to other rebels. Around the same time a peasant rebellion known as the Tonghak (meaning 'Eastern Learning') Uprising threatened domestic stability in Korea. Supported by the Japanese, the Tonghaks defeated the Korean army in 1893 and advanced on Seoul, the Korean capital.

The Korean king requested assistance from the Chinese, who prepared to send in troops. The Japanese acted swiftly, however, and sent 8000 of their own soldiers to Korea. Japanese troops arrived and demanded reforms, increasing the tensions. Chinese and Japanese forces clashed in July 1894. After this, the new, modern Japanese army quickly overran Korea, Manchuria and parts of China itself. The Japanese took control of the telegraph system, occupied Seoul, and broke into the royal palace and arrested the king. The Japanese navy also won the naval battles of the war, sinking ships that were carrying supplies and reinforcements.

Despite all international expectations, the Japanese won the war easily. Japanese military modernisation had been very effective, and Japanese forces were better equipped and prepared. By March 1895 the Japanese had invaded Shandong province and Manchuria and had captured positions that gave them control of the sea approaches to Peking (now Beijing). The Chinese sued for peace.

The Treaty of Shimonoseki and Triple Intervention

By the terms of the Treaty of Shimonoseki, which was signed in April 1895, China recognised the total independence of Korea. By the terms of a **lease**, it also granted control of the Liaodong (South Manchurian) Peninsula, Taiwan, and the Penghu Islands to Japan. The Liadong Peninsula included the strategically important port of Lüshun (at that time called Port Arthur by Westerners). China had to open four of its ports to Japan for trade and pay 200 million taels (8 million kg) of silver in war **reparations**.

> **KEY TERMS**
>
> **Lease:** An agreement by which land is given, for a specific period of time, in return for payment.
>
> **Reparations:** Money that one country has to pay another as compensation for war damage.

Victory in the war had confirmed Japan's status as a major world power, but the harsh terms of the peace treaty caused concern abroad. Russia, in particular, was angry at Japan's acquisition of the Liaodong Peninsula and Port Arthur, and at the impact of the treaty on China. Russia had its own reasons to be concerned, since it wanted to expand its own influence in the region and was anxious about Japan's growing strength. France and Germany also had economic interests and ports in China, and they were easily persuaded to join Russia in applying diplomatic pressure on Japan. Within just three days, the European powers insisted that Japan give up its claim on the Liaodong Peninsula – they did not want Port Arthur to fall under Japanese control. Japan was not in a position to refuse; it agreed to give up the Liaodong Peninsula in exchange for another 30 million taels of silver.

It was not surprising that Japan was unable to resist the combined pressure of Russia, France and Germany. Few countries could have resisted this pressure. However, the situation made clear that Japan was not yet able to pursue its foreign and domestic policies without interference by the great powers. Humiliated, and mindful of Port Arthur, the Japanese decided to build more warships and wait for the opportunity to gain revenge against the Russians.

The Anglo-Japanese Treaty, 1902: causes and consequences

The British believed that an alliance with Japan would be helpful for preventing Russian expansion in East Asia, where Britain and Russia frequently came into conflict over Afghanistan and India. The British were also concerned to stop any other European country from interfering in China or Korea. Britain was emerging from its period of 'splendid isolation' (see Section 1.1). It was seeking opportunities to strengthen itself because of the growing challenge from Germany and the constant need to protect its interests in Africa, India and the rest of the empire. It was also very important to refocus the Royal Navy's attention on home waters.

Britain had refused to join in the Triple Intervention in 1895, and the prospects for friendly relations with Japan seemed to be confirmed by the joint response to a rebellion against foreign influence in China (known as the Boxer Rebellion) in 1899–1901. Japan was aware of Britain's status as one of the world's great powers and was attracted by the idea that other nations would be impressed and intimidated by the alliance. The British and Japanese governments decided to adopt a common approach to the problems posed by Russian expansion in East Asia. During 1901, negotiations took place between the British foreign secretary (Henry Petty-Fitzmaurice, Fifth Marquess of Lansdowne) and the Japanese ambassador to London (Hayashi Tadasu).

The Anglo-Japanese Treaty was signed in 1902, and it was due to be renewed every five years. It was aimed mainly at defence against an expansion by either Russia or France in East Asia. It confirmed:

- the neutrality of China and Korea
- the interest of Britain in China, and the interest of Japan in China and Korea
- the rights of both Britain and Japan to protect their interests in China and Korea
- that Britain and Japan would remain neutral if either country went to war over China or Korea
- that Britain and Japan would provide support if either country found itself at war with two or more other countries.

Britain regarded the Anglo-Japanese Treaty as protection against Russian expansion, but for the Japanese, the Alliance was a major triumph. Japan could now count on British support in a war against Russia if any other country, such as France or Germany, sided with the Russians. Moreover, the signing of the Alliance marked the first time that Japan had been recognised as an equal by one of the major European powers.

France, Russia and the USA were concerned by Britain's new alliance. The agreement between Britain and Japan may have emboldened Japan in its dealings with Russia in 1903–04, and certainly the two sides shared intelligence information before and during the Russo-Japanese War of 1904–05 itself. The alliance was renewed in 1905 to add further clarification about the responsibilities of both countries after the war between Japan and Russia, and it also laid the way for Japanese involvement in the First World War, on the British side.

The Russo-Japanese War, 1904–05

Immediately after the 1895 Triple Intervention at the conclusion of the Treaty of Shimonoseki, Russia began building a railway along the Liaodong Peninsula, strengthening the port facilities at Port Arthur. The peninsula offered Russia a warm water port, and the railway was critical to Russian strategic goals.

By 1900 Russia occupied the whole of Manchuria. Russian expansion in East Asia caused alarm in Japan. Russia clearly had ambitions to seize Korea, which had been under Japanese control since the Treaty of Shimonoseki in 1895. The loss of Korea would greatly damage the Japanese economy and make Japan itself more vulnerable to a Russian attack. Control of Port Arthur was one thing, but control of large areas of Manchuria was quite another.

By leasing Liaodong under the Treaty of Shimonoseki and pursuing its ambitions for control of the land along the Korean border, Russia had brought itself into Japan's sphere of influence. In the aftermath of the Triple Intervention, many in Japan felt anger at the disrespect they had been shown by the West. Japanese resentment at Russian conduct and the popular feeling that the Japanese government should have acted more strongly against foreign pressure led to riots in Tokyo.

After the signing of the Anglo-Japanese Treaty with Britain in 1902, Japan felt strong enough to seek a settlement with Russia. In June 1903 Japan proposed that Russia and Japan should recognise each other's interests in Manchuria, ensuring peace in the region. Convinced of their military superiority, the Russians refused to do this. Instead, they demanded the establishment of a neutral buffer zone. The Japanese government again saw this as an insult and an attempt to block their plans for expansion in the region. It set about preparing for war. On 8 February 1904, the Japanese navy carried out a surprise attack on the Russian fleet at Port Arthur. Two Russian battleships and a cruiser were destroyed by Japanese torpedoes.

In May 1904, the Battle of Yalu River was the first major land battle of the war. Japanese troops captured a Russian position after crossing the river. This battle highlighted Russia's problems and demonstrated that Japan had become a major military power. Japanese troops drove the Russians back towards Port Arthur.

After a siege lasting 156 days, the Japanese captured Port Arthur. The siege cost Russia 6000 men, but cost Japan 14 000 men. The Russians surrendered Port Arthur on 2 January 1905. At the Battle of Mukden (February–March 1905) the Russians faced a stubborn enemy and withdrew after suffering exceptionally heavy losses.

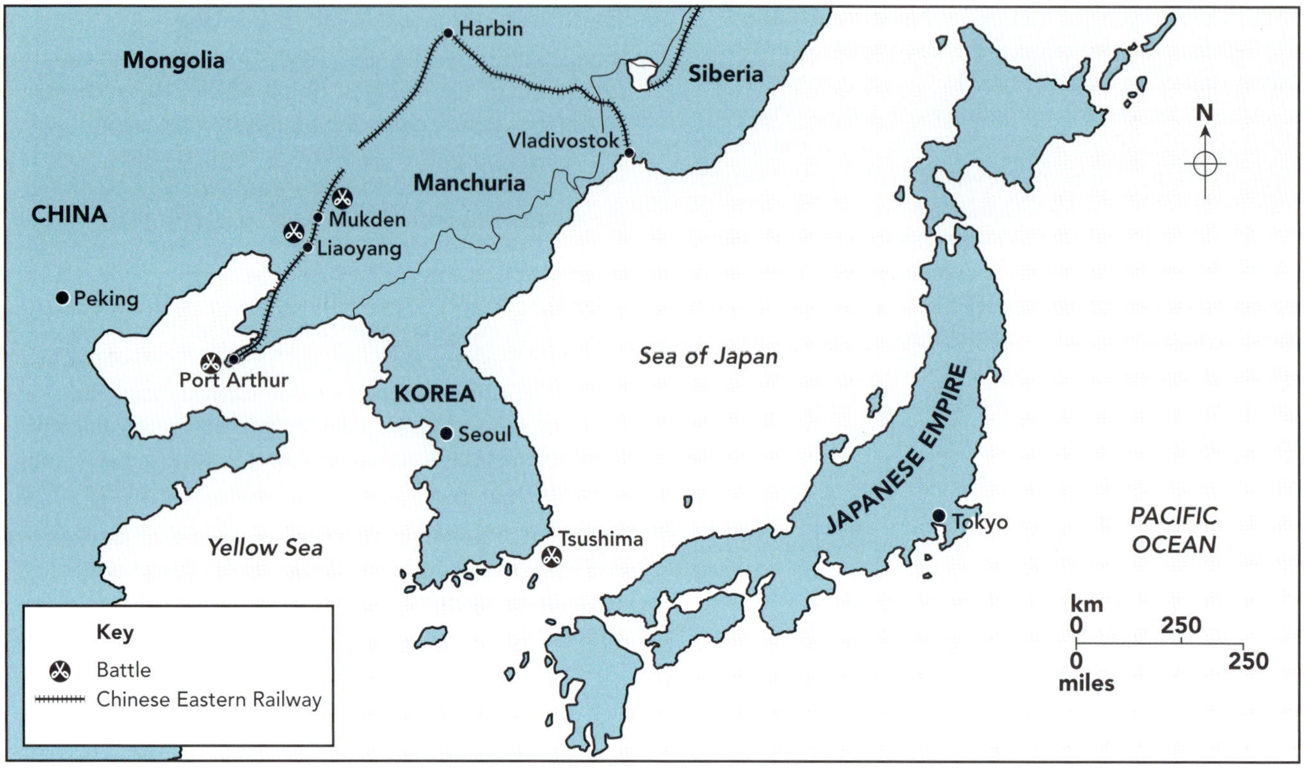

Figure 1.26: Map showing the Russo-Japanese War, 1904–05.

Figure 1.27: Japanese soldiers laying siege to Port Arthur, 1904.

The Japanese siege of Port Arthur succeeded in stopping Russia's East Asia naval forces from leaving their port, so the Russians sent their Baltic Fleet. The fleet sailed halfway around the world, in a voyage that took six months. The Russians encountered British fishing trawlers in the North Sea and fired at them, causing a diplomatic incident and slowing the Russian fleet's progress. In early May 1905, having arrived in the China Sea, the fleet headed for Vladivostok. The Japanese intercepted it and sank, seized, or put out of action eight battleships, nine cruisers, six special-service steamers, and a number of other ships in the Baltic Fleet. Altogether they killed about 4000 Russians and captured three admirals and 7300 sailors.

US President Theodore Roosevelt mediated the negotiations of the peace treaty, which was signed in September 1905 and known as the Treaty of Portsmouth. Russia recognised Korea as part of the Japanese sphere of influence, agreed to withdraw from Manchuria, handed over its 25-year lease to Port Arthur to the Japanese and gave the south of Sakhalin Island to Japan. The Japanese defeat of the Russians shocked the world and demonstrated Japanese power.

Reasons for Japan's victory

Russian troops' morale suffered as the defeats mounted up. Japanese soldiers fought with great determination, and they were well led. Russian leadership was often chaotic and incompetent. Russian soldiers were not well supplied, whereas Japanese industrial and military reforms ensured that Japan's men were well equipped. Japanese victories enabled Japan to raise more credit in order to continue to supply its men, while Russian defeats had the opposite effect on the nation's finances. Political disruption and unrest at home undermined the Russian war effort.

ACTIVITY 1.25

Figure 1.28: Cartoon published in the French magazine *Le Petit Parisien,* 1904.

Study the cartoon in Figure 1.28. It shows other countries looking on while the champion of Europe (Russia) on the left, takes on the champion of Asia (Japan) on the right. Consider the following questions in pairs or small groups.

a Why was this illustration published in 1904? Why was a French magazine commenting on these events?

b How is Russia depicted in the illustration?

c How is Japan depicted in the illustration?

d What is the meaning of the map on the floor of the ring?

e Which of the two countries did the artist believe was most likely to achieve victory in the conflict between Russia and Japan? How do you know?

f Do you think the artist considered Japan a major world power in 1904? Explain your answer.

g Who are the figures sitting around the edge of the ring? Why are they so interested in what is happening?

British intelligence assisted the Japanese. Japan's small navy was equipped with several British-supplied warships which had been recently constructed, in comparison to Russia's larger but older fleet. Japan's military leaders were trained in Britain and well versed in modern tactics. They were promoted on merit and achievement, whereas in Russia, traditions and social status dominated military thinking. Unlike the Russians, the Japanese respected the enemy and were aware of their strengths and weaknesses.

ACTIVITY 1.26

Consider the statement 'Japan's victory in the war of 1904–05 was the result of Russian weakness rather than Japanese strength'. To what extent would you agree with this statement?

a List the factors that enabled Japan to defeat Russia in the Russo-Japanese War of 1904–05.

b Look at your list.

  i Identify points that agree with this statement.

  ii Identify points that disagree with this statement.

  iii Decide whether, on balance, you agree or disagree with this statement.

c Prepare and deliver a presentation to explain and justify your decision.

Japan's role in the First World War and global position by 1918

Japan welcomed the outbreak of the First World War. It saw the war as an opportunity to prove its strength again, to expand its imperial possessions and to gain an advantage over some of its regional rivals. By the end of the war, Japan had successfully increased its international status, benefited economically and achieved recognition as an ally of the victorious entente powers.

Contribution to global war

On 7 August 1914, Japan offered to assist Britain in the Pacific and the British government accepted the offer. Japan wanted to build an empire in the Pacific, and the government offered to enter the war on the side of Britain and **the Allies** in return for control of Germany's territory in the region. Japan demanded that Germany should withdraw all its ships from Chinese waters and surrender its imperial possessions in China within a month. Germany did not respond, and Germany's ally Austria-Hungary also refused to respond to Japanese messages, so the Japanese declared war on Germany and its allies (the **Central Powers**) on 23 August 1914.

KEY TERMS

The Allies: The term that the British Empire, the French, the Russians, and later the Americans used to describe their own military alliance during the First World War. Because of the Triple Entente, signed in 1904–07, these countries were also known as the Entente powers.

Central Powers: The term used by the Allies to describe the military alliance of Germany, Austria-Hungary, Bulgaria and the Turkish Empire during the First World War. Because of the Triple Alliance, signed in 1882, these countries were also known as the Triple Alliance powers.

The Japanese navy contributed to Allied naval activities all over the world. Its primary role was to secure the sea lanes of the South Pacific and the Indian Ocean against the German navy. In the Indian Ocean, Japanese ships protected the groups of ships (known as 'convoys') carrying troops from Australia and New Zealand. In return for British recognition of Japan's claims to German colonies in Asia and the Pacific, Japan sent destroyers to South Africa and the Mediterranean. The Mediterranean was critical for Allied supplies. It was the short route to the Suez Canal and the Indian and Pacific regions of the British Empire and also the main sea route connecting Allied troops in North Africa and the Middle East with ports in Europe. On over 300 different occasions, the Japanese navy provided protection from German and Austrian submarine attacks, escorting hundreds of Allied transport ships as they sailed through the Mediterranean. In 1917 and 1918, when the Allied navies were seriously threatened by the Central Powers' submarine operations in the Mediterranean, Japanese involvement was critical in maintaining the security of these vital supply routes.

While the Western powers were fully occupied fighting the war in Europe, Japan took advantage of their absence from East Asia in a number of ways:

- Japan began to supply the East Asia region with goods that the European countries could no longer provide. During the war years, 1914–18, Japan's exports of cotton cloth increased threefold. Japan also greatly expanded its heavy industry to fill the gap left by the absence of European imports of iron, steel and chemicals.

- To assist with this surge in exports, the Japanese merchant fleet almost doubled in size during the war years.
- The Japanese shipbuilding industry was also boosted by the fact that Japan supplied Britain and the Allies with shipping and other goods throughout the war.

Japan's role in the Pacific

Japan played a key role in the Pacific from the beginning of the war. At the start of the war, Germany had control of territory in China. Its port and naval base was at Tsingtao, which was guarded by around 4000 troops and some battleships. After the British requested Japanese assistance, on 15 August, Japan issued an ultimatum to the Germans: they had to withdraw all German warships and hand over control of the port of Tsingtao to the Japanese within a week. When the Germans ignored the ultimatum and the deadline passed, Japan declared war on Germany.

The seizure of German possessions

Perhaps the most famous Japanese contribution to the war was the occupation of the Shandong Province in late 1914 and the Twenty-One Demands which followed. After the Japanese ultimatum to Germany, Japan began preparing to capture the German port and naval base at Tsingtao. The Japanese imposed a blockade starting on 27 August 1914. Over the course of a week, the Japanese presence increased. On 2 September, 23 000 Japanese soldiers landed in China's Shandong Province and surrounded the port at Tsingtao. From 4 September, Japanese aircraft began a series of air raids (including the first air raids launched from ships and the first night-bombing raids) against German forces. Japanese forces quickly occupied German territories and surrounded Tsingtao. Britain sent 1500 men to assist the Japanese, and together their forces numbered 50 000. The Japanese used very effective artillery and trench warfare tactics to weaken the Germans. Out of ammunition, outnumbered and exhausted, the Germans surrendered Tsingtao on 7 November 1914. The port of Tsingtao remained under Japanese control until the end of the war.

Meanwhile, during October 1914, the Japanese navy captured several German island colonies in the Pacific. The Japanese seized the Mariana, Caroline, Palau and Marshall Islands, with almost no resistance from the small number of German colonial personnel who were posted to these islands. There were small clashes between the defenders and landing Japanese troops but the colonial troops could do little to stop the Japanese.

The Japanese achieved their war aim of expanding imperial interests with the occupation of Shandong and the South Pacific islands. For some in the Japanese government, though, Japan's new position of strength was an opportunity on which to capitalise.

In January 1915, the Japanese Minister in Peking (now Beijing) presented a list of 21 demands to the Chinese. They were a collection of stringent demands for economic, territorial, diplomatic and political **concessions** from China. The 'Twenty-One Demands' were designed to dramatically increase Japanese political and economic power and influence over much of China. In effect, China would cease to be an independent country. When the Chinese initially refused to accept these demands, Japan issued an ultimatum on 7 May 1915:

The Japanese ultimatum concluded as follows:

> Despite the attitude of the Chinese Government, the Imperial Government of Japan, still warmly attached to the preservation of peace in the Far East, is still hoping for a satisfactory settlement in order to avoid the disturbance of relations. The Imperial Government hereby again offer their advice and hope that the Chinese government, upon this advice, will give a satisfactory reply by 6 p.m. on 9th day of May. It is hereby declared that if no satisfactory reply is received before or at the specified time, the Imperial Government will take steps they may deem necessary.
>
> **From the ultimatum delivered to the Chinese Minister of Foreign Affairs by the Japanese Minister, 7 May 1915.**

KEY TERM

Concession: Something that is allowed or given up to one party in a dispute to get their agreement in other areas. To give something up in this way is to concede it.

Following this ultimatum, the Chinese finally agreed to the Japanese demands on 8 May 1915.

Initially, only the USA objected on China's behalf – the rest of the international community was occupied with the war, or did not notice the harshness of Japanese demands. The USA's objection related to an agreement between the USA and the other colonial powers interested in China that dated back to 1899–1900 (see Section 1.4). In the so-called 'Open Door notes', the agreed principle stated that the foreign powers would not try to gain a special trade advantage in China. In 1915, therefore, the Americans felt that the Japanese Twenty-One Demands broke the agreement that the 'door' for trading with China would remain 'open' for all. Under pressure from the USA, followed by Britain and other countries with a trading interest in China, Japan was eventually forced to reduce its Twenty-One Demands. However, even the revised demands granted Japan similar rights in China to those enjoyed by the other great powers. Between 1916 and 1918, Japan provided the Chinese with a series of loans that further increased its financial, commercial and economic influence over China.

Intervention in the Russian Civil War

In 1917, Russia experienced two major political revolutions. In the first, Tsar Nicholas II was forced to abdicate (step down as emperor) in March 1917, and a Provisional Government took control temporarily. The Japanese government cautiously established formal relations with the new Provisional Government, because the Russians promised to follow the same foreign policy commitments made by the tsar.

In the second revolution, the Provisional Government was overthrown and the **Bolshevik Party**, took power, led by Vladimir Lenin and Leon Trotsky, following a political revolt in the Russian capital, Petrograd, in October 1917. The Bolsheviks were **communists**, and they were strongly opposed to cooperating with the capitalist Allied countries in what they regarded as a war between imperialist powers.

The Bolsheviks refused to continue any of the previous government's foreign policies, including fighting in the First World War. They, therefore, signed an **armistice** with the Germans and withdrew from the fighting. The new government agreed to Germany's peace terms and signed the Treaty of Brest-Litovsk with Germany in March 1918 (see the Introduction to Chapter 2).

The Americans, British and French were alarmed at the loss of Russia as a fighting ally, and they formulated plans to send troops to Russia to retake control of supplies they had recently sent to the Russian government, and then to assist the anti-Bolshevik forces in the **civil war** that was developing there.

KEY TERMS

Bolshevik Party: A communist party led by Lenin, which seized power in Russia in the second Russian Revolution in October 1917.

Communist: Supporting (or someone who supports) communism, a system of social, political and economic organisation in which all property is owned by the community and each person contributes according to their abilities and receives whatever they need.

Armistice: An agreement between all sides in a war to stop fighting for a certain time (also known as a truce).

Civil war: A war between people, groups or armies from the same country.

The first Japanese personnel to arrive in Russia landed at Vladivostok in January 1918. The Americans proposed that the Japanese join them in sending more troops to Russia in July 1918. The Japanese government agreed to send troops, but actually sent a much larger force than requested, and decided to keep their troops under their own control, rather than have them join in with the international forces. In total, over 70 000 Japanese personnel were sent to Russia. The Japanese involvement in the Russian Civil War was known as the 'Siberian Intervention', since most of the foreign soldiers occupied land in Siberia. This involvement lasted from January 1918 until June 1922 (much longer than the interventions by other powers).

Some people in the Japanese army saw the Russian Civil War as an opportunity to increase Japan's territory and power. They attempted to gain control of Siberia and sent troops to seize two railway lines: the Trans-Siberian Railway (almost 4000 km to the city of Irkutsk) and the Chinese Eastern Railway (which was under Russian control). Throughout 1919, the Japanese army supported anti-Bolshevik armies fighting in the east of the country and ignored criticism that they were interfering in Russian politics. Japanese businesses started to see

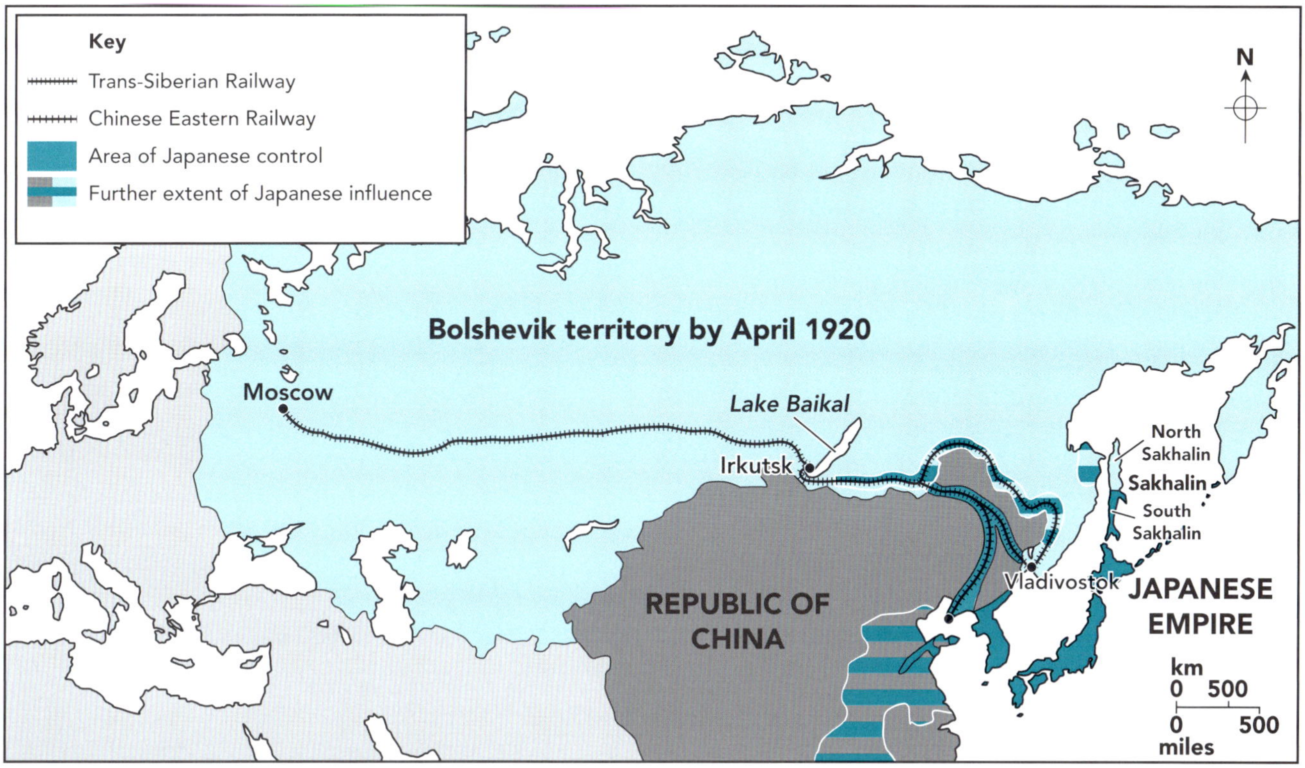

Figure 1.29: The Japanese intervention in the Russian Civil War, 1918–22.

opportunities for development, so they opened offices in cities in Siberia and around 50 000 Japanese people moved to work in them. Japanese control was not secure, but it was increasing.

By 1920, the Bolsheviks (known as 'the Reds' during the Russian Civil War) were in control of much of the country and the various anti-Bolshevik armies (known collectively as 'the Whites', although they were not a united group and there was no coordination between their forces) were being defeated one by one. The Japanese fought off Red attacks and supported anti-Bolshevik forces in the east in 1920, but the Reds occupied more territory.

In March and April 1920, at the town of Nikolaevsk, a Japanese army base containing around 350 soldiers, and a community of around 450 Japanese who had settled since 1918, the Japanese soldiers found themselves surrounded by an army of Bolshevik supporters. The Japanese soldiers initially indicated they would allow the Reds to occupy the city, but as the occupation began they launched an attack on the Reds. The attack failed, most of the soldiers died, and the Reds executed all the Japanese soldiers and civilians who survived. In response, the Japanese invaded the northern half of Sakhalin (an island between Japan and Russia where Japan had occupied the south since 1905 and the Treaty of Portsmouth). In addition, the Japanese government committed to staying in Siberia until the fighting was over, even after the Americans announced they would withdraw (the last US troops left in April 1920).

In 1921, however, the Japanese began negotiating with the Reds and prepared to leave. Japan's position grew weaker as negotiations failed to deliver any benefits for the Japanese, and the anti-Bolsheviks they supported collapsed. In early 1922, there were large Bolshevik attacks against the Japanese at Vladivostok, and in June the Japanese announced they would withdraw. The last Japanese soldiers left Vladivostok in October 1922. A peace agreement was signed in 1925, and the Japanese handed northern Sakhalin back to the USSR (Lenin's government formally changed the name of the country from Russia to RSFSR in 1921 and then USSR in 1922).

ACTIVITY 1.27

a How did Japan benefit from the First World War?

b Why would Japan's increasing power and influence over China be of great concern to the Western powers?

c Initially, China refused to agree to Japan's Twenty-One Demands. Why do you think the Chinese government finally accepted the demands on 8 May 1915?

d When Japanese representatives attended the peace conference, held at Versailles, in Paris, at the end of the First World War in 1919, they felt aggrieved that the representatives of Britain, France and the USA did not treat them with equal respect.

  i Why do you think that the British, French and Americans might have behaved in this way?

  ii Do you think that the Japanese had earned the right to be considered equals in the post-war peace-making process? (You may wish to revisit this question after you have studied the peace conference in more detail in Chapter 2.)

e Construct a timeline of all the events that helped Japan to increase its military and diplomatic power since the 1850s.

f Which of the events would you say was the most important? Write a paragraph to explain your judgement and support it with evidence.

g Compare your ideas with those of one of your classmates. Do you agree with their judgement? Why / why not?

Reflection

Compare your analysis for question **d** with that of another student. How did you decide whether Japan was right to be offended in 1919? Did you include the same or different examples as your partner? Discuss the similarities and differences with your partner. What did you learn from this discussion? Having discussed, would either of you alter your approach if you were to attempt a similar exercise again? If so, how?

KEY CONCEPT 1.3

Cause and consequence

Historians seek to explain why certain events or circumstances occurred, and to evaluate their possible consequences. Consider these issues relating to the emergence of Japan as a major world power with expansionist aims.

- **Cause:**

  Look at the reasons why Japan's power increased. To what extent did this change occur as a result of Western involvement in Japan?

- **Consequence:**

  In small groups, discuss the rise of Japan as a country of military, economic and diplomatic significance.

  Why did Japan's victories in the First Sino-Japanese War and the Russo-Japanese War surprise and concern the major European nations?

1.4 Why did the USA emerge as a world power and what was the impact on international relations?

Historians describe what happened to the indigenous peoples of America between 1492 and 1900 as a consequence of colonists moving from Europe, as a genocide. Few of the settlers who moved to America saw their colonisation as a destructive force, though. They rejected the colonisation of the 'Old World' and felt strongly that their new republic should not pursue imperial policies. The first European settlers in America had escaped from European countries, and the War of Independence (1775–83) had been fought to relieve Americans from the oppression of colonial rule.

In 1823, US President James Monroe stated that the Americas were independent, and that European powers should not consider colonising them. His warning, which came to be known as the Monroe Doctrine, effectively said that the entire western hemisphere (the part of the earth containing the American continents and the oceans surrounding them) was the USA's sphere of interest and positioned the USA as the protector of both American continents. This justified American isolationism from European affairs, but many people thought that it also justified American expansionism. These people saw European powers scrambling for colonial possessions in Africa and Asia and wished to warn them not to interfere in the affairs of the Americas.

Changing attitudes to overseas expansion

In the final 20 years of the 19th century, the USA did embark on policies of colonial expansion in the Pacific and Caribbean, and it began to take a much more active role in Latin America as well.

Impact of the closing of the frontier on US foreign policy

For much of the 19th century, American energy had been mostly spent on 'westward expansion'. Settlers had moved west from the first colonies on the east coast of the continent, building railways and new settlements, pushing indigenous peoples into marginal areas further and further to the west, and creating new states. Many settlers saw it as their mission to bring civilisation to the 'wild west' and were believers in the idea of 'Manifest Destiny'. The main ideas underpinning Manifest Destiny were that:

- US expansion to the Pacific Ocean was logical and inevitable
- aggressive US nationalism was desirable
- the USA had the 'divine right' to continue expanding westwards until it had spread from the Atlantic to the Pacific
- the USA had a duty to spread its Christian values and culture
- incorporation into the USA would bring liberty and freedom to other North American territories.

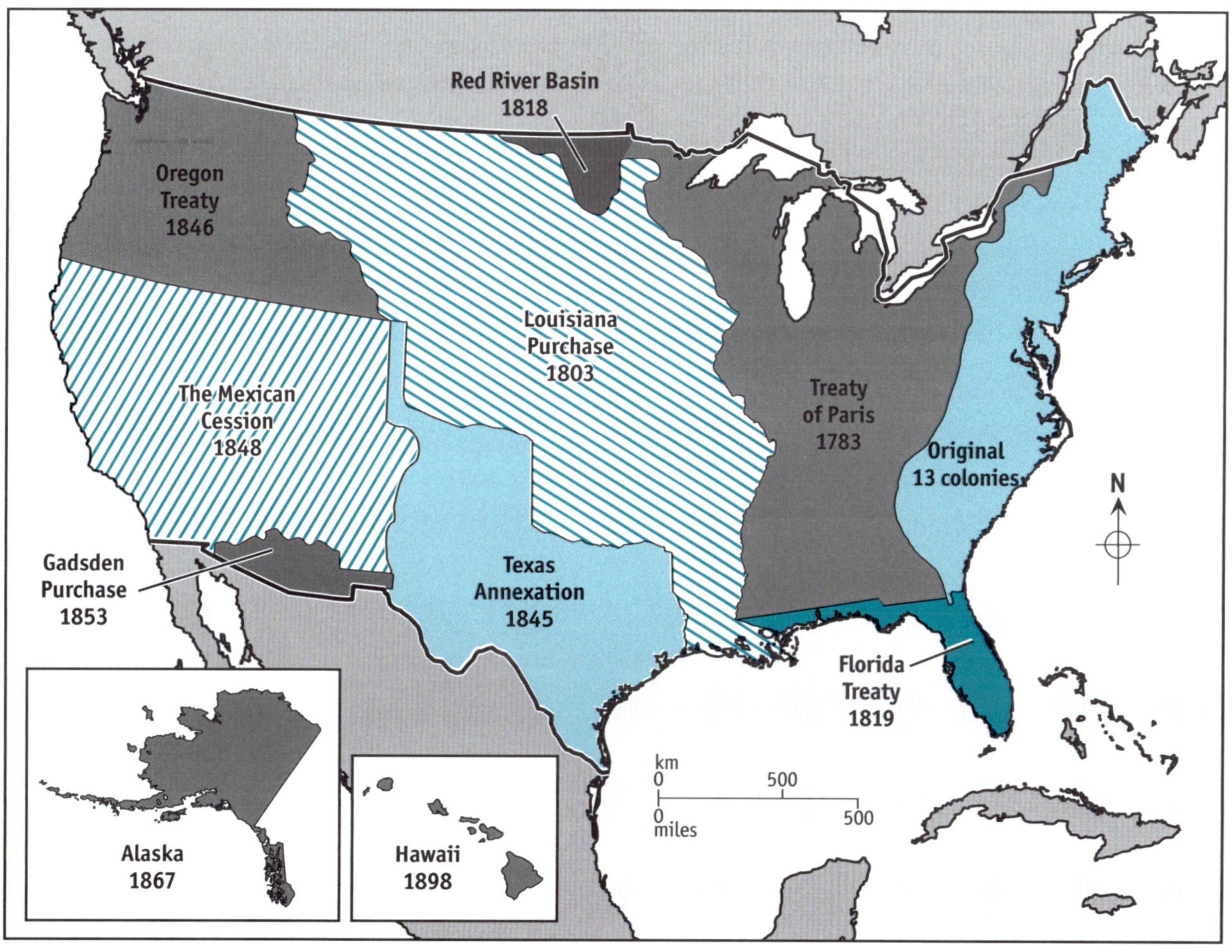

Figure 1.30: The expansion of the USA in the 18th and 19th centuries.

The US government wanted to encourage people to settle in areas that it termed the 'frontier' – areas that were wild, remote, dangerous and largely unexplored. To do this:

- The government sent in the US Army to fight the indigenous peoples, who resented the attempts of white settlers to occupy their land. The US government saw the indigenous peoples as 'uncivilised savages' and used brutal methods to deal with what they called the 'Indian problem'. Gradually, the indigenous peoples were murdered, worn down, killed in armed conflict or forcibly removed and confined to small areas reserved specifically for them to govern and live on (known as reservations). By 1900, as a consequence of the atrocities committed by settlers from Europe and their descendants, fewer than 350 000 Native Americans were left.
- The government sold land to settlers on which they could live and earn a living. The Donation Land Claim Act of 1850 allowed white settlers to take ownership of up to 640 acres of land in Oregon without charge. This was followed by a series of Homestead Acts. The first of these was passed in 1862 and made land available to those willing to improve and farm it. As a result, more and more settlers were encouraged to move westwards, settle on farms and push back the frontier.

ACTIVITY 1.28

Use the information here and any resources available to you to research American 'westward expansion' across the North American continent. Collect some research notes on the following questions, and then discuss your findings in small groups.

a Make a list of the various methods used by the USA to enable it to expand across the entire North American continent.

b How did the USA justify this expansion?

c Why did the USA establish the Monroe Doctrine in 1823?

The 1890 census, a detailed government survey of the American population, revealed that settlements had been established across the entire USA. With no 'untamed' areas left in which to settle, the government announced that the frontier was closed.

In 1893, the historian Frederick Jackson Turner published an essay entitled 'The Significance of the Frontier in American History', in which he described the 'closing' of the American frontier. He meant that the line between American civilisation and 'wilderness' had reached the western coastline. He also explained his 'frontier thesis', which strongly put forward his personal belief that the process of the settlement and colonisation of the North American continent had contributed to the development of American culture, with its strong elements of **democracy**, **egalitarianism**, physical strength, simplicity, openness and honesty.

KEY TERMS

Democracy: A system of government where the whole population have some political power. People govern themselves, usually through representatives who are chosen periodically in elections.

Egalitarianism: Belief in the principle that all people are equal and deserve equal rights and opportunities.

With westward settlement completed, Americans looked for new directions in which to expand. Many senior American politicians and clergymen began to argue that it was the USA's duty to spread democracy and Christianity to 'less fortunate' and 'backward peoples' in the world. For example, in his book *Our Country,* published in 1885, the clergyman Josiah Strong claimed that Americans belonged to the 'superior' Anglo-Saxon race, which should 'civilise' the 'savage races'. Those who argued in favour of American expansionism were very familiar with British imperialist ideas, and they also thought that acquiring territory was a way to find security and protection. For some people, the idea of Manifest Destiny justified American expansionism. Because some Americans believed that American democracy and capitalism were superior to the outdated monarchies and backward economies found in other countries, some Americans felt they had a moral duty to extend their control in all directions, not just westwards.

ACTIVITY 1.29

a According to the historian Frederick Jackson Turner, why did the closing of the frontier have such a major impact on the USA?

b In what ways might the closing of the frontier encourage the USA to seek overseas territorial possessions?

Development of naval power

The leaders of the USA were aware that they were descendants of colonists from Europe. They had also experienced the weak position that naval inferiority had led to during the American War of Independence. As a result, American leaders saw naval power as fundamental to the security and success of their nation. In the 1880s, the USA began building a modern battle fleet.

Mahan's *The Influence of Sea Power upon History*

Many people played small roles in expanding American power, but the man who had the biggest influence was a naval officer. In an influential book, *The Influence of Sea Power on History* (1890), Alfred Thayer Mahan argued that the world's most powerful nations had always been naval powers.

Mahan's argument highlighted that the USA had a strategic need for a strong navy, and, therefore, that it also required overseas possessions to act as supply bases offshore. Mahan also argued that the USA needed a cross-continental canal to connect the Atlantic and the Pacific Oceans.

Mahan's theory won support in the USA and Europe among backers of naval forces and colonial expansion. The idea of using naval forces to achieve colonial expansion inspired Kaiser Wilhelm II of Germany. American politicians including **Theodore Roosevelt**, 26th President of the USA (1901–09), took up Mahan's ideas, and in the 1890s the programme of shipbuilding in the USA increased. By 1900, the US Navy was the third-largest in the world.

KEY FIGURE

Theodore Roosevelt (1858–1919)

Roosevelt became president of the USA in 1901 and was re-elected by a landslide in 1904. He believed that the USA should play a major role in world affairs, and he supported the move towards US imperialism. He negotiated the Treaty of Portsmouth which ended the Russo-Japanese War in 1905. For this he was awarded the Nobel Peace Prize.

Building of The Great White Fleet

The 'Great White Fleet' was the name for a group of American battleships that completed a 14-month voyage around the world between 1907 and 1909. (The name arose because the ships' hulls were painted white.) The voyage reflected President Roosevelt's commitment to building a modern navy and demonstrating American

Figure 1.31: America's Great White Fleet.

naval power. It was an opportunity to make friendly visits to extend American power, but also to demonstrate the US navy's growing strength.

The fleet consisted of 16 battleships, and numerous other small escort vessels, all built between 1900 and 1906. They represented some of the best naval technology in the world at the time they were built, although by the time the voyage began they had clearly been overtaken by the new class of Dreadnought battleships being built in Europe.

Rapid economic growth

In the 1890s, America was fast developing an industrial economy. American industry had grown rapidly in the years after the Civil War of 1861–65 and this period was known as the 'Gilded Age' because of the amount of wealth created at that time. Between the end of the Civil War and the end of the century, the amount of railway track in the country increased by over 500%, and the amount of mined coal increased by 800%. A number of inter-related factors made such huge increases possible:

- The USA had large quantities of vital raw materials, such as coal, iron ore and oil.
- The population grew (from 31.5 million in 1880 to 76 million in 1900), partly because of increasing immigration from Europe and Asia. This increase in population provided both labour and consumers.
- New methods for the mass-production of manufactured products were introduced.
- A lack of government regulation enabled employers to manage their workforce in any way they chose.
- Large-scale, highly profitable companies were developed. These were known as corporations and trusts.
- Farming was mechanised. This mechanisation enabled the mass-production of wheat and other crops.
- A railway system was developed that became one of the most comprehensive railway systems in the world. This railway network facilitated the transportation of raw materials and finished products.
- Investment capital was made available through banks and the **stock market** in New York. By 1880, the New York Stock Exchange on Wall Street had become the second-largest money market in the world.
- The government encouraged the growth of American industry by protecting it from foreign competition. Tariffs were imposed on imported foreign-manufactured goods to ensure that they were more expensive than home-produced ones; these tariffs could be as high as 50% of the cost of the imported goods.

KEY TERM

Stock market: A place where shares are bought and sold. Companies sell shares to raise the money (capital) required to establish their factories and businesses. People buy shares in a company as an investment to gain from its subsequent profits.

The economic cycle and the Panic of 1893

Despite these economic strengths, the US economy suffered from an unstable banking system and overdependence on the domestic market. Anyone could set up a bank and small-scale banks would often invest unwisely on the stock market. Railway speculator Jay Cooke's company borrowed $100 million, and when it went bankrupt in 1873 the knock-on effects destroyed hundreds of banks. In 1893, bankruptcies in industries ranging from banks to railways sparked a crisis, which caused a shortage of cash. Industry laid off workers and unemployment rose from 3.7 million in 1892 to 12.3 million in 1894.

In 1893, people who had invested money in American companies began selling their shares in the companies. When lots of investors sell their shares at the same time, a crisis can begin. In 1893, the crisis triggered an **economic depression**. As is usual in a depression, there was a significant and sustained drop in economic activity, with a rise in unemployment, and a fall in production and trading.

KEY TERM

Economic depression: A situation when demand for goods and services drop, investment declines, prices fall and unemployment rises.

Many people feared that they had already invested too much money, and that American firms had already produced goods which would go unsold, and this prompted the thought that new markets would need to be found. For example, large-scale farmers in the south and west argued that they needed access to overseas markets in order to sell all their products and maximise their profits. They campaigned against the government's policy of protecting American industries from foreign imports by imposing high tariffs. They argued that this policy both prevented them from selling their products abroad and also increased their costs due to the high price of imported agricultural machinery.

Asia (especially China) was seen as a new market for American goods. An aggressive nationalism developed, partly because of a belief that an overseas empire could also provide manufacturers with cheap raw materials. Overseas expansion and the unifying effects of **patriotism** were regarded as potential relief for the labour tensions and unrest that grew during the depression of the 1890s.

KEY TERM

Patriotism: Love for and pride in your country.

ACTIVITY 1.30

Why were some American entrepreneurs able to become enormously wealthy during the late 19th century?

a Make a list of possible reasons.

b In pairs, compare lists and then re-arrange them into an order of significance – what you consider to be the most important reason at the top, and the least important at the bottom.

The building of the Panama Canal

Theodore Roosevelt was very skilful in foreign affairs. He understood when to threaten force and when to manoeuvre gently behind the scenes and wrote that he was fond of the proverb 'Speak softly and carry a big stick'. He saw the world as being divided between 'civilised' and 'barbaric' nations, and thought it was the duty of the 'civilised', Christian nations such as the USA to help the 'backward' and 'lawless' countries. He also saw it as entirely right that the USA should involve itself in Central America.

Geographically, the USA was a Pacific and an Atlantic power, but as a result of the Spanish–American War, the USA also became a Caribbean power. With this development came a revival of the long-discussed plans for a canal through the Isthmus of Panama.

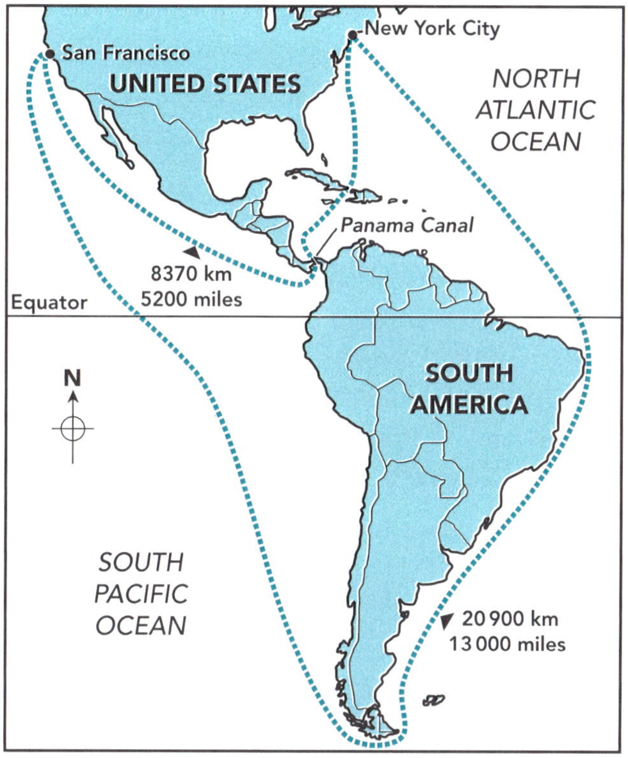

Figure 1.32: Map showing the Panama Canal. The opening of the Panama Canal greatly shortened the sea journey between the Atlantic and Pacific oceans.

The French diplomat (and builder of the Suez Canal in Egypt) Ferdinand de Lesseps had obtained a lease on Panama from the Colombian government, but the canal had not been completed. In 1889 de Lesseps negotiated a sale of the plans to the American government. The Colombian government threatened to stop the plans by refusing to allow access to the land around the planned canal, but Roosevelt intervened. In November 1903 a US-organised Panamanian independence movement led a revolution against the Colombian government. The uprising was inspired by Roosevelt and planned by Philippe Bunau-Varilla, an employee of the Panama Canal Company. Roosevelt sent the US cruiser USS *Nashville* to prevent the Colombian government from re-taking Panama. The USA quickly recognised the independent Panama government and negotiated with it for control of a 16 km-wide (10-mile-wide) strip across the Isthmus of Panama. The USA was granted control of the Canal Zone forever for $10 million and $250 000 pa in rent. Work began in 1907 and the Panama Canal opened to traffic in 1914. It reduced the journey between east and west coasts by nearly 13 000 km.

The Spanish–American War, 1898

By 1830 most Spanish colonies in South America had won their independence, but the fight for Cuban independence lasted much longer. In December 1895, Cuban rebels staged another uprising, and the Spanish sent almost 100 000 troops to crush the rebellion. The rebels were outnumbered and suffered cruel treatment from the Spanish when they were caught. However, they fought on, winning some support from ordinary Cubans and some sympathy in the USA.

Reasons for the Spanish–American War

A number of factors led to the Spanish–American War.

Increasing US interest in Central and Latin America

American presidents had always taken an interest in the affairs of countries in Latin America and the Caribbean, especially as they began to acquire independence in the 19th century, but in the years after the Civil War imperial dreams were forgotten. The Monroe Doctrine and discussions about pan-American cooperation suggested that the USA might one day take a more active role in Central and South America, and the development of the Panama Canal project increased American interest and involvement in Central America. By the 1890s America's growing imperial vision, backed up by the increasing power of the US navy, contributed to a sense that the USA was paying more attention to its closest neighbours.

In the years after the American Civil War, US businessmen invested $50 million in Cuban sugar and tobacco, and by the 1890s 90% of all Cuban sugar and almost 90% of all Cuban exports went to the USA. Almost half of the goods imported into Cuba came from the USA. Indeed, plans for the USA to acquire Cuba had been discussed before the Civil War, and in 1881, the US Secretary of Defence, James G. Blaine, wrote that if Cuba ever ceased being Spanish-controlled, it 'must necessarily become part of America'. American interests in Cuba were so significant by the 1890s that the fate of Cuba became a matter of some concern. The Cuban independence movement Cuba Libre had strong connections with Florida, and US politicians including the Secretary of State at the time, Richard Olney, had financial interests in Cuba.

'Yellow' journalism

A consequence of the US economic boom of the 1880s was the rise of the 'yellow press', so-called because of the colour in which a popular cartoon strip was printed in the *New York World* and the *New York Journal*. The name came to describe a group of popular newspapers that published low-quality, sensationalised and scandalous stories about sport, crime and political corruption, with bold headlines, lavish use of pictures, unresearched claims from unverified sources and faked interviews. Events in Cuba featured in the 'yellow press' during the Cuban War of Independence of 1895. Stories exaggerating the harshness of Spanish rule, or the heroism of Cuban revolutionaries proved to be very popular with readers.

The sinking of the Maine

Although the USA officially remained neutral in the war between Spain and the Cuban rebels, it sent a battleship, the Maine, to Cuba to protect US citizens who had been caught up in the fighting. Only weeks after it arrived, in February 1898, an explosion on board sank the Maine. The ship was completely destroyed, and 268 American sailors were killed. Although the early reports suggested that the explosion was accidental, William Randolph Hearst, a journalist with the *New York Journal*, immediately blamed Spain. He urged the government to war with the slogan 'Remember the Maine'.

Newspapers published pages of exaggerated and distorted information about the incident, and about Spanish involvement in it. Americans were whipped into a frenzy of anti-Spanish hysteria, and the chances of a peaceful resolution disappeared quickly as US politicians came under pressure to avenge the loss.

The closing of the frontier and the publication of Mahan's book in 1890 encouraged many Americans to believe that the USA should extend its influence. Arguably the most important of these was Theodore Roosevelt. Appointed Assistant Secretary of the Navy in 1897, he continued the process of developing the size and strength of the US navy. A year before the sinking of the Maine, he had argued that it was in the USA's best interests to force the Spanish out of Cuba.

President McKinley, 25th President of the USA (1897–1901), did not want war, but Roosevelt was already preparing for it. He ordered US naval vessels to occupy key ports, such as Manila Bay in the Philippines, with the aim of denying Spanish ships access to safe harbours and supplies.

Figure 1.33: The image, published in US newspapers, of the explosion that sank the USS Maine.

ACTIVITY 1.31

To five hundred thousand Cubans starved or otherwise murdered have been added an American battleship and three hundred American sailors lost as the direct result of the weak policy of our government toward Spain. If we had stopped the war in Cuba when duty and policy alike urged us to do, the Maine would have been afloat today, and three hundred homes, now desolate, would have been unscathed.

It was an accident, they say. Perhaps it was, but accident or not, it would never have happened if there had been peace in Cuba, as there would have been if we had done our duty. And it was an accident of a remarkably convenient kind for Spain. Two days ago we had five battleships in the Atlantic. Today we have four. A few more such accidents will leave us at the mercy of a Spanish fleet.

From an article in the *New York Journal*, 7 February 1898.

Study the extract from the article.

a Which of the following statements about the article do you feel are true, and which are false? Make notes which explain your reasoning.

- i The article believed that the US government had been right to keep out of the war between Cuba and Spain before the Maine incident.
- ii The article argued that the US government should have intervened in the war between Cuba and Spain even before the Maine incident.
- iii The article wanted its readers to believe that Spain had deliberately destroyed the Maine.
- iv The article wanted the US government to declare war on Spain.

CONTINUED

SPANISH TREACHERY!

DESTRUCTION OF THE WARSHIP MAINE WAS THE WORK OF AN ENEMY

b These two headlines appeared on the front pages of two other US newspapers on the same day. List the features they have in common.

Anti-Spanish feeling was increased by a letter written by the Spanish Ambassador in Washington, which criticised the President. In April 1898, McKinley asked **Congress** for authorisation to intervene in Cuba. There was a significant anti-imperialist element in Congress, however, and they were anxious to clarify that the USA had no intention of taking over Cuba. The Teller Amendment, a joint resolution (firm decision) of both houses of Congress, confirmed that US involvement was not to 'exercise sovereignty, jurisdiction or control' over Cuba, but to aid Cuba's 'liberty and freedom'.

KEY TERM

Congress: A congress is a formal meeting between delegates. In the context of US politics, 'Congress' refers to two institutions which, together, form the law-making branch of the federal (national) government. Congress meets in the Capitol building in Washington DC. The two institutions (the Senate and the House of Representatives), which occupy one end each of the Capitol building, have slightly different roles. The Senate takes more responsibility for American foreign policy.

Historians have debated the reasons for this decision, and a variety of different arguments have been suggested:

- It was inspired by an aggressive and patriotic press campaign that inflamed public opinion following the Maine incident.
- It was intended to protect American business interests in Cuba.
- It was inevitable, because of the misrule of the Spanish and the geographical closeness of Cuba to the USA.
- The USA feared an independent Cuba that it could not control.
- The USA desired more territory in order to extend its commercial interests.
- The US government wanted to distract the American people from the effects of the economic depression.

The Spanish–American War, April–August 1898

The US Secretary of State, John Hay, called this war a 'splendid little war'. Despite America being unprepared for the conflict, it was over remarkably swiftly and for the loss of fewer than 400 men. The first American attack was in May 1898 in the Philippine Islands, a Spanish colony in the Pacific. The American navy sank ten ships and captured the capital, Manila. In Cuba, in June, the Americans landed 17 000 troops. These troops included Theodore Roosevelt, who, delighted at the prospect of the war, had resigned his post as assistant secretary of the navy and formed a volunteer cavalry unit known as the 'Rough Riders'. The troops won several key victories, famously at San Juan Hill. In July, Santiago fell, and an armistice was signed.

Impact of the Spanish–American War

Spain asked for peace after losses in Cuba and Philippines, and the Treaty of Paris was signed in December 1898. Cuba was granted independence, but US troops stayed for four years, and an American governor was put in charge, to help establish stability and assist with the writing of a Cuban constitution. Before recognising Cuban independence, however, President McKinley insisted that the Platt Amendment (to the Cuban Constitution) of 1901 must be approved by the Cubans. This Amendment declared the USA had the right to intervene in Cuba to maintain its stability and independence at any time; that Cuba could not make treaties that would limit its independence; and that the USA would decide whether or not Cuban independence was in danger. The Cuban Constitution also granted the USA the right to maintain a naval base at Guantanamo Bay. American troops were withdrawn in 1902, and a new government was set up and run by Cubans. The USA continued to dominate the economy until 1959.

The Treaty of Paris also forced Spain to hand control of its other former possessions, including Puerto Rico and Guam, to the USA, and said that Spain would sell the Philippines to the USA for $20 million.

In addition, the Treaty of Paris confirmed the USA's acquisition of Hawaii. Following a series of trade treaties commencing in the 1840s, Hawaii had become important to the USA as a base for supplying American whaling vessels and a source of sugar cane. By 1870, American interests dominated much of the local economy. In 1887 the USA established a naval base at Pearl Harbor. Realising the strategic importance of Hawaii to American trade with East Asia, and in line with its new imperial policy, the USA formally annexed Hawaii in 1898, during the Spanish–American War.

The Treaty of Paris made clear that the USA had begun to follow policies designed to extend its global influence. It had become an imperial power.

America's interest in these new possessions was less to do with acquiring natural resources, and much more to do with trade. Puerto Rico and Cuba were gateways to Latin America, and important bases from which American naval power could be projected. As Mahan's vision had suggested, America's new colonies could be used to facilitate trade with Asia. In 1899, shortly after the end of the war with Spain, Secretary of State John Hay called for European powers to grant equal access – or an 'Open Door', as he put it – to commercial markets in China.

Anti-imperialists, such as the **Democratic** presidential candidate William Jennings Bryan, protested against acquiring foreign territories. They argued that this was a betrayal of the USA's isolationist traditions. However, the president, the **Republican** William McKinley, defeated Bryan in the 1900 presidential election. This suggests that most of the American public supported the USA's move towards imperialism.

KEY TERM

Democrats and Republicans: The two major political parties in the USA are the Republican and Democratic (or Democrat) Parties.

Theodore Roosevelt returned from the war in Cuba as a hero and won election to the position of governor of New York. He was selected as McKinley's choice for the vice president's position in the 1900 presidential election. When McKinley was assassinated just six months into his second term, Theodore Roosevelt became the 26th and youngest President of the USA (1901–09). As president, Roosevelt pursued expansionist policies in Latin America, building the Panama Canal and issuing the Roosevelt Corollary to the Monroe Doctrine. A corollary is a proposition that follows from something already agreed. This addition to the Monroe Doctrine stated that to preserve order the USA had the right to intervene in the affairs of other countries in Latin America in cases of 'chronic (serious) wrongdoing or impotence'. 'Impotence' meant that America had the right to intervene if the government of another country was incapable of ruling effectively. 'Wrongdoing' usually refers to criminal activity, but in this context, Americans could define what represented a crime.

Roosevelt explained the purpose of the Corollary in a speech in December 1904:

> All that this country desires is to see the neighboring countries stable, orderly, and prosperous. Any country whose people conduct themselves well can count upon our hearty friendship. If a nation shows that it knows how to act with reasonable efficiency and decency in social and political matters, if it keeps order and pays its obligations, it need fear no interference from the United States. Chronic wrongdoing, or an impotence which results in a general loosening of the ties of civilized society, may in America, as elsewhere, ultimately require intervention by some civilized nation, and in the Western Hemisphere the adherence of the United States to the Monroe Doctrine may force the United States, however reluctantly, in flagrant cases of such wrongdoing or impotence, to the exercise of an international police power.
>
> **From a speech by President Roosevelt to Congress, December 1904.**

Taft and Dollar Diplomacy

Roosevelt won the 1904 election, but did not stand for a third term in 1908, and William Taft became his successor. Taft, 27th President of the USA (1909–13), believed that US investment in Latin American countries would be welcome and would be beneficial for all those who lived there, while undermining European influence in the areas where this influence still remained. Taft stated that he would 'substitute dollars for bullets', meaning that he would use foreign policy to provide markets with which US companies could do business. As a result, US economic power would influence foreign affairs to the USA's advantage. This policy became known as 'Dollar Diplomacy'.

Taft knew that several Central American nations still owed debts to countries in Europe. He, therefore, offered to pay off these debts. But not all countries wanted to transfer their debts to the USA. When Nicaragua rejected the offer of American loans to pay off its debt to Great Britain, Taft sent a warship to the region and intervened to replace the Nicaraguan president with someone more sympathetic to the USA. Similarly, when Mexico appeared to be ready to allow Japanese companies to make a major investment in Mexico, Taft encouraged Henry Cabot Lodge, a senior Senator and member of the Foreign Relations Committee, to propose another extension of the Monroe Doctrine. The Lodge Corollary said that America would not only oppose foreign state influence in the western hemisphere; it would also stop investments by corporations.

In Asia, Dollar Diplomacy was successful in working with the Chinese government to develop the railway network. However, Taft's efforts to extend the Open Door policy further into Manchuria were unsuccessful, and brought the USA into conflict with Japan. When Taft's presidency came to an end in early 1913, the USA was considered a major world power. America's imperial policy direction was set, and military intervention and economic coercion (threats and forceful persuasion) had been established as tactics for achieving it.

The Philippine–American War, 1899–1902

Many Filipinos and Puerto Ricans had welcomed the prospect of American intervention in the 1890s. These people saw American intervention as a way of breaking Spanish domination, as a method of getting access to American wealth, or as protection against rebellious nationalist movements. Filipinos had been engaged in war with Spain since 1896. However, once it became clear that the USA did not intend to acknowledge the Philippines' declaration of independence, fighting broke out again, this time with America.

Reasons for the Philippine–American War

There were several reasons for the Philippine–American War.

US expansion into the Pacific

A US naval force was stationed in Hong Kong in case war should break out with Spain. When the USA declared war against Spain in April 1898, this force sailed to the Philippines and defeated the Spanish fleet in Manila Bay on the morning of 1 May. The Filipinos rose up and declared their independence. They proclaimed a provisional republic with a young nationalist leader and general, Emilio Aguinaldo, as president. After a bloodless battle with the Spanish in August, US troops occupied the capital, Manila, but Aguinaldo's supporters controlled the rest of the country.

Controversy over US motives and actions

Some Americans believed that the USA had no right to exercise control in a country where the people wanted self-government. But McKinley decided to retain possession of the islands, claiming that the intention was for 'benevolent assimilation'. The official US justification said that the intention was to create 'an enlightened system of government under which the Philippine people may enjoy the largest measure of home rule and the amplest liberty'. McKinley's government argued that its aim was to 'uplift and Christianise' the people of the Philippines (even though most of them were Catholic already).

The first shots of the war were fired in February 1899, when American naval forces bombarded the Philippines. As soon as they had control in the Philippines, the Americans introduced their own government, and American rule brought some improvements, including the building of schools, hospitals, roads, sewage systems, an elected assembly and the promise of self-rule.

During this three-year-long war, American soldiers committed crimes against the local population. They destroyed homes, crops and other property, captured and tortured prisoners, and murdered and raped local civilians. Information about these crimes did appear in newspapers, and the troops were strongly criticised by anti-imperialists back in America.

Filipino resistance

Aguinaldo and the rebels used guerilla tactics throughout 1899 and 1900, but Aguinaldo was captured by the Americans in March 1901. He formally surrendered but his men continued fighting into 1902. It took over 70 000 American soldiers to crush the rebellion and to capture

Aguinaldo. Over 4000 US soldiers died, and over 20 000 Filipino combatants, as well as perhaps 200 000 civilians, were killed during the war.

Figure 1.34: Members of an American Army unit prepare for action in 1899, during the Philippine-American War.

Impact of the Philippine–American War

From the beginning, US presidents and their representatives in the Philippines argued that their mission was to prepare the Philippines for independence. Nevertheless, American conduct in the Philippines War prompted the formation of an Anti-Imperialist League in the USA, which published criticisms of US policy in Cuba and the Philippines. The Democrat Party was also inspired to nominate William Jennings Bryan to run against McKinley in 1900 on an anti-imperialist platform. Bryan criticised McKinley for placing the USA in the 'un-American' position of crushing the Filipino independence movement with force.

At the same time, supporters of an American imperial foreign policy also adopted the language of freedom to describe the aims they wanted the USA to pursue. They saw the USA as providing a 'benevolent' type of imperialism, which aimed to spread freedom and bring progress to cultures that they believed were 'backward'. At the beginning of the 20th century, the USA seemed set to become one of the world's great imperial powers.

ACTIVITY 1.32

Figure 1.35: Cartoon published in the American magazine *Puck* in 1906.

Look carefully at the cartoon in Figure 1.35, which was published in an American magazine in 1906. Write answers to the following questions.

- a Who is depicted as captain of the American ship?
- b What do you think the American ship is meant to represent?
- c Why is the ship's gun drawn so large?
- d The character on the left is holding a document which says 'Claims'. Who or what does this character represent?
- e Why is the character in the middle crying?
- f The card at the end of the gun says 'Monroe Doctrine'. Why do you think these words are attached to the gun?
- g Do you think the cartoonist was being critical of America? Explain your answer.

ACTIVITY 1.33

a Construct a timeline of the main events in American foreign policy between 1890 and 1914. Beside each entry on the timeline, indicate whether American policy was isolationist or not.

b Arrange a discussion with your classmates.

- **i** One side should construct a case in support of the idea that American policy was motivated by isolationism.
- **ii** The other side should construct a case in opposition – they might like to argue that American policy was always interventionist.
- **iii** At the end of your discussion, write a paragraph to summarise the case you feel was stronger. Remember to include evidence in support of your ideas.

ACTIVITY 1.34

Figure 1.36: 'That's A Live Wire, Gentlemen!' a US cartoon from 1902. The figure on the right is commonly known as Uncle Sam, and he is usually drawn as a representative of the USA. On the left, Kaiser Wilhelm represents Germany, and John Bull represents Great Britain.

For each of the following questions, there are numerous possible answers. Try to go beyond the most obvious answers and discuss your ideas with a partner.

a What do you think the 'live wire' represents? What other lines might the cartoon's original readers have thought of, when they saw this image?

b This cartoon was drawn in 1902. What does this cartoon suggest about American attitudes to these European powers at that time? Why do you think Americans had these attitudes at this time?

c What does the cartoon suggest about American attitudes to American policy at this time? How might a critic of imperialism of all kinds comment on this cartoon?

The USA's entry into the First World War

From 1901 to 1920, US Marines conducted multiple military interventions in Caribbean nations, with over 20 separate landings during this period, but mostly the public did not support intervention in international affairs beyond the western hemisphere. When the First World War broke out in June 1914, this reluctance to intervene was tested.

Reasons for the USA's entry into the First World War

Woodrow Wilson was President of the USA during the First World War. The war originated with the murder of the heir to the throne of Austria-Hungary at the end of June 1914, but during July a crisis arose as threats and alliances pulled in more countries. At the beginning of August 1914, Germany put its war plan into action and attacked Belgium and France, and Russia and Britain declared war on Germany. The members of the Triple Entente joined forces to defend each other against attacks from the Central Powers, and war broke out among the European nations and their empires.

Wilson was appalled. At this point, however, he felt that the war was a European conflict which the USA should not get dragged into. Most Americans agreed with him.

KEY FIGURE

Woodrow Wilson (1856–1924)

The Democrat Woodrow Wilson was elected as president in 1912 and narrowly won a second term in 1916. He made the decision to bring the USA into the First World War in 1917. He considered himself to be a mediator between rival European nations and played a leading role in the peace negotiations at the end of the war. Wilson suffered a stroke in 1919 but continued to serve as president until 1921.

Figure 1.37: Europe in 1914, showing the division between the members of the Triple Alliance and the Triple Entente.

US relations with Germany, Britain and France

American society was sharply divided by the outbreak of war. British-Americans sided with the Triple Entente, as did many other Americans who associated Britain with democracy and liberty. Language, culture and history meant that most Americans supported the Triple Entente powers. The USA also had a long friendship with France dating back to the War of Independence. British **propaganda** was very effective at showing the Triple Entente as a group of decent and democratic nations defending Europe from the unprovoked aggression, and it also highlighted German war crimes in Belgium and France.

The USA was also home to around eight million Americans of German descent. These Americans naturally sympathised with the Central Powers, as did other Americans who felt anti-British or anti-Russian for family reasons. These included Irish Americans, who resented Britain because of the political problems in Ireland, and many Jewish and Polish Americans who were descended from people who had escaped from Russian persecution. Even many Americans who did not have a strong family connection did not want to see the USA allied with autocratic Russia (where the tsar ruled harshly and without paying attention to the wishes of the people).

In 1916, Wilson proposed a peace conference to Sir Edward Grey (the British foreign secretary), indicating that if the Allies agreed to the peace proposals and the Germans did not, then the USA might join the war on the Allied side. Wilson offered his services as a mediator but neither the Allies nor the Central Powers took him seriously and the suggestion came to nothing.

KEY TERM

Propaganda: Communication designed to influence an audience to support a specific action or political agenda. It does so by spreading ideas, information or rumours in ways that appeal to people's beliefs and feelings.

Wilson's policy

Wilson declared American neutrality in 1914, and from then until 1917 his main foreign policy aim was to keep the USA out of the war. He argued that 'There is such a thing as a nation too proud to fight' and said that the USA should remain neutral in thought and deed, to demonstrate that the USA was superior, and that there were other ways to resolve conflict. He campaigned for and won re-election to the Presidency in 1916 on the basis of a promise to keep the USA out of the war.

Twice, in early 1915 and again in early 1916, Wilson sent his chief foreign policy advisor, Colonel Edward M. House, to Europe to meet with the British, French and German leaders. Wilson instructed House to try to find a way to facilitate an end to the war. In May 1916, Wilson publicly promised US involvement in a post-war international peace organisation, and in January 1917, he gave a speech in which he called for 'peace without victory' and the establishment of a 'League of Peace' that would include the USA.

Despite Wilson's efforts to end the war, and his attempts to keep the USA out of it, the war had an impact on the USA almost from the beginning. As a neutral power, the USA insisted on its right to trade with both sides, but the British navy had blockaded German ports since 1914, so American trade was almost exclusively with the Entente powers. Any ships carrying goods towards Germany were intercepted by British ships, but the British Royal Navy was under orders to buy the entire cargo at pre-war prices and release the vessel unharmed.

The war, and the demand for American goods of all kinds, created a boom in US industry and agriculture, and the USA loaned money to the Europeans to help them finance the war. By 1917, the USA had loaned $2 billion to the Allies and $27 million to the Germans.

Anti-war pressure groups

The official policy of neutrality in the war was supported by Americans from across all sectors of society. America already had some prominent pacifist organisations, and they rushed to coordinate and join together to strengthen their message. The most important and largest of these was the American Union against **Militarism** (AUAM), which was intended to act as an 'umbrella organisation' for **progressive liberals**, **trade unions**, and church groups.

Some **socialists**, the IWW (Industrial Workers of the World), and some **radical** farming groups felt that the mainstream pacifist messages were too moderate. They argued that the conflict was an 'imperialist war' and blamed the war on capitalism.

KEY TERMS

Progressive: Supporting (or someone who supports) social reform.

Liberal: Believing (or someone who believes) that government should allow as much personal and economic freedom as possible.

Trade union: An organisation formed with the aim of improving the treatment of workers in a specific field of work.

Militarism: The belief that a country should use force and its military to achieve its foreign policy goals.

Socialist: Supporting (or someone who supports) socialism – an economic and political philosophy that pursues social ownership of the means of production (for example, factories), as opposed to private ownership.

Radical: Supporting (or someone who supports) drastic or complete change.

Poor, rural areas tended to be strongly anti-war, especially among the white population, who feared that the wealthy Wall Street elite would lead them into a destructive war.

Leaders of most religious groups often opposed American involvement in the war. Methodists and Quakers are examples of religious groups who strongly and publicly opposed the war, on grounds of pacifism.

Important women's organisations also spoke out against the war. The National Woman's Party was led by **Alice Paul.** This organisation made multiple anti-war protests at the White House, arguing that the USA had political problems to solve at home, including the issue that women were not allowed to vote in elections, and, therefore, it had no business intervening in foreign wars. The Woman's Peace Party started in 1915 and quickly attracted over 40 000 members. It led a pacifist campaign, and its leader, Jane Addams, met Woodrow Wilson to discuss the war on several occasions.

Henry Ford supported the pacifist cause by chartering a ship in 1915 to conduct a large-scale private peace mission, where many activists and public figures joined him to sail to Europe to meet with leaders on both sides. Ford fell ill, and although the mission continued, it was unsuccessful.

KEY FIGURE

Alice Paul (1885–1977)

Alice Paul was an American women's rights activist who campaigned for women's rights to vote in Britain and the USA. She was arrested and imprisoned numerous times in Britain and the USA. She formed the National Woman's Party in the USA in 1916. She was one of the leaders who campaigned for changing the US Constitution to allow women the vote in America in 1920.

Actions of German U-boats including the sinking of the Lusitania

In response to the British naval blockade, the Germans adopted the tactic of submarine warfare. In February 1915, the Germans announced that any ships carrying supplies for the Allied war effort would be sunk without warning. The implications for American ships travelling across the Atlantic soon became clear.

Many cruise ships travelling across the Atlantic from America carried passengers but also transported ammunition and other goods for the Entente powers. The Germans knew this and regarded them as fair targets in wartime. On 7 May 1915, therefore, a German submarine sank the British cruise ship Lusitania. Over 1000 people died, and among them were 128 Americans. American public opinion was furious. Wilson refused to over-react but insisted that the German government must apologise for the sinking, promise to avoid any future sinkings of ships carrying Americans and compensate US victims. He sent the German government three notes in which he made the American position clear: the USA would regard any future sinking as a 'deliberately unfriendly' act.

Wilson's response caused a split in the US government. The Secretary of State, William Jennings Bryan, resigned on 9 June 1915. Bryan was a pacifist who firmly supported American isolationism and he believed that the president's warning was too strongly worded. He thought that it was likely to be seen as suggesting that the USA would soon declare war against Germany.

Bryan's argument was supported by other people who were totally opposed to entering the war. Bryan was replaced by Robert Lansing, who was convinced that the USA could not remain neutral forever and would eventually have to enter the war against Germany.

Images of the sinking liner were used frequently in British propaganda in the USA.

Figure 1.38: A British propaganda poster 'Take Up the Sword of Justice' (1915), intended to motivate Americans to support joining the war on the Allied side.

In 1915, a strong 'preparedness' movement developed, behind ex-president Theodore Roosevelt, and former secretaries of war Elihu Root and Henry Stimson. It argued for the USA to build up strong naval and land forces for defensive purposes, based on the assumption that the USA would have to fight sooner or later. The preparedness movement inspired Wilson to embrace proposals to issue warnings to Germany and encouraged him to begin to build up American land and naval forces over the long-term.

In August 1915 another U-boat sank the liner *Arabic*, with the loss of 44 passengers and crew, including three Americans. The sinking made the American public angry again, and again prompted official protests from the government. The German government insisted that its campaign against Allied shipping was legitimate but abandoned unannounced attacks on merchant and passenger vessels in September 1915. This reduced the risk of war with America for a time.

By January 1917, however, Germany's situation was increasingly desperate and unrestricted submarine attacks started again. The campaign had a huge impact on Allied imports, but in response, on 3 February, President Wilson cut diplomatic relations with Germany.

The Zimmermann Telegram

When the USA finally declared war in 1917, this was not solely because of events in the Atlantic. A threat much closer to home played at least as significant a role.

In March 1917, British spies intercepted a telegram message from the German foreign minister, Arthur Zimmerman, to the German ambassador in Mexico. The telegram suggested to the Mexican government that if Mexico joined the war by attacking the USA, Germany would ensure that at the end, Mexico got back territories (New Mexico, Texas and Arizona) it had lost to the USA in the 1840s.

The British showed the USA government a copy of the 'Zimmermann Telegram'. After the recent series of attacks on American ships by German U-boats, Wilson felt the time for a change in policy had come. He held a meeting on 20 March, at which all his closest colleagues agreed that the USA should enter the war.

On 2 April 1917, Wilson requested a declaration of war against Germany from Congress, arguing that Germany had declared 'nothing less than war against the government and people of the United States'. Permission was granted by 82–6 in the Senate and 373–50 in the House of Representatives. Wilson promised to make the world 'safe for democracy' and on 6 April the USA declared war on Germany.

There was a huge outpouring of patriotic feeling. Large numbers of young men rushed to enlist. Concerned about opposition to the war from pacifist groups, President Wilson created the Committee on Public Information (CPI) with the aim of promoting the USA's war effort with a massive pro-war publicity campaign. Wilson organised a massive anti-German propaganda campaign, while huge sums of money were raised by taxation and borrowing to fund the war effort.

ACTIVITY 1.35

- a Why didn't the USA enter the First World War in 1914?
- b What evidence suggests that American public opinion remained opposed to US entry into the war in 1916?
- c Why did the USA declare war on Germany in April 1917?

ACTIVITY 1.36

- a Look back over the reasons why America entered the war, and the work you have done on this topic. Work with a partner.

  One person should make a list of all the reasons why Americans did not want to join the First World War at the beginning of the war.

  The other person should make a list of all the reasons why USA eventually did enter the war.
- b Use both lists to consider the following statement: 'America's decision to enter the First World War came as a surprise.' How far would you agree with this statement? Construct an essay plan for an answer to this question. Make sure that your answer addresses both sides of the argument.

Impact of US intervention

In 1917 the USA had a small army: it sent only 84 000 US soldiers to Europe by March 1918. It took time for the USA to build up a large enough fighting force to make a significant difference. Before the end of the war, around 1.5 million American men volunteered for active service. In addition, the Selective Services Act in May 1917 changed the law to make it compulsory for men aged 21–30 to join the armed forces (this kind of policy is called 'conscription'). Congress increased the conscription age to 45 in 1918. Eventually almost 4 million men were conscripted into military service, and almost 2.5 million of them served on the Western Front by the end of the war. By the summer of 1918 there were about 2 million American men in France, and reinforcements were arriving at a rate of 10 000 a day.

Some historians have argued that the arrival of American troops made little difference to the eventual outcome of the war, suggesting that the Allies had already established a strategic advantage. However, American troops unquestionably helped the Allies to resist the large-scale German attacks of spring 1918 and to defend Paris when it was under threat later in 1918. At a time when Germany was unable to increase the size of its fighting forces, the Americans provided large numbers of fresh reinforcements, who were greeted enthusiastically by war-weary Allied soldiers. US forces formed an important part of the counter-attack in late summer 1918, halting the German attack at Chateau-Thierry and Belleau Wood. In September 1918, the Allied commander General Foch launched the Argonnes Offensive, and American troops played a key role in pushing the Germans back at St Mihiel. Over 100 000 Americans were killed on the Western Front. In addition, during the course of the war, 21 498 US Army nurses served in the USA and overseas.

At sea, Allied shipping losses had been high in early 1917, but they fell by two-thirds after the USA joined the war. The US navy played an important role in ensuring that the German U-boats were finally defeated in the Atlantic. This defeat meant that vital supplies (such as food, iron, steel and munitions) for Britain and France, as well as US soldiers, could cross the ocean. American shipyards could build new ships at such a rate that they could more than replace every ship the Germans sank.

The strength of the US economy was vital to Allied victory. The USA spent $35 billion on the war. After entering the conflict in April 1917, the US Treasury provided $10 billion in long-term loans to Britain, France, and other allied nations.

Wilson's Fourteen Points

In January 1918, President Wilson delivered a speech to the US Congress in which he outlined the USA's war aims and his vision for the future. In some ways, this speech represented the most significant intervention in the war, because it led, indirectly, to the German decision to request an armistice later in the year.

The President said:

> The USA entered this war because **violations** of right had occurred which made the life of our own people impossible unless they were corrected and the world secure once and for all against their recurrence. What we demand in this war, therefore, is that the world be made fit and safe to live in; and particularly that it be made safe for every peace-loving nation which, like our own, wishes to live its own life, determine its own institutions, be assured of justice and fair-dealing by the other peoples of the world as against force and selfish aggression.
>
> **From a speech by President Wilson to Congress, 8 January 1918.**

KEY TERM

Violating/violation: Breaking or acting against something, for example a law, agreement (such as a treaty), or something that should be treated with respect.

In his speech, Wilson listed what became known as his 'Fourteen Points', which, he argued, should form the basis of peace negotiations once the First World War ended. These reflected Wilson's thinking about why the war had broken out and how it had been conducted. They were also part of the way in which Wilson justified the war to the American people. Wilson wanted the post-war world to see:

1. no more secret treaties between countries
2. nations able to sail and trade freely on the sea
3. protectionist barriers to trade removed and countries practising free trade
4. nations reducing their armed forces
5. rival imperial claims settled by negotiation rather than conflict, recognising the wishes of the native people
6. Russia reintegrated into world diplomacy and land lost to Germany restored
7. land taken from Belgium during the war returned to it
8. France freed from German occupation and land taken from France by Germany in 1871 returned to France
9. Italian frontiers redrawn to match the nationality of the local people
10. peoples in Austria-Hungary given the right to self-government and independence (known as self-determination)
11. all foreign forces withdrawn from the Balkan nations
12. peoples in the former Turkish (Ottoman) Empire given independence, and the Dardanelles made free to shipping
13. an independent, self-governing Poland with access to the sea
14. an international organisation in which member nations could discuss their disagreements and deal with them by negotiation rather than war: a League of Nations.

When the Germans agreed to an armistice, they did so on the understanding that the peace treaty would be based on the principles laid out in Wilson's Fourteen Points. The armistice came into effect with a ceasefire that began at 11 a.m. on 11 November 1918.

ACTIVITY 1.37

Which of the following statements most accurately reflects President Wilson's aims in listing his Fourteen Points? Reach a judgement, and prepare an argument to support your decision, including reference to detailed supporting evidence. Discuss your answers in small groups.

a. Wilson wanted to prove that the USA was now a world power.
b. Wilson wanted to avoid future wars.
c. Wilson wanted the USA to control Europe after the war.
d. Wilson wanted to punish Germany for causing the war.

For the USA, the First World War was both short and successful. No fighting had taken place on American soil, and many of its industries had expanded to meet increased wartime demand. In addition to supplying its allies with vital resources, the USA had been able to extend its markets in areas such as South America and East Asia, formerly dominated by European nations. Prior to 1917, Britain had funded its war effort by taking out loans from private American banks. Following its declaration of war against Germany, the US government itself provided loans to Britain and the Allies. These loans would have to be repaid with interest once the war was over.

The war had proved to be highly beneficial for the American economy and American business. By 1918, the USA was unquestionably the greatest financial power in the world. Moreover, its president clearly believed that the USA had both the right and the responsibility to play a leading role in negotiations leading to the post-war peace settlement.

Not only had the USA emerged as a major world power, by 1919 it had arguably become the most powerful and important. Wilson and other American diplomats led the peace treaty negotiations, which began in Paris in January 1919, and in doing so they shaped the post-war world.

KEY CONCEPT 1.4

Change and continuity

Look back at this section, and the work you have done on it. To what extent do you think that America changed its attitude to isolationism? In small groups, discuss whether America's attitude to getting involved in world affairs changed during this period, or whether isolationism remained a key principle in American political thinking. Remember to make a judgement and find detailed examples to support your judgement.

KEY CONCEPT 1.5

Interpretations

Most American historians at this time either argued that America did not have an empire, or (if they accepted that it did have an empire) they said that America was a reluctant (unwilling) imperial power.

Many historians saw America's slowness to enter the First World War (along with its refusal to join the League of Nations after 1919 and avoidance of any involvement in European affairs in the 1920s – see Chapter 2) as evidence that pointed to the conclusion that America was not an expansionist power. When America had become involved in international affairs, they suggested, it was out of humanitarian concern for others.

In the 1950s, a historian called William Appleman Williams wrote a controversial book that opened a debate about the nature of American imperialism. He argued that America was less reactive and more deliberately expansionist than previous historians had suggested.

Look back on the information in this section. Work with a partner and think about America's growth as a world power.

- What is the evidence that America only reluctantly got involved in affairs abroad, and what is the evidence that suggests America became involved more willingly?
- What events suggest that America only got involved when its own interests were threatened, and what events tell a story of a country more ambitious to expand its interests abroad?

Practice questions

Source-based question

Read the sources and then answer **both** parts of the question.

SOURCE A

When I realised that the Philippines had dropped into our laps, I confess I did not know what to do with them. And, one night it came to me:

1 That we could not give them back to Spain – that would be cowardly and dishonourable.

2 That we could not turn them over to France or Germany, our commercial rivals in the Far East – that would be bad business.

3 That we could not leave them to themselves – they were unfit for self-government.

4 That there was nothing left for us to do but to take them and to educate, uplift, civilise and Christianise the Filipinos.

The next morning, I sent for our map maker and told him to put the Philippines on the map of the USA; there they are, and there they will stay while I am president.

From Republican President William McKinley, speaking in an interview, 1899.

SOURCE B

We believe that the policy known as imperialism is hostile to liberty and tends towards militarism. We reaffirm that all men, of whatever race or colour, are entitled to life, liberty and the pursuit of happiness. We insist that the subjugation of any people is criminal aggression. We condemn the policy of the US government in the Philippines in pursuit of un-American gains. We denounce the slaughter of Filipinos as a needless horror and protest against the extension of American territory by Spanish methods. We demand the immediate ending of the war against liberty, started by Spain and continued by us.

We urge the US government to announce to the Filipinos our purpose to concede to them their

CONTINUED

independence for which they have so long fought and which is theirs by right. The USA has always protested against the doctrine of international law which permits the domination of the weak by the strong. The USA cannot act upon the belief that might makes right.

From a statement by the American Anti-Imperialist League, 1899.

SOURCE C

The Philippines are ours forever. And just beyond the Philippines are China's unlimited markets. We will not abandon this opportunity or renounce our part in the mission of our race to civilise the world. God has marked us as His chosen people to lead the regeneration of the world. Our largest trade in the future must be with Asia. The Pacific is our ocean and is the ocean of the commerce of the future. China is our natural customer. Most future wars will be conflicts for commerce. The power that rules the Pacific, therefore, is the power that rules the world. And, with the Philippines, that power is and will forever be the USA. Two years ago we had no commercial, naval or military base in the Pacific. Today, we have the Philippines, located at the most commanding commercial, naval and military point in the ocean, rich in natural resources and peopled by a race which civilisation demands shall be improved.

From a speech by Republican Senator Albert Beveridge, 1900.

SOURCE D

This nation has always been quick to express its sympathy with those who were fighting for civil liberty. We believe in the principles of self-government and, if we now reject this belief, the USA will lose prestige and influence among other nations. The argument that this earth belongs to those who have the power to acquire it does not justify the taking of the Philippines. The spirit which justifies the forcible annexation of the

CONTINUED

Philippines will justify the seizure of other islands and the domination of other people, and with wars of conquest we can expect a growth of our army and navy. This will impose a large financial burden on our people. Those who support imperialism argue that it will benefit our commercial interests. This is an argument based upon the theory that war can be rightly waged for financial advantage, and that it is profitable to purchase trade by force. I favour the expansion of trade by every legitimate and peaceful means, but I am not willing to gain trade by human blood. It is not necessary to own people in order to trade with them.

From a speech by Democratic Senator William Jennings Bryan, 1900.

1 a Read Sources **A** and **B**.

Compare the views in the two sources regarding the USA's actions in the Philippines. **[15 marks]**

b Read **all** of the sources.

How far do Sources A to D support the view that Americans were in favour of the USA becoming an imperial nation? **[25 marks]**

Essay-based questions

Answer **both** questions. Answer **both** parts of each question.

2 a Explain why Japan was victorious in the Russo-Japanese War of 1904–05. **[10 marks]**

b To what extent was the adoption of Western technology the main reason for Japanese modernisation during the 19th century? **[20 marks]**

3 a Explain why the USA entered the First World War in 1917. **[10 marks]**

b 'Victory in the war against Spain (1898) was the main reason for the USA's emergence as an imperial power.' How far do you agree? **[20 marks]**

Improve this answer

1 a Read Sources **A** and **B**.

Compare the views in the two sources regarding the USA's actions in the Philippines.
[15 marks]

In the late 19th century, public opinion in the USA was divided over the issue of imperialism, and these two sources reflect that division. Source B is clearly opposed to imperialism, which it claims threatens 'liberty', involves the 'domination of the weak by the strong' and goes against American beliefs and traditions. As a result, it condemns the actions of McKinley's government in the Philippines, describing it as 'criminal aggression' and 'needless slaughter'.

So far, this answer has nicely set up the difference between the sources. The opening sentence provides contextualisation, showing how the two sources fit into the contemporary wider debate within the USA regarding the issue of imperialism and American involvement in it. It has addressed only Source B in any detail, however.

President McKinley clearly recognised that there was likely to be opposition to US involvement in the Philippines, which is why he uses Source A to stress that the USA did not deliberately seek control over them – they simply 'dropped into our laps' following victory in the war against Spain. McKinley then proceeds to justify US control over the Philippines by suggesting that his government had no choice – the Philippines could not be given back to Spain or to commercial rivals such as France or Germany.

The answer has now outlined some key points from Source A. The answer is fully focused on the topic of the question, but there is still no comparison of the sources. Any similarities and/or differences are left up to the reader to find.

The main difference between the two sources is that, whereas Source B argues that the Filipinos deserved liberty and freedom, Source A claims that they were unfit to govern themselves and therefore needed the USA to 'educate, uplift, civilise and Christianise them'. Therefore, while Source A highlights the positive aspects of imperialism (in much the same way as European nations had justified their imperialistic actions in Africa and Asia), Source B stresses its negative aspects.

This answer demonstrates good understanding of the views expressed in the two sources. Contextual knowledge is used effectively in the final sentence, showing how McKinley's attempt to justify US imperialism in the Philippines was based on the same arguments as those used by imperialistic European nations.

There are three main areas in which the answer could be improved:

- There could be more comparisons between the views, and the answer might acknowledge that both sources contain some similar ideas. Both Sources A and B recognise that allowing independence for the Philippines was an option, although they clearly differ on whether that would have been the best course of action.
- There needs to be some attempt to explain why the two sources express such contrasting views. This could be achieved by stressing that President McKinley was a Republican, a party which supported US expansion through imperialism. Conversely, Source B comes from the American Anti-Imperialist League, which, as the name clearly implies, was totally opposed to imperialism.
- The reasons why some Americans opposed imperialism are clearly expressed in Source B. Further contextualisation could be provided by explaining why other Americans, such as McKinley and his Republican Party, supported it by looking at the economic, political and strategic advantages they hoped to achieve by taking control of the Philippines.

Now, having read all of these points, write your own improved answer to this question.

Improve this answer

2 a Explain why Japan was victorious in the Russo-Japanese War of 1904–05. **[10 marks]**

Arguably, the most important factor in Japan's victory was Russian arrogance and complacency. Russia considered itself to be a major European power and was convinced that Japan posed no real threat to its interests in East Asia. As a result, Russia refused to negotiate with Japan over their conflicting interests in Manchuria and Korea. Moreover, the Russian base at Port Arthur was totally unprepared for any Japanese attack.

This is a good start, suggesting that the answer is going to be fully focused on the requirements of the question, and analytical rather than simply descriptive. It begins with the most important factor, although it does not provide very much detail or depth of analysis. The significance of the point about complacency (which is presumably connected with the example of Port Arthur) is not explained.

Once the Japanese had taken Port Arthur, they had gained control over the local seas, enabling them to move troops around without resistance. Russian soldiers, on the other hand, had to undergo a lengthy journey across Asia. This gave the Japanese the time and opportunity to move into Manchuria. The Japanese troops were well-led, totally organised and better-equipped than their Russian counterparts. Tired after their long journey, and lacking effective leadership, the Russians finally lost Mukden after a three-month siege.

This paragraph illustrates the interconnection between two causal factors. The connection is not fully explained, but the answer implies that the writer understands not only that the loss of Port Arthur was part of the Russian defeat in itself, but that its effects also made any future recovery or Russian victory much less likely.

The main Russian fleet was in the Baltic Sea, and had a long way to travel in order to engage with the Japanese. It encountered problems with the British fleet in the North Sea and, because of Britain's 1902 alliance with Japan, was refused access to the Suez Canal. Its slow-moving ships, laden down with coal, were forced to go round the southern tip of Africa. The fleet did not reach the Straits of Tsushima until May 1905, by which time the Japanese navy was fully prepared. The slow-moving, outdated Russian ships were no match for Japan's modern warships.

The reasons why it took so long for the Russian Baltic fleet to reach the Straits of Tsushima are explained here. It is implied that Russia lost the war because of its naval disadvantages, but there is no explicit link back to the question until the final sentence, so the reader has to think about why these details might be relevant.

Japan's rapid modernisation and industrialisation in the second half of the 19th century had enabled it to develop the military capability to defeat a major European power in war. While Russia relied on outdated ships, weapons and military tactics, Japan could deploy a thoroughly modern army and navy. However, there is little doubt that Russia (in common with most of the other major European powers) had grossly underestimated the Japanese.

This paragraph sets the fact that the Japanese had up-to-date military equipment in the context of Japan's rapid modernisation and industrialisation in the second half of the 19th century. Japan's modern weapons are contrasted with Russia's outdated equipment, and the contrast is effective. The link back to the point made in the first paragraph works well, and reinforces the judgement made about the importance of that main idea at the beginning.

Now, having read all of these points, write your own improved answer to this question.

SELF-EVALUATION CHECKLIST

After working through this chapter, complete the table.

You should be able to:	Needs more work	Almost there	Ready to move on
explain the various motives for the 'Scramble for Africa' by European countries			
outline the processes involved with the colonisation of Africa			
analyse different impacts of colonialism on Africa			
explain ways that African peoples resisted European colonisation			
explain why European powers attended the Berlin Conference and assess its outcomes			
assess the reasons for rivalries between colonial powers in the late 19th and early 20th centuries			
describe the outcomes of treaties, conferences and crises after 1900			
evaluate the state of European empires and major alliances in 1914			
explain the nature of Japanese relations with the Western Powers			
analyse the reasons for rapid modernisation and military development in Japan			
explain why international recognition of Japan occurred and when it occurred			
evaluate Japan's role in the First World War and explain its global position by 1918			
explain why attitudes to overseas expansion changed in America after 1890			
analyse the reasons for, and impact of, the Spanish-American War (1898)			
analyse the reasons for, and impact of, the Philippine-American War (1899–1902)			
analyse the reasons for, and impacts of, the USA's entry into the First World War.			

> Chapter 2

International relations, 1919–29: conflict and cooperation

KEY QUESTIONS

This chapter will help you to answer these questions:

- Why was there such extensive dissatisfaction with the peace settlements of 1919–20?
- Why was the League of Nations created and what challenges did it face in the 1920s?
- How and why did international tensions remain high after the Versailles settlement?
- How and why did international relations improve from 1924 to 1929?

Timeline

Oct 1917 Bolshevik Revolution in Russia

Jan 1918 President Wilson's 14 Points Speech

Mar 1918 Treaty of Brest-Litovsk (Germany and Russia)

Oct 1918 German request for armistice

Jan 1919 Opening of the Paris Peace Conference at Versailles

Jun 1919 Treaty of Versailles

Sep 1919 Treaty of Saint-Germain

Nov 1919 Treaty of Neuilly

Jun 1920 Treaty of Trianon

Jun 1920 Treaty of Sèvres

May 1921 Treaty formally ending the war between the USA and Germany

1921–22 Washington Conferences

Apr 1922 Rapallo Pact (Germany and the USSR)

1922–23 World Disarmament Conference

Jan 1923 French occupation of the Ruhr

Aug 1924 The Dawes Plan

Oct 1925 Locarno Conference

Aug 1928 Kellogg-Briand Pact

Sep 1929 The Young Plan

GETTING STARTED

Working in pairs or small groups

a Use Chapter 1 (Section 1.4) and any other resources available to you to do a little background research and identify the reasons why the following countries went to war in 1914, or joined in before it ended: Germany, France, Britain, Russia, Austria-Hungary, Italy, Turkey, Japan, the USA.

b Look at the map in Figure 2.1 that shows Europe at the start of war in 1914. Now compare it with the maps in Figures 2.6 and 2.7 and identify the new countries that have been created by the peace treaties of 1919–20, which you will study in this chapter. What is the same? What is different?

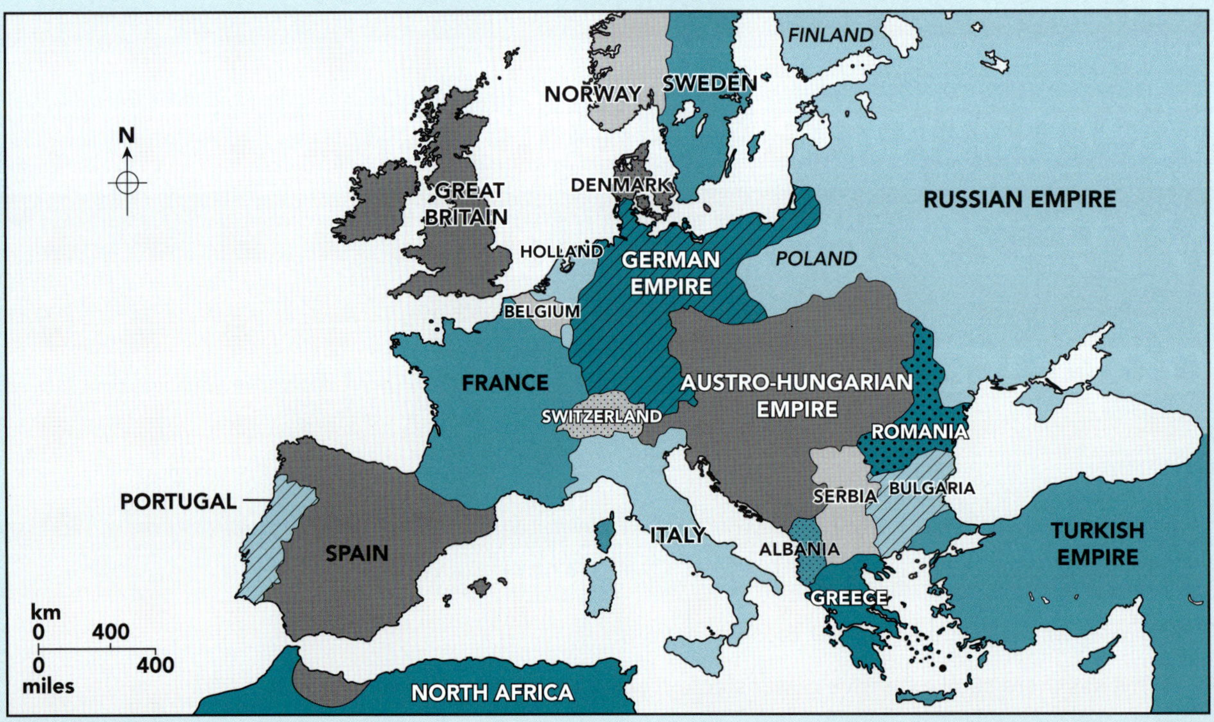

Figure 2.1: Europe in 1914.

Introduction

In January 1919, a group of men met in the great Palace of Versailles, near Paris in France, to make the peace that ended what became known as the First World War. These men faced a challenging task. The murder in 1914 of the heir to the Austrian throne had led to a worldwide conflict. France, Britain, Russia, Italy and the USA had fought against Germany, Austria-Hungary and the Turkish Empire, from 1914 to 1918. About 20 million soldiers and about the same number of civilians had died.

The situation in 1918

The end of the war did not bring stability. The political effects of the First World War were devastating. Revolutions occurred throughout the former Austro-Hungarian and Turkish empires. Like the German Empire, these empires collapsed into chaos. An influenza epidemic in 1918–19 caused a further 2.5 million deaths in Europe. During the war, Germany's enemies had successfully prevented food from reaching into Germany and Austria-Hungary, so millions in central Europe were starving by the end of 1918. Serious social unrest was breaking out in countries such as Italy, Germany and Hungary and there were fears of revolution. Several million refugees were now in search of homes and security. The winning allies had to adjust their economies from making weapons to more peaceful products and they also owed $176 billion, mainly to the United States, which they had borrowed to pay for the war.

Meanwhile, revolution had already taken place in Russia in 1917 (see Chapter 1, Section 1.3). Russia had initially taken part in the war on the Allied side. In October 1917, led by Vladimir Lenin and Leon Trotsky, the Bolshevik party had overthrown the Russian government and set up a new government based on communism. The new revolutionary government had withdrawn from the war, by signing the Treaty of Brest-Litovsk with Germany in December 1918. The terms of the treaty were extremely harsh. Russia lost large areas of territory, including areas containing much of its best farmland, raw materials and heavy industry. Russia lost 25% of its population, 25% of its industry and 90% of its coal mines. Later, in 1918, countries still fighting Germany remembered these huge penalties that Germany had imposed on Russia for being the 'losers' in their war.

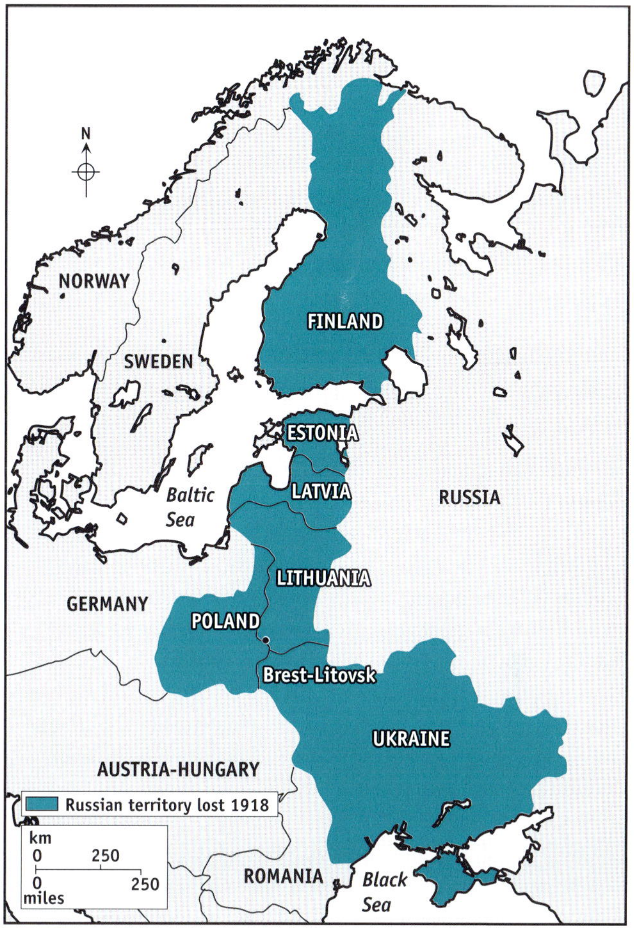

Figure 2.2: Territory lost by Russia as a result of the Treaty of Brest-Litovsk with Germany in 1918.

By the end of 1918, Lenin and the Bolsheviks were engaged in the Russian Civil War against other revolutionary parties and supporters of the Russian monarchy. Other nations, such as Britain, France, the United States and Japan, provided some support to these anti-Bolshevik groups – either because they feared revolution in their own countries or because they wanted to seize Russian territory. The Bolshevik government seemed determined to spread communism as far as possible throughout the world, so the Western powers now viewed Russia as a threat. This situation made it even more difficult to achieve peace and stability.

The peace settlement and beyond

The American president, Woodrow Wilson, was determined to bring about a fair and lasting peace but he met resistance from European politicians, who were equally determined to gain revenge and ensure that their own countries would be safe from another German attack. As a result, the peace settlement that emerged between 1919 and 1920 consisted of terms imposed by the victorious nations on the defeated countries. Inevitably, nations that lost territory and had to pay compensation to the victors were resentful. Old tensions and rivalries remained, while many potential new ones were created.

A lasting peace seemed even more unlikely when, despite Wilson's encouragement, the US Senate refused to accept the settlement agreed at the Paris Peace Conference. The USA, now the leading economic and industrial power in the world, was not prepared to support the peace terms or join the new **League of Nations** which was created to keep peace in the world. It was equally significant for future international stability that Russia was not invited to the peace talks and took no part in the negotiations for the treaties that would define the post-war world.

KEY TERM

League of Nations: An international organisation, of which every country in the world could be a member, designed to provide solutions to problems and disputes between nations.

All countries were keen to avoid the horrors of another war, and many attempts were made to improve international relations during the 1920s, including the establishment of the League of Nations. For a time, these seemed to be successful and were greeted with both enthusiasm and relief. However, tensions continued to simmer beneath the surface of the post-war world.

2.1 Why was there such extensive dissatisfaction with the peace settlements of 1919–20?

In January 1918, when US President Woodrow Wilson had outlined his vision for future world peace in his 'Fourteen Points' speech (see Chapter 1, Section 1.4), the First World War was still happening, and its outcome was not clear. Wilson had hoped his speech would encourage Russia to remain in the war. He had also hoped that the speech would prompt Germany and its allies to seek a peace settlement.

Instead, Russia withdrew from the war in March, allowing Germany to move large numbers of troops to the west and start a new attack on France. The war, therefore. lasted until a series of military defeats led Germany to ask for an armistice in November 1918. The German Kaiser, Wilhelm II, then abdicated and Germany became a republic (known as the Weimar Republic).

When the new German government requested peace terms, it hoped that the terms would be based on Wilson's Fourteen Points. However, the situation was now very different to that of January 1918. In addition, the German government seems to have been unaware that the Fourteen Points had never been written into a formal agreement or that the British and French had not supported the Fourteen Points and were likely to press for harsher terms.

The negotiations at Versailles

In January 1919, representatives of nearly 30 victorious nations met at Versailles, near Paris, the place where Germany had imposed harsh peace terms on France after a previous war (the Franco-Prussian War of 1870–71). The aim of this Paris Peace Conference was to develop a settlement that would finally end the First World War, and prevent such a war from ever happening again.

Because of the political and social chaos across Europe, it was essential to reach decisions quickly. The principal decision makers at Versailles were a 'Council of Four', consisting of President Woodrow Wilson (USA), Prime Minister Georges Clemenceau (France), Prime Minister David Lloyd George (Britain) and Prime Minister Vittorio Orlando (Italy). In reality, Italy had little influence. Orlando's inability to speak English greatly restricted his participation in negotiations. Also, once it became clear that Italy would not receive all its territorial claims, Orlando temporarily withdrew the Italian delegation from the conference in anger. As a result, the main decisions were taken by the 'Big Three'.

Figure 2.3: The Council of Four at the Paris Peace Conference. From left to right, Lloyd George (Britain), Orlando (Italy), Clemenceau (France) and Wilson (USA).

Key issues in agreeing the treaties

The peacemakers at Versailles faced a series of challenges. They had to end a world war, decide on the terms of the peace settlement and deal with the problems arising from the collapse of several major European empires.

The aims of the Big Three

Perhaps the most significant factor shaping the decision-making process was the disagreements between the USA, France and Britain over how the defeated Germany should be treated.

Wilson, representing the USA:

- wanted a more lenient peace, based on the Fourteen Points and his slogan 'peace without victory'
- wanted to avoid causing resentment in Germany that might lead to war in future.

The USA had joined the war late, in 1917. As a result, the USA had suffered far less than its European allies during the war. In fact, the USA had greatly benefited from war economically and had lent large sums of money to the British to enable them to fund their war. Wilson firmly believed that imposing a harsh treaty on Germany would cause resentment and make future conflict more likely. He did not understand that the ideas in his Fourteen Points were not in line with opinions in Europe in 1918 and 1919. For example, the Fourteen Points had included the idea that nations should have the right to govern themselves. This idea had already been abandoned by the British and the French, as they had promised South Tyrol to Italy in 1915 and had agreed to give parts of the Turkish Empire to France in 1916.

Wilson thought that the greed and selfishness of the rival European nations had been a major contributing factor to the outbreak of the First World War and saw himself as a mediator (go-between) between these nations. Wilson could not understand how anyone else could not accept his views and values. He felt that Germany was not solely responsible for causing this terrible war. However, Wilson had very little understanding of the complex problems facing Europe in 1919. Also, he could no longer claim to fully represent the government of the USA, as his political party, the Democratic Party, had lost control of the Senate in the elections of 1918. Under the US Constitution, the Senate had the right to reject any treaty the President made. The war had become increasingly unpopular in the USA. The Republican Party strongly opposed American involvement in the Paris peace talks as many Republicans believed that these were largely European matters and did not wish to be drawn in to any more European wars. By the time Wilson arrived in Paris, the Republican Party held a majority in the Senate. As Theodore Roosevelt, a former Republican president, pointed out: 'Our allies and our enemies and Mr. Wilson himself should all understand that Mr. Wilson has no authority to speak for the American people at this time.'

Georges Clemenceau, representing France:

- wanted to destroy Germany economically and militarily
- wanted to avenge France's humiliating defeat in the Franco-Prussian War of 1870–1871
- wanted the return of Alsace and Lorraine, regions of France taken by Germany in 1871
- wanted reparations (compensation) from Germany.

KEY FIGURE

Georges Clemenceau (1841–1929)

Clemenceau was a French politician who served as prime minister of France in 1906–09 and 1917–20. In line with French public and political opinion, he insisted on a harsh settlement being imposed on Germany at the Paris Peace Conference.

Large areas of northern France had been destroyed in the bitter fighting since 1914. Nearly 2 million French soldiers and civilians had died in the war and millions more were permanently injured. When the German army retreated across France in 1918 they had deliberately destroyed everything which might be valuable, such as coal mines and canals. Paris had been shelled only months before the peacemakers sat down to make peace.

Clemenceau wanted to ensure that Germany could never again threaten French borders. He was keen to secure a guarantee of British and American support in the event of any future German attack against France.

The domestic politics of the victorious powers also played an important part in the final terms. Clemenceau was an elected politician who had to respond to public opinion. French public opinion was not in sympathy with the ideals and principles present in Wilson's Fourteen Points. The French people were demanding revenge for what they had suffered.

David Lloyd George, representing Britain:

- wanted a less severe settlement
- wanted to ensure that the German navy was no longer a threat to British domination of the seas or able to threaten Britain's colonial interests in South or East Africa.
- believed that it was in British interests to allow Germany to recover quickly as Germany was a potentially important consumer of British exports.

KEY FIGURE

David Lloyd George (1863–1945)

Lloyd George was the British prime minister from 1916 to 1922. He became a very powerful and charismatic wartime leader who played an important part in ensuring that Britain and France did not lose the war against Germany.

Like Clemenceau, Lloyd George was an elected politician. British public opinion was strongly anti-German, and Lloyd George had just won an election on the promise that he would 'make Germany pay'.

However, Britain's overseas trade needed to recover. Britain had been the world's leading exporter in 1913 but, by 1919, it had been overtaken by both the USA and Japan. Also, the First World War had cost Britain over £3.25 billion (estimated). Britain desperately needed to increase its trade, and Germany provided a potentially valuable market for British exports. Also, there was less bitterness towards Germany in Britain than in France.

So, Britain sought a settlement that would punish Germany so that Germany did not threaten British interests – but one that would also make it possible for both Britain and Germany to recover economically in future.

Lloyd George's knowledge and understanding of European affairs was very limited, his experience as a minister before 1916 had been on domestic affairs. He had little awareness of the possible implications of some of his decisions for the peoples of central and eastern Europe. In addition, he often disagreed with the French on major issues. For example, he was personally more sympathetic towards the Russian Revolution then the French were. France was owed a lot of money by Russia and Lenin was refusing to pay it back.

Representation of other powers

The peacemaking process was dominated by the 'Big Three', Wilson, Clemenceau and Lloyd George, but 32 nations were actually represented in Paris. Many were allies of the British, such as Australia, or countries such as Poland and Belgium that had suffered from Germany's actions during the war. These countries played no real part in the outcome. Russia was not invited. It was in the middle of a civil war and the 'Big Three' were angry at Russia's departure from the war against Germany in early 1918. The 'Big Three' also feared that a communist revolution would spread to other countries and refused to have any diplomatic relations with Russia's Bolshevik government. Germany, Austria and Turkey, the defeated nations, were not allowed to have any role in the negotiations and were just informed of the terms that would be imposed on them.

ACTIVITY 2.1

Either on your own or in pairs, try to answer these questions. For each question, identify three key points which are important to your explanation. Place these points in order of importance. Suggest reasons why you have placed them in that order.

a Explain why the Treaty of Brest-Litovsk played a significant part in the final stages of the First World War.

b Explain why not allowing Germany to participate in the peacemaking was likely to be damaging to the outcome.

c Explain why the choice of Versailles, in France, was not a good choice of location for making the peace.

ACTIVITY 2.2

Figure 2.4: 'European Baby Show', cartoon from the *Detroit News*, 1919.

Study the cartoon in Figure 2.4. Discuss the following questions in pairs or small groups:

a Who is the main character depicted in the cartoon?

b What is the context of the cartoon?

c Why is the main character labelled as 'judge'?

d Why are the European nations shown as babies?

e How accurate a picture of the peace settlement does the cartoonist portray?

Key terms of the treaties

Under these circumstances, it is perhaps unsurprising that the settlement that emerged from the Paris peace talks did not resemble Wilson's vision of a 'fair and just settlement'. Five separate treaties were agreed, each dealing with one of the First World War's defeated nations. These were:

- the Treaty of Versailles with Germany
- the Treaty of Saint-Germain with Austria
- the Treaty of Neuilly with Bulgaria
- the Treaty of Sèvres with Turkey
- the Treaty of Trianon with Hungary.

All these nations had been German allies in the war.

The Treaty of Versailles

The Germans hoped for a reasonable settlement based on Wilson's Fourteen Points, which had been widely publicised in Germany. They were disappointed.

The principal terms which affected Germany's territory (land) were:

- Alsace and Lorraine were returned to France.
- Eupen and Malmédy went to Belgium.
- North Schleswig returned to Denmark. (Germany had taken it from Denmark in 1864.)
- The Saar Valley, a heavily industrialised region, would be administered by the new League of Nations for 15 years. During this period, France could take the coal from its coal mines as compensation for the German destruction of French coal mines. After 15 years, a **plebiscite** would determine whether it should belong to France or Germany.
- The Rhineland, part of Germany along its border with France, would be demilitarised, meaning that no troops could be stationed there. This decision gave France the security that it wanted. It meant that Germany would be unable to defend this part of its border or use it as a starting point for invading France.
- Much of West Prussia went to Poland. Poland was given access to the sea through the 'Polish Corridor', which divided Germany from its province of East Prussia.
- The port of Memel (modern Klaipėda) went to Lithuania.
- Estonia, Latvia and Lithuania, which Germany had gained through the Treaty of Brest-Litovsk, were removed from German control and were established as independent states.
- Germany lost its African colonies, which became **mandates** under League of Nations supervision.

KEY TERMS

Plebiscite: A referendum (vote) in which local people express their opinion for or against a proposal relating to a constitutional issue.

Mandates: Overseas territories taken from the defeated countries at the end of the First World War. Responsibility for these territories was passed to other countries, which would administer them on behalf of the League of Nations.

For Germany, these territorial losses were both economically devastating and politically humiliating. The country was geographically split in two by the 'Polish Corridor', lost control of the major industrial region in the Saar and was forced to return the economically lucrative Alsace and Lorraine to France. Many German-speaking people moved from areas that now came under the control of other countries. Those who remained were often persecuted for Germany's role in the war.

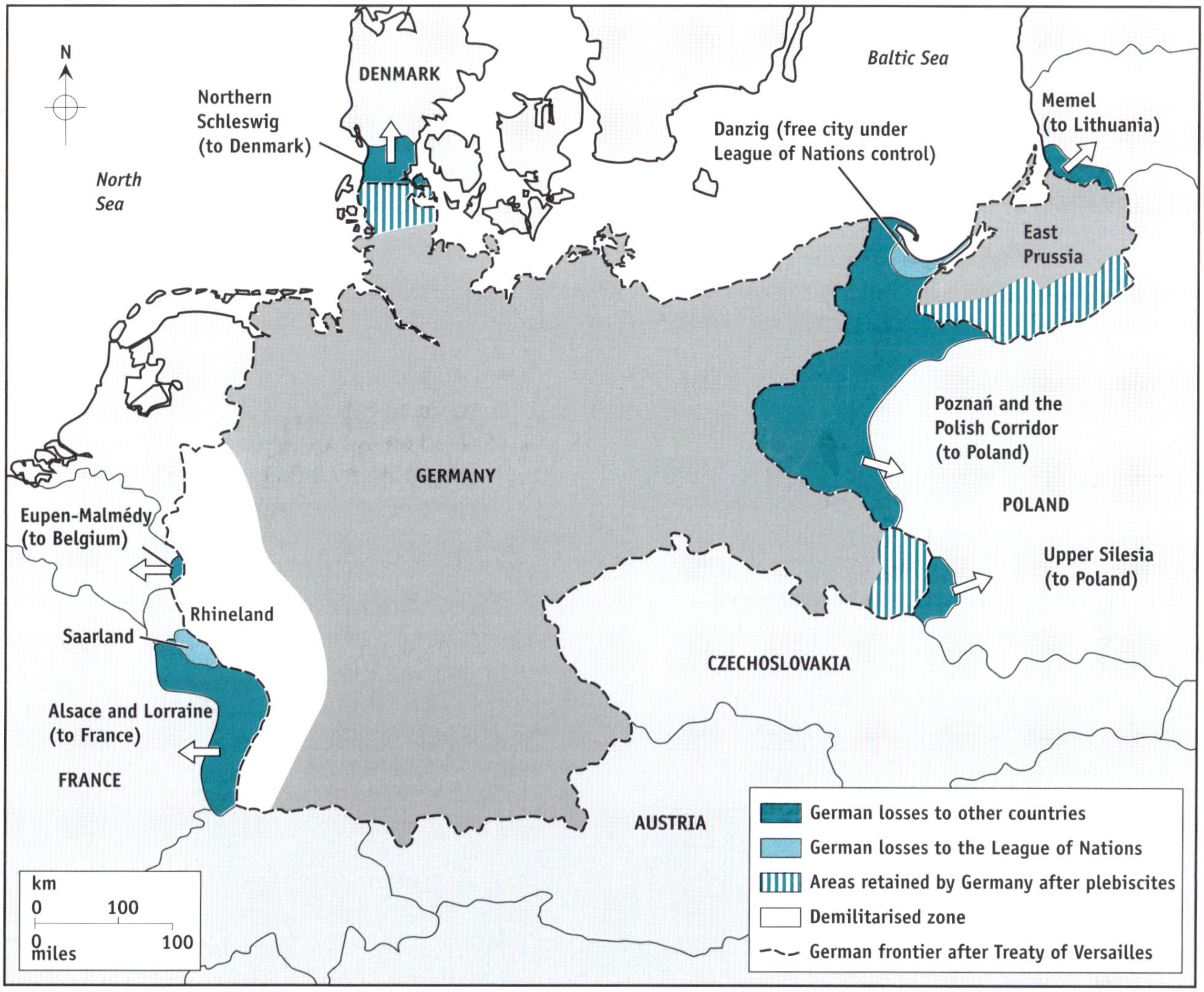

Figure 2.5: The European territory lost by Germany as a result of the Treaty of Versailles.

The Treaty of Versailles contained further terms, including the following:

- The German army was limited to a maximum of 100 000 troops and was not allowed tanks or military aircraft. The navy was allowed no submarines and a maximum of six battleships. These restrictions were intended to weaken Germany's armed forces so much that it could not pose a threat to other European countries in the future. The restrictions were deeply humiliating for a nation with a proud military tradition.
- Anschluss (union) between Germany and Austria was forbidden. This term aimed to prevent the two German-speaking countries uniting and forming a powerful nation in central Europe.
- The 'War Guilt Clause' blamed Germany and its allies for the outbreak of the First World War. The Germans had to accept that Germany alone was guilty of causing the war. The victorious nations imposed reparations on Germany for the damage the war had caused, and the War Guilt Clause provided legal justification for making Germany pay these reparations. Imposing reparations on Germany was also intended to weaken the country economically so that it could not threaten other countries in the future.

The treaties of Saint-Germain, Neuilly, Trianon and Sèvres

Having finalised the Treaty of Versailles with Germany, the Paris Peace Conference now turned its attention to the other defeated nations (Austria-Hungary, Bulgaria and Turkey). In many ways, Wilson's notion of giving independence and **self-determination** to the peoples who formerly belonged to the Habsburg, Turkish and Russian empires was becoming a reality. The disintegration of those empires had already resulted in the emergence of new states. The Paris peacemakers had the difficult task of trying to formalise the resulting chaos. Their decisions formally confirmed the existence of new national states: of these, the main new states were Yugoslavia, Poland, Czechoslovakia, Austria and Hungary. These states became known as the **successor states**. Again the 'losers' were not allowed to negotiate and were just presented with the terms.

KEY TERMS

Self-determination: The principle that people of common nationality should have the right to form their own nations and govern themselves.

Successor states: Newly formed states whose territory and population were previously under the sovereignty of another state.

Each of the defeated nations was dealt with separately through a series of four treaties.

- **The Treaty of Saint-Germain** was signed with Austria in September 1919. By the terms of this treaty, Austria lost territory to Czechoslovakia, Yugoslavia, Romania, Poland and Italy. The formerly great Austro-Hungarian Empire, which had dominated central and eastern Europe and the Balkans since the 16th century, came to a humiliating end.
- **The Treaty of Neuilly** was agreed with Bulgaria, which had been a German ally in the war, in November 1919. Bulgaria lost territory to Greece, Yugoslavia and Romania. It had to reduce its army to no more than 20 000 and was instructed to pay reparations of over $400 million.
- **The Treaty of Trianon** with Hungary (June 1920) stated that Slovakia and Ruthenia were to become part of Czechoslovakia. Hungary also lost Transylvania to Romania, and Croatia and Slovenia to Yugoslavia.
- Under the terms of **the Treaty of Sèvres**, signed in August 1920, Turkey lost territory to Greece and Italy. Other parts of the former Turkish Empire

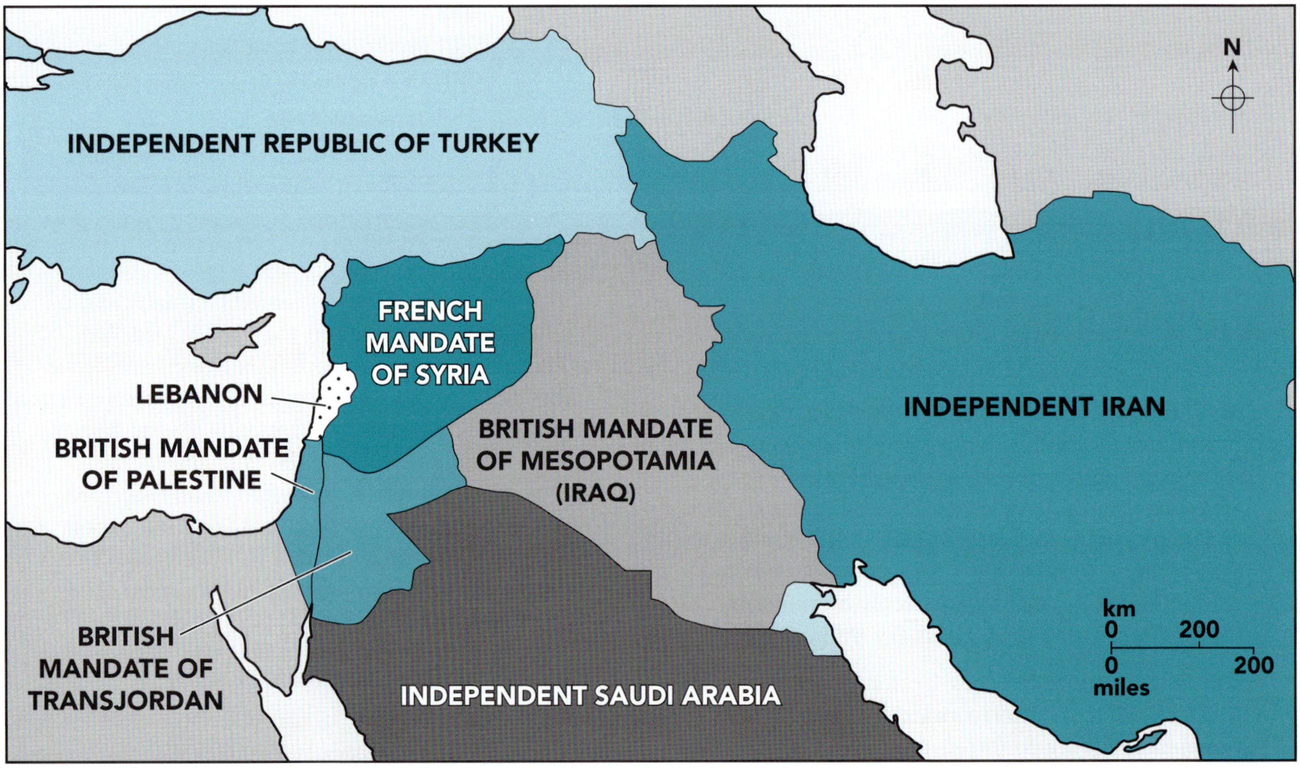

Figure 2.6: Map of the Middle East after the Treaty of Sèvres in 1920.

Figure 2.7: A 1920s map of Europe, showing the new national borders agreed in the peace settlements. The Austro-Hungarian and Turkish empires were broken up. Nine new countries were created: Austria, Czechoslovakia, Estonia, Finland, Hungary, KSCS, Latvia, Lithuania and Poland.

were given as mandates: Syria was given to France, and Palestine, Iraq and Transjordan were given to Britain (see Figure 2.6). The treaty also stated that the Dardanelles were to be permanently open to all shipping. The Turkish National Movement was established, led by Mustafa Kemal later known as Atatürk. It aimed to overturn the terms of the Treaty of Sèvres and expel foreign soldiers from the country. By October 1923, both these things had happened, and the new Republic of Turkey was proclaimed, with Atatürk as its first president.

Difficulties created by the treaties

All the treaties were to create new problems. Redrawing the map of Europe, satisfying the demands of the victors and managing the collapse of empires came at a cost. For example 1.6 million people who considered themselves Hungarian would now be living under a foreign government in Romania. Many who saw themselves as Germans found themselves in the new state of Czechoslovakia. Also, many of the newly created boundaries would make it impossible for some countries, such as Austria and Hungary, to be able to survive economically.

There was the expectation that the new nations would become **liberal democracies**, like Britain and France, but this transition to a new form of government could be difficult in countries like Poland and Yugoslavia where there was no tradition of democracy or popular elections. Creating a government which was acceptable to the majority of the population was a challenge. Some of the new nations such as Czechoslovakia faced the difficulty of having no common language, which led to communication difficulties. What should be the 'official' language? Some even had different railway systems which would have to be coordinated.

KEY TERM

Liberal democracy: Where a government is elected and implements liberal principles such as the rule of law, protection for individual rights and liberties and freedom of speech.

In Hungary a radical communist dictator, Béla Kun, seized power in 1919, murdering all his opponents and invading Czechoslovakia and Romania in order to gain more territory for his new nation. Another major challenge came in 1920 when Poland attempted to invade Ukraine and seize territory there but was driven out by the Russians. The range of difficulties was enormous.

Boundaries created by the settlements

None of the representatives of the Big Three at Versailles had much knowledge or understanding of the complexities involved in creating boundaries, and these complexities were not important to their voters. Wilson's Fourteen Points had offered some suggestions about what might happen to the area. For example:

- Poland should be given 'secure access to the sea'.
- The peoples of the former Austro-Hungarian Empire should be given every opportunity for 'autonomous development', or the right of a people to develop in their own way.
- The contested boundaries between Italy and Austria should be drawn 'along clearly recognisable lines of nationality'.
- The territories in the Middle East which had been part of the Turkish Empire should also be given the 'opportunity for autonomous development'.

These had seemed sensible at the time, but many problems arose when actually trying to put these ideas into practice.

In redrawing the map of Eastern Europe, the peacemakers had left around 30 million people living in minority groups under foreign rule. This situation made border disputes inevitable as many reluctant members of these new nations wanted boundaries to be redrawn so they could be part of their 'own' nation. Examples of difficulties created by the new boundaries are as follows:

- **Yugoslavia** was formally established in December 1918. Yugoslavia was made up of the previously independent kingdoms of Serbia and Montenegro, together with territory that had been part of the old Austro-Hungarian Empire. It now became home to people of varying **ethnic** and religious backgrounds – Serbs, Croats, Bosnians, Slovenes, Magyars, Germans, Albanians, Romanians and Macedonians, Orthodox and Roman Catholic Christians, Jews and Muslims. In some cases these groups had got on well together. However, in other cases there had been long-term rivalries and bitter conflict and these tensions led to great resentment when these groups were included in the same nation.

KEY TERM

Ethnic: Relating to a group of people who share a common history and culture.

- **Poland** had been controlled for more than a century by foreign powers, such as Germany and Austria and most recently Russia. In November 1918, Poland re-emerged as an independent nation with new boundaries. Of Poland's population of 27 million, fewer than 18 million were Poles and more than 1 million were German who did not want to be Poles. Wilson's promise to give Poland access to the sea meant that East Prussia was cut off from the rest of Germany. This situation infuriated the Germans, who wanted a different boundary.
- **Czechoslovakia** emerged from the collapse of the Austrian Empire in October 1918, and its existence as an independent state was confirmed by the Paris peace settlement. In addition to Czechs and Slovaks, Czechoslovakia now

contained former Russians, Hungarians, Poles, Jews and more than 3 million German speakers. The German-speaking populations of Bohemia, Moravia and the Sudetenland made up a sizeable minority group that persistently claimed it was being discriminated against.

- **Austria** was landlocked and most of its industrial areas were given to Poland and Czechoslovakia by the Treaty of Saint-Germain. This redistribution of territory caused enormous economic problems for Austria. Its new boundaries made Austria economically **unviable** and dependent on foreign loans to survive.

KEY TERM

Unviable: Unlikely to work; having no chance of success. (Something that can work is known as 'viable'.)

Inconsistent application of national self-determination

Maintaining a commitment to self-determination was not as straightforward as Wilson had hoped. Wilson had believed that nationality could be determined by language, but this idea was too simplistic for the complicated situation in eastern Europe, where there were so many ethnic groupings, all with conflicting ambitions. Because so many people in eastern Europe were left living as minority groups in foreign countries, many people naturally felt that self-determination applied only to the victors.

While it was not difficult to apply the principle of self-determination to Estonia, Latvia and Lithuania, it was much more difficult in the case of Germany. The need to make Czechoslovakia a viable nation meant that it was given the largely German-speaking and strategically and industrially important area known as the Sudetenland. The loss of the Sudetenland angered the Germans. The Germans in the Polish Corridor felt that the principle of self-determination did not apply to them as they were on the losing side. The area which became Yugoslavia was made up of so many different nationalities and racial groups that the only way to create a nation that might be in any way viable was to ignore the principle totally.

Reactions of the victors and defeated powers

Many historians are critical of the Paris peace settlement of 1919–20, which had both short- and long-term effects on international stability. They argue that the five treaties were based on a series of compromises that satisfied none of the countries involved. Representatives of the victorious nations drew up the peace terms, while the defeated nations had to accept the terms imposed upon them. In addition, it was not only the defeated nations that were frustrated and angry at the peace settlement. France, Russia, Italy and the USA, countries that had played a significant role in the Allied powers' victory, were also disappointed.

The victors: France, Britain, the USA, Italy and Japan

Amongst the victorious powers there was little satisfaction with the peace settlements and often bitter disappointment.

France

Generally, French public opinion was disappointed that France's huge sacrifice had produced so little return. However, people also felt enormous relief that the killing was over and were willing to try to make the peace work. The return of the provinces of Alsace and Lorraine, which had been taken by Germany in 1871, was important to France as these provinces contained valuable resources.

However, France had wanted and expected a much harsher settlement imposed on Germany. Indeed, Clemenceau had argued for the creation of an independent Rhineland state and proposed that Germany should be broken up to permanently weaken it. France feared that the settlement left Germany strong enough, both economically and politically, to threaten the security of France again. This fear dominated French foreign policy throughout the 1920s.

Most important to the French people was the payment of reparations. Germany had imposed reparations on France after France's defeat in 1871. The First World War had devastated large parts of northern France, including French industry there, and the French people wanted compensation. Ultimately, they were disappointed that this wish was unfulfilled.

Britain

Britain's reaction was mixed. The British did not feel the passionate desire for revenge that existed in France. Some people felt strongly that the peace terms were too harsh, especially the reparations demanded from Germany, and that these terms might lead to further disputes. The idea of a League of Nations to prevent a repeat of the war was very popular, and the demand by some politicians during an election in 1918 to 'Hang the Kaiser' did not arouse much interest. The slogan 'Homes fit for Heroes' aroused much more interest, by promising to provide decent homes for returning soldiers.

The military were pleased that the German navy was no longer a threat, and British trade routes were secure. Most of the former German colonies in Africa came under British control – however, these colonies were of little commercial value, and getting responsibility for parts of the former Turkish Empire in the Middle East actually added to Britain's problems.

The overall reaction was of huge relief that the war was finally over. Later, however, Britain realised that its economy had suffered great damage during the war. This damage was largely responsible for a major depression.

ACTIVITY 2.3

> The Fourteen Points were both contradictory and imprecise. Trying to apply them to specific situations in Europe was bound to lead to the peacemakers being attacked for violating [breaking] them in some respect. The Treaty, however, represents a breach of faith with a defeated and broken enemy who had laid down their arms on the assurance of a Wilsonian peace. The terms of Versailles are unnecessarily harsh over the Saar and the Polish corridor – and the cruellest part of it all is the Anschluss. The Treaty is a French peace – a Clemenceau peace.
>
> **From an open letter to the British government by the Leaders of the League of Nations Union in Britain, May 1919.**

Read the extract from the letter carefully. Either on your own or in pairs, consider these questions:

a How accurate was the view on the Fourteen Points?

CONTINUED

b How accurate was the comment that, 'The Treaty was a breach of faith with a defeated and a broken enemy who had laid down their arms on the assurance of a Wilsonian peace'?

c Why could the comments about the Saar, the Corridor and the Anschluss be seen as unfair criticism of the Treaty?

d How justified is the comment that the Treaty was a 'French peace – a Clemenceau peace'?

The USA

The US President Woodrow Wilson had played a leading role in determining the terms of the Paris peace settlement and made strenuous efforts to convince the American people to support them. However, public opinion in the USA was largely opposed to the settlement. Many Americans believed that its terms were too harsh on Germany and that this situation would cause resentment and encourage the desire for revenge. Most argued that to support the settlement and, in particular, to join the League of Nations, would inevitably involve the USA in future wars. The US Senate, dominated by Wilson's Republican political opponents and anxious to damage Wilson, refused to **ratify** the peace settlement, and the USA subsequently signed its own separate treaty with Germany. The USA had played a vital role in the drafting of the actual Treaty of Versailles, but they never actually signed it.

KEY TERM

Ratify: To give formal acceptance to something.

Italy

Despite its membership of an alliance with Germany and Austria-Hungary before the war, Italy did not enter the First World War when it began in 1914. However, in April 1915 Italy signed the Treaty of London with Britain, France and Russia in return for promises of major territorial gains along the Adriatic coast, which would be taken from the Austro-Hungarian Empire after victory was achieved. The Italians also trusted in a vague promise that Italy would get a share of the reparations paid to the Allied powers by Germany.

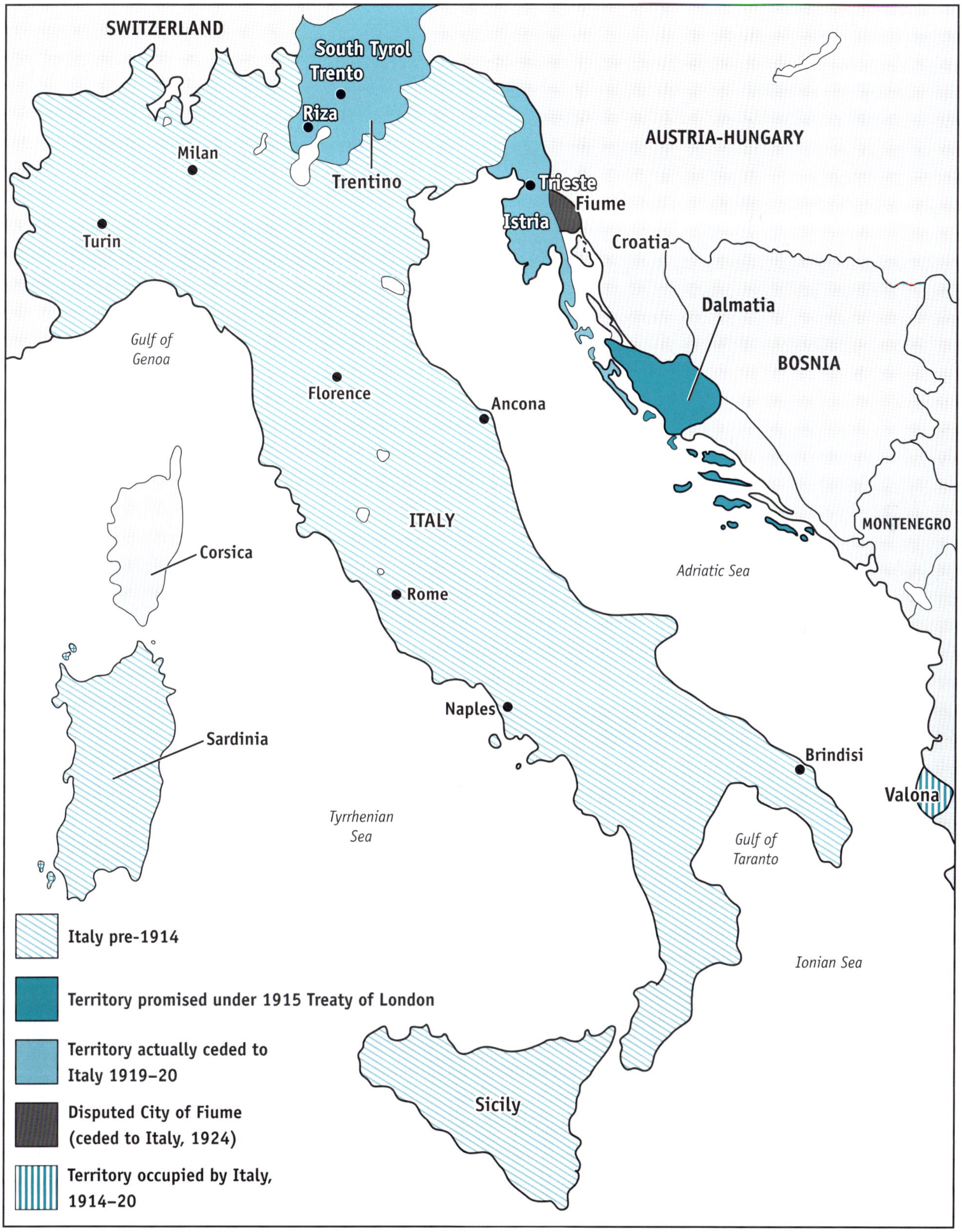

Figure 2.8: Territory promised to Italy under the terms of the Treaty of London in 1915.

Italy thus joined the war on the side of Britain, France and Russia. Italy's involvement in the war was not very significant militarily, but it was expensive for the Italians in both human and financial terms. Over 600 000 Italian soldiers were killed and 950 000 seriously wounded. The Italian government spent more money in the three years of war than it had in the previous 50 years. Once the war was won, the Italian people expected the promises made in the Treaty of London to be honoured.

To most Italians, the Paris peace settlement was a bitter disappointment. The major decisions had been taken by the 'Big Three', Wilson, Clemenceau and Lloyd George. The Italian delegation, led by Prime Minister Orlando, had been largely ignored and humiliated. Although Italy had gained Trentino, South Tyrol, Istria and Trieste, its claims to parts of Dalmatia, Albania, Fiume, Adalia (Antalya on the south Turkish coast) and some of the Aegean islands had been denied.

The Italians felt that other countries, especially Yugoslavia, had gained at Italy's expense. In addition, when the other victorious powers decided to postpone discussion about the details of German reparations until 1922, the Italians assumed (correctly) that they would get nothing, and this caused great anger. Although Italy had been on the winning side, it had reason to feel unhappy with the peace treaties. That unhappiness caused later major problems for international peace.

ACTIVITY 2.4

Either on your own or in pairs, consider the following question, 'Explain why Italy was disappointed by the outcomes of the peace settlements in 1919.'

a Identify at least three reasons for Italy's disappointment, and then analyse which you think was the most important, and why.

b Do you think Italy was justified in feeling disappointed? Why? Do you think Italy was treated fairly?

Japan

Japan had entered the war in 1914 on the side of France and Britain. Japan played little part in the detailed negotiations at Versailles in terms of Europe and the Middle East. However, Japan did gain substantially from the overall treaties. Japan saw its presence at Versailles as important, because it demonstrated its status as a 'Great Power' alongside the USA and France. In addition, Japan gained control of the former German colonies in China, and international acceptance of its growing presence in Manchuria. (Figure 3.8 in Chapter 3 shows how Japan's presence in Manchuria had grown by 1931).

Japan had good reason to be pleased with the peace treaties because it had achieved its expansionist ambitions in China. However, Wilson did not agree to Japan's request for a racial equality clause in the League of Nations Covenant (the terms that the League members agreed to). This clause would have guaranteed equal treatment for people of all races. Many of Wilson's political supporters in the southern states of America, which had formerly allowed the 'owning' of enslaved people, would not have accepted such a clause. The refusal to include a racial equality clause caused anger and resentment in Japan and damaged its relationship with the USA for years.

The defeated powers: Germany and its allies

For the First World War's defeated nations, the implications of the peace settlement could be seriously damaging. Bulgaria was much reduced in size and the Bulgarian economy was severely damaged by the terms of the Treaty of Neuilly. Turkey no longer controlled its once great empire and remained under the authority of an Allied army of occupation. It also felt humiliated.

Austrians and Hungarians also were angry at the way in which the Paris peace settlement had divided up the territories of the former Austrian-Hungarian Empire among newly formed nation states. They argued that the First World War's victorious nations had created new boundaries without considering cultural, language-related and ethnic factors. The Austrians and Hungarians had requested that plebiscites should be held to find out the wishes of local people, but these requests had been ignored. The refusal to hold plebiscites added to the sense that only friends of the victors would enjoy self-determination.

Germany

Germany had not been allowed to participate in the peace negotiations. Its representatives were members of the new German government. These representatives were still expecting a peace settlement based on the Fourteen Points of January 1918, unaware that France and Britain had not supported the Fourteen Points. Germany also expected to keep the territory that it had gained through the Treaty of Brest-Litovsk. When the German representatives were informed of the terms of the peace settlement, they were horrified.

There is arguably some justification for the German objections:

- At a time of intense political instability, 100 000 troops (the number allowed) might not be enough even to maintain law and order within Germany itself, and would fail to defend the country against external attack. Also, while Germany was forced to disarm (give up its weapons), it was clear that no other major European powers intended to do so – this difference in treatment meant a threat to German security. Germany had a strong military tradition and did not like seeing it destroyed.
- Although they were set up as mandates under the supervision of the League of Nations, Germany's former colonies in Africa were effectively taken over by Britain, France and South Africa. The reallocation of colonies seemed like more prizes to the victors.
- Millions of people who were German in terms of their language and culture now lived under foreign rule in countries such as Poland and Czechoslovakia.
- Although East Prussia was part of Germany, it was separated from the rest of the country by the Polish Corridor.
- The War Guilt Clause caused particular resentment in Germany because of the complicated series of events that had led to the outbreak of war in 1914. The Germans felt that other nations should share some part of the blame.
- The amount established for reparations was extremely high and virtually impossible for Germany to pay.

However, many historians have argued that, because they had ignored Wilson's Fourteen Points when inflicting the Treaty of Brest-Litovsk on Russia, Germany had little right to expect those points to form the basis of their own peace settlement. In fact, in Europe Germany lost only territory that it had gained as a result of previous wars and remained potentially the strongest economic power in Europe.

ACTIVITY 2.5

Figure 2.9: A cartoon titled 'The Reckoning', published in a British magazine in 1919. The newspaper the figure is holding is headed 'Allies' indemnity demands'. The caption at the bottom says, 'Pan-German. "Monstrous, I call it. Why, it's fully a quarter of what we should have made *them* pay, if *we*'d won."'

Look at the cartoon in Figure 2.9.

a What point is the cartoonist making?

b How valid do you think the point is?

c To what extent can the cartoon be seen as showing anti-German bias?

The terms of the Treaty of Versailles caused great resentment in Germany. Nevertheless, Germany had to accept the treaty – failure to do so would have meant the continuation of war and an attack on Germany itself. The German people were starving, and many were dying in a flu pandemic. There were battles on German streets between former soldiers and communists. The Germans were in no position to renew fighting. The German representatives signed the Treaty of Versailles on 28 June 1919 because they felt that they had no alternative. In doing so they accepted the loss of some 70 000 square kilometres (27 000 square miles) of former German territory, containing some 7 million people.

The army had ultimately been responsible for Germany's defeat in the war. However, the army commanders were able to convince many in Germany that defeat was not their fault and that they had been 'stabbed in the back' by the new civilian government after the Kaiser had abdicated. German resentment against the Treaty of Versailles, and the idea of the 'stab in the back' against the German military, had major implications for the future.

ACTIVITY 2.6

President Wilson had called for a 'peace without victory'.

a In pairs, discuss the reasons why the First World War's defeated nations would have been disappointed and angry about the outcomes of the Paris Peace Conference.

b What do you think were the possible implications of their disappointment and anger?

c Make out a case both for and against imposing the terms that were imposed on Germany and its allies.

The position of Russia

Russia was not invited to send representatives to the peace conference and was not consulted at all about the terms of the settlement. This exclusion from international affairs left Russia feeling increasingly isolated and angry, with much of its former territory in eastern Europe divided up amongst newly created nations, including the Baltic states of Lithuania and Estonia. Lenin's new communist government did not forget that the countries that wrote the Treaty of Versailles also sent their troops to Russia in 1919 to try to stamp out the communist revolution.

Involved in the bitter civil war in Russia, Lenin took little interest in events in Versailles. In 1919 he set up the Communist International, an organisation that aimed to spread revolution throughout Europe and the world. Lenin's action gave a clear indication of his intentions and his attitude towards the other powers.

Reparations

The peace settlements created many controversies. However, two issues caused the most debate and anger: the question of 'war guilt' and the requirement for Germany to pay reparations. These two issues possibly had greater implications for the future than any other issue.

The question of 'war guilt'

Perhaps one of the most controversial parts of the whole Versailles settlement was what became known as the 'War Guilt Clause'. The clause was set out as Article (clause) 231 of the treaty.

Article 231 of the Treaty of Versailles stated:

> The Allied and Associated Governments affirm, and Germany accepts the responsibility of Germany and her allies for causing all the loss and damage to which the Allied and Associated Governments and their nationals have been subjected as a consequence of the war imposed upon them by the aggression of Germany and her allies.

In signing the Treaty of Versailles, Germany accepted its own responsibility, and that of its allies, for causing the First World War and for paying for the damage it had caused to the victors.

Considering the tensions that had built up in Europe during the late 19th and early 20th centuries, and the complicated events that led to war in 1914, it may seem unreasonable that the victorious nations expected Germany and its allies to accept full responsibility for the war. The Germans certainly thought so. However, including the War Guilt Clause in the Treaty of Versailles provided legal justification for expecting Germany and its allies to pay reparations.

The issue of size and payment

Germany's enemies had suffered greatly during the First World War, both economically and in human terms. France, in particular, demanded compensation. France had suffered most during the war. Many of the war's major battles had taken place on French soil – whole towns and villages were destroyed, and France's main industrial region in the north had been devastated. Reparations would enable reconstruction, both in France and in other countries such as Belgium which had been badly affected by the war.

The issue of reparations caused disagreement among the 'Big Three' at Versailles. Wilson was entirely opposed to inflicting reparations on the defeated nations, arguing that doing this would cause resentment and instil in Germany a desire for revenge. This situation had happened with Germany and France in 1871 – but the French had paid reparations then. Also, Germany had taken productive territories such as Ukraine from Russia in 1918 as compensation. Clemenceau, therefore, believed that the Germans should now pay high reparations in their turn. In addition to providing compensation for war damage, Clemenceau viewed reparations as a way of keeping Germany weak so that it could never threaten France again. Lloyd George agreed with the principle of reparations but wanted to keep them as low as possible so that the German economy could recover quickly and reestablish its trading links with Britain.

After long debates, the Paris Peace Conference finally agreed to impose reparations on Germany and the other defeated nations. The task of setting the amount that each country would have to pay was given to a Reparations Commission that would meet in 1921. However, it was already clear that most of the reparations requirements would be imposed on Germany and Bulgaria. The treaties of Saint-Germain, Trianon and Sèvres recognised that Austria, Hungary and Turkey had very limited resources and would find it difficult to pay reparations.

When the Reparations Commission met in 1921 it considered the resources available to each of the defeated nations and listened to the views of their representatives before deciding how much each country should pay. Because of the major economic problems facing Austria and Hungary, no reparations were imposed on them. Limited reparations were imposed on Turkey, but these were eliminated under the terms of the Treaty of Lausanne in 1923. A figure of £100 million was set for Bulgarian reparations but only a small amount of this had been paid by 1932 when the requirement was abandoned.

As a result, the heaviest burden in terms of reparation payments fell on Germany, which was instructed to pay a total of £6.6 billion. The German representatives at meetings of the Reparations Commission were horrified. They argued that Germany was in no position to meet such demands, as the war had devastated its economy.

The German representatives were not alone in criticising such a high reparations demand. The British economist **John Maynard Keynes**, who had attended the Paris Peace Conference, argued that reparations at such a high level would add to the economic problems facing post-war Europe. In particular, he argued that reparations would lead to high **inflation**. However, Clemenceau's demands for reparations won. Keynes's prediction that German reparations would cause economic problems in Europe was accurate. Similarly, President Wilson's fears that imposing reparations on Germany would lead to resentment and the desire for revenge turned out to be correct.

KEY FIGURE

John Maynard Keynes (1883–1946)

Keynes was the leading economist of the early 20th century and was a member of the British delegation at the Paris Peace Conference. In his book *The Economic Consequences of the Peace* (1919), he argued that reparations were vindictive and would lead to problems because Germany would be unable to keep up with the payments.

KEY TERM

Inflation: A process that leads to an increase in the price of goods and services. It drives down the value of income and savings, discouraging investment and causing demands for increased wages. This loss of value in turn leads to higher prices, an inflationary spiral that can result in increased unemployment.

ACTIVITY 2.7

> The Treaty includes no provisions for the economic rehabilitation of Europe – nothing to make the defeated Central Empires into good neighbours, nothing to stabilise the new states of Europe, nothing to reclaim Russia. It is an extraordinary fact that the fundamental economic problems of a Europe starving and disintegrating before their eyes, was the one question in which it was impossible to arouse the interest of the Four. Reparation was their main excursion into the economic field, and they settled it without considering the economic future of the states whose destiny they were handling. Clemenceau was preoccupied with crushing the economic life of his enemy.
>
> **From J. M. Keynes, *The Economic Consequences of the Peace*, 1919.**

a What was the main reason for Keynes' objection to reparations?

b To what extent do you think this was unfair criticism of the 'Big Three'?

ACTIVITY 2.8

Work in two groups. Imagine you are at a meeting of the Reparations Commission. One group should represent France; the other group should represent Germany.

a The 'French' group should make out a case explaining why the reparations expected from Germany are fully justified.

b The 'German' group should explain why reparations are both unjustified and likely to be harmful to future international relations.

c Each group should present its case to the class.

d Now, as a class, evaluate the two arguments. In the context of 1919, who do you feel had the stronger case? (Alternatively, you could do this activity in pairs.)

CONTINUED

Reflection

How did you decide which case was the stronger? What criteria did you use to base your conclusion on? Think about any difficulties that you faced in trying to weigh up the two arguments? How did you ensure that you reached a balanced judgement?

Considering the disappointment of the First World War's victorious nations, the resentment of those that had been defeated and the problems faced by the 'successor states', it is easy to see why many historians are critical of the Paris peace settlement. However, such criticisms do not fully consider the difficult circumstances that faced the men responsible for drawing up the settlement. Satisfying the competing demands of the victorious nations was almost impossible. In eastern Europe, the peacemakers had to recognise situations that had already emerged following the disintegration of the Hapsburg, Turkish and Russian empires towards the end of the war. In fact, far fewer people were living under foreign rule in 1920 than had been the case in 1914. As an American delegate at the peace talks claimed: 'it is not surprising that they made a bad peace: what is surprising is that they managed to make peace at all.'

ACTIVITY 2.9

Many people in Germany and in other countries felt that the Treaty of Versailles was not 'fair' on Germany, and that it was not a 'just' treaty either. Those two words, 'fair' and 'just' often appear in essay questions about the Versailles Treaty. Work out carefully what you think a 'fair' and a 'just' treaty would be in the context of 1919 (the two words can mean quite different things!). Get a clear definition in your mind of those words. Then draw up a plan for each of the following essays. Make sure that you set out a clear case 'for' and 'against' each statement, indicating the main points you would make. (Plan your argument – don't just list facts!)

a 'Versailles was a fair treaty as far as Germany was concerned.' How far do you agree?

b 'Germany was unjustly treated by the Treaty of Versailles.' How far do you agree?

ACTIVITY 2.10

Working in a group, allocate the role of a defence and a prosecution lawyer for each of the 'Big Three' over their roles in the making of the Peace Settlement.

a Which of the two roles in each case would you find most challenging? Why?

b Which of the two roles in each case would you find the easiest? Why?

c If you are the defence lawyer for your allocated country:

  i Identify the three main points you would use in the defence.

  ii Identify the three points which you think the prosecution would focus on. How would you counteract them?

d If you are the prosecuting lawyer for your allocated country:

  i Identify the three main points you would use in the prosecution.

  ii Identify the three main points which you think the defence would focus on. How you would counteract them?

KEY CONCEPT 2.1

Interpretations

The Treaty of Versailles has generated much debate among both people who were involved at the time and later historians.

> The settlement of 1919 was an immense advance on any similar settlement made in Europe in the past. In broad outline it represents a peace of reason and justice and the whole fabric of the continent of Europe depends on its maintenance.
>
> **From *Diplomatic History* by James Headlam-Morley, a British historian involved in the drafting of the Versailles Treaty, 1927.**

> The Treaty includes no provisions for the economic rehabilitation of Europe – nothing to make the defeated Central Empires into good neighbours, nothing to stabilise the new states of Europe, nothing to reclaim Russia ... It does not promote any economic solidarity amongst the Allies themselves. There is no arrangement for restoring the disordered finances of Europe, or to adjust the systems of the Old World and the New. It is a disaster.
>
> **From *The Economic Consequences of the Peace* by the economist J. M. Keynes, who was involved in the peace negotiations at Versailles, 1919.**

> The Versailles Treaty was not exceptionally harsh considering how thoroughly Germany had lost a long and bitter war.
>
> **From Sally Marks, *The Illusion of Peace*, 1976.**

> The Versailles Treaty of 1919 was one of the most outrageous treaties in history. It was an act of plunder perpetrated by a gang of robbers against a helpless, prostrate and bleeding Germany. Amongst its provisions, it required Germany and its allies to accept full responsibility for causing the war, disarm and make substantial territorial concessions.
>
> **From an article 'The Treaty of Versailles, the Peace to end all Peace', by Alan Woods, 2009.**

Look back at the information in this section. Work with a partner and analyse why these British historians, two of whom were involved in the Treaty of Versailles, and two writing decades later, have come to such different conclusions about the treaty. Why do you think that historians, even after many years of research, looking at the same facts, still disagree? Which interpretation do you think is correct? Why?

2.2 Why was the League of Nations created and what challenges did it face in the 1920s?

The First World War was the first large-scale conflict to take place between industrialised nations. It was warfare on an unprecedented scale. For the first time, the number of civilian deaths matched those of military personnel. The war was later called 'the Great War', and 'the war to end all wars'. Anti-war feeling spread across the world after 1918, together with a determination that such a disaster must never be allowed to happen again. Even while the war was still happening, statesmen in many countries had concluded that there must be major changes in the way that international relations were conducted to avoid a similar disaster in the future.

Creation of the League of Nations

Many people think that creating a League of Nations was Wilson's own idea, but this was not the case. As early as 1915 (before the USA entered the First World War), the 'League to Enforce Peace' was established in Philadelphia by a group of leading citizens, including former US president William Howard Taft. At a conference in Philadelphia in 1915, the League proposed an international agreement in which participating nations would agree to 'jointly use their economic and military force against any one of their number that goes to war or commits acts of hostility against another'. Also in 1915, in Britain, a 'League of Nations Society' was founded in London with similar aims. In 1916, a senior British politician, Lord Robert Cecil, submitted a **memorandum** to the British government proposing an international organisation to settle disputes between nations and help preserve world peace. Leon Bourgeois and Paul Hymans had made similar proposals to their governments before 1918. These two men later represented France and Belgium respectively at the Paris Peace Conference.

Wilson's Fourteen Points

By the end of 1917, the United States had joined the war as an ally of France and Britain. In a speech to the Congress of the United States in January 1918, President Wilson put forward the idea that, after the war ended: 'A general association of nations must be formed under specific **covenants** for the purpose of affording mutual guarantees of political independence and territorial integrity to great and small states alike.'

Later Wilson included this statement in his 'Fourteen Points' speech. By doing so, the President made it clear that he supported the idea of creating an international organisation designed to prevent future wars. Wilson intended that every independent nation in the world would be a member of this organisation. He believed that such an organisation would be able to resolve disputes between nations, prevent larger nations from showing aggression towards smaller ones, and avoid the deaths of millions in future wars. He advocated the idea, but he left it to others to work out how it might work.

KEY TERMS

Memorandum: A short report, written specially for a person or group of people, containing information on a particular subject.

Covenant: A written, formal and binding agreement.

Inclusion in all the treaties

At the Paris Peace Conference in 1919, Wilson acted as chairman of a multinational commission set up to agree the rules by which the new League would operate. The commission consisted of two representatives each from the USA, Britain, France, Italy and Japan, together with one representative each from Belgium, China, Portugal and Serbia. Representatives from Czechoslovakia, Greece, Poland and Romania were later added.

While there was strong support for the idea of establishing a League of Nations designed to ensure future international peace, there was less agreement between delegates about how the League should be organised. After much negotiation and compromise, delegates at the Paris Peace Conference finally agreed on the precise wording of the Covenant of the League of Nations. This document outlined the League's aims, structure and methods of working. The opening section of the Covenant stated that member states were committing themselves to 'promote international cooperation and to achieve international peace and security' and that they were accepting the 'obligation not to resort to war'. When a nation signed the Covenant it agreed to obey the rules imposed on members of the League.

On 28 June 1919, Part I of the Treaty of Versailles formally established the League of Nations.

Wilson insisted that the Covenant of the League of Nations should also be included in each of the separate peace treaties that emerged from the Paris Peace Conference. By signing the Covenant, over 40 states became the founder members of the League. These included France, Britain, Italy and Japan. Others joined later. However, there were significant absentees such as Russia, Germany and the USA.

Figure 2.10: A 1919 cartoon depicting the formation of the League of Nations.

The aims of the League of Nations

Essentially the League had three main aims. These were to:

- prevent future wars
- administer the post-war peace settlements
- promote international cooperation.

Preventing future war

Many statesmen, including Wilson, believed that the horrors of the First World War could have been avoided if there had been an international organisation designed to settle disputes between nations before they developed into large-scale wars. The League aimed to prevent future war by a number of methods.

- The League would promote **disarmament.** Article 8 of the Covenant begins 'Members of the League recognise that the maintenance of peace requires the reduction of national armaments to the lowest point consistent with national safety'. There had been a serious 'arms race' in the years before 1914. Germany, France and Russia had built up large armies, while the Germans and the British had expanded their navies. The slaughter of both soldiers and civilians in the war had horrified many people. Terrible new weapons such as poison gas had increased the threat. The idea of disarmament was that nations could keep armies and navies large enough to defend themselves, but not to attack other nations.

KEY TERM

Disarmament: Reducing the size of armies, navies and air forces, as well as certain military resources such as submarines and tanks.

- The League would abolish secret diplomacy. Wilson strongly believed that the main cause of the First World War was the secret diplomacy that had led to the Triple Alliance between Germany, Austria-Hungary and Italy, and the Triple Entente between France, Russia and Britain. In fact, both these alliances had been created by a series of treaties that were mainly defensive rather than aggressive. If everyone had understood this, and known full details of these treaties, the alliances would have caused less fear and suspicion about the possible motives of the countries involved. Under Article 18 of the Covenant, any future treaty entered into by a member state would have to be registered with and published by the League of Nations. The terms would be known to all. This openness would avoid unnecessary fears that some nations were secretly plotting against others.
- Under Article 13 of the Covenant, member states agreed to **arbitration** by the League of Nations members for any dispute between them. The League would investigate the dispute, considering the rights and wrongs of each nation involved. It would then give a judgement on how the dispute should be settled. The League's decision would be binding on both parties, meaning that both the countries involved in the dispute had to obey it. It was hoped this system would avoid a repeat of what had

happened in 1914, when a dispute between Austria and Serbia had developed into the First World War.

- The League would develop **collective security**. This term meant that member states would work together against any country that seemed to be a threat to peace because it was acting aggressively or ignoring decisions made by the League. Cooperation could take the form of **economic sanctions** or, if these failed, joint military action. Collective security was a fundamental part of the League's role. It was designed to ensure that when a small nation seemed threatened by a larger and more powerful one, other nations would work together to defend it. This would give the League the ability to enforce its decisions if needed.

KEY TERMS

Arbitration: The settling of a dispute between two parties by an impartial third party.

Collective security: The idea that if any member state of the League of Nations was threatened, all the other member states would work together to defend it.

Economic sanctions: Refusing to trade with a nation, hoping that such economic pressure will force the nation to act differently.

Administering the post-war peace settlements

Another role of the League of Nations was to ensure that the terms of the peace treaties were carried out. The League did this in two main ways:

- **Arranging plebiscites.** For example, the Treaty of Versailles set out that the League of Nations should administer the Saar Valley (a major industrial area of Germany) for a period of 15 years. The intention was to compensate France, which could take coal from it as the Germans had destroyed many of France's coal mines during the war. After 15 years a plebiscite would be held so that local people could decide whether the area should belong to France or Germany. (The League administered the area until 1935, then organised the plebiscite. The Saar region voted to return to Germany.)
- **Organising mandates.** As a result of the peace treaties of 1919 to 1920, many colonies were taken away from the defeated nations such as Germany and Turkey. Where the peacemakers felt that these territories were not yet ready for full independence, they agreed to run these colonies as mandates (see Section 2.1). The administration of these mandates was entrusted to another country (known as the Mandatory) appointed by the League of Nations. The idea was to prevent these former colonies collapsing into chaos as there was no government there. The League established a Mandate Commission to review the progress of each mandated territory. The Mandatory had to submit an annual report to the League. This system was outlined in Article 22 of the Covenant. It worked reasonably well.

Promoting international cooperation

The League of Nations aimed to actively work towards improving relations between member states and the lives of their citizens. The League would achieve this by:

- repatriating (sending home) prisoners of war and resettling refugees (a huge problem in 1918)
- improving working conditions and wage levels throughout the world through an International Labour Organization (ILO)
- providing loans to new countries, such as Austria and Hungary, to ensure their economic survival
- encouraging the development of education in all countries
- promoting improvements in public health, such as the prevention and control of disease.

The structure of the League of Nations

The most important parts of the League of Nations organisation were the General Assembly and the Council. These were supported by other institutions, including the Secretariat, the Permanent Court of International Justice, and various commissions and committees established to investigate and deal with specific problems.

The General Assembly

The General Assembly met annually in Geneva, in Switzerland. This location was selected because Switzerland seemed to symbolise the desire for peace. It was a traditionally neutral country that had taken no part in the First World War. Switzerland was also the base for the **International Red Cross**. Each member state could send up to three representatives to meetings of the Assembly, and each state was able to cast one vote. The Assembly's main role was to decide general policy, to deal with the admission of new members of the League and to handle the organisation's

Figure 2.11: Delegates at the first meeting of the League of Nations General Assembly, 15 November 1920. The League started work in early 1920, but the General Assembly met for the first time in November 1920.

finances. Any decision taken by the Assembly had to be **unanimous**; in other words, a single country could prevent a decision being taken by voting against it. This requirement led to problems later, as a single nation could prevent the League from taking action.

KEY TERMS

International Red Cross: An organisation founded in Geneva, Switzerland, in 1863 with the aim of easing the suffering of people affected by war and armed conflict across the world. The International Committee of the Red Cross has been awarded the Nobel Prize on three occasions, in 1917, 1944 and 1963.

Unanimous: Agreed by everyone.

The Council

The Council was a smaller body. The Council's main functions were to settle political disputes between nations and oversee all parts of the organisation. The Council was the League's executive – its main decision-making body. It held four regular sessions each year, with extra meetings (known as extraordinary sessions) being called in times of emergency. The Council met 107 times between 1920 and 1939. As with the General Assembly, decisions taken by the Council had to be unanimous (again, the unanimity rule caused problems later). It was hoped that members of the Council would act in the interests of all nations and put the aims of the League and the need for peace above the interests of their own country.

The Council was made up of permanent and non-permanent members:

- **Permanent members** – there were four original permanent members: Britain, France, Italy and Japan. These were seen as the 'winners' in the First World War, which did not always make them popular with the 'losers'. The USA would have been a permanent member but decided not to join the League of Nations. Germany became a fifth permanent member when it joined in 1926. When Germany and Japan left the League in 1933, the Union of Soviet Socialist Republics (USSR, or Soviet Union) joined as a permanent member.

- **Non-permanent members** – initially, there were four non-permanent members, elected every three years by the General Assembly. The aim was to ensure that the major world powers should not dominate proceedings and that all nations could be represented at the highest level in the League. The first non-permanent members were Belgium, Brazil, Greece and Spain. The number of non-permanent members increased to six in 1922, nine in 1926 and 11 in 1933.

The Secretariat

The Secretariat carried out the day-to-day work of the League, such as preparing agendas, publishing reports and dealing with essential routine matters. It was based in Geneva and directed by a Secretary-General. The first Secretary-General was the British diplomat Sir Eric Drummond, who held the post from 1919 to 1933. The Secretariat was not a decision-making body. It could advise and recommend, but it its role was to carry out the wishes of the Assembly and the Council.

The Permanent Court of International Justice

The Permanent Court of International Justice was based at The Hague in the Netherlands. The Permanent Court was designed to deal with legal disputes between states. This court had been created before the First World War and its role was continued under the League of Nations.

The Permanent Court consisted of 15 judges of different nationalities who were elected for a period of nine years by the General Assembly. The Court was one of the League's successes. It handled 66 cases by 1939 and was continued by the League's replacement, the United Nations, after the Second World War. Its success showed that there was a real need for a 'referee' between nations as well as an organisation which could make the rules that set out relationships between nations. The Permanent Court was particularly good at dealing with complex disputes over borders between nations.

Commissions and committees

The League of Nations established a number of commissions (also known as agencies) and committees to deal with specific problems. The main commissions dealt with issues such as the mandates, disarmament, refugees and slavery. There were committees for matters relating to international labour, health, child welfare, drug problems and women's rights. The intention was that where conflicting national interests might prevent a resolution of international issues, the commissions and agencies would work for the overall benefit of the countries and people involved. Their role was to rise above specific national interests and solve problems from a broad, international perspective.

ACTIVITY 2.11

Either on your own or in pairs, consider the following questions:

a Explain why the League of Nations was created.

b Explain how the League was structured to carry out the intentions of those who created it.

The aim of this activity is to for you to practise explaining quite a complex issue simply and clearly. For both questions try to identify three or four specific points which you feel are most important to explaining the answer. Write them down in order of importance and add a couple of sentences of supporting detail for each point to demonstrate your understanding of the point.

Weaknesses of the League

During the 1920s, the League enjoyed some success in resolving international disputes, but it was clear that its powers and authority were limited. There were several reasons for the League's weaknesses.

Restricted membership

The League of Nations was intended as a global organisation. However, of the world's major powers at the time, only Britain, France, Italy and Japan were members of the League throughout the 1920s. The USA never joined, Germany was not allowed to join until 1926, and Russia did not become a member until 1934. So, three of the world's major powers were unrepresented in both the Council and the Assembly, and this lack of representation inevitably led to the feeling that the League did not fully represent 'world' opinion.

The USA's refusal to join the League of Nations

It is, perhaps, the supreme irony that the USA rejected the post-war peace settlement and the League of Nations, despite the fact that its president had been so instrumental in the creation of both. By the time Wilson returned to the USA from the Paris Peace Conference, the Republican Party had gained control of the Senate.

Despite all Wilson's attempts to convince the American people of the League's importance, to both the world and the USA, the Senate voted against him on 19 November 1919. Most Americans wanted to ensure that the USA did not become involved in another war. They did not want the USA to commit to a possible conflict by agreeing to the terms of the Covenant. The USA's refusal to join the League significantly damaged the League's chance of success, reducing both its credibility and its financial security.

Most Republican senators shared the views of Henry Cabot Lodge:

> The independence of the USA is not only precious to ourselves but to the world ... I have always loved one flag, and I cannot share that devotion with a mongrel banner created for a League. Internationalism ... is to me repulsive ... The USA is the world's best hope, but if you fetter her in the interests and quarrels of other nations and the intrigues of Europe, you will destroy her power and endanger her very existence ... We would not have our country's vigour exhausted, or her moral force abated by everlasting meddling and muddling in every quarrel which afflicts the world.
>
> **From a speech by Senator Henry Cabot Lodge to the Senate Foreign Relations Committee, on 12 August 1919.**

ACTIVITY 2.12

THE ACCUSER

Figure 2.12: Cartoon, *World Journal Tribune*, 22 March 1920. The figure on the left is labelled 'Humanity', the figure on the right 'U.S. Senate' and the figure below it 'Treaty of peace'.

Look at the cartoon in Figure 2.12.

a What point is the cartoonist making in this 1920 cartoon?

b Using your contextual knowledge, to what extent do you feel this point is a fair comment on the Senate's refusal to support the Treaty of Versailles?

Leadership

Another weakness in the structure of the League was the lack of clear and consistent leadership. There was a Secretary-General, based permanently in Geneva, but he was seen as a servant or an administrator of the League, rather than as a leader.

Leadership, therefore, had to come from the Council. However, although the Council met four times a year, its membership was constantly changing. The changes in membership made consistent policymaking difficult. For example, between 1919 and 1929 the British had five different foreign secretaries, who were its Council members. These men came from different political parties and held different views on the role of the League and on British foreign policy. There was never a consistency of views or policy within the Council.

Voting processes

The Covenant of the League of Nations stated that all decisions must be unanimous in both the General Assembly and the Council. The requirement for unanimity meant that a single vote of the Assembly could prevent a country from taking an action which it felt was essential to its security (but which might lead to war). Every country had the right of veto – the ability to prevent a decision being reached and acted upon.

The need for everyone to agree also slowed down the League's decision-making process. In addition, many decisions made by the Council had to be ratified by the General Assembly, which met only once a year. The infrequency of meetings could slow the process further. As a result, the League appeared both slow and indecisive at times.

Enforcement difficulties

It was frequently difficult to enforce decisions made by the League of Nations, for a number of reasons. First, the League was an integral part of the widely unpopular post-war peace treaties. Many people felt that the League was an organisation created by the victorious nations for their own benefit. The fact that none of the defeated nations was initially allowed to join the League reinforced this perception.

Second, the authority of the League of Nations was frequently weakened by other organisations. For example, a '**Council of Ambassadors**' had been established to administer the post-war treaties until the League of Nations was fully operational. In practice, this Council continued to function until 1931. On several occasions the Council of Ambassadors disagreed with the League's decisions and ignored them (as in the Corfu Incident, discussed here and in Section 2.3). There were also occasions when countries such as Britain and France chose to ignore the League entirely, preferring to make separate agreements. This was the case with the Locarno Treaties of 1925 (see Section 2.4).

KEY TERM

Council of Ambassadors: An intergovernmental agency founded in 1920 with the task of implementing the terms of the Paris peace settlement and mediating territorial disputes between European states. Chaired by the French foreign minister, the other nations represented were Britain, Italy and Japan. Because of its decision not to ratify the Paris peace settlement, the USA had observer status only (it could oversee the rulings of the Council of Ambassadors but had no power to change them).

Most importantly, at times countries discovered that their commitments to the League of Nations conflicted with their own national interests. There were several incidents in the early 1920s in which national interests meant that the League either took no action or failed to resolve a dispute.

The Polish seizure of Vilna, 1920

The first successful challenge to the League of Nations' authority came early in the League's existence, in 1920. A dispute arose between Poland and Lithuania, two countries whose borders had been defined by the settlement agreed at the Paris Peace Conference. Vilna (Vilnius) was the capital of Lithuania, but its population was mainly Polish. In 1920, Polish troops occupied the city. Following a request by Lithuania, the League of Nations ordered Poland to remove its forces and tried to arrange a plebiscite to decide the region's future. Although the Polish government initially agreed, it subsequently reinforced its troops in Vilna, and, in 1922, it annexed the city and its surrounding area.

Poland had effectively defied the League of Nations, and the territory remained in Polish hands until 1939. In this case, the role played by Britain and France was the key to the League's failure. Both Britain and France supported Poland's claim to Vilna. France was very keen to keep Poland as an ally in case of any future conflict with Germany. Without the support of these two major powers, the League of Nations was powerless to enforce its decision. An underlying weakness of the League of Nations thus became clear as early as 1920. Britain and

France were putting their own national interests ahead of their commitment to the League.

The Treaty of Riga, 1921

Russia had dominated Poland before 1914. In 1920, Poland invaded Russian territory. Defeated and in the middle of a destructive civil war, the Russians had no choice but to sign the Treaty of Riga. By this treaty Poland gained 80 000 square kilometres of Russian territory.

The League of Nations took no action against Poland's open aggression. There were two main reasons for this. First, Russia was not a member of the League at that time. Second, both Britain and France hoped that Poland would win. Russia's communist government was unpopular in Britain and France and both Britain and France had sent their own troops to Russia to try to prevent communism taking over. So, naturally Russia saw the League as hostile to its interests.

The invasion of the Ruhr, 1923

The Ruhr was Germany's most important industrial region. When Germany failed to pay war reparations, in January 1923 France and Belgium invaded the Ruhr, to take its coal, iron ore and timber as compensation. By taking this action, two members of the League of Nations were breaking the rules which they had promised to obey by signing the Covenant of the League. Both France and Belgium were represented on the League of Nations Council – France as a permanent member, Belgium as a non-permanent member. Since decisions of the Council had to be unanimous, the representation of France and Belgium meant that the League was unable to deal with this incident. In the end, the Dawes Plan of 1924 led to the withdrawal of French and Belgian troops from the Ruhr region. The Dawes Plan was initiated by the USA, which was not League member. The League of Nations had played no part in either preventing or ending this crisis.

The Corfu Incident, 1923

In August 1923, Italy blamed Greece for the death of three Italian officials who were engaged in a League of Nations attempt to resolve a disputed border between Greece and Albania. The new Italian prime minister, Mussolini, demanded compensation and sent Italian troops to invade the Greek island of Corfu as revenge. Greece appealed to the League of Nations against the Italian aggression, and the League ordered the Italian troops to withdraw.

Mussolini refused to accept that the League had the authority to deal with this issue. He threatened to withdraw Italy from the League and referred the matter to the Council of Ambassadors. The Council decided that Greece should pay considerable compensation to Italy.

This incident exposed two fundamental weaknesses of the League of Nations. First, as a member of the League of Nations Council, Italy was in a position to prevent the League from taking action. As on other occasions, the national interests of member states could be given greater importance than enforcing the authority of the League. Second, the League's decision was effectively overruled by another body – the Council of Ambassadors.

The Corfu incident also demonstrated that while the threat of sanctions might work against small states, it did not work against larger states such as Italy. The League's Secretary-General wrote 'the Corfu crisis has weakened the moral authority of the League. The authority of the League has been challenged in a sphere precisely that for which it was created. This challenge has brought into question the fundamental principles which lie at the root of the new world order established by the League.' It was an unfortunate incident which clearly demonstrated the problems which faced the League.

Figure 2.13: A British cartoon titled 'The Latest Caesar'. It suggested that Mussolini had imperial ambitions and was prepared to use force to achieve them. He is portrayed with one foot on Italy and one on Corfu. The caption at the bottom is formatted like a line in a play and says: 'Sig. Mussolini (*a bit above himself*), "I do bestride the narrow world like a colossus."

Collective security after 1923

The League's ability to confront aggression and threats to world peace depended entirely upon the notion of collective security – League members working together to impose economic sanctions or, in the worst case, taking military action against a threatening nation. Collective security was reflected in Article 11 of the Covenant, which stated 'Any war or threat of war, whether immediately affecting any of the Members of the League or not, is hereby declared a matter of concern to the whole League, and the League shall take any action that may be deemed wise and effectual to safeguard the peace of nations.'

As the League had no army of its own, the League initially expected member states to provide troops if military action became necessary.

The system was established by Article 16 of the Covenant:

> Should any Member of the League resort to war in disregard of the Covenant, it shall be deemed to have committed an act of war against all other Members of the League, which hereby undertake immediately to subject it to the severance of all trade or financial relations.
>
> It shall be the duty of the Council in such case to recommend what effective military, naval or air force the Members of the League shall severally contribute to the armed forces to be used to protect the Covenant of the League.
>
> **From Article 16 of the Covenant of the League of Nations.**

However, a resolution passed in the Assembly in 1923 decided that each member state could decide whether or not to provide armed forces in a crisis. If a nation did not want to fight to enforce a League decision, then it did not have to. The resolution clearly weakened the entire principle on which collective security was based. It became unlikely that any state would actually send troops to fight elsewhere. For example, why should Dutch troops go and fight the Turks in Iraq because the Turks wanted some part of their old empire back? Why should Dutch troops die, and Dutch taxpayers support some conflict in which they had no interest, hundreds of kilometres away? The resolution removed one of the major ways of preventing aggression.

In the final analysis, the League of Nations was only as strong as the willingness of its member states to support it and the principles on which it was built. That willingness was often weak, as politicians put their own, and their countries', interests before the needs of the 'greater good'.

Collective security and the League's involvement in the resolution of post-war disputes

Under the principle of collective security, members of the League would act together to take economic and, if necessary, military action against any country that was a threat to peace.

The intention was that any dispute between nations should be referred to the League, which would carefully review all the issues involved. The League would then decide how to resolve the dispute. If a country refused to accept the League's decision and began preparing for war, the League would ask its members to impose economic sanctions against it. Sanctions might include cutting all trade of food, fuel or arms with that country. If economic sanctions did not have the desired effect, League members would collectively threaten military action. It was assumed that aggressive countries would back down when confronted by the combined strength of the League's member states.

This system enabled the League to play a key role in the successful resolution of a number of international disputes during the 1920s. The reason for the League's success in dealing with these disputes was that all the parties involved accepted the League's arbitration and decisions. These were relatively minor disputes, and none of them directly involved any of the world's major powers. In some cases, pressure from the major powers, such as France and Britain, was important in persuading the minor powers to obey the League's rulings. However, the following examples showed both that the League had a vital role in keeping the peace, and that it was capable of carrying out that role.

Figure 2.14: A British cartoon from 1920 demonstrating the hope that the League would bring peace. The angel on the left represents Peace; the female figure on the right represents the League of Nations. The caption at the bottom says: 'Peace. "This is my temple and you are its priestess. Guard well the sacred flame."'

The Teschen dispute, 1920

With its large deposits of good quality coal, the Teschen (Cieszyn) area had been one of the wealthiest and most industrialised regions of the former Austro-Hungarian Empire that had collapsed in 1918. The Teschen area was also an important railroad centre. Before the Austro-Hungarian Empire absorbed it, the area had been Czech, so Czechoslovakia had a distant claim to it. However, the majority of the population was Polish, though some Germans and Czechs also lived there. Even before the war ended in 1918, both Poles and Czechs had tried to claim this vital area and gain control of it, because of its economic importance. In 1919, both countries again claimed the region and violence broke out between them. Both countries saw the area as vital for their economies. The League studied the dispute, listened to both sides, and made a decision. It split the region between the two countries in 1920, drawing up clear boundary lines between the two nations. Although neither Poland nor Czechoslovakia was entirely satisfied with the League's decision, both accepted it, and the fighting ceased. Neither country was strong enough in 1920 to challenge the decision, and pressure from Britain and France made it sensible to accept the decision.

The Aaland Islands dispute, 1921

The League was equally successful in resolving a dispute over the Aaland (or Åland) Islands (a group of some 6500 small islands situated midway between Sweden and Finland in the Baltic Sea). Although the population of the islands was almost exclusively Swedish-speaking, the Aaland Islands had belonged to Finland since the early 1900s, when Finland had been ruled by Russia, and the newly independent nation was determined to keep them. However, most local inhabitants wanted the islands to become part of Sweden. The Swedish government raised the issue with the League of Nations.

After detailed consideration, the League of Nations decided that the islands should remain with Finland. Both Finland and Sweden accepted the League's decision, and the threat of war was averted.

The Swedish government was not pleased with the decision. Its disappointment is clear from its response to the League:

> It is with profound disappointment that Sweden learns of the League's decision. In supporting the cause of the people of the Aaland Islands, Sweden was not influenced by the desire to increase its territory. It only wished to support the just aspirations of the island population to reunite itself to its mother-country. This population has declared its unanimous wish not to be bound to a country to which it had been joined by force. Sweden had hoped that the League, which was established to assure justice in international relationships, would have favoured a solution in line with the principle of self-determination. It had hoped that the League of Nations would have filled, at least on this occasion, the role of the champion and defender of right. The League's decision will shake the confidence that countries which support international law have in the League of Nations. Sweden loyally accepts the decision but hopes that the day will come when the aspirations of the people of the Aaland Islands will be triumphantly vindicated [upheld].
>
> **From the Swedish government's response to the Council of the League of Nations, 24 June 1921.**

This response was cleverly worded. For example:

- The response claims that Sweden had not been 'influenced by the desire to increase its territory' and that it was simply supporting the wishes of the local population to be governed by Sweden rather than Finland. The response states that Finland had gained the Islands 'by force'. This wording implies that Finland, rather than Sweden, had been the aggressor state.
- The response implies that, in making its decision, the League was not acting in the 'role of champion and defender of right' or supporting 'justice in international relationships'.
- The response claims that the League's decision was not 'in line with the principle of self-determination', which had been one of President Wilson's key objectives.
- The response claims that the League's decision was not in line with international law and that it would 'shake the confidence that countries which support international law have in the League of Nations'.
- The response implies that the League's decision would not bring an end to the dispute, because the Aaland Islanders would continue to seek justice.
- Despite all these points, the response makes it clear that 'Sweden loyally accepts the decision' reached by the League of Nations.

Looking at the Swedish government's response in isolation, you might easily conclude that the League of Nations had made a major mistake in deciding to leave the Aaland Islands in the possession of Finland. However, the Swedish government's response is biased – it looks at the problem of the Aaland Islands only from its own viewpoint. In fact, there were logical reasons for the League's decision. The judgement was based on detailed consideration of all the issues by a specially appointed commission and provided the outcome that was most likely to ensure future peace in the islands. The judgement also contained specific guarantees to protect the rights of Swedish people in the islands to maintain their own language and culture.

The Upper Silesian coalfields dispute, 1921

Upper Silesia was an important industrial region with major coalfields. Both Germany and Poland claimed the area because of its economic importance and the people of Upper Silesia were divided over whether they wished to be part of Germany or Poland. A local plebiscite failed to solve the issue, and this failure led to a series of local riots from 1919 to 1921 between the rival nationalities there. France backed Poland, hoping that it might be an ally against Germany in the future, while Britain and Italy backed Germany.

ACTIVITY 2.13

The many different reactions to the Council's decision on Silesia were predictable. The League's members congratulated themselves for an outstanding performance. They feel the League has really worked well. One called it 'the first step in the geometry of peace.' Poland is very satisfied. Germany, on the other hand, is not. It ignores the fact that the League gave her two-thirds of the total area and three fifths of the population in Upper Silesia. The German government and press were violently opposed to the Council's action. Their government threatened to resign. The British Foreign Secretary was plagued by visits from German officials, and he finally lost all patience with the German Ambassador. He told him 'if I were a German, I would make the best of it.' The German people did not share this view.

The League's decision deprived Germany not only of much agricultural land but also many of the industrial resources of Upper Silesia.

Neither France nor England was satisfied by the League's proposal. The French were upset because Poland did not receive all of the industrial area. The British were disappointed at the small area allotted Germany. Yet this mutual dissatisfaction with the League's action was unimportant since both powers had agreed to accept the League's recommendation without question. Upper Silesia has been provided with a viable boundary and enabled the League of Nations to pass its first test involving the major Allied powers.

From a note by an official in the British Foreign Office, November 1921.

CONTINUED

Either on your own or in pairs, read again the section on the Upper Silesia question and then answer the questions. You will need contextual knowledge to answer the questions fully.

a Why do you think the Silesia decision was called 'the first step in the geometry of peace'?

b Why were the French upset because Poland did not get all of the industrial area?

c Why were the British disappointed at the small areas allotted to Germany?

d To what extent do you feel that this British official has given a balanced and accurate picture of the solution to the Upper Silesia question? What other points could he have made?

(Although it was not long since the end of the First World War, Britain was more sympathetic towards Germany than France was.)

Because of this indecision among the 'victors', Britain and France referred the issue to the League of Nations. After carefully considering the case, the League decided to divide the area between Germany and Poland and drew up the new boundary. Neither country was happy with the result, but both accepted it, and the League monitored the frontier for the following 15 years to ensure that peace remained. This is a good example of the League at work, both in making the decision and monitoring the situation afterwards to prevent any more conflict.

Figure 2.15: A poster published during the Silesia plebiscite urging Upper Silesians to join Germany. The caption at the top says 'This is what will happen to you if you join Poland!' The child and the woman are shown pulling a plough. The caption at the bottom says 'We farmers vote for Germany!'

The Yugoslavia–Albania border dispute,1921

Also in 1921, the League had to deal with open warfare between Yugoslavia and Albania when Yugoslav troops invaded Albania in November 1921. This conflict was caused by disputes between the two countries over territory on their joint border. The League of Nations sent a commission, consisting of representatives from Britain, France, Italy and Japan, to investigate the cause of the disagreement. On the basis of the Commission's recommendations, the League of Nations judged in favour of Albania. Yugoslavia complained bitterly but had no alternative but to withdraw its troops. This resolution was another success for the League and its methods. Yugoslavia was unable to resist.

The Memel issue, 1923

The port of Memel (modern Klaipėda) and the surrounding area were placed under the control of the League of Nations by the Treaty of Versailles. The area had been part of Germany before 1914, but most of the population were Lithuanian. (This is a good example of the complex task that faced the peacemakers in 1919.) However, Lithuania claimed the region and invaded it in 1923.

The League decided that the area around the port should belong to Lithuania, but that Memel itself should remain an 'international zone'. Lithuania accepted the decision. The action taken by the League of Nations was a success in the sense that it prevented bloodshed and provided a solution to a challenging problem. Some people criticised the League's decision because it seemed to condone the fact that Lithuania had been able to gain land by the use of force. However, there was no easy solution and the problem was contained.

The Greco-Bulgarian border dispute, 1925

Following another border dispute, Greece invaded Bulgaria in 1925. Bulgaria wanted to avoid open conflict, so ordered its troops to offer only token resistance and appealed to the League to deal with the issue. Bulgaria's action was a clear indication that Bulgaria hoped that the League would find a peaceful settlement to the dispute. The League condemned the invasion and called for Greece to withdraw and pay compensation to Bulgaria. Greece complied with the League's decision.

ACTIVITY 2.14

a Look carefully at the disputes, which the League played a major part in solving. Do a little more research into each of these (in particular the disputes over the Aaland Islands, the Yugoslavia–Albania border, Memel and the Greco-Bulgarian borders).

b Copy and complete the table to identify the main reasons why there was a peaceful solution in each case.

Dispute	Reasons for peaceful solution
Teschen dispute	
Aaland Islands dispute	
Upper Silesian Coalfields dispute	
Yugoslavia–Albania border dispute	
Memel issue	
Greco-Bulgarian border dispute	

c Now look at the reasons you have identified. To what extent was the League responsible for achieving a peaceful solution?

Role and impact of the agencies

In addition to preventing wars and resolving disputes between nations, the League of Nations had other roles, including providing financial assistance and encouraging economic cooperation. The League provided vital financial assistance to many countries facing economic difficulties. For example, the League arranged loans for Austria and Hungary when these new nations faced bankruptcy in 1920 and sent commissioners in 1922–23 to advise on how best to spend the money (rather like the role of the International Monetary Fund after 1945). These actions helped Austria and Hungary achieve some economic recovery and political stability. The League also organised financial assistance to other central and eastern European countries. One British diplomat said that this assistance 'prevented them from going communist like the Russians'. The League also did good work in overcoming the problems imposed by the German reparations. This work led to the Dawes and Young plans (see Section 2.4).

In many ways, the League's most successful achievements were the work of its commissions or agencies, and these were continued after the Second World War by the United Nations, which replaced the League.

These commissions achieved some notable successes during the 1920s. They organised the repatriation (return to their own countries) of some former 400 000 prisoners of war. They set up refugee camps to deal with the thousands of refugees displaced by the war and found permanent homes for them. They began the process of getting nations to work together to prevent or cure diseases such as malaria and leprosy. They closed down a number of Swiss companies that were selling illegal and dangerous drugs and arranged for the freedom of some 200 000 enslaved people, as well as putting pressure on all members to ban any form of enslavement. However, there were some failures as well. Little progress was made during the 1920s in persuading nations to disarm, restricting working hours for industrial workers or extending the rights of women.

International Commission for Refugees

Under its first director, the Norwegian, Fridtjof Nansen, the International Commission for Refugees helped to resettle over half a million former prisoners of war who had been left in Russia at the end of the First World War. There were also hundreds of thousands of refugees in Europe as a result of the collapse of the Russian, Austrian and Turkish empires. In 1922, the commission

Figure 2.16: Armenian refugees waiting for food in 1920. The League played a key role in preventing famine after the collapse of the Turkish Empire in 1918.

introduced the Nansen passport, the first internationally recognised identity card for stateless refugees. During 1923, violence erupted in Turkey and the commission helped to find homes, food and jobs for almost one-and-a-half million refugees. It also worked closely with other agencies to prevent the spread of diseases such as typhoid and cholera.

In the 1930s the commission played an important part in assisting those fleeing from Nazi Germany. One recent historian wrote 'The League, more than any other single international institution in the 20th century, founded an international system to manage the challenge posed to nation states by refugees. It created a regime based on asylum, assistance and burden sharing that continues into the 21st century'. This commission was continued by the present United Nations.

The International Labour Organization

The International Labour Organization (ILO) was created by the League of Nations and financed through the League. Under the leadership of Frenchman Albert Thomas, the ILO was relatively successful in improving working conditions around the world. One of its aims was to prevent the type of working conditions in factories that enabled communists to gain supporters for their radical ideas. Governments were persuaded to fix maximum working hours (per day and per week), to establish minimum wage levels, to provide sickness and unemployment benefits and to introduce old-age pensions. For example, in 1928 the ILO's decision to establish a minimum wage was ratified by 77 countries. By the end of the 1920s, social security schemes were common in Europe. Such measures made an enormous difference to the lives of underprivileged people. There was also a focus on the prevention of child labour and better working conditions for women.

However, not all of the ILO's decisions were successfully implemented, For example, its attempts to ban night work and ensure that workers received paid holidays were rejected. One delegate argued that such schemes would require his country 'to commit industrial suicide'.

The Health Organization

As well as dealing with specific problems, such as the health risks posed by large numbers of refugees in Turkey, the Health Organization achieved a great deal in investigating the causes and possible prevention of epidemics. Although the USA was not a member of the League of Nations, it played a major part in the work of the Health Organization and provided substantial funds for it.

The Health Organization succeeded in combating a typhus epidemic in Russia and preventing it spreading to other countries. It carried out research on diseases such as leprosy, and following its research, vaccines were introduced worldwide for diseases such as tuberculosis, diphtheria and tetanus. The organisation played a major role in focusing attention on the prevention and treatment of tropical diseases.

By 1939, the organisation was working on a wide range of beneficial activities ranging from funding pioneering medical research to providing medical care in remote communities. Like the Commission for Refugees, the organisation's work was continued after the Second World War, as the World Health Organization (WHO), part of the United Nations. The Health Organization demonstrated clearly what might be achieved by countries working together to solve problems like infectious diseases which did not respect national boundaries.

The Slavery Commission

A commission was set up in 1924 to attempt to end the practice of enslavement, which still existed in some parts of the world, and also to end the practices where children were forced to work, or women were forced into prostitution. This commission had some success at fighting enslavement. For example, over 200 000 enslaved people were freed in countries such as Burma and Sierra Leone in the late 1920s, and enslavement was abolished in Jordan, Iraq and Nepal. The commission was less successful at ending child labour, however, as the practice was too deep-rooted in many countries, and often families depended on it for their survival.

The Disarmament Commission

The second major role given to the League on its foundation was to arrange disarmament. Point 4 of Wilson's Fourteen Points called for 'the reduction of national armaments to the lowest point consistent with domestic safety'. Many felt at the time that, in the words of a British delegate to the Versailles Treaty, 'If there is an excess of guns around, there will always be a chance of them getting fired off.' It was accepted that the arms 'race' before 1914 had been a significant factor in increasing the tensions between nations, even if it did not actually cause these tensions. A Disarmament

Commission with a permanent Secretariat was created to try to achieve disarmament. The commission faced a challenging task, which ultimately failed.

Because major powers such as Germany, the USA and Russia were not members of the League, and other countries held many different views on the subject, the League could achieve little in the 1920s. There were serious divisions between France and Britain. The French government saw Germany as the biggest threat to peace and wished to defend itself against any German rearmament. The British government at times saw France as a bigger threat to European peace and was also determined to retain its naval superiority over other nations which might threaten its trade and empire.

In 1925, the Disarmament Commission put forward a draft treaty to control armaments, but the Assembly did not consider it as there was no agreement by the major powers about what it should contain. However, in 1925 the League Council itself started to work on the issue of disarmament, and invited the countries outside the League (Russia, Germany and the USA) to join in and prepare for a world disarmament conference. Five years of long and difficult negotiations followed. The negotiations eventually led to the World Disarmament Conference in Geneva in 1932 (see Chapter 3, Section 3.1), but in the 1920s, the Disarmament Commission failed to achieve one of the great objectives behind the creation of the League.

The Mandates Commission

The Mandates Commission supervised the territories that had been taken from Germany and Turkey at the end of the First World War. Supervision was intended to ensure that these territories, in the Middle East and Africa for example, were well governed and adequately prepared for their own independence. The commission ensured the efficient administration of the Saar region until 1935, and then arranged a plebiscite in which the local people voted to return to Germany.

The commission also successfully managed the issue of the port of Danzig. In Point 13 of his Fourteen Points, Wilson had promised Poland 'free and secure access to the sea'. This promise caused a problem for

Figure 2.17: Meeting of the Disarmament Commission in 1924.

the peacemakers as the Poles did not have any access to the sea. The solution was to give them the largely German city and port of Danzig, which obviously annoyed both the German inhabitants of Danzig and also Germany as a whole. However, the League did not actually give Danzig to Poland, but made it into a Free City, administered by the League but with economic links to Poland. This compromise worked reasonably peacefully until Hitler seized it in 1939.

The Mandates Commission demanded regular reports from the mandatory powers such as Britain and France to ensure that they were following the strict rules laid down by the League. Although the commission did not have the power to carry out inspections to ensure the accuracy of these reports, there is clear evidence that the mandatory powers treated these territories differently from their other overseas possessions. For example, Britain allowed its mandate of Tanganyika (part of modern-day Tanzania) to purchase American goods that were cheaper than the British equivalent.

Critics of the mandates argued that too little was done to prepare these territories for future independence and that the mandates simply gave the victorious powers the prizes of war. Some mandates proved to be enormous and costly challenges.

ACTIVITY 2.15

Working in pairs or in a group, consider the following question:

'The work of the League's independent agencies and commissions was its greatest success in the period between 1919 and 1929.' How far do you agree?

a Think carefully about your criteria for 'success' in this context.

b Identify what could be seen as the 'successes' of the agencies and commissions.

c Identify what could be seen as the 'successes' of the League in other areas.

d Draft an opening paragraph of a response to this question. Your answer should make it clear why you have reached your conclusion, and why your 'side' is more correct than the 'other' side.

2.3 How and why did international tensions remain high after the Versailles settlement?

International tensions remained high in the post-war years for a number of reasons. The disagreements at Versailles among the USA, Britain and France increased when the US Senate rejected the peace settlement and refused to join the League. Russia remained isolated as fears of communist-style revolution spread across Europe. France's fear of Germany remained, while Britain began to feel some sympathy towards Germany over the terms of Versailles. Many nations were very dissatisfied with the new arrangements for Europe's new borders, and political leaders started to take advantage of that dissatisfaction.

Crises and tensions

A series of incidents between 1919 and 1923 demonstrated that the peace treaties had not removed all the sources of tension among the nations of Europe.

Fiume

The First World War had a serious and damaging impact on Italy, one of the 'victorious' powers of the war. Italy had borrowed heavily to finance its involvement in the war, and its attempts to repay its debts led to damaging inflation. The value of the Italian lira fell from five to the dollar in 1914 to 28 to the dollar by 1921. In addition, the cost of living increased steeply, which hit the poor hardest. Italy also faced disruption in its industry as production shifted from producing war materials to meeting peacetime needs. Unemployment was already high, but the return of more than 2 million soldiers from the war made it rise further. Many Italians felt strongly that they had made a huge sacrifice during the war against Germany and Austria and had not been sufficiently rewarded for it by the Treaty of Versailles.

A series of weak governments were unable to solve these problems. This failure led to disorder. Strikes organised by trade unions in 1919 and 1920 quickly turned into rioting and looting. In many industrial cities, workers took control of their factories and established councils to manage them. When the Italian Communist Party was formed in January 1921, it seemed that a revolution would soon break out in Italy.

Formed in 1919, under the leadership of **Benito Mussolini** the Italian National **Fascist** Party had gained a reputation for violence. Its black-shirted members regularly attacked communist headquarters and newspaper offices. Nevertheless, the party had achieved increasing support from the sections of Italian society that most feared communism – industrialists, landowners, middle-class property owners, the Roman Catholic Church and King Victor Emmanuel III. In 1922, the Communist Party called for a **general strike**. Faced with the threat of revolution, the king asked Mussolini to form a government. Italy became the world's first fascist state and Mussolini established a dictatorship which controlled Italy until 1943.

KEY TERMS

Fascist: Supporting (or someone who supports) fascism, a political philosophy which believes in state control over all aspects of society and the economy and is heavily nationalistic. In a fascist state, power is held by a small elite, usually under the direction of a dictator, and political opposition is banned. A fascist government maintains power through control of the country's armed forces.

General strike: A national strike, or refusal to work, by all the workers in major industries, such as transport, energy and manufacturing, in a country on the same day.

KEY FIGURE

Benito Mussolini (1883–1945)

Mussolini led the fascist movement in Italy, forming the Fascist Party in 1919 and ruling Italy from 1922 to 1943. He swiftly established a dictatorship and launched a campaign to control all aspects of Italian life. His decision to support Hitler during the Second World War proved disastrous, and he was dismissed by the king in 1943. Mussolini was executed by communists in 1945.

In line with the aggressive nationalism which was a feature of fascism, Mussolini made it clear that his aim was to make Italy 'great, respected and feared'. He declared 'The 20th century will be a century of Italian power.' He was determined to restore Italian pride, which had been badly damaged during the First World War, and promised a return to the great days of the old Roman Empire.

In March 1923, Italian troops took possession of the Adriatic port of Fiume. This action defied the Paris peace settlement, which had declared Fiume a 'Free City', to be used jointly by Italy and Yugoslavia. Both Italians and Yugoslavs lived in Fiume. Italy simply claimed Fiume, although it left a small part of the city to the Yugoslavs. The League of Nations and the other powers took no action (See Section 2.2). The League's inaction set an unfortunate example. A larger power, a leading member of the League, was able to use force against a smaller, weaker, nation, and successfully seize territory. The seizure made Mussolini more popular in Italy and encouraged him to take similar actions later.

Corfu

In August 1923, four Italian officials were killed while monitoring a border dispute between Greece and Albania (see Section 2.2). Mussolini believed that Greece was responsible for the deaths and ordered Italian troops to bombard, and afterwards occupy, the Greek island of Corfu. Greece appealed to the League of Nations, which instructed Italian troops to withdraw from Corfu. Mussolini refused to accept the League's authority. He had been in power for only a year, and his position was not yet secure. He needed to demonstrate to the Italian people how tough he was. Mussolini persuaded the Council of Ambassadors to overrule the League's decision.

Britain and France saw Mussolini as a useful ally against communism, and France did not want to offend a possible ally against Germany. So, Britain and France were not prepared to take strong action against Mussolini. As a result, the League did nothing and the Italian occupation continued until Greece paid substantial compensation. Mussolini's refusal to abide by the decisions made at the Paris Peace Conference caused concern throughout Europe.

ACTIVITY 2.16

When Italy sent its troops into Corfu to get compensation, the Greeks appealed to both the League and the Conference [Council] of Ambassadors to get them removed. However, this gave Mussolini the opportunity to play off the two organisations against each other to ensure he got what he wanted. The British representative at the League said that 'this appeal is life and death for the League, and we must be prepared to use force to get the Italians out. The British Foreign Secretary said, 'we must support the League as this is the first occasion that a small nation has appealed to it against the aggression of a Great Power', and, in a note to the Prime Minister he said, 'Italy's conduct is violent and inexcusable. If we don't back up the Greek appeal to the League, the League may as well shut up its doors.'

The French, however, viewed the attack differently and encouraged the Italians to resist. The Italians were supporting their invasion of the Ruhr. The British Foreign Secretary said in Parliament 'the French are not behaving honestly and are supporting the Italians, there is a desire to help Mussolini to save face.' He seemed determined to use force to uphold the role of the League. However, within weeks the British attitude had changed. They did not want a war in the Mediterranean. They felt that sanctions would not work and damage their trade. The British navy was involved in keeping the peace and preserving British interests in the Eastern Mediterranean and wanted no threat there or to the Suez Canal.

From *International Relations Since the Peace*, written by a British journalist and historian, 1925.

a Identify three reasons why Mussolini was able to achieve his objective in Corfu.

b Why did the British change their minds over Corfu?

c How balanced and objective a view of the Corfu incident is this source?

The Ruhr crisis

Earlier in 1923, France and Belgium's invasion of the Ruhr region in Germany was a greater threat to both the peace of Europe and the peaceful implementation of the terms of Versailles. The German economy was exceptionally weak after the war. Germany had lost valuable territory and industrial areas, and, like Italy, had suffered disruption when millions of soldiers returned to peacetime life, and German industry had to switch from making war materials to meeting peacetime needs. The actions of France and Belgium, therefore, greatly increased Germany's economic problems.

In January 1923, angered by Germany's failure to make reparations payments, French and Belgian troops occupied the Ruhr – one of Germany's most important industrial regions – aiming to seize coal, iron and timber by way of payment. This invasion was a clear breach of the Covenant of the League of Nations. The German government ordered a policy of **passive resistance**. This policy meant that miners and factory employees refused to work and industry in the Ruhr stopped. Although the French and Belgians largely failed in their aim to seize goods from German factories and mines, the economic effect of the loss of output from such a vital industrial region was catastrophic for Germany. Germany was already suffering from rising inflation, and the Ruhr crisis made this worse. The economic impact made it even less likely that Germany would be able to meet its reparations requirements in the future.

Figure 2.18: French soldiers invade the Ruhr.

KEY TERM

Passive resistance: Taking an action which does not involve any violence to prevent your opponents achieving their objectives: for example, refusing to work or sitting down and blocking a road.

German hyperinflation and the reparations issue

Despite deciding to isolate itself politically from Europe, the USA continued to have a major effect on European economies. During the First World War, the USA had provided large loans to assist its European allies. Now it insisted on the full repayment of these war debts. For most European countries, damaged by the effects of war and struggling to rebuild their economies, the only way to meet these debt repayments was by ensuring that Germany paid its reparations.

Following its defeat, Germany claimed that it was in no position – politically, socially or economically – to meet these demands for reparations. Fighting on the Western Front during the First World War had taken place mainly in France and Belgium, and Germany emerged from the war with most of its industrial infrastructure undamaged. However, Germany had borrowed heavily to finance its war effort, and the combined effects of repaying these debts and meeting reparations requirements were disastrous for the German economy. Much as Keynes had predicted (See Section 2.1), German inflation spiralled out of control. The value of Germany's currency (the mark) fell dramatically, as shown in Table 2.1.

Early 1921	\$1 = 90 marks
Early 1922	\$1 = 320 marks
December 1922	\$1 = 7400 marks
November 1923	\$1 = 4.2 trillion marks

Table 2.1: Changing value of the German mark from 1921 to 1923.

Germany's currency became almost worthless. In January 1922, a loaf of bread cost 250 marks; by November 1923, the price had soared to 200 000 million marks. Germany was suffering from an extreme form of inflation that economists call hyperinflation. This caused enormous hardships to its population. Germany's Weimar government was faced with numerous uprisings and struggled to maintain control over the country. The government was not strong enough to control wages and prices and simply issued paper money, which rapidly became worthless, and made the problem worse.

Figure 2.19: German children using banknotes as building blocks during the hyperinflation crisis, 1923. How reliable do you think this photograph is?

Eventually the invading armies withdrew from the Ruhr and, with the support of the USA (through the Dawes Plan; see Section 2.4), the situation calmed and the German economy recovered. However, the crisis did not improve relations between France and Germany.

Relations between Britain and France were strained as a result of their different attitudes towards German recovery and the Ruhr crisis. As at Versailles, Britain was keen to reestablish a trading partnership between the two countries, and encouraged Germany's economic revival. In contrast, France was determined to keep Germany as weak as possible for as long as possible. Britain opposed the French actions in the Ruhr, considering these actions effectively an act of war. Interestingly, Italy supported the French actions in return for French support over Italy's role in Corfu. Again, national interests were more important than the interests of peace and security.

ACTIVITY 2.17

Read the article and then, working either on your own or in pairs, consider the two questions.

In January 1923 the French President issued the following statement: 'France has no intention of holding the Ruhr permanently. She means to stay there until she is paid, or has assurances that she will be paid. We intend to hold this mining and industrial area until Germany fulfils its agreement. It may be a matter of five years before Germany gives sufficient proofs of its sincerity of paying reparations, at present there is none. It may be considerably less if the German government reorganizes its financial system on a sound basis and obtains a foreign loan which would be applied on the reconstruction of the devastated regions of France. But France is determined not to give up its claims in the Ruhr until our just claims are met.'

In Britain criticism of France was acute, and it became fashionable there to explain all of England's troubles to the occupation of the Ruhr. The Foreign Secretary entered into a verbal duel with the French President about the legality of the occupation, arguing that it was illegal, which encouraged the Germans to hope for active help from England against France and so stiffened passive resistance. The English see the French using it just to ruin Germany and possibly remain there permanently. The English agree that a foreign loan may be necessary for the Germans in the short term to pay off the French, but still see reparations as a simple desire for revenge and as little to do with their reconstruction. They feel that the Germans will, if treated reasonably, pay the reparations due.

From an article by an American journalist, 1925.

a Compare the French and English views on the French invasion of the Ruhr.

b Reflecting on the author and date, how useful do you consider the source to be when analysing the Ruhr invasion? Using your contextual knowledge, how perceptive do you think the author was?

Ethnic, political and economic problems in the successor states

The new 'successor states' that emerged when the peacemakers redrew the boundaries of central and eastern Europe faced many problems. A country which made 'sense' in terms of nationality might not be able to survive economically. Also, there was a serious agricultural depression (a situation where prices fell and crops were overproduced) throughout the region in the 1920s, resulting in continuing economic instability.

Drawing the new national boundary lines caused immense ethnic tension in the region which lasted until and beyond the Second World War. People of the same ethnicity could be scattered across several different possible 'new' countries. People who saw themselves as members of one nationality found themselves in the same country as other nationalities who had been bitter enemies in the past. There could be serious religious divisions within nations, among people of Protestant, Catholic, Jewish and Muslim religions, for example. There had been terrible attacks against Jewish people in much of eastern Europe in the years before the First World War and **antisemitism** was deeply rooted in some areas.

KEY TERM

Antisemitism: Hostility towards, and discrimination against, Jewish people.

The new states also faced political problems. There had been no democracy in any of these new states before 1914, as they were ruled by autocratic monarchs. The new states were expected suddenly to become democratic republics, electing their own leaders, although they had no tradition of elections or popular representation. A total of 75% of the inhabitants of the regions were poor rural farmers, who wanted to see land reforms and an end to the power of aristocratic landlords.

In practice, only one of those new democracies survived until 1939. It was hardly surprising that instability and tension dominated the region and continued to play a key role in the buildup to the Second World War.

Hungary

Although once an independent nation, Hungary had become part of the Austrian-Hungarian Empire and had been ruled from Vienna. After the departure of the Austro-Hungarian emperor in 1918 there was political chaos in Hungary, and the communist party seized control under Béla Kun and announced the creation of the Hungarian Soviet Republic in 1919. The events in Hungary horrified the peacemakers at Versailles. Fear of communism and revolution spread across Europe. The new Hungarian government launched attacks on both Romania and Czechoslovakia to expand Hungary's territory, and also started a brutal campaign known as the 'Red Terror' to murder all its opponents. The French intervened to defeat the Hungarians and a new military leadership took over. This leadership started the 'White Terror' to murder all the communists in 1921. This situation was not a good start for a new nation.

The new government hated the terms that the peace imposed on Hungary. The country was economically weak and relied on foreign loans for survival. About 25% of people who saw themselves as Hungarian were placed in other states. About 50% of territory seen as Hungarian was given to other states such as Romania, always seen as a long-standing enemy. A strongly authoritarian and antisemitic leader, Horthy, emerged to rule Hungary between the two world wars. Horthy was determined to revise the terms of the treaties. By the 1930s the Hungarians could see clearly that Germany under Hitler was a model that they could follow.

Czechoslovakia

Czechoslovakia was perhaps one of the few success stories of the successor states. However, Czechoslovakia still had problems. The new state, part of the former Austro-Hungarian Empire, emerged in October 1918.

Figure 2.20: Map showing one of the problems facing the successor states – the different languages spoken in Czechoslovakia.

It was recognised as an independent state by the peacemakers in 1919. However, as well as containing Czechs and Slovaks, the new country contained Russians, Hungarians, Poles and Jews, and, most significantly, over 3 million German speakers who did not like being Czechs. There were also divisions between the Czech-dominated area, which was more industrialised and Protestant, and the Slovak-dominated areas, which were more agricultural and Roman Catholic.

These problems became more significant in the 1930s in the build-up to the Second World War. However, in the 1920s Czechoslovakia benefited from good leadership and was able to survive economically. As a result, Czechoslovakia developed a working democracy which survived until Hitler destroyed it in 1939.

Poland

Poland had been dominated by other countries, especially Russia, since 1795, but re-emerged as an independent country in 1918. The treaties confirmed its independence in 1919. However, Poland's existence was always under threat because it had no geographical barriers against its hostile neighbours, Russia and Germany.

Like other successor states, Poland contained a large number of minorities who had no wish to be Polish. Eighteen million of the 27 million population were Polish. There were many new 'Poles' who saw themselves as German or Ukrainians. In addition, Poland was a country with a very strong Roman Catholic tradition, but 3 million Jewish people lived there too, and this led to considerable ethnic and religious tension. There had been serious antisemitism there before 1914, and that antisemitism continued.

With a large rural and agricultural population Poland was also economically weak. There was little industry in the country and the 1920s were a time of high inflation. The new rulers had no experience in economic management. Poland had no tradition of democracy or democratic institutions, and democracy did not last long in this ethnically and religiously divided country. By 1926 a strongly nationalist dictator ruled the country.

Yugoslavia

Yugoslavia was formed from territory taken mainly from two independent countries, Serbia and Montenegro, and also included some parts of the former Austro-Hungarian Empire. It contained a mix of different ethnic and religious groups, and its people spoke many different languages. Approximately 40% of the population were Serbs, but there were also Croats, Bosnians, Slovenes, Hungarians, Macedonians, Kosovans and Albanians. In many cases there was a long history of conflicts between the various groups. For example, there had been religious tensions between Greek Orthodox and Roman Catholic Christians, Jews and Muslims.

Geographically and economically the country did not work well. Slovenia had the most wealth and Kosovo had the greatest degree of poverty. In addition, Yugoslavia was bordered by seven different countries: Italy, Austria, Hungary, Romania, Bulgaria, Greece and Albania and most of these hoped to seize some of Yugoslavia. This did not lead to a sense of security. Democracy failed because there were so many divisions and no democratic traditions to build on. Yugoslavia became a dictatorship under a king in 1929, and democratic processes were banned.

Austria

Before 1914, Austria's capital, Vienna, had been the centre of a major European empire. Its armies had been defeated in Italy in the west and against Russia in the east, and the empire collapsed in 1918. Much of Austria's territory went to independent nations such as Czechoslovakia and Hungary. There were hardly any ethnic or religious minorities in Austria as the vast majority of the population were ethnic Germans who spoke German. Austria was economically very weak as much of its industry and agriculture had gone elsewhere and it became very dependent on foreign loans. Helping it to survive was one of the first tasks of the new League of Nations. Austria considered that uniting with Germany (Anschluss) might be a possible solution to its economic problems and give it greater status in Europe. However, the Treaty of Versailles did not allow this union. France would not tolerate such a powerful potential combination to its east.

ACTIVITY 2.18

a Consider questions **i** and **ii**. Draft a possible plan for each answer.

i Why was drawing up the boundary lines between nations along 'clearly recognisable lines of nationality' so difficult for the peacemakers?

ii Should all the problems facing the successor states be seen as the responsibility of the peacemakers?

b Compare your plans with a partner.

For Question **i**:

- Does your partner's plan show that they have understood the problems facing the peacemakers in trying to resolve this issue? (The main problem was that it was a fine idea in theory, but it did not work in practice).
- Has your partner provided three or four examples, such as Poland and Czechoslovakia, which clearly illustrate the problem?

For Question **ii**:

- Has your partner structured their plan in two columns? One column should suggest reasons why the problems facing the successor states are the fault of the peacemakers. The other column should list points suggesting why they are not.
- Has your partner provided factual examples to back up each point?

The aims and impact of international treaties and conferences of the early 1920s

Although considerable tension arose from the peace treaties, no country wanted another war. Between 1921 and 1923, several attempts were made to avoid conflict, resolve disputes and revise and fill in gaps left by the treaties.

The 'Little Entente', 1921

The 'Little Entente' was an early example of nations working together to preserve the peace and establish greater economic cooperation. The Little Entente was a series of agreements (not formal treaties) between Yugoslavia and Czechoslovakia (two of the newly formed post-Versailles nations) and Romania. Although an 'old' nation, Romania had various concerns about the implications of the peace treaties. The primary aim of this *entente* was national security. The members wished to keep their new boundaries and their independence safe from external threats. They were particularly worried by the **revisionist** approach of Hungary, which wanted to expand on the boundaries laid down by the treaties. Austrian and German revisionism also concerned them. Their focus was cooperation and mutual support and the alliance was defensive, not aggressive. France was later to link up to this group, hoping to counterbalance what it saw as a growing threat from Germany. The Little Entente was a good example of regional cooperation for mutual benefit.

KEY TERM

Revisionist: Wishing to change something, or someone who wishes to change something.

The Washington Conference, 1921–22

Although the USA did not sign the Versailles treaties and did not join the League, it played an important role in international relations after 1920, particularly when its own interests were involved. The USA was concerned about growing tensions in East Asia and the Pacific arising from Japanese expansion in the region. The USA had substantial economic interests in the area, as well as colonies in the Philippines. There was a fear in the USA and beyond that another naval arms race in the region might lead to war. In 1921 the USA invited nine nations to Washington DC to discuss possible reductions in the size of their navies and the situation in East Asia. The nations met for the Washington Naval Conference: Britain, Japan, France and Italy (the major League powers) and also Belgium, China, Portugal and the Netherlands.

ACTIVITY 2.19

HONOURABLE RATIO;
OR, NAVAL CONVERSATIONS IN LONDON.
"THIS DESPICABLE CREATURE DOES NOT FIND HIS SEAT SO SATISFACTORY AS YOU TWO ILLUSTRIOUS PERSONS FIND YOURS!"

Figure 2.21: A British cartoon illustrating the Washington Naval Conference. It is titled, 'Honourable Ratio; Or, Naval Conversations in London.' The caption below the title says, 'This despicable creature does not find his seat so satisfactory as you two illustrious persons find yours!'

Look at the cartoon in Figure 2.21.

a What is the relevance of the 5 5 3 in the cartoon?

b What point is the cartoonist making?

c How valid is the point that the cartoonist is making?

The Washington Naval Conference led to a series of treaties, which at the time seemed to guarantee peace and reduce tension in East Asia.

- **The Five Power Treaty** (signed by the USA, Britain, France, Japan and Italy) – Japan agreed to withdraw from some of its recently acquired Chinese territory and to limit its navy to three-fifths the size of the British and US navies. In return, the Western powers agreed not to develop any new naval bases near Japan. All five countries agreed to limit the number and size of their warships.
- **The Four Power Treaty** (signed by USA, Britain, France and Japan) – the four countries agreed to respect each other's rights in the Pacific and East Asia, and to deal with any future disagreements by negotiation rather than military action. The USA, France and Britain all had colonies in the region.
- **The Nine Power Treaty** (signed by all nine countries attending the conference) – this treaty guaranteed protection for China against invasion and agreed to uphold the 'open door' policy which allowed equal opportunity for all countries seeking to trade with China.

The treaties arising out of the Washington Naval Conference undoubtedly reduced tensions in East Asia. All of the countries involved had been willing to compromise in the interests of maintaining peace. However, the treaties were far from perfect. For example, although the Five Power Treaty limited the tonnage of each nation's large warships, it did not include all types of warships. As a result, there was a race to build smaller warships that could be used if war broke out. Also, the treaties lacked a means of enforcement – they did not specify what action would be taken if a country violated the agreements it had made.

ACTIVITY 2.20

SOURCE A

The agreements made at the Washington Conference have placed the USA in danger. The USA has sacrificed itself to bring about peace. It should be pointed out that such treaties cannot be regarded as a guarantee against war, since similar agreements have failed many times in the past.

From the *American Army and Navy Journal*, 1922.

SOURCE B

If the Washington Conference fails it will not be due to the Japanese. It would have been fair to give equality to Japan. The USA should have granted this. The delegates should have been reminded of the opening address in which the President urged the delegates to be unselfish and think responsibly about the future of the world.

From the writing of a Japanese businessman in 1922.

CONTINUED

SOURCE C

The Washington treaties are not a means of reducing the American fleet, but a way of increasing the efficiency of the American navy. The same holds true for Britain and Japan. Of the 1.65 million tons to be destroyed, over half are ships so old that they can no longer be considered fit to fight.

From an article by William H. Gardiner, 'A Naval View of the Conference', *Atlantic Monthly*, April 1922. Gardiner was president of the US Navy League.

Considering these sources and using your own knowledge, to what extent does each source view the Washington Naval Conference as a success?

Think carefully about what the criteria for 'success' are in this context. Should the success criteria include the fact that it actually took place? Or the fact that it involved the Americans?

The Genoa Conference, 1922

At the suggestion of Lloyd George, the British prime minister, representatives of over 30 European countries met in Genoa, Italy, in April to May 1922, to discuss ways of easing the post-war economic problems that were seriously affecting most European countries at the time. France was represented by its prime minister, Poincaré. Despite their political and diplomatic isolation, both Germany and Soviet Russia were invited to the conference. This was because Lloyd George believed that including Germany and Russia was vital to achieving the aim of 'the economic reconstruction of Europe, devastated and broken into fragments by the agency of war'.

The different attitudes of Britain and France towards Germany are clearly shown by this extract, from a British political magazine:

A major issue is at stake regarding the forthcoming conference in Genoa. M. Poincaré wants the physical security and prosperity of France by means of holding Germany down and taking large reparations from her and meanwhile maintaining an expensive army and navy. On the other hand, Mr. Lloyd George stands for toleration, **conciliation** and cooperation with Germany. M. Poincaré has tried to prevent the Conference altogether. Mr. Lloyd George told him that Britain would carry on in any case, and that if France refused to attend she would be the greatest loser. M. Poincaré probably felt that he could not afford to forfeit the good opinion of the world by not attending.

From 'France and the Genoa Conference', *The Spectator*, 4 March 1922.

KEY TERM

Conciliation: Trying to reach a peaceful settlement to a dispute and reduce tension.

The conference focused largely on the issue of German reparations. With serious internal economic problems, Germany was struggling to keep up with the payments. Britain was interested in restoring its German trading links. Britain, therefore, argued that the massive reparations imposed on Germany would undermine European economic recovery and should be reduced. However, France feared a revival of German power and opposed anything that seemed to weaken the terms of the Treaty of Versailles, and, therefore, insisted that reparation payments should be made in full.

The Genoa Conference achieved nothing. The USA was still pursuing its isolationist policy and was determined to avoid involvement in European affairs, so it did not attend. Because of France's unwillingness to compromise, Germany withdrew from the conference. Feeling increasingly isolated and sensing an opportunity to develop their relationship with Germany, the Russians also withdrew. National self-interest appeared to be the dominant factor. It is worth noting that this conference was not managed by the League of Nations.

The Rapallo Pact, 1922

The First World War and the Paris peace settlement had left both Germany and Bolshevik Russia isolated and vulnerable. The foreign ministers of Germany and Russia had attended the Genoa Conference, and they continued to hold joint discussions in Rapallo, Italy, once the Genoa conference broke up. These discussions led to a treaty (also known as the Rapallo **Pact**) in 1922 by which Germany recognised the Bolsheviks as the **legitimate government** of Russia. (Germany was the first foreign government to do so.) The negotiations also agreed to renounce (give up) all territorial claims against each other, and to 'cooperate in a spirit of mutual goodwill in meeting the economic needs of both countries'.

KEY TERMS

Pact: A formal agreement. It could mean a treaty between two or more countries, as in the case of the Rapallo Pact, or an agreement to recommend a course of action, as in the case of the Hoare–Laval Pact (see Chapter 3, Section 3.2).

Legitimate government: A government that is accepted both by the people of the country and also by other nations as having a right to rule that country.

The treaty made increased trade between Germany and Russia possible and, thus, greatly benefited both nations economically. The treaty also led to industrial and military collaboration that enabled Germany to evade many of the terms of the Treaty of Versailles. Major German companies, such as Krupp, built factories in Russia which produced the tanks, artillery, aircraft and other military equipment that the Treaty of Versailles had banned them from manufacturing. Germany also organised military training in Russia for German officers who had been dismissed from the army because the Treaty of Versailles had reduced the size of the German army. Russia's major weakness during the First World War had been the lack of modern military equipment and training. The Russian armed forces were now able to learn from German military expertise and technological skills. The two 'outcasts' of Versailles were now working together, not to progress world peace, but in their own, military, interests.

The Rapallo Pact caused great concern elsewhere in Europe, particularly in France and Poland. The French, fearful of communism spreading from Bolshevik Russia and determined to keep Germany weak and isolated, felt threatened by the increasingly friendly relations between these two countries. The Poles were aware that both Germany and Russia claimed parts of the territory that comprised post-First World War Poland. As Poland shared a border with Germany to the west and Russia to the east, Poland's security was clearly under threat. Moreover, Poland's own hopes of territorial expansion into both Germany and Russia were reduced. The Rapallo Pact inevitably increased the tension in Europe.

Figure 2.22: A cartoon from a German satirical magazine commenting on the Rapallo Pact. It shows Germany and Russia emerging from the grave and coming to life again.

The Treaty of Lausanne, 1923

The Treaty of Sèvres had never been formally ratified. Although the Turkish government had signed the treaty, Greece refused to do so because of its claims to more former Turkish territory. This issue became more complicated when the Turkish National Movement, under the leadership of Mustafa Kemal, gained control over Turkey. Kemal's government rejected the Treaty of Sèvres, claiming some of the territory that the treaty had taken from the former Turkish Empire.

Representatives of all the countries involved met in Lausanne, Switzerland. They aimed to prevent this situation from leading to further border disputes. Discussions were tense, and there were constant protests from the Turkish representatives. Nevertheless, agreement was finally reached, and the Treaty of Lausanne was signed on 24 July 1923.

The opening words of the treaty read:

> France, Britain, Italy, Japan, Greece and Romania of the one part and Turkey of the other part, being united in the desire to bring to a final close the state of war which has existed in the East since 1914, being anxious to re-establish the relations of friendship and commerce which are essential to the mutual well-being of their respective peoples, and considering that these relations must be based on respect for the independence and sovereignty of states, have decided to conclude a Treaty for this purpose.
>
> **From the opening words of the Treaty of Lausanne, 1923.**

The treaty settled the borders of Turkey, Greece and Bulgaria. It also formally recognised the independence of the Republic of Turkey, with Kemal as head of state. Turkey's requirement to pay reparations was ended. The treaty meant that another challenge to the peace settlements had succeeded; and Germany noted the ending of reparations for Turkey.

ACTIVITY 2.21

Look carefully at the Washington Naval Treaties and the Rapallo Pact.

a Which one do you think was more important to international relations in this period? Why?

b Do some research once you have studied the 1929–39 period and compare the short-term effects of the two treaties with their long-term impact. Was one more important in the short term rather than the long term? Did one contribute more than the other to increasing tensions between nations? Did either have consequences which those taking part did not intend?

Reflection

Compare your analysis for this task with that of another student. How did you decide on which agreement was more important? Did you take the same approach to your partner? If not, how did your approach differ, and how did this lead you to a different answer?

Changing relationships between the major powers

The ending of the First World War led to global economic chaos. Countries such as France and Belgium needed to rebuild their industrial infrastructure following the devastation of war damage. Britain had lost over 40% of its merchant fleet during the war, significantly reducing its ability to trade. At the same time, these countries had to repay their war debts to the USA. War debts and reparations requirements meant that the German economy declined into a period of hyperinflation. Japan had gained major economic advantages from the war, but now found that it faced renewed commercial competition from other countries. The USA had also gained many economic benefits during the war but found that its trading opportunities were reduced because of economic weaknesses elsewhere in the world.

Unemployment rose as wartime production ceased and soldiers returned from the war. Economic hardships led to social problems, which, in turn, posed the threat of civil disturbance and revolution. In these circumstances, it is not surprising that international tensions remained high in the immediate post-war period and that relationships between former allies and former enemies changed in many ways.

Key changes in the international situation included the USA's move towards a more isolationist policy; the gradual acceptance of the communist regime in Russia; and Japan's rise to power in East Asia. The treaties arising from the Washington Naval Conference helped to reduce Western concerns about the situation in East Asia, but soon increased tension between the USA and Japan, as Japan saw the treaties as an incentive to expand its influence in East Asia, and the USA increasingly saw this as a threat to the USA. The treaties achieved little in terms of reducing tensions in Europe. The French refusal to compromise at the Genoa Conference undermined Britain's attempt to improve relations between France and Germany. Failure to reach agreement on the issue of German reparations and the subsequent French invasion of the Ruhr industrial area caused further instability. In addition, the failure of the Genoa Conference led to closer relations between Germany and Russia, resulting in the Rapallo Pact, which was widely seen as a threat to stability within Europe. Stability was further threatened by the Treaty of Lausanne, the first international agreement to demonstrate clearly that the Paris peace settlement could be successfully challenged and amended.

The European nations: Britain, France, Germany and Italy

Although Britain and France had been allies during the First World War, the relationship worsened after 1918. France had been invaded by Germany twice in the space of less than 50 years. After the humiliating defeat in the Franco-Prussian War (1870–71) and the devastating effects of German aggression between 1914 and 1918, France's main priority was to ensure that Germany could never again become a threat. At the Paris Peace Conference, Clemenceau had demanded that the peacemakers impose a harsh settlement on Germany, and to some extent the Treaty of Versailles had met his demand.

Lloyd George did not support the French determination to destroy Germany (so long as the Germany navy stopped being a threat to Britain). Many people in Britain felt that the Treaty of Versailles was not only harsh on Germany, but also contained issues which might lead to future conflict. Some of these people had joined a League of Nations Union to support the idea of the League and to ensure that 1914–18 was the 'war to end wars'.

A fundamental and long-lasting problem was that Britain wanted a possible ally in some circumstances, while France wanted a binding alliance that would commit Britain to supporting France, with military force if needed, at all times. Lloyd George did not want always to have to support France in strictly enforcing the terms of the Treaty of Versailles. So, he insisted that Britain would only make a binding commitment to back France with force if the USA agreed to commit to this as well. When the USA refused to sign the treaties and join the League of Nations, Lloyd George was able to avoid such a commitment. So the USA's decision not to ratify the treaty meant that France no longer had the guarantee of American and British assistance if Germany behaved aggressively towards France in future.

As the 1920s progressed, there were further quarrels between Britain and France over reparations and the mandates that Britain and France took over in the Middle East. At the same time, Britain and France developed different relations with Germany and Italy. France continued to follow a tough and uncompromising policy towards Germany throughout the period from 1919 to 1929. The aim of this policy was to ensure that Germany remained too weak, both militarily and economically, to pose a threat to French security. For this reason, France insisted that Germany should pay the full amount of reparations. This approach is clearly demonstrated by French refusal to compromise at the Genoa Conference (see earlier in this section). Since Germany had to pay the reparations over a period of 66 years, the French could feel certain that Germany would remain economically weak for a long time – too weak to plan any further aggression against France.

When Germany fell behind in its reparations payments, France was prepared to adopt extreme measures to force the Germans to pay and sent troops to occupy the Ruhr region in 1923. The occupation of the Ruhr was effectively an act of war. It severely damaged France's relations with Britain, which wanted to encourage the recovery of the German economy. The worsening of relations with Britain made France feel more isolated and insecure. The 1920s also saw a change in relations between Britain, France and Italy. France sympathised with Italy's anger over its treatment at Versailles and saw Italy as a potential ally against Germany. Britain had its own interests in the Mediterranean and viewed Italy as a possible threat in that region. So Mussolini's invasion of Corfu in August 1923 caused more tension between Britain and France, and illustrated how international relations were changing.

Figure 2.23: German coal being taken to France. The British felt strongly that this action would only lead to further tension.

The USSR and the challenge of communism

Russia remained a cause for concern throughout the 1920s. No one had had to deal with a communist regime before. Many capitalist countries were concerned because in March 1919 communists from all over the world had been invited to a conference in Moscow. This conference marked the creation of the Third International or **Comintern**, an organisation which aimed to achieve a communist revolution throughout the world. Its chairman, Grigori Zinoviev, proclaimed that 'in a year the whole of Europe will be communist'. When the Comintern met in 1920 it had delegates from 37 different countries. The number of countries represented at the Comintern caused much concern in many capitals. In the political and economic turmoil Europe faced just after the war, widespread revolution seemed genuinely possible. Even in the USA, fear that revolution might spread from communist Russia led to a nationwide panic, known as the Red Scare, in 1919 and 1920.

KEY TERM

Comintern: An organisation created by Lenin in 1919 with the aim of spreading communism and starting a worldwide anti-capitalist revolution. The term is short for Communist International.

However, by 1921, hopes of a worldwide communist revolution under Russian leadership were disappearing. Attempted revolutions in both Germany and Hungary had failed. So, Lenin began to accept that Russia's future depended on a degree of peaceful coexistence and some economic cooperation with other countries.

In March 1921, Britain signed a trade treaty with Russia in order to help its own economy but was reluctant to have any further dealings with the new communist state. However, France remained deeply resentful of Bolshevik success in Russia. The Bolshevik government's refusal to repay Russian debts to France resulted in great anger. French concerns regarding Bolshevik Russia were heightened when the Rapallo Pact was signed in 1922, restoring full diplomatic relations between Russia and Germany and ending the political and economic isolation of both countries. Both France and Poland saw an alliance between Russia and Germany as a threat to themselves.

In the period between 1919 and 1923 Russia slowly began to emerge again as a major power. By the end of 1922, Lenin and the Bolsheviks had defeated their opponents in the Russian Civil War and created the USSR. They now ruled a vast territory which spread from the Baltic Sea in the west to the Pacific Ocean in the east.

Many countries were still deeply suspicious of the USSR's 'revolutionary' potential, and many people saw evidence of a communist threat to their own countries, but increasingly the USSR became accepted as another nation which other nations would have to negotiate with. Russia's invitation to the Genoa Conference in 1922 had given it a 'seat at the table' with the other great powers. Recognition and respectability were slowly arriving for communist Russia.

ACTIVITY 2.22

Read Sources A and B, and then consider the two questions.

SOURCE A

On February 21, 1923, reports came from Moscow that Litvinov, Commissar of Foreign Affairs, had made a significant speech in the Kremlin. He blamed the tension between Britain, other Western Powers, and Russia on the activities of supporters of the former Tsar. He defended the Chinese policy of the Soviet Government with dignity and frankness, showing that while sympathetic towards the national aspirations of the Chinese it was not trying deliberately to provoke anti-foreign sentiment in China which might damage British trade or influence there, any more than in Chile or Nicaragua. The latter referring to fears from the United States that there is a plan to export communism to Central and Southern America. He argued that support for the British working class in their struggle with poverty and oppression is not designed to cause unrest in Britain or be seen as an attack on the British Government. He reminded his listeners that it was not long since British soldiers that had been sent to Russia to defeat the Revolution, had been withdrawn.

From an article by an American historian, 1927.

CONTINUED

SOURCE B

The British Government calls the attention of the Soviet Government to its agreement on June 4, 1923, 'not to support with funds, or in any other form, persons or bodies or agencies or institutions whose aim it is to spread discontent or start rebellion in any part of Britain and its Empire and to impress upon its officers and officials full and continuous observance of these conditions.'

Violations of this understanding have emerged recently. They range from speeches by Russian officials which threaten British interests in Persia. There has been support for British workers going on strike in Britain which has inflicted real damage on our economy. The support for nationalist movements in India is in clear breach of the agreement, and the open support for socialism in China will damage not only the peace there, but our commercial interests as well.

From the British Note to the Government of Russia, 23 February 1923.

a Compare the views in the two sources on the causes of tension between Britain and Russia in this period.

b How great an impact did the tension between the newly emerging communist state in Russia and France, Britain and the USA have on international relations?

The USA: isolation or involvement

Despite President Wilson's leading role in negotiating the peace treaties, public opinion in the USA had been divided on whether the USA should ratify the Paris peace settlement and join the League of Nations. Most Democratic Party senators supported President Wilson's argument in favour of internationalism – that the USA should play a full and active part in international affairs. Most Republican Party senators opposed internationalism and argued in favour of isolationism – that the USA should keep out of international affairs unless its own interests were at stake. In November 1919, the US Senate rejected the Paris peace settlement and refused to allow the USA to join the League of Nations.

The USA's decision not to ratify the Paris peace settlement had major implications for international relations after 1919. It made the treaties that emerged from the Paris Peace Conference seem less legitimate and seriously damaged the credibility of the proposed League of Nations. It also increased France's feelings of insecurity. The French now had no guarantee of American support if Germany recovered and attacked France. In addition, Britain used the decision as an excuse to cancel its own commitment to support France if necessary. Britain was clearly seeking to avoid serious involvement in European affairs as its interests lay elsewhere in the world with its large empire and colonies. With no guarantee of American or British help, France was left feeling betrayed and vulnerable.

The relationship between the USA and the European powers was further complicated because, during the war, the USA had provided its European allies, such as Britain and France, with sizeable loans. These loans had to be repaid with interest once the war was over. In 1919, Britain and France urged the USA to cancel these debts. They pointed out that the USA had benefited economically from the war, and that its post-war economy was in a much better state than their own. However, the USA insisted that the loans should be repaid in full. American President Coolidge said 'They hired the money – didn't they'. European nations were already suffering from major economic problems in the period immediately following the First World War. The need to repay their debts to the USA increased their financial problems. In order to repay these debts, countries such as Britain and France depended on the reparation payments they were due to receive from Germany, which Germany could not provide.

Failure to ratify Versailles and join the League did not mean that the United States withdrew into total isolation from world affairs. In 1921 it made a separate peace with Germany. And it played a part in world affairs when it felt that this best suited its own interests – in the Washington Naval Conference of 1921 to 1922, for example.

KEY CONCEPT 2.2

Significance

Historians are likely to regard something as 'significant' if it had important consequences or if it tells us a lot about what was happening in a particular place, at a particular time. The failure of America to join the League of Nations could be seen as a particularly significant event in the period 1919–23.

Discuss with a partner any reasons why this event could be described as significant.

- What does it tell us about American foreign policy at the time?
- What were the implications for international relations in this period?
- Why should this decision be seen as an important one which needs to be taught

Emergence of Japan: internal issues and the effect on international relations

As you learned in Chapter 1, Japan had emerged from a period of isolation in the course of the 19th century. It had also industrialised and modernised and developed into a major military power in East Asia. Japan had made great efforts to resist foreign powers trying to control it and aimed to become an imperial power itself. In the 19th century it had attempted to invade mainland Asian territories such as Korea, Manchuria and parts of China but these attempts had not succeeded. However, the alliance with Britain in the Anglo-Japanese Treaty of 1902 and Japan's victory over Russia in the Russo-Japanese War of 1904–05 showed that Japan was now a major, and ambitious, power in East Asia. As an ally of Britain it had joined the war against Germany in 1914 and provided support for the allies during the war. It had, therefore, gained a seat at the negotiating table at Versailles in 1918 to 1919, and was now clearly seen as one of the 'Great Powers'.

During the 1920s Japan faced a series of major domestic problems. It was attempting to move from an absolute monarchy under the emperor towards a democracy, while experiencing considerable economic difficulties.

Agricultural depression throughout much of the 1920s and a collapse in the prices for Japan's principal exports, textiles (woven goods), resulted in economic decline and unemployment. This situation contributed to political instability throughout the decade.

The large and growing army and navy were playing an increasingly important role in politics and disliked taking orders from democratically elected politicians. The military wanted to expand Japan's growing empire on the Asian mainland. They needed more raw materials and oil for their weapons and warships and knew that they would have to take these from other countries in East Asia. The military wanted to expand, initially into China and then into South East Asia, in the search for these materials. By the end of the 1920s, the Japanese military had begun to dominate decision-making in Japan. This situation became a seriously destabilising factor in international relations.

The USA viewed Japan with suspicion, seeing it as a potential rival for dominance in the Pacific and as a commercial rival as well. Relations between the two countries were not improved when Wilson and other leaders refused to include the proposed racial equality clause in the Covenant of the League of Nations. In 1924, America banned Japanese immigration into the United States. The ban caused more anger in Japan.

Japan was fully involved as an equal in the Washington Naval Conference in 1922. Arguably, Japan benefited more than any other nation from this conference. The treaties allowed Japan to build up its larger warships to a total of 300 000 tons (the Americans were allowed 500 000 tons). The Japanese were persuaded to abandon their 1902 alliance with Britain, and instead they signed a treaty with the USA, Britain and France. Under the terms of this treaty, the four powers agreed to settle all disputes in the region peacefully.

Superficially, by the end of the decade, tension had eased in East Asia. However, political instability in Japan, together with the determination of Japan's increasingly powerful military leaders to expand its territory, meant there was still potential for a major crisis in international relations.

Figure 2.24: One of the new Japanese battleships built in the 1920s. The Japanese naval programme included building eight like this one. The Washington Naval Conference of 1922 now permitted this. The Japanese started to build new aircraft carriers as well.

ACTIVITY 2.23

In this task you will identify and explain factors which had a major impact on international relations.

Consider the following important developments in the 1920s:

a the emergence of Japan as a major power

b the establishment of communism in Russia

c The USA's refusal to join the League of Nations.

Working in pairs, identify two or three reasons why each one of those developments affected international relations in the 1920s. Consider both the way in which other nations viewed each development and also the possible threat to peace that each development represented. Which development do you think represented the greatest threat to peace? Why?

ACTIVITY 2.24

Prepare for a debate on the statement: 'The Versailles settlement was solely responsible for international tensions remaining high between 1920 and 1924'.

CONTINUED

Work in two groups.

a One group should identify and develop causes of tension which can be directly linked to the international tensions of 1920–24. These might include reparations, the harsh terms imposed by the victors, the absence of Germany and Russia from the peace conference at Versailles, the failure to separate ending the war from making the peace and the way in which the issue of self-determination was tackled.

b The other group should identify other factors which caused the tension, such as the Fourteen Points, the impossibility of dealing with the collapse of European empires without breaching the principle of self-determination, the rise of communism, post-war economic dislocation and the role of individuals such as Mussolini and Béla Kun.

c Hold a full class debate on the issue and try to come to an agreed conclusion as to the extent to which the Versailles settlement should be seen as responsible.

2.4 How and why did international relations improve from 1924 to 1929?

After 1924 there was a general relaxation in tension and the period saw an improvement in international relations. There were several serious attempts to resolve disputes and reduce the likelihood of conflict.

Economic recovery and improved relations

At the beginning of 1924, international relations remained extremely tense, particularly in Europe. European nations were struggling with the economic problems resulting from the First World War, and these nations were more divided than united. Border disputes continued to break out as countries challenged the decisions made at the Paris Peace Conference. French and Belgian soldiers were still occupying German territory in the Ruhr.

The economies of the major European nations had been devastated by the First World War. In addition to physical damage, some countries had lost their export markets, mainly to the USA and Japan. The high costs of fighting a war had resulted in high taxation, extensive foreign borrowing and rising inflation. To finance the war effort, countries had left the **gold standard**, a system by which countries agreed to convert paper money into a fixed amount of gold. Leaving the gold standard enabled these countries to print more paper money but had the serious effect of weakening the value of their currencies, leading to inflation.

However, slowly the economies of European nations began to recover as they adapted to peacetime conditions. Realising that private businesses would be unable to finance the reconstruction of infrastructure and industry, governments took the lead. For example, both France and Britain appointed ministers of reconstruction to encourage the process. Financial constraints severely hindered the work of these ministers, but gradually economic confidence was restored. Businessmen were increasingly willing to invest money again. Members of the public were willing to lend money to governments that offered guaranteed interest rates. In 1925, Britain returned to the gold standard. France did the same in 1926 and Italy in 1927. By 1928, virtually all of the world's nations had returned to the gold standard. This led to an increase in international trade. Economic confidence was gradually restored, employment rose, poverty decreased, and social problems declined.

In the USA, as in Europe, the ending of the First World War had initially led to a period of high inflation and rising unemployment. Nevertheless, the USA had emerged from the war as the world's leading economy, with its industries and infrastructure undamaged. The USA had gained new markets, and the demand for war material had encouraged it to increase manufacturing production and efficiency.

The USA also benefited when its former European allies repaid their war debts. The USA experienced an economic boom, indicated by a massive rise in **consumerism**. New factories were built in the 1920s and mass-produced cars, radios, vacuum cleaners and refrigerators at prices many could afford, as prices dropped, and real wages increased.

Despite its outward commitment to a policy of isolationism, the USA played a significant role in easing international tensions during the 1920s. Its vast financial resources helped to overcome the problem of German reparations and consequently led to an improvement in relations between France and Germany.

KEY TERMS

Gold standard: A monetary system where a country's currency or paper money has a value directly linked to gold.

Consumerism: Where the focus of the economy is on the interests of consumers (ordinary citizens), that is, on producing things which improve the quality of life of individuals, as opposed to producing things like tanks or battleships.

The Dawes Plan (1924) and its effect on international relations

By 1924, it had become more important than ever to find a solution to the problem of German reparations. There were three main issues:

- French and Belgian troops were occupying German territory. This was effectively an act of war which posed a clear threat to peace in Europe.
- Germany claimed that it was unable to make the reparation payments that the Treaty of Versailles required.
- The USA continued to insist on full repayment of the loans it had made to Britain and France during the war; Britain and France argued that they could only afford to repay these debts if they received reparation payments from Germany.

To address these problems, a conference was held in London during 1924. The chairman of this conference was the American banker Charles Dawes. Representatives from the USA, Britain, France, Italy and Belgium attended the conference. The League of Nations played no part in it. The plan that emerged from this conference is known as the Dawes Plan.

The Dawes Plan had four main parts:

- It was agreed that French and Belgian troops should withdraw from the Ruhr as quickly as possible, and that the region should be returned to full German control. This would help Germany's economic recovery. However, France and Belgium would continue to receive reparations from Germany.

- Germany's reparation payments were restructured. Although the total amount Germany would have to pay was not reduced, it was agreed that its annual payments would be restricted to what 'she could reasonably afford'.
- It was agreed that Germany's national bank, the Reichsbank, should be restructured and supervised by representatives of the other countries attending the conference.
- Germany received a sizeable foreign loan, mainly from the USA. The loan was intended to stabilise the German economy so that Germany would be better able to meet its reparations requirements in the future. These reparations would enable countries such as Britain, who had borrowed large sums from the USA to fund the war, to repay the Americans.

The Dawes Plan seemed to mark a significant change in French policy towards Germany. Previously, France had adopted a hardline attitude, insisting that Germany paid reparations on time and in full. France's approach had been one of the main reasons for the failure of the Genoa Conference and the French occupation of the Ruhr. The new French willingness to compromise opened the way for further negotiations designed to reduce tensions between France and Germany. However, much depended on the willingness of the USA to make substantial loans to Europe.

Stresemann and German recovery

Gustav Stresemann was one of the leading politicians of the Weimar Republic. Although he was chancellor for only three months in 1923 his work was central in ensuring economic recovery. As foreign minister he did much to improve relations with Germany's former enemies and restore Germany's position as a major European power.

KEY FIGURE

Gustave Stresemann (1878–1929)

Stresemann was chancellor of Germany in 1923 and foreign secretary from 1924 to 1929. He played a key role in the German economic recovery in the 1920s and in the rehabilitation (restoration) of Germany in international affairs.

Stresemann played a vital role in ending the occupation of the Ruhr by France and Belgium, stabilising German currency and ending inflation. His work restored confidence in the Weimar system of government as well as in the German economy. Investment increased and employment improved.

However, there were still weaknesses in the German economy. For example, it depended heavily on US loans, and there was both an adverse **balance of payments** and a **budget deficit**. Those weaknesses became clear when economic crisis happened in 1929.

Perhaps Stresemann's greatest success lay in the field of foreign policy. His main hope was to achieve a revision of the Treaty of Versailles in Germany's favour. He helped Germany develop a working relationship with its former enemies and he was active in revising the terms of the treaty through the Young Plan, the Treaty of Locarno, and the Kellogg–Briand Pact (see later in this section). Stresemann also played an important part in easing reparations and reestablishing Germany's position as a major, and respectable, European power.

KEY TERMS

Balance of payments: The difference between the money coming into a country and the money going out of it. An adverse balance of payments occurs when a country pays out more money to import goods and services than it brings in by exporting goods and services.

Budget deficit: When a government is paying more money to run the country than it is receiving in taxes.

German entry into the League of Nations

Perhaps one of Stresemann's greatest achievements was to gain membership of the League of Nations for Germany. Stresemann negotiated Germany's entry to the League as part of a wider treaty at Locarno in 1925 (see later in this section). In fact, as well as becoming a member, Germany was given a seat on the Council of the League, which enabled Germany to play a dominant role in making League policy.

German entry into the League of Nations was a clear signal to other nations that Germany was now accepted as a 'respectable' nation, with the same status as powers such as Britain and France. Many people saw this as a major step forward in reducing the tension in Europe.

However, it also enabled Germany to advance its plans to revise the Treaty of Versailles to the east of Germany.

The Young Plan

The Young Plan was inspired by the USA. Despite the Dawes Plan, the USA knew that once Germany had made its full annual reparations payments to Britain and France, it would not be able to afford its interest payments on US loans. As a result, a committee met in Paris to discuss the possibility of reducing the figure that had been agreed for reparations immediately after the peace talks. The chairman of the committee was Owen Young, an American who had worked on the Dawes Plan.

Negotiations were not easy, especially as the Germans added new demands, including the return of the Polish Corridor and Upper Silesia to Germany. Stresemann took every opportunity to try to revise the Treaty of Versailles. However, the outcome of these negotiations throughout 1928 and 1929 was the Young Plan, which reduced the final sum of German reparations from £6.6 billion to £2 billion. Reducing the amount was an admission that the figure set in 1921 was too high and unrealistic. In addition, the international controls over the German economy that the Dawes Plan had established were dismantled. These were significant steps for Germany and went a long way towards easing tension across Europe.

The Young Plan was probably the best example of France's apparent new willingness to compromise. By 1929, the French appreciated that continuing to insist on full reparations would leave France isolated and less secure. Also, both Britain and France realised that Germany would only be able to pay reparations at all if it received American loans. This situation meant that Britain and France had to agree with the Young Plan.

The final details of the Young Plan were resolved in a series of conferences at the Hague (known overall as the Hague Conference) in 1929–30. As part of the Young Plan, the Hague Conference finally dealt with the issue of French military occupation of the Rhineland, ending it five years earlier than laid down in Versailles. It was hoped that the Young Plan would settle the reparations issue for good. However, a major economic crisis in the USA after 1929 made it unlikely that the USA would be able to continue to play a major role in Europe's finances.

ACTIVITY 2.25

SOURCE A

While some in the German Nationalist Party see the Young Plan as something designed to 'enslave the German people' and were determined to defeat it in the Reichstag as there was no rejection of the war guilt clause as part of the process, more moderate views have risen to the fore. The real benefit of the Plan was that it would ensure the withdrawal from the Rhineland and free Germany from that provision of the Treaty. Germany would be free to put her economy in order. With the reductions in reparations and much better management of the economy and taxation by the present government there should not be an issue there. A short-term American loan would also improve the payments to Britain, France and Belgium. There will be a time when foreign governments cease to impose these terrible burdens on the German people, and we will see this Plan merely as another step on the process of ending the mutilated 'peace' of Versailles.

From an article by the President of the Reichsbank who negotiated the Young Plan on the part of Germany, 1930.

SOURCE B

Our Plan achieved much. Germany's debts have been massively reduced. They went from one-third to one-quarter of what they were under the Dawes Plan. That was a great reduction. We got all foreign control out of Germany. Nobody wants a foreign controller in their country, that was great too. We put Germany on her own. All the atmosphere of war and the machinery of the hated Versailles have disappeared. The next thing is the amount of burden put upon Germany. Lots of newspapers say that we still have put on Germany a much greater burden then she can bear. That is nonsense. The British and the French have got huge national debts because of the War, the Germans have hardly any. The depreciation of the mark has wiped it out. The Germans will owe America some money for a while, not pleasant, but quite bearable.

From an article by a member of the American team who negotiated the Young Plan, 1931.

CONTINUED

a Compare the two views of the Young Plan and its impact on Germany.

b Look at the provenance of the two sources, the authors, their positions, the dates of publication. What reservations might you have about the validity of what they wrote? Why might their views have particular value to a historian?

Aims and impact of international proposals, treaties and conferences

With a background of economic recovery and increasing political and social stability in much of Europe in the later 1920s, serious attempts were made both to solve some of the problems left by the peace treaties and to put into practice some of the ideals which the League of Nations represented. Some attempts at problem solving, such as the Locarno Treaties, were successful (at least in the short term), while those which attempted to put the ideals of the League's Covenant into practice, such as the Geneva **Protocol**, had limited success.

KEY TERM

Protocol: A written proposal which, if agreed by all nations, would become a binding agreement.

The Geneva Protocol, 1924: support and opposition

One unfortunate failure was the Geneva Protocol of 1924. The prime minister of Great Britain, MacDonald, proposed this plan, with French support. MacDonald had been a pacifist (someone who believes in peace and is unwilling to fight) and had refused to fight in the First World War. The Geneva Protocol was a highly idealistic plan. Its aim was that all future disputes between nations would be dealt with by the League of Nations Permanent

Figure 2.25: League of Nations members waiting to hear proposals from the British prime minister, Ramsey MacDonald, about the Geneva Protocol in 1924.

Court of Justice (See Section 2.2). The rulings of the Court would be final. All nations collectively would have to enforce these rulings, by sanctions or by force if necessary. The proposal meant that one nation might have to send soldiers to fight in a dispute that did not affect it in any way. The intention was to encourage disarmament and increase security for nations. It would add real power and authority to the League of Nations.

Although it passed the Assembly when it was first proposed, the Geneva Protocol failed the following year. Playing a large part in the opposition was the new British foreign secretary whose party had replaced MacDonald's in power at the end of 1924. Nations were not prepared to give up their right to act in their own interests if they wanted to. The fact that Russia, Germany and the USA were not in the League made it probably unworkable as well.

The Locarno Treaties, 1925

The resort of Locarno in Switzerland was the setting for a series of agreements designed to improve stability and security in Europe. The original idea of holding the Locarno Conference came from Gustav Stresemann, the German foreign minister, who wanted to restore German prestige and privileges as a leading European nation. To achieve this, he was willing to accept some of Germany's losses in the Treaty of Versailles.

The most significant outcome of the Locarno Conference was that Germany, France and Belgium promised to respect their joint frontiers. This agreement meant that these borders in the west, agreed at the Paris Peace Conference, were jointly confirmed and accepted. Germany, France and Belgium could not take military action unless it was purely defensive.

In addition, a Treaty of Mutual Guarantee was agreed. This treaty stated that Britain and Italy would assist any country that suffered an act of aggression in violation of the Locarno Treaties. This meant that Britain promised to help France if Germany attacked it. So the agreement finally gave the French some of the security they had wanted for so long.

Mussolini's aggressive actions in Fiume and Corfu during 1923 had caused concern across Europe. At Locarno, Mussolini adopted a more cautious and diplomatic approach, creating good working relationships with representatives from Britain, France, Germany and Belgium. Despite his ambitious foreign policy aims, Mussolini recognised that, in the 1920s, Italy was in no position, economically or militarily, to challenge the major European powers, Britain and France. He also realised that as Italy was the only fascist nation and had a reputation for aggressive foreign policies, it was in danger of becoming isolated. In the 1920s, being isolated made a nation vulnerable. Mussolini played an important role in achieving the agreements reached at Locarno, gaining a reputation as a statesman with whom other European nations could safely negotiate. His involvement was a sign that Mussolini's Italy was being accepted by the other leading European nations as a major power. Even if Italy was not yet either 'great' or 'feared' as Mussolini hoped, at least it was 'respected'.

The Locarno Conference seemed to mark a major turning point in international affairs, symbolised by the effective working relationship that had developed between Stresemann and **Aristide Briand**, the French foreign minister.

KEY FIGURE

Aristide Briand (1862–1932)

Aristide Briand was a leading French statesman in the 1920s. He was prime minister several times in the early 1920s and foreign secretary from 1926 to 1932. Briand was always determined to make the new international system work, both for France and in the interests of peace.

To emphasise Germany's good intentions towards France, Stresemann accepted the permanent loss of Alsace, Lorraine, Eupen and Malmédy. In doing so, he hoped to win assurances from Germany's former enemies that there would be no further attacks such as the invasion of the Ruhr. Germany promised that the Rhineland, the area nearest France, would remain demilitarised – in other words, that it would not place its own troops there. This was extremely important to France. The talks also enabled Germany to be accepted as a member of the League of Nations in 1926.

The treaties were greeted with relief and enthusiasm across Europe. One British politician suggested that while 'The Great War ended in 1918, the Great Peace did not begin until 1925'. The three foreign ministers who negotiated them, Chamberlain of Britain, Briand of France and Stresemann of Germany, were awarded the prestigious Nobel Peace Prize in 1926.

Achievements

In some areas the Locarno Treaties were a real success. Germany was now restored to equality with the other major powers, and it was clear that Germany was negotiating with Britain and France to maintain peace in Europe. Germany was now a member of the League of Nations and could play a role in resolving further disputes, and (it was hoped) upholding the Covenant of the League. The borders between France and Germany and between Belgium and Germany were guaranteed. Mussolini seemed to be playing a more responsible role in European international relations than previously. There was a widespread feeling in Europe that tensions had relaxed, and that the Locarno Treaties were a reason for optimism.

Failures

However, the Locarno Conference did not achieve lasting success. Stresemann was able to hide his strong revisionist aims. Although he guaranteed Germany's western boundary, he made no promise about Germany's eastern borders. He was still determined to overturn the Treaty of Versailles in the east, and Germany's entry to the League and seat on the Council put him in a strong position to do that. France and Britain were only interested in the western boundary guarantee and appeared unconcerned about what happened to the east of Germany. This apparent concession to Germany over the eastern borders angered several of the new nations in Eastern Europe, such as Poland and Czechoslovakia, who felt threatened by it. This anger weakened the chances that these countries might ally with France to limit German expansion.

German public opinion was against the Locarno Treaties. Many Germans felt that Stresemann had made too many concessions. German resentment led to the growth of strongly nationalistic and increasingly aggressive political parties in Germany.

In addition, the treaties were negotiated independently of the League of Nations. Many people felt that this weakened the League. The organisation set up to keep the peace had played no part in what some people saw as a major step towards peace.

ACTIVITY 2.26

Look carefully at the Dawes Plan and the Locarno Treaties.

a Copy and complete the table for each one to identify the benefits to international relations in one column, and possible criticisms or failings in the other.

	Benefits	Problems
Dawes Plan		
Locarno Treaties		

b Did either the Dawes Plan or the Locarno Treaties do anything more than just bring some short-term gains? Did either bring any real long-term benefits? Should one be seen as much more important than the other?

ACTIVITY 2.27

SOURCE A

Figure 2.26: Europe making a positive step forward. A British cartoon from 1925 by David Low. A female figure with the word 'EUROPA' on her skirt is stepping from one rock to another. The rocks in the bottom left say 'Dawes' then 'Locarno'. The one in the bottom right says 'Disarmament'.

CONTINUED

SOURCE B

Figure 2.27: Depicted, from left to right, Briand, Austen Chamberlain (British foreign secretary) and Stresemann. A British cartoon from 1925 by the same cartoonist as Source A (David Low).

Study the cartoons in Figure 2.26 (Source A) and Figure 2.27 (Source B), by a British cartoonist, on the Locarno Treaties.

a In Source A, who does 'Europa' represent?

b In Source A, what is the link between Dawes, Locarno and Disarmament?

c In Source B, why has the cartoonist shown the three characters standing on pieces of paper?

d In Source B, what is the cartoonist suggesting about Briand's attitude to the treaties?

e In Source B, what is the cartoonist suggesting about Chamberlain's role in the treaties?

f To what extent is the cartoonist making a different point about the treaties in the two cartoons?

The Kellogg–Briand Pact, 1928–29

The Kellogg–Briand Pact was another attempt in the 1920s to reduce international tension and achieve some of the hopes of the peacemakers of 1919. The pact was the work of the long-serving French foreign minister, Briand.

Purpose

Despite the Locarno agreements, the French still felt insecure. In 1927, Briand proposed a pact between France and the USA to outlaw war altogether. Initially, US President Calvin Coolidge and Frank Kellogg (the US Secretary of State, who was in charge of foreign affairs) opposed the idea. Coolidge belonged to the Republican party, the party that had opposed Wilson's Treaty of Versailles and US membership of the League. Coolidge and Kellogg were concerned that such an agreement might force the USA to intervene if France was threatened. However, the USA did not wish to seem opposed to international peace, so it agreed to be involved, on the condition that all other major nations took part, too, and that no direct American commitment would result from any agreement.

The result was the Kellogg–Briand Pact of 1928, which was subsequently signed by over 60 nations, including the USA, France, Britain, the USSR, Germany, Italy and Japan. The Kellogg–Briand Pact officially came into effect on 24 July 1929. By signing the pact, nations renounced war and agreed to settle disputes by peaceful means. For France, the pact appeared to provide protection from future German aggression. For Germany, the USSR and Japan, the pact offered international recognition as equal and trustworthy partners. Britain saw the pact as another way of preserving international peace and stability, separate from the League of Nations. All countries agreed on the aim of having no more wars and settling disputes peacefully.

Limitations

The pact did not indicate what steps might be taken against a country that broke the agreement. The USA only signed the pact on condition that the USA retained the right to self-defence and would not have to act against any nation that broke the agreement. It was easy for Kellogg to sign the pact, as the USA made no formal commitment and retained its isolationist policy. In practice the Kellogg–Briand Pact was worthless.

Figure 2.28: French Foreign Minister Aristide Briand (seated left) and American Secretary of State Frank Kellogg (seated right), the architects of the Kellogg-Briand Pact. Who do you think was the intended audience for this photograph?

The Hague Conference, 1929, and the dispute over the evacuation of the Rhineland

The Hague Conference finalised the details of the Young Plan (see earlier in this section) and ended French occupation of the Rhineland five years earlier than had been planned under the Treaty of Versailles. All French troops were evacuated (taken away). Despite its success in these areas, the Conference revealed that France and Britain still disagreed over many issues, and that Germany continued to feel anger at the remaining reparations and some of the terms of Versailles. Nevertheless, the Hague Conference was a good example of how nations could work together to solve major problems.

Developing relations between the major powers

As a result of the agreements reached in the period 1924–29, relations between the major powers were significantly improved. However, underlying tensions remained.

France and Germany: the role of Stresemann and Briand

Both Stresemann and Briand had been leaders of their countries before becoming foreign ministers. Both men played an important part in achieving a working relationship between their countries and dealing with the problems that remained after 1924, including the issue of reparations. Both men faced serious domestic challenges to their apparently conciliatory policies towards each other's country. Many people in France disliked making any concessions to Germany. Many people in Germany hated the Treaty of Versailles and wanted to destroy all the terms that the treaty had imposed on Germany.

France's new spirit of cooperation with Germany was clearly reflected in the Locarno Treaties, the Kellogg–Briand Pact and the Young Plan, which were largely due to the influence of Briand. However, Briand ensured that French security was always emphasised. Like many in France, he remained suspicious of German intentions. Briand continued the policy started with the Little Entente of 1921, signing further treaties with Romania in 1926 and Yugoslavia in 1927, which resulted in a network of alliances in eastern Europe. Briand also strongly encouraged the development of an effective League of Nations. Neither strategy was particularly effective. France's Little Entente partners were relatively weak and it soon became clear that the League of Nations only had the power to enforce its decisions on minor issues.

Arguably Stresemann was both more dominant and more successful than Briand. He played a key role in enabling Germany to take a more critical part in international relations, including gaining membership of both the League and its Council. He was also able to pursue a clearly revisionist policy and reduce reparations at the same time. Stresemann was a central figure in the negotiations over the Dawes and Young Plans, which were very beneficial to Germany. He managed to avoid giving any promises that Germany's eastern borders could not be changed.

Both Briand and Stresemann were awarded the Nobel Peace Prize for their work at Locarno for helping the cause of peace. Possibly Stresemann deserved it less than Briand. A determinedly revisionist Germany grew in strength.

ACTIVITY 2.28

Working in pairs, draw up a plan for the question 'Stresemann did more harm than good to international relations between 1924 and 1929'. How far do you agree?

- a Identify areas where Stresemann did 'harm' and then 'good', thinking carefully about what those two words mean in the context of the period.
- b Make sure each factor you identify, for example the Locarno Treaty, fits into one of the two categories and that you can explain it.
- c Try to reach a firm judgement for which you can argue a good case.

Italy and the impact of Mussolini's ambitions on international relations

One country seemed to threaten the prospect of peace in Europe. By 1929 Mussolini had become a dictator in Italy. He was encouraging an aggressive nationalism as his foreign policy. When he was trying to gain power in Italy in the early 1920s, Mussolini had become popular by promising to revise the Treaty of Versailles in Italy's favour. He had presented the treaty as a 'mutilated peace' which had not given Italy the rewards it deserved. Mussolini's aggressive tendencies had become clear in the Fiume and Corfu affairs and in his hostility to some of the principles of the Covenant of the League of Nations.

Mussolini appeared as a European statesman in his work on the Locarno Treaty, but by the late 1920s he was clearly trying to widen his appeal to the Italian people. He did all he could to increase the Italian army and navy – this was not in the spirit of the League or of keeping the peace. He made aggressive speeches stating that the Mediterranean ought to be 'an Italian sea' ('Mare Nostrum', literally 'our sea') and these speeches worried the British, who had colonies in the Mediterranean. Mussolini also had territorial ambitions towards Yugoslavia and Albania. He began to increase Italy's control over Libya, which the British felt might threaten their control over the important Suez Canal. He wanted to expand the Italian Empire in East Africa.

While France remained sympathetic to Mussolini's ambitions (always looking for support against Germany), Britain and countries that wanted to uphold the Covenant, were less sympathetic. However, by the end of the 1920s it was mainly talk on Mussolini's part, and no action.

Shifting relations with the USSR

The USSR remained largely isolated throughout the 1920s while the Bolshevik regime established itself in power and possible leaders struggled for supremacy. There was a major debate within Russia in this period about whether the government should focus on developing socialism within the USSR itself (a policy known as 'socialism in one country') or on spreading socialism in other countries. It became clear by 1929 that the focus would be on developing socialism within the USSR. This direction led to a change in attitude towards the USSR, as European countries saw the USSR as less of a threat to capitalism and democracy. However, although Britain, France and Italy had restored diplomatic relations with the USSR by 1924, these countries still feared the spread of communism. In particular, the USSR's close relations with Germany following the Rapallo Pact in 1922 caused concern across Europe. The USA also distrusted the USSR and did not establish diplomatic relations with it until 1933. The Russians still resented the fact that they had not been allowed to attend the Paris Peace Conference or join the League of Nations. They increasingly saw the League as a means of preserving the international power and influence of Britain and France.

French relations with Russia also remained tense. Although France restored formal diplomatic relations with Russia in 1924, it made little attempt to improve the relationship. France had been deeply concerned about the Rapallo Pact. The French believed that this treaty would increase the risk of revolution spreading from communist Russia and would also assist German economic and political recovery. French concerns increased in 1926 when Russia and Germany signed the Treaty of Berlin, extending the Rapallo agreement for a further five years.

Fear of revolution was always a major factor when European powers considered their relationship with Russia. Nevertheless, by 1929 European countries were beginning to accept that the communist regime in the USSR was there to stay and that perhaps it was less of a threat than they had feared. There was a feeling that the time had come to permit the USSR to play a greater role in European affairs. However, by 1929 a new leader had emerged in Russia: **Joseph Stalin**, a ruthless dictator whose views on foreign policy had a major influence on the course of international relations in the next decade.

KEY FIGURE

Joseph Stalin (1878–1953)

After the death of Lenin in 1922, Stalin started a long campaign to succeed him. By 1929 he had achieved this and he then ruled Russia as a dictator. He was probably one of the most ruthless and brutal dictators of modern times. His main concern between 1929 and 1935 was to modernise Russia and build up its economy and armed forces.

Improved relations: reality or illusion

In terms of reducing international tension, it appeared that considerable progress had been made between 1924 and 1929. Prior to 1924, the League of Nations had already been successful in settling several border disputes. By 1929, France was beginning to adopt a less hardline approach towards Germany, even to the point of accepting reduced reparations payments under the Young Plan. Germany had formally accepted at least some of the terms of the Treaty of Versailles, and the Locarno Conference seemed to symbolise a new era of friendly relations within Europe. All the major powers had renounced war by signing the Kellogg–Briand Pact – these even included the USA, which had steadfastly refused to join the League of Nations.

However, there was still some progress to be made. For example, the French still deeply distrusted Germany and they had accepted the Young Plan largely because of international pressure. Tensions remained.

The European powers

Reviewing international relations in 1929 in Europe, there were grounds for both optimism and pessimism. The creation of the League of Nations had provided a system for preventing war and solving disputes between nations. Some potential conflicts had been avoided, and territorial disputes settled. Problems such as reparations had been overcome. Countries had, to some extent, recovered from the terrible social and economic impact of the First World War. Autocracies had gone and working democracies were being established. While there was still unhappiness at the way in which boundaries had been drawn between nations in central and eastern Europe, these boundaries were gradually being accepted and made to work. The hatred between France and Germany was declining and a working relationship was being established. The threats from Russia and communism seemed to be lessening as well. There was still a desire to revise the Treaty of Versailles, but there seemed to be less anger about it.

There were also grounds for pessimism. The League had not always succeeded in solving disputes, and some weaknesses in its ability to solve problems had emerged. Several major treaties had been signed without the League's involvement, and it was clear that nations would often put their own interests ahead of the League's hopes of maintaining peace. Major powers such as America and Russia were still not members of the League. Liberal democracy was not making much progress in Europe and authoritarian and aggressively nationalistic governments were emerging. Strongly nationalist political parties that disliked the idea of the League were also developing in some countries. In Europe, much depended on the willingness of able statesmen to work together to maintain the peace.

KEY CONCEPT 2.3

Change and continuity

Historians study patterns of development over time, identifying and analysing areas of continuity and areas of change. Reflect carefully on the attitude of both Britain and France towards Germany, their former enemy, in the 1920s.

- How much continuity of policy was there?
- Was there any fundamental change of policy?
- If there was continuity, why did this happen?
- If there was change, why did it occur?

Look also at the attitudes of France, Britain and Germany towards the USSR in the 1920s, remembering that in the First World War Russia had been an ally of Britain and France and an enemy of Germany.

- To what extent was there change in the attitudes of France, Britain and Germany?
- Was there continuity of policy?

Japan and the USA

In East Asia there were signs of growing tension. Democracy was weak in Japan and an aggressive, nationalist, expansionist militancy was growing, determined to expand out from Japan and colonise other countries. Japan was aiming to gain both China and parts of South East Asia, which had the raw materials its economy needed. Japan's intentions worried both the British and the French, who had colonies there. The USA, too, increasingly saw Japan as a threat, because of the USA's vast commercial interests in the region and its colonial possession in the Philippines. There were growing concerns about China's weakness and the probability that Japan would become the dominant power in East Asia. The Washington Naval Conference had weakened the American and British navies but permitted the Japanese navy to expand. Japanese shipyards were producing a growing fleet of battleships and aircraft carriers (an important new weapon of war).

Immediate impact of the Wall Street Crash

In 1929 an economic crisis occurred in the USA which suddenly ended the improvements in international relations. In October, the American stock market crashed. Thousands of American citizens were financially ruined. Many banks were forced to close down as people rushed to withdraw their savings. This was the Wall Street Crash. Severe economic depression set in – first in America and then around the world. After the First World War, the USA had replaced Britain as the economic powerhouse of the world, and its loans and investments were crucial to European economic health. Stock markets and prices collapsed throughout the world, and especially in Europe.

Unemployment soared in Germany, France and Britain. Poverty grew. Economic instability led to social instability, which led, in turn, to political instability. **Right-wing** politicians who had little time for democracy or the ideals of the League of Nations now had powerful arguments to win over voters. Democracy had failed them. International relations in Europe and East Asia changed fundamentally after 1929, and this economic crisis was a driving force behind that change.

KEY TERM

Right-wing: Describing people or groups, often strong nationalists, whose political beliefs are based on an ordered society that values tradition and discipline. They usually oppose socialism and communism, believing that social inequality is natural and desirable, and because both pose a threat to private property.

FINAL STOCK QUOTATIONS ON PAGES 38, 39, 40, 41 THIS EDITION

Complete Wire Reports of UNITED PRESS, The Greatest World-Wide News Service

The Pittsburgh Press

STOCKS EXTRA
Complete Markets

FIFTY-TWO PAGES — PITTSBURGH, PA., THURSDAY, OCTOBER 24, 1929 — THREE CENTS

SELLING PANIC WRECKS STOCK EXCHANGE; NEW YORK FRENZIED

Grundy Defends Lobbying

PITT, TECH, W. & J. COMMERCIALIZE SPORTS, IS CHARGE

American colleges and universities are commercializing sports and athletics on a large scale, according to charges made today by the Carnegie Foundation for the Advancement of Teaching.

Several schools in Pittsburgh and Western Pennsylvania are named in the report of the Foundation.

Briefly, the charges are that universities and colleges are maintaining students through their courses in return for their athletic ability.

Only 28 of 112 schools investigated are found to be "simon pure" in the matter, according to the Foundation's report, which covers 369 pages.

Denial of "athletic subsidy" was made by University of Pittsburgh officials, but Dr. Thomas S. Baker, Carnegie Institute of Technology, admits that the sport "has taken on some of the aspects of big business."

Cause of Shooting

REGARDS WORK AS FULFILLING PARTY PLEDGE

Senators Listen Unwillingly to Tariff View Exposure.

WILDEST DAY IN HISTORY OF MARKET RUINS SCORES; LOSSES TO BE IN BILLIONS

Leading Financiers Frantically Call Conference As Sales Break All Known Records; Threaten To Close Exchange; Almost Every Stock on List Hard Hit.

By W. W. Forster,
Press Financial Editor.

In the wildest day in stock market history with tickers running over three hours late, sales being chalked up at the astounding rate of 16,000,000 shares per day and with rumors of the closing of the New York stock exchange, billions of dollars were wiped from security values and huge fortunes literally blown away as market panic reigned today.

At 3 p. m. sales for the day had crossed the 12,000,000 mark and at the close were announced as 12,880,900. Indications were that the tickers would not halt finally before 7 p. m.

The market closed the day, a battered hulk. A stock panic surely was in progress and consternation gripped Wall Street, despite a spirited rally in the last hour of trading.

Rumors were flying thick and fast and so furious was the activity on the floor of the New York exchange that officers of the institution considered halting activities.

PANDEMONIUM MARKS SELLING AVALANCHE.

There was a literal avalanche of selling. Frenzied traders fought on the floor to sell their holdings at the best available figure. They paid little heed to prices. It was pandemonium and no mistake.

Rumors of financial disaster, of stock exchange firms being in a shaky position, of government intervention and similar stories shook the exchange to its very foundation.

A report from the treasury department at Washington that the market's decline was not due to unsound business conditions, had only a momentary effect. The list again plunged down until paper losses stood at a reported figure of $10,000,000,000.

The seriousness of the market situation was made more tense when it was announced that a conference was being held in the offices of the J. P. Morgan Co. to take immediate action

RACE RESULTS

LAUREL.

FIRST SNOW HERE

Downfall Accompanies Sud-

Figure 2.29: An American newspaper headline on the Wall Street crash of October 1929.

ACTIVITY 2.29

Consider the proposition:

'There was a real improvement in international relations between 1924 and 1929.'

Form two groups.

- **a** One group should argue that there was a real improvement.
- **b** The other group should argue that there was not.
- **c** Each group should research the issue and prepare their argument. Make sure that you cover all areas, including East Asia and the Middle East as well as Europe and the Americas.
- **d** Be prepared to present a clear (and obviously one-sided) argument lasting no more than ten minutes. Take care to identify the points which your opponents might make against you and think about how you can challenge them.

Practice questions

Source-based question

Read the sources and then answer **both** parts of the question.

SOURCE A

I have always been a sincere advocate of an agreement between the leading nations to set up the necessary international machinery that would bring about a practical abolition of war. But it is inadvisable to join a League of Nations that would make it necessary for the USA to maintain a standing army. This would be needed to support new and independent governments that it is intended to establish among semi-civilized people. This could involve the USA in wars in Europe, Asia and elsewhere. Rather, we should disarm the defeated nations and then follow the example by disarming ourselves. If the world is disarmed there will be no more world wars. Nations should be left entirely independent to decide their own affairs.

From a letter written by Senator George Norris (Republican) to an American newspaper, the *Nebraska State Journal*, 18 March 1918.

SOURCE B

The Republicans are trying to defeat the plan for a League of Nations, which, if organised, will reduce military armament among all the great powers, and make war almost, if not completely, impossible. If the Senate destroys the League of Nations, then the USA must begin at once to arm on a greater scale than any other nation in the world, because we must be strong enough to beat all comers. This means a navy in the Atlantic big enough to overcome the combined navies of at least three European powers. It means a navy in the Pacific bigger than Japan. It means the greatest standing army we have ever had. If we want to promote human slaughter and increase taxation, we should defeat the League of Nations. If we must abandon the glorious ideas of peace for which this nation has always stood, we must do so with full knowledge that the alternative is wholesale preparation for war.

From a public speech by Senator William G. McAdoo (Democrat), 1919.

SOURCE C

An American cartoon, published in 1919, commenting on the implications of joining the League of Nations.

SOURCE D

I am in favour of the League of Nations Covenant, of which our gallant and noble President is the proposer. I believe Mr. Wilson will be able to accomplish the fulfilment of the Covenant despite all opposition. The League of Nations idea is a very delicate matter to handle, and no-one but our President, who possesses the necessary qualities, could really be at the head of it. The abuse and discredit given to our President by the Republicans would make one imagine that these men lack intelligence. They know the Covenant is good for humanity; they should boost the League instead of criticising it. Their criticism of every move President Wilson makes implies that they are foolish or influenced by political motives. The League of Nations will alleviate all

CONTINUED

unrest, discontent and anxiety, and will make the world safe for democracy. The League would promote commerce, civilisation and brotherly love. I sincerely hope our President sees his way clear, and happy will I be the day the Covenant is accomplished and put into operation.

From a letter to an American newspaper, the *Evening Public Ledger* (Philadelphia), 28 March 1919.

1 a Read Sources **A** and **B**.

Compare the views of Senators Norris and McAdoo on whether the USA should become a member of the League of Nations. **[15 marks]**

b Read **all** of the sources.

To what extent do Sources A to D support the view that the League of Nations would be more likely to cause wars than prevent them? **[25 marks]**

Essay-based questions

Answer **both** questions. Answer **both** parts of each question.

2 a Explain why the Dawes Plan was developed in 1924. **[10 marks]**

b 'The Locarno Treaties of 1925 greatly reduced tension between European nations.' How far do you agree? **[20 marks]**

3 a Explain why France occupied the Ruhr region of Germany in 1923. **[10 marks]**

b 'The structure of the League was the main reason for its weakness in the 1920s.' How far do you agree? **[20 marks]**

Improve this answer

1 b Read **all** of the sources.

To what extent do Sources A to D support the view that the League of Nations would be more likely to cause wars than prevent them? **[25 marks]**

The sources do support the view to some extent that the League would cause wars, but they also make some points which suggest that they might help prevent them. On the whole they are not really in favour of America joining the League.

This is not a very strong opening paragraph. Using phrases such as 'to some extent' and 'on the whole' and 'not really' suggests vagueness and indecision. The student should either come up with a firmer answer – or simply get on with the analysis of the sources and leave the 'firm' answer to a reasoned conclusion at the end of the response.

Source A is a letter from a Republican Senator in March 1918. In it he suggests that joining the League might be a good idea in principle – it might lead to the 'abolition of war'. However, he also feels that it would mean that America had to keep a large army and could lead to America getting involved in wars in Europe and Asia. He suggests that a better solution would be to disarm the enemy and then America would disarm and there would be no more wars. So, the source does not entirely support the view.

This paragraph suggests some grasp of the source, with the comment about agreement in principle but that joining the League could lead to wars in practice. The response shows that the Senator is a little undecided on the point. However, there is no comment there at all about the provenance of the Source. What is the relevance of the date? There is no comment on the fact that he is a 'Republican' – or why it is relevant that the author is a Senator. The paragraph needs an evaluation of the source and also evidence of relevant contextual knowledge.

Source B is a speech by a Democratic Senator in 1919 and clearly supports the view. While Source A suggests that joining the League will mean that America has to build up its armed forces, this source argues the opposite. He feels that if America does not join it will have to increase its army and navy, seeing a threat from Japan. He argues that a failure to join means that 'the alternative is a wholesale preparation fo war.'

As with the preceding paragraph, this paragraph shows a sound grasp of the source and there is a good choice of relevant quotes. There is a clear link back to the question and it is all relevant. However, as with the description of Source A, there is a lack of comment on the provenance of the source. There needs to be contextual knowledge (background to the date) and serious source evaluation. What is the significance of the fact that it is a public speech by a Democrat – and also a Senator?

Source C is a cartoon which is clearly very hostile to the League of Nations and does not want America to join it. The League is represented as an angry-looking man whipping the horse marked 'peace'. The point about the 'affairs of the world' suggests that the League would lead to America getting more involved in world affairs which could mean being involved in wars as well.

This is slightly too descriptive of the cartoon, but the student has grasped the overall point that the cartoonist is making. There could be more explanation of the caption about the 'cart having precedence' and the signpost at the bottom of the cartoon. Comment about the significance of the date would help as well. The focus is descriptive rather than analytical. There needs to be more evidence of reflection on the source's provenance and validity.

Source D is a letter to a newspaper which strongly supports President Wilson and criticises his Republican opponents. The author argues that the Covenant 'is good for humanity' and 'will make the world safe for democracy.'

This is rather a brief comment which does shows a grasp of the source and has used some relevant quotes (and not just copied out large parts of the source!). However, it is not carefully linked to the question and needs a sharper focus. Again, it is descriptive and lacks evaluation and comment on the provenance. What is the value of the source? Does it make a strong point in opposing the view about causing wars?

In conclusion some of the sources support the view, and some do not, but the support side is stronger than the other.

This is a weak ending and does little more than repeat the opening paragraph. There is no 'right' way to answer this sort of question, but good responses demonstrate a sustained judgement from the start. Once you have carefully studied the sources, reflected on the provenance of all the sources and considered of the context of each source, then write a clear answer with broad reasons in the opening paragraph. Then, if you feel that the sources overall strongly support the view, follow that opening paragraph with full details of the sources that best support this judgement. Comment on the provenance and context of each source and fully evaluate it. Then write another paragraph discussing sources which do not support the view, again with comment on provenance and context, and suggest why you feel that case is weaker. Remember that you must use and evaluate every source.

When you have studied these comments, write your own answer to the question.

Improve this answer

3 b 'The structure of the League was the main reason for its weakness in the 1920s.' How far do you agree? **[20 marks]**

The structure of the League was a major reason for its weakness and for its inability to deal with some of the challenges that arose in the 1920s. While it was a good idea to require that decisions had to be unanimous, it was difficult to get any decisions made in practice. Different countries had different views on issues. However, there were other reasons for the League's weakness such as the absence of important countries from membership and that some countries on the Council acted too much in their own interests and not in the interests of keeping peace.

This is quite a good start. There is focus there – the question is clearly understood – and there are points made both for and against the statement. There is no sustained judgement yet, but the answer is going in the right direction. The analytical approach is good.

One of the major reasons for the League's weakness was the fact that all the decisions made by the Council had to be unanimous. This meant that a single member of the Council, for example France, could prevent any action being taken. For example, when France invaded the Ruhr, a breach of the League's Covenant, nothing could be done to stop the invasion or start any action against it, as France refused to vote for such an action. Also, the structure gave too much power to the Council, and too little to the Assembly, which represented all member nations. This gave the impression that the League was being run in the interests of the members of the Council and their nations. Another weakness was that, although designed to prevent war, the Covenant did allow members to go to war – war was not totally outlawed.

This is sound. It is clear what the paragraph is about – it is about the reasons for the League's weaknesses. There are good, clear, relevant points made and the information is accurate. It is perhaps a little theoretical? It would be helpful to provide one or two more facts to back up those points. The analytical approach is sound, and the paragraph shows understanding, but demonstrating some knowledge would improve the answer.

However, there were other reasons why the League proved to be weak, and those reasons were probably more important in explaining its weakness. One of the world's greatest powers, the USA, was not a member. Not only was the USA the major economic power in the world after 1918, it had showed its military strength in the First World War and was also a major power in the Pacific. Germany was not allowed to join until 1926, and the USSR was not allowed to be a member initially either. Having such major powers excluded was also a weakness. Many nations felt that the League was dominated by European nations, France and Britain, and they ran the League in their own national interests and not in the interests of peace. The failure of the League to deal effectively with problems such as Corfu and Vilna in the early years after its formation also weakened it. Mussolini simply ignored its instructions and did as he wished, and the Vilna affair showed that Council members put their own national interests ahead of those of the League's. It was seen often as being run by the winners of the war in the interests of the winners. Another problem which led to weakness was that it was very difficult for an elected politician, the British foreign secretary for example, to take a decision in the Council which might help bring peace, which would damage the interests of the country which elected and paid him.

This is good. Again, the paragraph's intention is clear from the start, and it also suggests that an answer about 'the main' reason is coming. The paragraph makes some very clear points – all relevant and accurate and (in contrast to the previous paragraph) backed up with good and relevant detail. The level of understanding is clear and there is no irrelevance in the paragraph. A little more supporting detail would help convince the reader that there was really an excellent grasp of the topic.

While the structure of the League did lead to weaknesses, these could have been overcome with goodwill and a lot of effort. However, with the absence of major nations from membership and the way in which national leaders put what they saw as the interests of their country ahead of trying to achieve the objectives of the League, it was always likely to fail.

This is good also. It does not just repeat what is said before but sums up the issue well. There is an answer there and it is well supported.

When you have studied these comments, write your own answer to the question.

SELF-EVALUATION CHECKLIST

After working through this chapter, complete the table.

You should be able to:	Needs more work	Almost there	Ready to move on
explain the problems faced by peacemakers in 1919			
discuss the solutions peacemakers proposed to the problems they faced during negotiations			
identify the terms of the peace treaties			
analyse the causes of opposition to the peace treaties			
examine the reasons for the creation of the League of Nations			
identify the challenges faced by the League of Nations			
describe the structure and role of the League of Nations			
analyse the successes and failures of the League of Nations			
explain the reasons for international tensions from 1920 to 1923			
identify crises that reflect international tensions in this period			
analyse the relationships between the major powers during the early 1920s			
discuss the reasons for economic recovery and the impacts of this on international relations			
identify the aims and outcomes of key international proposals, treaties and conferences in this period			
judge the extent to which international relations improved in the period from 1924 to 1929			
analyse the reasons for optimism in international relations in 1929.			

> Chapter 3

International history, 1929–39: the rise of extremism and the road to war

KEY QUESTIONS

This chapter will help you to answer these questions:

- How did the rise of extremism affect international relations?
- Why did the League of Nations fail to keep the peace in the 1930s?
- Why, and with what effects, did Britain and France pursue a policy of appeasement?
- Why did war break out in 1939?

Timeline

- **Sep 1931** Japan invades Manchuria
- **Feb 1932** Opening of the World Disarmament Conference
- **Jan 1933** Hitler becomes chancellor of Germany
- **Sep 1934** Russia joins League of Nations
- **Jan 1935** Return of the Saar region to Germany after a plebiscite
- **Mar 1935** Germany introduces conscription and begins open rearmament
- **Oct 1935** Italian invasion of Abyssinia
- **Mar 1936** German occupation of the Rhineland
- **Oct 1936** Rome-Berlin Axis (Italy and Germany)
- **Nov 1936** Anti-Comintern Pact (Germany and Japan)
- **Nov 1937** Italy joins the Anti-Comintern Pact with Germany and Japan
- **Mar 1938** Anschluss (union of Germany and Austria)
- **Sep 1938** Munich agreement over Sudetenland
- **Mar 1939** German occupation of Czechoslovakia
- **May 1939** Pact of Steel (Italy and Germany)
- **Aug 1939** Nazi-Soviet Pact
- **Sep 1939** German invasion of Poland/outbreak of Second World War

GETTING STARTED

Reflect on international relations between the ending of the First World War and the Young Plan of 1929.

a Identify what you think were the principal threats to peace in 1930.

b Explain which one you think was the most serious threat to peace – and why.

c Identify the strengths and weaknesses of the League of Nations as a peacekeeper and consider what was needed to enable it to play that role more effectively in the future.

Introduction

The gradual improvement in international relations from 1924 to 1929 owed much to the USA's economic strength and its willingness to lend money to other countries. For example, France accepted the Dawes Plan and withdrew from the Ruhr because American loans ensured that Germany would meet its reparations requirements. France's actions greatly reduced tensions between the major European nations, leading to agreements at the Locarno Conference in 1925 that seemed to guarantee future peace in Europe. The Young Plan also helped to resolve the difficult issue of reparations. By 1929 memories of the 1914–18 war were beginning to fade, and European economies were recovering. The tensions caused by the collapse of old empires, the creation of new nations and the redrawing of national boundaries had begun to ease.

However, the Wall Street Crash of October 1929 meant that the USA's post-First World War economic boom ended suddenly and dramatically. The Crash led to serious economic depression and unemployment, both in the USA and across the world. The period between 1929 and until about 1936 was known as the **Great Depression**. It had catastrophic effects on the global economy as US loans were called in and European countries were unable to pay their debts.

KEY TERM

Great Depression: The period between c.1929 and c.1936 when many national economies collapsed. There was rapid deflation, mass unemployment and serious poverty in almost every developed nation.

As the economic crisis worsened and poverty and hardship increased, many people became disenchanted with elected governments as they believed that these governments were incapable of solving their problems. Instead, they adopted extremist political ideas, such as the ideas of communism and fascism. At the same time, many middle-class people grew increasingly concerned about the adverse effects on their livelihoods of social disorder and the threat of revolution. They wanted governments capable of restoring order and protecting their interests.

Even in countries with well-established forms of constitutional government, such as Britain, France and the USA, support for fascist and communist organisations grew during the 1930s. In these countries, democracy was able to survive. However, in countries that lacked a strong democratic tradition, such as Germany, Japan and Spain, democratic forms of government collapsed.

Political extremism often led to aggressive nationalism that did little to encourage the League's ideas of disarmament and cooperation between nations. Dictators tried to gain popular support for their regimes by making territorial gains, while democratic nations were too involved in dealing with poverty and mass unemployment to worry about what was happening abroad. The 1930s was a troubled era.

KEY TERM

Political extremism: When people are attracted to radical political ideas such as fascism on the 'Right' or communism on the 'Left', rather than to liberal democracy.

3.1 How did the rise of extremism affect international relations?

The economic crisis resulted in large-scale unemployment, which in turn led to social unrest and political extremism in many countries. Popularly elected governments in democracies often struggled to cope with these challenges and some governments collapsed. Those that survived, such as in the USA and Britain, had to put economic survival and recovery before preserving peace abroad and maintaining good international relations. Voters wanted jobs and security for their families and they were less concerned about the wider issue of world peace.

Impact of the Great Depression on political ideologies and intentions

The Great Depression had worldwide effects. The political effects were especially far-reaching in Germany and Japan, but also had an effect on the foreign policies of democracies such as the United States and Britain.

The collapse of support for democracy and rise of Nazism in Germany

The impact of the Great Depression on political extremism and international relations is most obvious in **Adolf Hitler**'s rise to power in Germany. Hitler seemed an unlikely political leader as he was just one more unemployed soldier with a limited education and little hope of finding employment in 1919. However, his skill in delivering frenzied, almost hypnotic, speeches gained him a small group of supporters, and by 1921 he had become the leader of the National Socialist German Workers' Party (the Nazi Party). To begin with, its members were mainly the unemployed and soldiers returning from the First World War. These men were disenchanted and had little hope for the future so they might have turned to communism, but instead they were drawn to Hitler's magnetic speeches.

KEY FIGURE

Adolf Hitler (1889–1945)

Austrian-born Hitler moved to Munich in 1913 and won medals for bravery in the First World War. He later adopted an extreme right-wing nationalist outlook and joined the German Workers' Party (later the Nazi Party). After years of commanding only a tiny amount of support, Hitler's party grew in popularity and he was appointed chancellor of Germany in 1933, quickly establishing a dictatorship. His policies contributed to the outbreak of the Second World War in 1939.

Hitler was heavily critical of Germany's democratic post-war Weimar constitution. He argued that the constitution produced weak governments and poor leadership and that it was failing to deal with the growing threat of communist revolution. Hitler claimed that politicians had betrayed the country by seeking peace when Germany could still have won the First World War. These politicians had agreed to the humiliating Treaty of Versailles, which Hitler argued was the cause of all Germany's post-war problems.

Well-organised and violent gangs of Nazi supporters, known as **stormtroopers**, attacked the meetings of rival political parties. Far from hiding these violent methods, Hitler boasted about them. The authorities were so worried about the possibility of a communist revolution that they did little to stop them. When the head of the Munich police force was told that such gangs were causing bloodshed throughout the city, he replied that it was a pity there were not more of them.

In 1923, the Nazi Party attempted a 'national revolution', which is known as the Munich **Putsch**. The 'putsch' tried to take power in Germany and throw out the democratically elected government. The putsch was easily put down, and Hitler was arrested and sentenced to prison.

KEY TERMS

Stormtroopers: Nazi gangs that specifically used violence against Hitler's opponents.

Putsch: An attempt to overthrow a government using violence.

Hitler learned one important lesson from the Munich Putsch: to take power, violence did not work, and legal methods had to be used. He used his time in prison to put his ideas on paper, writing a book called *Mein Kampf* (*My Struggle*). The main ideas set out in the book later had a major influence on international relations when Hitler became Germany's leader. These ideas were:

- All the terms of the Versailles treaties should be rejected as far as they affected Germany.
- The Weimar government was to blame for Germany's defeat in 1918 (not the German army).
- Germany must rearm.
- Germany and Austria should unite in Anschluss.
- Germany should expand to the east.
- Communism should be destroyed.
- Jews were responsible for most of Germany's problems.

Hitler was released from prison in 1924 but initially struggled to find support for his ideas. American loans under the Dawes Plan of 1924 had helped to stabilise the German economy, and Germany was developing better relations with other European nations through the Locarno Treaties and Stresemann's work. With the situation improving in Germany, there was less support for a political party built on extremist views.

In the May 1928 elections the Nazi Party gained only 810 000 votes out of 31 million.

However, the Wall Street Crash and the ensuing worldwide depression breathed new life into Hitler's political career. American loans, on which Germany's new prosperity was entirely dependent, suddenly stopped. The country was plunged back into economic chaos. Deflation damaged the economy, and unemployment rose to over 6 million. The able Stresemann had died in 1929, and the Weimar government seemed unable to manage the economic crisis. Support for the Nazis began to grow as they seemed to offer hope to the millions of unemployed. In the elections of 1932, the Party gained 37% of the total vote. Although they still did not have an overall majority in the German parliament, the Reichstag, the Nazis had become the largest single party. On 30 January 1933, Hitler was appointed chancellor of Germany.

Hitler became chancellor of Germany mainly through legal and constitutional means, by exploiting the very weaknesses within the German constitution that he had strongly criticised. However he also cleverly used various illegal and often violent methods to damage his opponents. Once in the position of chancellor, it did not take Hitler long to remove all political opposition, end the constitution through which he had been elected and establish the **Third Reich**.

Germany became a one-party, **totalitarian** state founded on extreme nationalism and the use of violence to maintain order and obedience. If Mussolini had established the world's first fascist state in Italy, Hitler had created the second. He was then in a position to implement the ideas listed in *Mein Kampf*, and he had considerable support within Germany to help him to achieve this. Inevitably, his views on the Treaty of Versailles, joining with Austria, German rearmament and eastward expansion had serious implications for international relations in Europe.

KEY TERMS

Third Reich: The term used by Hitler that linked the present with Germany's past glories. The First Reich (empire) was the Holy Roman Empire (962–1806). The Second Reich followed the unification of Germany in 1871 and lasted until 1918.

Totalitarian: A system of government that is centralised and dictatorial and requires complete obedience to the state.

ACTIVITY 3.1

Working on your own or in pairs, consider these two questions:

a Explain why Hitler was able to rise to power in Germany.

b Explain why Hitler's rise to power in Germany was such a threat to international relations in 1933.

For both questions, try to identify at least three separate points which you feel are important to the answer. Put them in order of importance and make sure that each one is supported by relevant detail.

The collapse of democratic government and rise of militarism in Japan

Democracy had only recently arrived in Japan. The Japanese people were used to a system in which the emperor held supreme power, and they had little experience of parliamentary democracy, of government by consent. Many believed that politicians were weak, corrupt and open to bribery. As unemployment and poverty grew on a large scale following the Wall Street Crash and the growing world-wide depression, the Japanese blamed the elected government for their misfortunes. They looked to the military, always influential in Japanese public life and politics, for solutions to their problems.

In September 1931, against the wishes of Japan's elected government, the Japanese army took control over the whole of Manchuria, part of China (see Section 3.2). This event led to the collapse of democracy in Japan itself. With the government unable to control Japan's armed forces, the emperor, Hirohito, replaced it with a Government of National Unity dominated by the military. As a result Japan became a military dictatorship that clearly intended to expand further into Asia.

These military rulers knew that Japan was short of the raw materials required to expand its army and navy and needed to seize other territories in Asia to get them. This situation caused great concern in a weak, unstable and highly vulnerable China but it also threatened the regional interests of European nations and the USA. As in Germany, a new aggressive nationalist leadership in one country created instability in the whole region.

Figure 3.1: Japanese generals announcing their illegal seizure of Manchuria.

ACTIVITY 3.2

Working on your own or in pairs, consider these two questions:

a Explain the reasons for Italy's change of direction in foreign policy in the early 1930s.

b 'Hitler's rise to power in Germany in 1933 was the greatest threat to peace in the early 1930s.' How far do you agree?

For the second question, copy and complete this table. In the first column, identify the points you would make if you were arguing that Hitler's Germany was the greatest threat to peace. In the second column, list any other factors that threatened the peace (you might include countries/dictators, or broader factors such as the Great Depression or the collapse of democracy). Which do think would be the easier case to argue? Why?

Hitler's Germany was the greatest threat to peace	Other factors that threatened the peace

Pressure on Mussolini for a change of policy in Italy

From 1924 to 1934, Italy's foreign policy was relatively cautious and diplomatic, despite Mussolini's aggressive speeches. Italy had reason to fear Hitler's intentions, particularly his desire to form a union between Germany and Austria. One of Mussolini's major concerns was the post-First World War weakness of Austria. Austria was a neighbouring nation and its lack of political, economic and military strength meant that it would provide Italy with little protection if Germany regained its power and showed signs of aggression. A revival of German military strength and ambition seemed increasingly likely when Hitler's Nazi Party gained power. Consequently, Mussolini provided support to the anti-Nazi Austrian government of Chancellor Dollfuss in the early 1930s. When Dollfuss was murdered by Austrian Nazis in July 1934, Mussolini sent Italian troops to the border between Italy and Austria to try to prevent a possible German invasion of Austria. France and Britain praised Italy's actions highly. Both countries increasingly saw Mussolini as a potential ally against Hitler's Germany.

By 1934, Mussolini was widely respected abroad. He had developed good relationships with Britain and France, played an important role at the Locarno Conference, and helped to prevent Hitler's hopes of uniting Germany with Austria in 1934. However, little progress had been made towards achieving Mussolini's ambitious international aims which he had boasted about after he came to power. Italy was neither 'great' nor 'feared' as he had promised the Italian people. In the early 1930s, although Italy was not affected as badly by the Depression as some countries, it was still facing economic and social problems, and Mussolini's popularity with the Italian people was declining. Mussolini, therefore, felt himself under pressure to adopt a more prestigious and aggressive foreign policy. He needed a propaganda boost, some spectacular overseas success that would unite Italians behind him. Mussolini had been increasingly impressed by the way Hitler had begun challenging the Treaty of Versailles by 1935, and how his actions had increased his popularity in Germany. He also saw the weak response to Hitler's aggressive foreign policy by the League of Nations and by Britain and France in particular (see Section 3.2). Mussolini became increasingly convinced that a close relationship with Germany would benefit Italy more than strong relationships with Britain and France.

Mussolini, therefore, changed the direction of his foreign policy. Rather than fearing and resisting the resurgence of German power, he began to support it and to imitate it in many ways. The diplomatic approach he had adopted between 1923 and 1934 was replaced by aggression and an even greater desire for glory. His new policies added greatly to the growing sense of crisis that was developing in Europe in the 1930s.

US foreign policy: involvement or isolationism

The traditional view of American foreign policy during the period 1919–39 is that the USA chose to remain isolated from world affairs. The fact that it refused to join the League or ratify the peace treaties reinforces this idea. However, this view is misleading, at least to some extent. For example, the USA played a vital part in preventing starvation in parts of Europe in 1918 to 1919. In addition, leading members of US governments in the 1920s realised that much of American prosperity depended on the USA's overseas trade and business. These politicians accepted that the best way to protect and increase business was by cooperating with other countries in keeping the peace, so trade could move freely. They kept a watch on international activities that threatened American interests (for example, Japan's expansion into China).

'Involvement without commitment' had, therefore, become the basis of American foreign policy, with a focus on the USA's commercial interests. This policy meant that the USA did cooperate with the League of Nations to some extent in the 1920s. The Dawes and Young Plans were inspired by the USA and American money was crucial for the recovery of Europe. The USA was largely responsible for the Washington Naval Conference and US Secretary of State Kellogg worked with Briand to produce the Kellogg–Briand Pact of 1929.

However, US policy changed in the early 1930s. Economic depression and mass unemployment were devastating the USA by 1932. Ordinary Americans were not interested in foreign affairs. A new president, **Franklin Roosevelt**, came into power in 1933 and his focus was on dealing with the economic and social crisis he faced at home. Roosevelt had no specific foreign policy ambitions. He suggested that America should aim to be a 'Good Neighbour', which could be interpreted in different ways and committed the USA to nothing. Public opinion and many in the US Congress preferred to remain isolated from the growing tension in Europe. Fears of American soldiers dying overseas in foreign wars were very strong in America at the time.

KEY FIGURE

Franklin Roosevelt (1882–1945)

Roosevelt was president of the USA from 1933 to 1945. His early years in office were dominated by the Great Depression and mass unemployment in the USA. He was under considerable political pressure during the 1930s to adopt isolationist policies, although he personally disliked the fascist dictators in Europe and was worried about the rise of Japanese power.

Although a US observer attended the World Disarmament Conference of 1932 to 1934, he played little part beyond observing. In 1935, Congress passed the Neutrality Act, which ruled that the USA would neither take sides nor sell arms to other nations in any conflict elsewhere. America remained firmly neutral in the armed conflicts that broke out later in the 1930s. This policy was significant for world affairs. For example, if the USA had supported either side in the Spanish Civil War or when Italy invaded Abyssinia in 1935 (see Section 3.2), the outcome might have been different.

ACTIVITY 3.3

Figure 3.2: 'A Good Time for Reflection', a US cartoon published in 1938. Uncle Sam holds a list of reminders about world wars: American casualties, unpaid war debts, economic collapse. The menacing figure on the left rises out of Europe and represents a 'war threat'.

Look at the cartoon in Figure 3.2.

a How well does this cartoon represent American attitudes towards international relations in the 1930s?

b Explain the references to 'unpaid war debts' and 'economic collapse'.

Failure of the World Disarmament Conference, 1932–34

A major element of the Covenant of the League of Nations was the hope that nations would give up large armies and navies, to prevent future wars. The League's Disarmament Commission had been working towards this objective throughout the 1920s, with little success.

Reasons for the conference

One of the most important of Wilson's Fourteen Points had asked for nations to reduce their armaments and military to 'the lowest point consistent with domestic safety'. By signing the peace treaties and the Covenant of the League, many nations committed to the idea of disarmament, but the idea proved very difficult to put into practice. Attempts to control the arms trade broke down over arguments between nations that made guns (often at great profit) and nations that did not, while countries that wanted to buy arms for defence resented being prevented from doing so.

The League's Disarmament Committee had achieved little success in the 1920s. The Washington Naval Conference of 1921 to 1922 had made a start, but nations soon found ways around the rules laid down there. The USA had tried to organise another conference on naval disarmament in 1927, but France and Italy refused to attend, and Britain and the USA disagreed about what could and should be achieved. Attempts to organise a more general disarmament conference in the late 1920s had also failed, largely over divisions between the British and the French, when Germany demanded the right to rearm unless other nations disarmed. The British were quite sympathetic to this German demand, but the French premier later said in 1931, 'The British have this idea, both false and dangerous, that land armies like ours are dangerous as they prepare for war, while their navy has a moral value as it prevents war. We will oppose this viewpoint categorically and we will avoid allowing the British and their allies to dominate the world.' (This comment gives a good picture of the relationship between the British and the French, who were supposed to be allies.)

In 1930, Britain, the USA, Japan, France and Italy attended a naval conference in London which aimed to continue the disarmament work started by the Washington Conference. The conference resulted in the Naval Treaty of 1930, in which Britain, the USA and Japan agreed to restrict the size and tonnage of their navies, although France and Italy refused to sign.

Meanwhile, the League Disarmament Commission had been preparing for a global disarmament conference for several years, and in 1931 the League Council finally called for a World Disarmament Conference to meet in Geneva in 1932, often known as the Geneva Conference.

Figure 3.3: The meeting of the World Disarmament Conference, 1932.

Effect of international events

There was much optimism when the Conference began, chaired by a former British foreign secretary. Over 60 nations were represented – including the USA and the USSR, although neither were members of the League. However, early optimism was not fulfilled. Despite lengthy discussions, the conference failed to achieve any significant decisions regarding disarmament. A key reason for this is that the timing of the conference could not have been worse. Three separate issues arose during the conference, all of which undermined discussions about disarmament.

- The depression that followed the Wall Street Crash of 1929 was beginning to have serious and damaging social and economic effects across the world. Faced with mass unemployment and hunger, governments had to focus on internal politics and not international relations. Many countries wanted to maintain their armaments because of the threat of internal revolution.
- In September 1931, Japan's army started to take over Manchuria (See Section 3.2). The League of Nations ordered the army to withdraw, but Japan continued to invade. Japan, then left the League in March 1933, and no sanctions were applied against it, either military or economic. Other countries felt that they needed to maintain their own armaments to protect themselves, if the League of Nations was powerless to prevent such aggression. Second, as well as defying the League of Nations, Japan was increasing the size and strength of its navy, thus breaking the commitments it had made at the Washington Conference. This situation seriously threatened US interests in East Asia, so the USA was determined to maintain its armaments, particularly its naval fleet, to protect those interests.
- In January 1933, Hitler gained power in Germany, causing alarm across Europe. Hitler had always made it clear that he intended to destroy the Treaty of Versailles, restore Germany's power and prestige and rearm. His ambitions posed a threat to other European countries, which wanted to maintain their armaments as security against possible German aggression.

ACTIVITY 3.4

Figure 3.4: A cartoon in an American newspaper, 1933.

Look at the cartoon in Figure 3.4.

- **a** Given the date of the cartoon, what incident is the cartoonist referring to?
- **b** The paper in the fist says 'League of Nations' at the bottom and 'Nine Power Treaty' and 'Kellogg Pact' at the top. What is this referring to?
- **c** What point is the cartoonist making?
- **d** Using your own knowledge, is the cartoonist making a fair point?

The attitude of major powers, especially France and Germany

In 1933, the World Disarmament Conference was already disrupted by events in Manchuria, and Hitler continued to challenge the whole idea of disarmament. His argument was that Germany had reduced its armaments to the levels set out in the Treaty of

Versailles but that none of the other major European nations had reduced their armies and navies in line with the commitments they had made at the Paris Peace Conference. He claimed that Germany was in no position to defend itself against foreign invasion. Hitler, therefore, insisted that, if other countries were not prepared to disarm, Germany should be permitted to increase its own armaments in the interests of self-defence.

ACTIVITY 3.5

SOURCE A

It has been remarked that huge armaments are not in themselves the evils to be feared; armaments are merely symptoms of the poor health of the international community. Until substantial progress in the solution of current international problems has been made, the hopes of disarmament supporters will not be realized. Responsibility for the failure of disarmament will naturally be placed upon the delegates to the Geneva Conference. Responsibility should be charged to the resurgence of aggressive nationalism. So long as there remains the probability of armed conflict, Manchuria, Hitler, and Polish Corridor affording evidence – nations will naturally regard as suicidal any reduction of their armed forces. The current distrust of national ambitions unpleasantly reminds us of the 'armed peace' of 1914. I am not yet justified in passing final judgment upon the Conference. Disarmament precedents are few in number and may take some years to succeed. This Geneva Conference is but the first of a series of meetings and is making its appropriate contribution. The stage may be dark, and the curtain may be down, but it is only the start of a process which could lead to peace. What is concerning however, for those who wish the Conference to be successful, is the lack of co-operation between the two leading nations in the Conference, Britain and France.

From an article by a member of the American team representing the United States at the World Disarmament Conference, written in December 1932.

SOURCE B

The Professor, who had recently returned from Geneva where he had been a member of the British delegation to the Disarmament Conference, addressed the League of Nations Union in Manchester. He was deeply pessimistic about the possibility of any good outcome from the talks. The change of government in Germany, he felt, was going to have profound implications for peace in Europe, and events in the Far East were also going to result in an increase of tension there and the likelihood of more conflict. It was tragic that the growth of nationalist forces throughout the world was not dissimilar to the events which led to the crisis in 1914. He stressed that there had been real co-operation with our main allies to collectively work for peace and that both the British and the French were more than prepared to set an example there if it furthered the cause of disarmament. When questioned he did agree that arms themselves did not lead to wars, it was the leaders of those nations which possessed the weapons that caused conflict.

From an article in a British newspaper, 11 November, 1933.

Compare the views in the two sources on the World Disarmament Conference.

a Copy and complete this table to identify the similarities and the differences. Where do the sources agree and disagree?

Points of agreement	Points of disagreement

b What do the different dates suggest?

c Why might the nationality of the two delegation members influence their views?

d Why might you view the second source in a different light from the first one?

ACTIVITY 3.6

Figure 3.5: A British cartoon commenting on the work of the Disarmament Conference. The donkey says 'I suggest that the first article in the draft Convention for World Disarmament should provide for the filing down of the beaks of doves and the prohibition of lethal weapons like olive branches.' Doves and olive branches were traditional symbols of peace.

Look at the cartoon in Figure 3.5.

a What point is the cartoonist making about the League's Disarmament Conference?

b How far do you feel that this is a fair comment?

Hitler's argument seemed reasonable to some of the delegates at the Disarmament Conference. However, the French government were still concerned that any revival of German military power posed a serious threat to France and refused to consider any French disarmament. Hitler, therefore, withdrew Germany from both the Disarmament Conference and the League of Nations in October 1933. Germany's actions inevitably led to the collapse of the conference.

The World Disarmament Conference failed. It was not possible to bridge the gap between the ideals of the Fourteen Points and the Covenant of the League on the one hand, and the demands of national security felt by many nations, the ambitions of some leaders and aggressive nationalism on the other – especially against a background of a world depression and political instability. Tension in Europe and East Asia was rising again.

ACTIVITY 3.7

In 1918, the German people, trusting in the guarantees of Wilson's Fourteen Points, laid down their arms after four years of valiant resistance in a war they had never wanted. Germany supported the concept of the League of Nations more enthusiastically than any other

CONTINUED

nation. This is why the German people accepted the absurd conditions of the Treaty of Versailles. Having suffered most from the consequences of war, our people faithfully supported the idea of restructuring relations between nations in the interest of ridding the world once and for all of similar horrors. The German people were convinced that the League would lead to a general international reduction in arms. While Germany fulfilled its obligations to disarm, other nations failed to perform theirs. Surrounded by highly armed nations of war, Germany was completely at the mercy of any threat which any of them might pose. Given other nations' refusal to disarm, the German government could not remain in the League.

From Adolf Hitler, 'Proclamation to the German People', Berlin, 16 March 1935.

Working in pairs identify:

a the points that Hitler makes which can be challenged

b the points which could be seen as accurate.

ACTIVITY 3.8

Consider the question 'The World Disarmament Conference failed because of the actions of Hitler'. How far do you agree?

a Working in pairs, copy and complete the table. In column one, list the main reasons why Hitler should take responsibility for the failure of the conference. In the second column, list all the other factors/countries/individuals that should also share responsibility.

Hitler's responsibility	Other factors

b Reflect on the 'How far' part of the question. Should Hitler be seen as having the greater part of the responsibility, or was he just one factor amongst many others of equal, or even greater, importance?

Changing relationships between the powers

The 1930s saw rapid changes in the relationships between all the major European powers. France remained deeply concerned with its own security. Germany under Hitler was determined to break free of all the restraints imposed on Germany by the Treaty of Versailles. Italy was increasingly anxious to fulfil Mussolini's promises to recreate a 'Roman' empire. Britain, less concerned with Germany than France was, was keen to keep open its Mediterranean trade route, which ran past Italy through to the Suez Canal. Britain was seeing Japan as a growing threat to its empire in South East Asia and India. The USA also had concerns over Japan's aggression in China. International relations were moving into a new era in a period of rapid change.

The London Naval Conference, 1930

When France and Italy refused to sign the naval treaty that resulted from the London Naval Conference of 1930, this was an early indication of a shift in relations between the former allied powers. The growing disagreements between France and Britain over many issues limited the chances of united action against aggression. Italy under Mussolini was beginning to adopt a more independent and aggressive position and the whole ideal of disarmament, which was fundamental to the League, was being marginalised.

The Stresa Front, 1935: membership and purpose

Increasingly worried by the situation in Germany under Hitler, France was keen to secure Italian support to try to contain Germany. The French foreign secretary, Laval, visited Mussolini in January 1935. Records of the meeting are not clear. However, Laval returned to France with the impression that he had Italy's support against German expansion or aggression. In return France would not oppose Italian expansion in East Africa, provided it could be done 'peacefully'. Mussolini's impression of what was agreed was less clear about giving support against Germany. However, he was convinced that he had been given freedom to expand the Italian empire in East Africa, and did not remember that he should use 'peaceful' methods to do so. This misunderstanding later caused serious problems.

In April 1935, a follow-up meeting took place, in Stresa, Italy, between the prime ministers of Britain, France and Italy. This second meeting produced a declaration which stated that the three powers opposed any change in the peace treaties which might threaten the peace of Europe. The declaration became known as the Stresa 'Front'. It reinforced the Locarno Treaty and clearly aimed to put a brake on Hitler's expansionist ambitions.

On the surface, the Stresa Front looked like a determined effort to restrain Germany and keep the peace. Actually, the appearance of unity between the three powers lasted only a few weeks. The French were still angry with the British for not agreeing to guarantee military support if France was attacked by Germany and immediately made a Treaty of Mutual Assistance with Russia to gain a possible ally to the east of Germany. This treaty worried the British, who were always suspicious of Russia's communism and its possible spread.

Britain, seriously worried about Japan's naval expansion in East Asia, further damaged its relationship with France by then making an agreement with Germany. This was the Anglo-German Naval Agreement which allowed the German navy to expand to up to 35% of the size of the British navy. The agreement would enable Britain, short of money, to build up her Far East fleet to hold back Japan's navy, while spending little on her army. The French were furious at this concession to Germany. France wanted a strong British army able to support France if attacked by Germany. The Naval Treaty, a clear breach of Versailles, further damaged any hopes of disarmament and could be seen as further encouraging Hitler's ambitions.

ACTIVITY 3.9

Figure 3.6: A British cartoon of 1935. The barrel is labelled 'Collective isolation' and the document being read is labelled 'British separate navy deal'.

Look at the cartoon in Figure 3.6.

a Which three countries are represented by the men in the barrel?

b What point is the cartoonist making by 'If the barrel had been stronger, my story would have been longer'?

The Rome–Berlin Axis, 1936

In 1936, Germany and Italy signed an informal, but well-publicised, agreement that marked another shift in relationships between the major powers. Mussolini believed that the Stresa Front had given him permission to expand in East Africa and invaded Abyssinia in 1935 (see Section 3.2). Britain strongly opposed the invasion, as it was publicly anxious to uphold the principles of the League, and also concerned about the threat to its own colonies in East Africa. Mussolini was furious at Britain's response.

Mussolini was clearly influenced and impressed by the way in which Germany had walked out of the League and the Disarmament Conference. In addition, Hitler was supporting Italy's initiative in helping the Nationalists in the Spanish Civil War. So, Mussolini made an informal agreement with Hitler known as the 'Rome–Berlin Axis'. European politics would now revolve around an axis (or line) based on these two powers. Both Hitler and Mussolini felt that they would greatly benefit from agreement and mutual support, and they both had their own expansionist aims: Hitler in eastern Europe and Russia and Mussolini in the Balkans, the Mediterranean and North and East Africa. No binding commitments were made, and the agreement was perhaps more symbolic than substantial, but the agreement made it clear to Europe and the wider world that international relations were changing.

These changes were not in the spirit of the Covenant of the League – two fascist dictators were taking a very different direction from the aims of the League of Nations.

The Anti-Comintern Pact, 1936–37

Later in 1936, the 'Axis' agreement was widened when Hitler made a pact with Japan that became known as the 'Anti-Comintern Pact'. In 1937, Italy joined them. The apparent aim of this agreement was to destroy communism (the ideology spread by the Comintern), but the three powers had their own, unspoken, aims. Hitler wanted to destroy communism, but he also wanted to expand to the east and destroy Russia. He wanted the wheatfields, oil and iron ore that lay there. Japan wanted to be free to expand into China because it was angered by Russian military support for China and it also resented Britain's empire in the east. Italy wanted to expand its 'empire' and to weaken Britain, a potential obstacle to Italian expansion in Africa. Again, nothing specific was agreed between the nations, but the pact made it clear to the world that a new group of powers was emerging.

All these powers were authoritarian dictatorships with expansionist agendas and by December 1937 all of them had left the League of Nations (see Section 3.2).

Figure 3.7: A Japanese propaganda poster showing children's joy at the signing of the Anti-Comintern Pact. The children are waving the flags of Germany, Italy and Japan, and the photos are of the leaders of the three countries.

ACTIVITY 3.10

Either on your own or in pairs, consider these two questions:

- **a** Explain the importance of the Rome–Berlin Axis and the Anti-Comintern Pact.
- **b** Did the Rome–Berlin Axis and the Anti-Comintern Pact have the same, or different, objectives?

The changing nature of relations with the USSR and its impact on foreign policy

A central element of changing international relations between the two world wars was the role of Russia. Torn apart by revolution in 1917, followed by an even more violent civil war which ended with Bolshevik victory in 1921, Russia's place in world affairs had a strong impact on international relations. There were four broad phases in Russia's approach to foreign policy between 1919 and 1939.

1. **The Civil War period, 1919–24**. The Comintern was set up and there was a policy to spread communism and revolution to the rest of the world. This policy failed but gave many nations a lasting suspicion that world revolution was a long-term objective of Russia. During this period, the French, British, Japanese and Americans all sent troops and munitions to try to restore the tsarist system and destroy communism. The communist leadership in Russia never forgot these actions.
2. **Defensive isolation, 1924–34.** Internal economic growth and the rise of the dictator Stalin dominated this period. Exporting communism was not the main focus. The aim was to create 'socialism in one country', not world revolution. Hatred of the 'West' did not decline, but the USSR took every opportunity to gain formal recognition by other powers, to make neutrality and non-aggression pacts with them and, if possible, to achieve trade deals to help Russia industrialise.
3. **Threats from the East and the West, 1934–39.** By 1934, once Stalin had achieved absolute power in Russia, he turned his attention to foreign affairs. Stalin saw two potential threats to Russia. The first was from Germany, because of its strong anti-communist message and because of Hitler's determination to expand to his east and destroy Russia. The second lay in Japan's determination to expand into China and Manchuria and also to eliminate communism. The Anti-Comintern Pact of 1937 reinforced these concerns. Stalin feared a war against Russia on two fronts, east and west. This fear led him to try to gain support in the west against Germany.
4. **Aggressive isolation, 1939–41.** Stalin saw that the other powers were failing to contain Germany and sensed that his military forces were in no position to defend Russia against either Germany or Japan (and certainly not both) So, he made an agreement with Hitler in 1939 to buy himself time to rearm. In the late 1930s, always afraid that his own military might overthrow him, he had executed the majority of senior officers in the Russian army, navy and air force. His armed forces were leaderless and weak in 1939.

The Soviet response to the rise of Nazism

Stalin's Russia had good reason to be concerned by Hitler's rise to power. As the only communist country, the USSR felt isolated and vulnerable. Its only formal alliance was with Germany that had begun with the Rapallo Pact in 1922. In view of the German Nazi Party's strongly anti-communist views, this relationship was now under threat.

Russian security was similarly threatened. In his book *Mein Kampf*, Hitler had argued that the German population was too large for the boundaries in which it was constrained. His stated solution was **Lebensraum** (gaining living room), meaning that Germany would take land to the east to provide more space for the expanding German population. The implication was clear – Hitler's long-term intention was to take land from Poland and the USSR.

KEY TERM

Lebensraum: Literally 'living room'. Hitler dreamed of the German people expanding eastwards and dominating much of east and central Europe. He wanted the farmland and the natural resources in those regions, such as coal, iron ore and oil.

Russia was dominated by a single man, Stalin, and Stalin's fears and suspicions were the major influences behind Russia's foreign policy after 1934. When Stalin saw the successful aggressions of Japan, Germany and Italy, and the failure of the League to prevent them, he became increasingly concerned for Russia's security and attempted to work with Britain, France and other countries to contain Germany. During the 1930s, Stalin publicly reduced support for local communist parties in Britain and France and support for anti-colonial movements in British and French colonies. In 1934, Russia joined the League of Nations.

In 1935, Stalin agreed a treaty of mutual assistance with Czechoslovakia and another with France (the French formally agreed the terms in 1936). These treaties promised that if Germany attacked Russia, then France and Czechoslovakia would come to the aid of Russia. In return, Russia would support France or Czechoslovakia if Germany attacked them. Stalin was looking for allies to his west. During the Spanish Civil War which broke out in 1936 (see Section 3.2), Russia helped the Republicans, who were supported by local communists.

However, on four separate occasions in 1938 Stalin asked Britain and France to join Russia in an international conference to deal with the growing tension in Europe but was ignored each time. Later in 1938, when Russia was not invited to the Munich Conference over the Sudetenland (see Section 3.3), the suspicious Stalin became convinced that Britain and France were actively cooperating with Hitler's Lebensraum ambitions. He decided he had to adopt different policies to ensure Russia's security.

The Comintern and fear of communism

Stalin's attempts to gain allies failed because amid the social and economic chaos of the Great Depression, political stability was under threat in both Britain and France. Extremist political parties were growing in popularity, and revolution seemed a distinct possibility. Under these circumstances, the British and French governments viewed Stalin's communist Russia with distrust and fear. Many British politicians saw Stalin's Russia as a bigger threat than Hitler's Germany. The Comintern, with its commitment to spreading communism, had been a very active force during the 1920s. It had supported the growth of communist parties in countries like Germany and Italy throughout the 1920s, as well as in East Asia, encouraging anti-colonial movements in French and British colonies. The Comintern had also tried to influence working-class movements in countries like Britain, encouraging members of the working class to rise against their capitalist bosses. Although Stalin publicly ordered the Comintern to reduce its activities in the 1930s, in order to gain allies, the dislike of Russia remained.

ACTIVITY 3.11

Either on your own or in pairs, consider these questions:

a Was Russia a real threat to Britain and France in the 1930s?

b Can Russian foreign policy between 1924 and 1939 be seen as consistent?

c Were Britain and France justified in their approach towards Russia after 1929?

3.2 Why did the League of Nations fail to keep the peace in the 1930s?

During the 1920s, the League of Nations had successfully resolved a number of international disputes, as outlined in Chapter 2. However, these were relatively minor problems that did not directly involve any of the most powerful countries. The League's inability to deal effectively with events that involved one or more major powers quickly became obvious after 1930.

The response of the League to major crises

It was events in East Asia that put the League and its Covenant to their first real test.

Manchuria, 1931–33

Japanese expansion in East Asia concerned the USA and European nations that saw Japan's increasing interests in China as a threat to their own trading rights. Their concerns were increased in 1931, when Japanese forces invaded Manchuria, an area of China in which Japan had extensive trading rights.

China appealed to the League of Nations, which ordered Japan to withdraw. When Japan refused to obey the ruling, the League appointed a commission to investigate the rival claims of China and Japan to the area. The commission was led by the British politician Lord Lytton, and consisted of four other members from Germany, Italy, France and the USA (the USA was prepared to participate because of its commercial interests). While the commission was carrying out its fact-finding mission and preparing its recommendations to the League, Japanese forces continued their armed takeover of Manchuria. In 1932, Japan claimed full control over Manchuria and renamed it Manchukuo.

The commission spent six weeks in Manchuria in early 1932, investigating the rival claims of China and Japan. The commission's report (the Lytton Report) was published in October 1932. It found fault on both sides but recommended that Manchuria should be returned to Chinese sovereignty under the oversight of the League of Nations. At a meeting in February 1934, the League of Nations voted in favour of accepting the Lytton Report's recommendations by a majority of 42 to 1. The only vote against was cast by the Japanese representative.

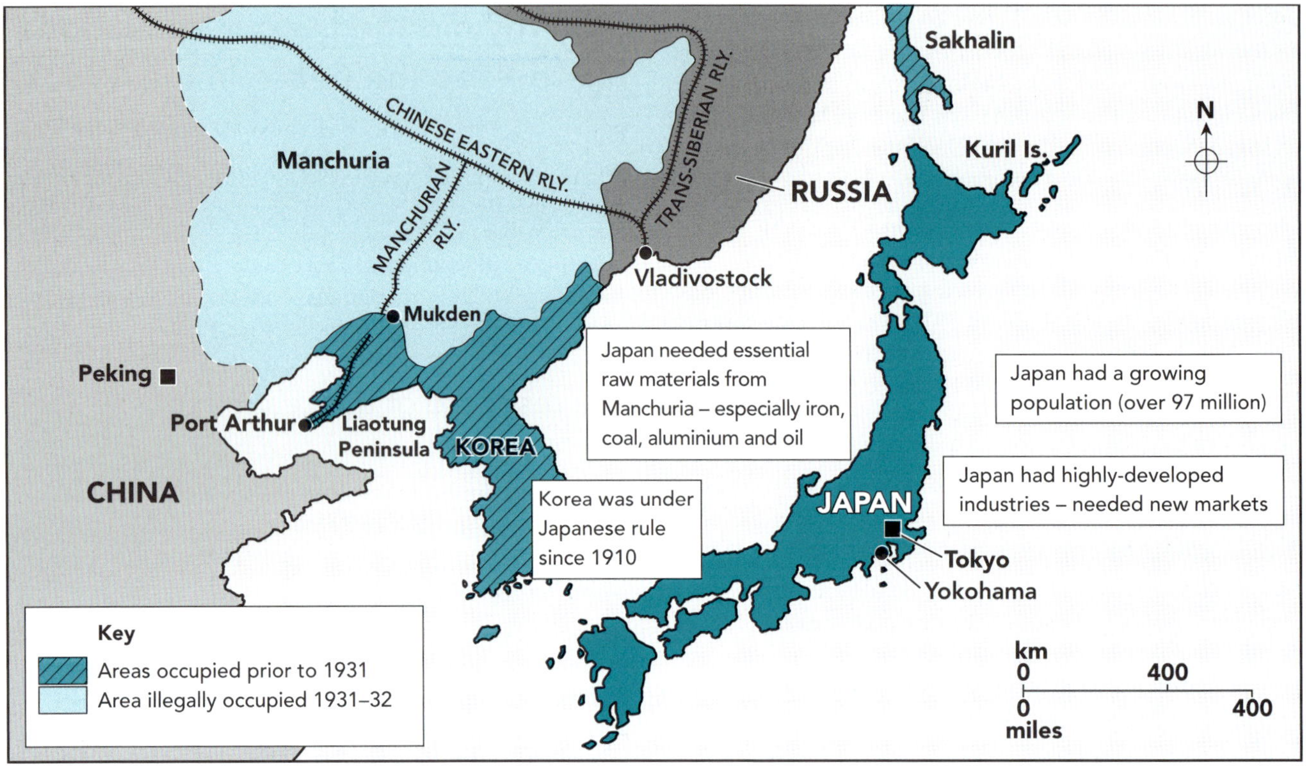

Figure 3.8: The Japanese occupation of Manchuria, 1931-32.

Refusing to accept the League's decision, Japan continued with its military occupation of Manchuria. Under the terms of its Covenant, the League should have taken action against Japan to remove its army from Manchuria. Nations looked to Britain and France to take the lead in implementing the League's instructions. However, at the height of the worldwide depression, Britain and France were in no position to impose economic sanctions on Japan and neither country was prepared to go to war over this issue. The only other power in a position to act was the USA. But the USA was not in the League and was facing mass unemployment and a collapse of its banking system at home. It, too, was unwilling to go to war.

Without the support of two of its most powerful members or of the USA, the League was powerless to do anything in response to Japan's highly aggressive actions. Encouraged by this inactivity, Japan continued its aggression in Manchuria and began a full-scale invasion of China itself. China's appeals to the League of Nations were greeted with sympathy, but no practical assistance. In March 1933, Japan left the League, having clearly succeeded in breaking the covenant which it had signed in 1919. Other nations soon followed.

Figure 3.9: A Japanese propaganda poster of 1933. The Japanese soldier on the right is holding a happy-looking Chinese child. The doves represent the peace that Japan is supposed to be bringing to China.

ACTIVITY 3.12

Figure 3.10: 'The Doormat', a British cartoon of 1932, commenting on the Manchurian Crisis. The pillar is labelled 'Geneva'. The female figure lying on the ground represents the League; the paper next to her says 'Honour of Nations'. The military figure marching over them represents Japan. The figure on the right is powdering the female figure's face from a box marked 'Face-saving Outfit'.

Look at the cartoon in Figure 3.10.

a What point is the cartoonist making?

b To what extent do you feel that it is a fair comment?

Abyssinia, 1935–36

In 1935, Italy demonstrated its new aggressive foreign policy by invading Abyssinia (modern Ethiopia), one of the few parts of Africa not yet under European control. Mussolini had long wished to expand Italy's empire, having promised the Italian people that he would recreate a great 'Roman empire'. Italy already held the protectorates of Eritrea and Somaliland and wanted to take over Abyssinia to make a larger and better-connected empire in north-east Africa. Italy had tried to invade Abyssinia in the 1890s, but its army had suffered a humiliating defeat in 1896 at the battle of Adwa. This time Mussolini was taking no chances, and in October 1935 his army attacked, supported by tanks, artillery, poison gas and aircraft. **Emperor Haile Selassie of Abyssinia** appealed to the League of Nations for assistance.

KEY FIGURE

Emperor Haile Selassie of Abyssinia (1892–75)

Haile Selassie was emperor of Abyssinia from 1930 to 1975. He tried to modernise Abyssinia by giving it a written constitution and abolishing slavery. The Italians drove him out in 1936.

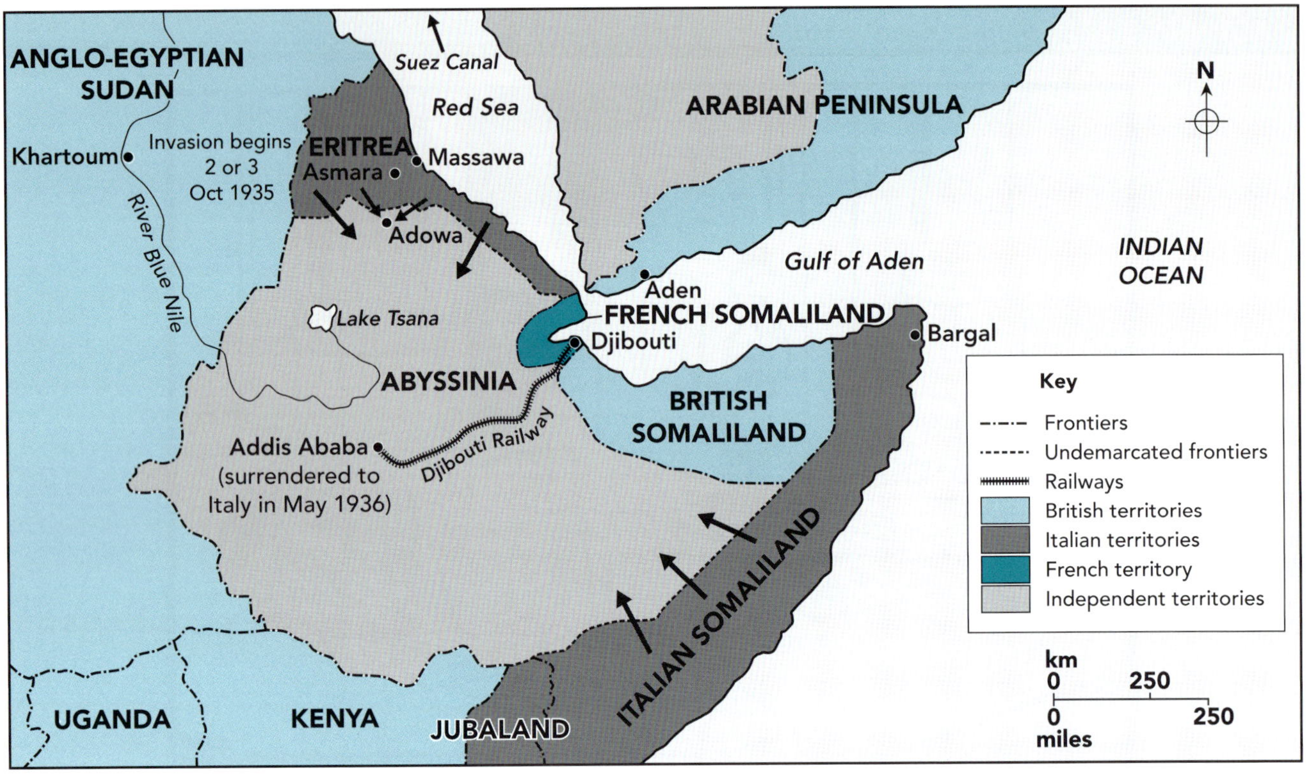

Figure 3.11: Abyssinia, 1935.

The situation confronting the League of Nations was clear. A powerful member of the League was displaying clear and totally unjustified aggression towards one of its weaker members. The League of Nations unanimously condemned this act of aggression and discussed what methods it should use to force Italy to withdraw from Abyssinia.

Again, however, the League's ability to take effective action was hindered by the national interests of its two most powerful members. Britain and France were reluctant to give their full support to Abyssinia for two main reasons:

1 Both Britain and France saw Italy as a vital ally against the growing power of Germany. The three countries had only recently formed the Stresa Front with the aim of resisting further German attempts to change the Treaty of Versailles.

2 Mussolini had suggested that Italy was prepared to go to war with any country which imposed sanctions against it. Neither Britain nor France was prepared to go to war, especially against a country that they viewed as an important ally for the future stability of Europe. They were even less willing to go to war to defend a distant African country, whose independence and security were of no direct interest to them. Also, as Mussolini stated, there was little difference between Italian actions in Abyssinia and earlier British and French methods of developing their own empires in Africa.

There were disagreements on the issue in both Britain and France and the internal political situations in France and Britain complicated the situation further. France was bitterly divided between conservative and socialist groups who disagreed strongly on foreign policy. The British were aware of the damage that events in Manchuria had done to the League and its Covenant, and both politicians and the public wanted a firm stand against Mussolini. However, Britain's prime minister from 1935, Stanley Baldwin, favoured a different approach to Mussolini than his foreign secretary. Also, the country was involved in a major constitutional crisis over the king's wish to marry a divorced American woman. These factors led to inconsistent foreign policy.

Initially, both Britain and France seemed to support and even encourage the League's decision to impose economic sanctions against Italy. Economic sanctions were the first weapon the League could use against aggressors. With their large naval fleets in the Mediterranean, Britain and France would be in a position to enforce any sanctions, and indeed Britain moved a large part of its navy into the Mediterranean to make its position clear. However, the sanctions actually imposed were very limited and did not apply to resources such as oil, coal and steel that were necessary to conduct a war. In practice, the sanctions had little effect on Italy's ability to maintain its fight for Abyssinia.

At the same time as publicly imposing limited sanctions, British and French diplomats were secretly meeting with their Italian counterparts to discuss ways of settling the Abyssinian problem without risking a war or imposing effective sanctions. (This was the kind of secret negotiation that Wilson had hoped to end with his Fourteen Points – see Chapter 2.) The outcome of these secret meetings was a proposal put forward jointly by Samuel Hoare, the British foreign secretary, and Pierre Laval, the French prime minister in December 1935. The proposal, known as the Hoare–Laval Pact, recommended partitioning Abyssinia in a way that would grant Italy effective control of the country. The emperor of Abyssinia and its people were not consulted.

When details of the Hoare–Laval Pact became known, the British and French governments faced a hostile reaction. Public opinion in both countries still largely supported the League of Nations and believed that action should be taken to end Italy's aggression towards Abyssinia. At the League itself, member states expressed their anger and disappointment that the pact was essentially recommending that Italy should be rewarded for its aggression. The British and French governments were forced to repudiate the pact and both Hoare and Laval resigned from their posts. Public opinion felt the League had been betrayed.

The League's limited economic sanctions against Italy remained in place, but they were ineffective in preventing Mussolini from acquiring a vulnerable African state and were quickly abandoned. Annoyed that the League had imposed any sanctions at all, Mussolini withdrew Italy from the League in 1937 and moved towards a closer alliance with Hitler's Germany.

ACTIVITY 3.13

Study the cartoon in Figure 3.12.

a What point is the cartoonist making about the attitude of France and Britain towards Mussolini's invasion of Abyssinia in 1935?

b Why did the cartoonist add the question mark after ('together?')?

c To what extent is this cartoon a fair comment on the policies of Britain and France towards Mussolini's invasion of Abyssinia?

Figure 3.12: A British cartoon of 1935 titled 'The Awful Warning' commenting on the British and French response to Mussolini's invasion of Abyssinia. The caption at the bottom is presented as a song verse. It says, 'France and England (together?): "We don't want you to fight, But by jingo if you do, We shall probably issue a joint memorandum Suggesting a mild disapproval of you."' The words are based on an earlier popular song that called for British military intervention in another country.

The British and French attitude towards the Manchurian and Abyssinian crises can be seen as selfish and damaging to the League's credibility, but it was also logical. The heaviest burden of any League action, either economic or military, would inevitably fall on Britain and France. Most of the other members of the League were small nations, lacking the financial and military resources to take effective action. There were many in both Britain and France who felt it would be foolish to go to war against Italy to defend an African country of little interest to either of them. Public opinion in both countries was divided on the issue, and both countries were still dealing with severe economic depression.

The lack of trust between Britain and France made the situation worse. France was politically divided between Left and Right, and increasingly concerned by the resurgence of Germany under Hitler, and so it was reluctant to take any action without the guarantee of British support. The Anglo-German Naval Agreement of 1935 convinced the French that Britain was an unreliable ally – by signing this agreement, Britain effectively supported German rearmament. British politicians viewed France as weak and offering no guarantee of genuine support in a crisis, as the Abyssinian crisis showed. Manchuria and Abyssinia clearly demonstrated the real weakness of the League. The League had no armed forces of its own to enforce its rules.

ACTIVITY 3.14

a In pairs or in a small group, consider the following questions:

i Explain why neither Britain nor France was prepared to impose effective sanctions against Italy over its invasion of Abyssinia.

ii 'The final nail in the coffin of the League of Nations.' How far do you agree with this view of the role of the League of Nations over the Italian invasion of Abyssinia?

Think carefully about the quote. Was it the 'final' nail? Are there other factors which are better candidates for that term? You might argue, for example, that the League's structure or the absence of the USA from in the League was more important.

CONTINUED

b i Put yourself in the position of the British foreign secretary. You need to justify your actions to **1** the League of Nations and **2** your own parliament.

What points would you make to the League which you would not make to your parliament? What points would you make to your own parliament which you would not make to the League?

Then repeat the process for the French foreign secretary. It may be useful to organise your notes into a table.

	Justifying your actions to the League	Justifying your actions to your parliament
British foreign secretary		
French foreign secretary		

ii Divide the class into two groups. Using your notes from part **i**, one group should write a speech for the British foreign secretary, justifying their actions; the other should write a speech for the French foreign secretary. You can decide if they are making the speech to the League of Nations or their own parliament.

iii One member of each group should present their case to the class. As a class, decide which nation had a better justification for inaction. Give reasons for your conclusion.

KEY CONCEPT 3.1

Significance

Historians are likely to regard something as 'significant' if it not only had a major impact on events at the time and had longer-term implications, but also if it tells us a lot about what was happening in a country at a particular time.

CONTINUED

- Discuss with your partner why the Hoare–Laval Pact could be seen as a 'significant' event. Does it merit that term?
- Does it tell us a great deal about what was happening in Britain and France at the time? What does it tell us?
- What were the short-term implications of the pact?
- What were the longer-term implications?
- Is it an event which really deserves to be studied when examining international relations between 1929 and 1939?

Changing attitudes of major powers towards the League of Nations

For the League of Nations to be effective, it required the full commitment of all the major powers. Only the major powers had the economic and military power necessary to enforce the League's decisions. During the 1930s, the major powers became less committed to supporting the League and more concerned with their own specific national interests. Disarmament and keeping the peace became less important.

Withdrawal from membership of Japan, Germany and Italy

In the years from 1933 to 1937, three members withdrew from the League of Nations.

Japan, February 1933

At the end of the First World War, Japan's democratically elected government seemed genuinely committed to the League and its principles, as demonstrated by its willingness to compromise at the Washington Naval Conference (see Chapter 2, Section 2.3). In addition, Japan's rise to world-power status was formally recognised when it became a permanent member of the League Council.

As democracy collapsed, the military dictatorship in Japan viewed membership of the League as holding back its ambitions for territorial expansion. Japan deeply resented the League's decision to support China's claim to Manchuria and immediately withdrew its membership and ignored the League's instruction for Japanese troops to withdraw.

THE ULTIMATUM.

JAPAN. "IF YOU GO ON SAYING I'M NAUGHTY, I SHALL LEAVE THE CLASS."

Figure 3.13: A British cartoon titled 'The Ultimatum'. It comments on the Lytton's Report's condemnation of Japan's attacks in Manchuria. The caption under the title says: 'Japan. "If you go on saying I'm naughty, I shall leave the class."'

Germany, October 1933

Hitler was strongly critical of the League, partly because it had been created by the Paris peace settlement. Hitler viewed the League as a way for Britain and France to maintain their power over Europe in general, and over Germany in particular. He deeply resented that Germany had not been permitted to become a member of the League when it was created and was only allowed to join in 1926 after formally accepting the terms of the Treaty of Versailles. Soon after he became chancellor of Germany in January 1933, Hitler attended the World Disarmament Conference to demand that either other nations should disarm to the same extent that Germany had been made to do in 1919, or that Germany should have the right to expand its armed forces for self-defence. When his demand was rejected, he angrily walked out of the Conference, and also left the League, seeing it as an obstacle to his ambitions for Germany.

Figure 3.14: A cartoon published in *Le Témoin*, a French satirical newspaper, in March 1935. A huge Hitler with a shadow of German militarism is shown looming above the members of the League of Nations.

Italy, 1937

Mussolini's Italy had never been a fully committed member of the League. As early as 1923, Mussolini had ignored the League's instruction to withdraw Italian troops from Corfu. Italy remained in the League only while it appeared to provide some guarantee of national security, and while it was in Mussolini's interests to maintain good relations with Britain and France. When the League imposed sanctions following Mussolini's invasion of Abyssinia, Italy withdrew its membership.

Three major powers had left the League by 1937. All three intended to follow their own expansionist agendas.

Admission of the USSR, 1934

In the 1920s, the USSR viewed the League of Nations with deep suspicion. The League had been established by the Paris Peace Conference, to which Russian delegates were not invited, and Russia was initially prohibited from becoming a member. To the Soviet government, it appeared that the League's purpose was to maintain the isolation of the USSR and the power of Europe's leading capitalist nations, Britain and France.

By 1934, however, circumstances had changed. The revival of Germany, and its rearmament under Hitler, posed a serious threat to the USSR's national security, while the USSR saw Japan as a serious threat in East Asia. With Germany and Japan no longer members of the League, it seemed a good moment to seek membership. In September 1934, the USSR joined the League as a permanent member of the Council. However, even as a member, the USSR remained heavily critical of the League, particularly regarding its failure to apply the principle of collective security in defence of its members.

ACTIVITY 3.15

The aggressor states such as Japan and Italy are now still weaker than a possible bloc of peace-loving nations, but the policy of non-resistance to evil and aggression, which the opponents of sanctions propose to us, can have no other result than further strengthening and increasing the forces of aggression. The moment might arrive when their power has grown to such an extent that the League of Nations, or what remains of it, will be in no condition to cope with them even if it wants to. With the slightest attempt of aggression, collective action as envisaged in Article 16 of the Covenant of the League of Nations must be brought into effect. The programme envisioned in the Covenant of the League must be carried out against the aggressor, decisively, resolutely and without any wavering.

From a speech by Maxim Litvinov to the League of Nations in September, 1934.

a What point is Litvinov making?

b Why is he referring to Japan and Italy as 'aggressor states'?

c Why is he putting forward this argument in 1934?

Negotiations taking place outside the League

By 1936, the League's authority had been undermined by several international agreements which the League had not organised, although they dealt with issues of disarmament, reparations and borders that the League had been set up to address. These agreements included the final stages of the Young Plan, the London Conference and also major events such as the Anglo-German Naval Treaty and the Stresa Front. None of these agreements involved the League. Perhaps the most significant set of negotiations which undermined the League was the Hoare–Laval Pact which allowed Mussolini's aggression in Abyssinia, even though Haile Selassie had appealed to the League to act to save his country from invasion. The hopes of the League's founders were fading fast.

ACTIVITY 3.16

Either on your own or in pairs, consider the following questions:

a Explain the importance of the withdrawals from the League by Japan, Germany and Italy.

b Which of the three withdrawals did the most damage to the credibility of the League as a peacekeeper? Why?

c Explain why Russia joined the League of Nations and why its joining was significant.

Responses to the Spanish Civil War

The next blow to the League's credibility came in Spain. As in Japan and Germany, democracy in Spain was a victim of the Great Depression. Since 1885, Spain had been governed under a constitutional monarchy. However, during the 1920s political divisions among monarchists, liberals, socialists, communists, anarchists (who rejected all forms of authority) and separatists (who wanted independence for the region in which they lived) had made it impossible for any elected government to provide effective leadership. In 1923, led by Don Miguel Primo de Rivera, army officers had carried out a bloodless coup, seeking to establish strong and stable government. With the support of King Alfonso XIII, parliamentary government was removed, and Rivera established himself as dictator. As the social and economic effects of the Great Depression hit Spain, Rivera lost the support of the army and was forced to resign. King Alfonso abdicated in April 1931, and the new Republic of Spain was proclaimed. In the political chaos that followed, no single party was able to gain control within the Spanish parliament. Right-wing groups (the Church, the army, wealthy landowners, industrialists and businessmen) formed a new party, the Spanish Confederation of the Autonomous Right (CEDA). **Left-wing** groups (socialists, communists and anarchists) decided to work with many liberals, in a group that became known as the **Popular Front**, to oppose the CEDA. Neither CEDA nor the Popular Front was able to form a government capable of addressing Spain's social and economic problems. Social order collapsed, and Spain experienced strikes, riots and appalling acts of violence.

KEY TERMS

Left-wing: Supporting the political 'left'; believing that all parts of society should share wealth and power.

Popular Front: A government made up of an alliance of many different left-wing groups and parties, such as communists, socialists and radical liberals.

In July 1936, with a Popular Front government in power in Madrid, a leading right-wing politician was killed by the bodyguard of a left-wing politician. The assassination convinced right-wing groups that a military dictatorship was the only way to overcome the increasing violence and stop a communist takeover. In July 1936, a group of army officers in Spanish Morocco began a revolt against the elected government. General **Francisco Franco** assumed leadership of the conflict. Within days, the revolt had spread to mainland Spain. However, many Spaniards resisted a military takeover and civil war began.

Anarchist trade unionists in Barcelona fought against and defeated the army insurgents. The government in Madrid issued workers with guns, which allowed them to overcome local army regiments fighting for the Nationalists. For the next three years, Spain was torn apart as Franco's right-wing Nationalists fought with the left-wing Republicans for control of the country. By 1939, the Nationalist victory was certain. Franco established a military dictatorship that included elements of fascism. There was now another fascist dictator in Europe, and again the League of Nations had failed to keep the peace.

KEY FIGURE

Francisco Franco (1892–1975)

Franco came from a military family, and by the time of the Spanish Civil War he had risen to the rank of general. He led the Nationalist rebels to victory against the Republican government in the war. Franco remained in power until his death in 1975.

Why the League of Nations did not respond

When civil war broke out in Spain in summer 1936, it was clear from the start that both Italy and Germany were supplying a large amount of military aid to the rebels under General Franco. The legitimate Republican government, therefore, appealed to the League to try to prevent such foreign intervention. The appeal led to discussion within the League about whether it was the League's role to intervene in what some nations saw as a purely internal Spanish matter. The League felt it had a responsibility to get involved when one nation attacked another, but not when the two sides in a conflict were both from the same nation. Many powers were also reluctant to get involved in a potentially complex and challenging dispute. So, many League members decided to ignore the issue.

The creation of the Non-intervention Agreement, 1936

Public opinion in Britain, France and the USA was divided over Spain. Some people saw Franco as another violent fascist dictator determined to seize power, while others viewed him as a vital barrier against the spread of communism. When the Republican government of Spain asked for British and French assistance against Franco and the military support he was receiving from Germany and Italy, British and French politicians in those countries adopted a pragmatic approach. France was worried that the civil war between Left and Right in Spain would spread across the border to France and that France would become involved. France, therefore, immediately acted to persuade the British (who were also anxious to avoid conflict) to try to prevent other nations from becoming involved in the civil war. Britain and France signed a Non-intervention Agreement which promised that they would not help either side. They then encouraged the League of Nations to establish a Non-intervention Committee. This committee was intended to ensure that no foreign aid, especially military aid, entered Spain to support either side.

Reasons for the failure of the Non-intervention Agreement

Becoming a member of the Non-intervention Committee required members to support the principle of non-intervention. Germany, Italy and Russia, among other nations, joined the committee. The committee had no powers and hoped to rely on its members to obey its rules. However, while Britain and France followed the rules of non-intervention closely, Germany, Italy and Russia completely ignored the rules and poured large amounts of military aid into Spain, with Germany and Italy being the biggest offenders. The USA did not join the committee. Some Americans fought on the Republican side, but the USA also provided supplies of oil to the Nationalists.

By the end of 1936, despite the intentions of the Non-intervention Agreement, the civil war was no longer an internal Spanish affair. It had become an international battleground for the rival ideologies of fascism and communism, with the League watching helplessly on the sidelines. Even though there was ample evidence of both Italian and German military support for Franco, the committee chose to ignore it to avoid having to recommend any actions to the League that might lead to the League having to intervene or get involved. However, ignoring what was clearly happening did even more damage to the credibility of the League.

The intervention of Italy, Germany and the USSR

By the end of July 1936, Franco's Nationalists controlled parts of northern Spain and the southern areas around Cadiz and Seville. The Republicans controlled the centre and north-east of Spain, most significantly the major cities of Madrid and Barcelona. Realising that taking full control of Spain would be difficult, Franco appealed to Mussolini and Hitler for assistance, claiming that he was fighting to prevent a communist revolution in Spain.

Neither Mussolini nor Hitler had any real interest in Spain, but both men could see the value of having a third fascist state in Europe, especially one that was situated on France's southern border. Consequently, from the start of the civil war, Germany and Italy secretly supplied Franco with military equipment and troops. Italy and Germany each had their own reasons for interfering in the Spanish Civil War:

- **Italy:** Mussolini was seeking military success and confirmation of his ability to lead Italy back to its former greatness, as a major power with a leading role in European affairs. Italy pretended to support the Non-intervention Committee, but it was impossible to hide the presence of some 50 000 Italian troops and over 750 Italian fighter planes around the battlefields of Spain. Within Italy, Mussolini boasted of the country's involvement in the Spanish Civil War. It provided propaganda material designed to maintain his popularity with the Italian people. Mussolini portrayed himself as leading the fight against communism, which he argued posed a major threat to the stability of Italy. He also knew that support for Franco would anger France and Britain.
- **Germany:** The Spanish Civil War provided an opportunity to test the efficiency and capability of Germany's rearmament programme. Many of Germany's new weapons, especially bombers, were tested in Spain and air force pilots gained valuable combat experience. Hitler also encouraged involvement in Spain to distract Mussolini from Germany's plans to force a union with Austria. To prolong the Spanish Civil War, Germany supplied Franco's Nationalists with men and equipment, and Hitler allowed German firms to sell arms to the Nationalists.

The involvement of Italy and Germany in what was basically a private, internal, Spanish affair later had a major impact on international relations.

While Italy and Germany aided the Nationalists, the USSR responded to the Republicans' appeal for assistance. Soviet leader, Stalin, also had an interest in prolonging the Spanish Civil War. Sensing that Germany posed the biggest threat to the security of the Soviet Union, Stalin had worked hard to maintain good relations with both Britain and France. While he did not want Franco to take control of Spain (which would pose another fascist threat to the Soviet Union), he knew that neither Britain nor France would tolerate a communist government in Spain. As a result, Stalin authorised just enough aid to ensure that the Republicans could maintain their resistance, but not enough to enable them to gain outright victory.

In the early stages of the Civil War, Spanish communist soldiers helped by Soviet advisors and tanks played an important part in preventing the Republic's defeat. This aid was followed in 1937 and early 1938 by large supplies of aircraft, arms and ammunition, as well as more advisors. The actual amount of aid sent is not known, because the USSR, as a member of the Non-intervention Committee, always denied that it was sending aid to the Republicans (just as the Italians and Germans denied that they were aiding the Nationalists).

However, by late 1938, the USSR was becoming concerned about its own security and diplomatic isolation, and stopped sending supplies and ammunition to the Spanish Republicans. This helped the Nationalist cause. In addition, Franco gained further support from Germany in exchange for a 40% share in the Spanish iron mines. These factors gave Franco the upper hand. In January 1939, Barcelona finally fell to the Nationalists. With the fall of Madrid two months later, Franco's victory was secured.

Figure 3.15: Republican propaganda poster. The USSR assisted the Republicans.

Figure 3.16: Nationalist propaganda poster. Germany and Italy supplied aid to the Nationalists.

The International Brigades and other volunteers

Despite the Non-intervention Agreement's aim of preventing foreign interference , the Spanish Civil War attracted volunteers from many countries. Franco's well-armed professional soldiers met determined, if disorganised, resistance. Many ordinary men and women in Spain, encouraged by communist and socialist leaders, enlisted and were given basic training in methods of warfare. They were supported by the International Brigades, communist-organised armies of foreign volunteers. British, French, Italian, German, Polish, Russian and American civilians poured into Spain by sea from Marseilles or along pathways across the Pyrenees to help fight Franco and fascism.

Not all volunteers were communists. Some were just driven by a desire to prevent the spread of fascism and others were in search of adventure. Some volunteers came to provide medical support to the wounded. At a time of high unemployment, there were many people who saw involvement in the Spanish Civil War as a way of escaping from poverty and boredom. Over 20 000 men came to Spain to fight for the Republic, and over 10 000 of them died there.

The lack of commitment of France and Britain

While the dictatorships were prepared to intervene in the Spanish Civil war, the democracies were not. America remained neutral and Britain and France were reluctant to participate. The British government was deeply worried about the spread of communism and much less concerned by fascism. There was strong sympathy for the Nationalist cause. Many people admired Mussolini and openly supported his intervention to support Franco. There were many British investments in Spain and investors feared that they might be seized by the 'Left' if they won. Republican supporters were in a minority. By stopping the Republic buying arms, Britain made the Republic more dependent on communist support, and also played an important part in its defeat.

In France the left-wing government in 1936 was initially sympathetic to the Republicans, but also strongly opposed to any war, so was reluctant to act. There was also huge support for Franco in parts of the French Assembly (parliament) and across the country. Many people were terrified that the war in Spain would spread over the Pyrenees into France. Inaction and non-intervention followed. Towards the end of the war, in late 1938, France became more supportive and opened its frontiers to the Republicans, but it was too late.

Figure 3.17: Defeated supporters of the Republic at the border between Spain and France.

In 1939 thousands of refugees poured into France, fleeing from Franco's troops, and the League of Nations' refugee agency dealt effectively with them. Ultimately the inaction of Britain and France had as much effect on the outcome of the Spanish Civil War as the actions of Italy, Germany and the USSR.

ACTIVITY 3.17

Spain is another victim of Fascist weapons . . . Events in Spain presented the Great Powers with a new problem. It was not a war between two countries, but a revolt against a constitutionally elected government, and the question was what attitude the other countries ought to adopt in these circumstances. The Great Powers chose neutrality ... an idea which originated in Britain ... At the beginning the war in Spain was regarded as a civil war. As there is no article in the Covenant to determine the League's attitude in a civil war, the non-intervention agreement was not in conflict with the Covenant. But when in August Italy sent army planes to Spain ... Spain's Foreign Secretary appealed to the Assembly in September. He pointed out the great

CONTINUED

danger to peace if it should become the custom for a country to support a rebellion in another country with military forces ... without any declaration of war. The Assembly demanded proofs. They were already available in the Non-intervention Committee in London ... Now it was evident that non-intervention was in conflict with the Covenant. In the face of a military attack on one of its members, the League of Nations has no right to declare itself passive. But the Assembly did not move.

From an article by a Danish journalist in 1937.

Look carefully at the journalist's comments.

In pairs or small groups, consider the following statements. Decide whether each statement is true or false and give reasons for your decision.

The Danish journalist:

a suggested that, when the Spanish Civil War initially broke out, the League of Nations had no right to intervene

CONTINUED

- **b** believed that the League of Nations had a responsibility to intervene in the Spanish Civil War once foreign countries, such as Italy, became involved
- **c** claimed that the League of Nations could not intervene in the Spanish Civil War because there was no evidence that other countries, such as Italy, were becoming involved
- **d** argued that Italy was effectively waging war against Spain
- **e** opposed fascism
- **f** supported communism.

Causes of the failure of the League of Nations

By the end of the 1930s, as political extremism spread throughout Europe and East Asia and international tensions rose, it was clear that the League of Nations was unable to keep the peace. As you have learned while studying Chapters 2 and 3 of this book, some weaknesses had been apparent since the League had been established but had become more problematic in the 1930s. Other pressures had arisen from the economic and social problems of the 1930s.

Inability to achieve widespread disarmament

Attempts to achieve worldwide disarmament in the 1920s had failed, although some progress had been made, for example in the treaties arising from the Washington Naval Conference of 1921–22. The World Disarmament Conference of 1932 had collapsed. The Anglo-German Naval Agreement had allowed the German navy to increase, and Hitler had begun the process of German rearmament. The Spanish Civil War showed that the League had failed to prevent international conflict.

Absence of major powers

In the early years of the League, the absence of Germany, Russia and the USA had limited its ability to act. Although Germany and Russia later joined the League, international cooperation was never strong. The withdrawal from the League of Germany, Italy and Japan during the 1930s significantly weakened the League's authority.

Reliance on Britain and France

The two most powerful members of the League, Britain and France, often put their own national interests before the 'greater good' of the League. This approach severely restricted the League's ability to act. This weakness had become obvious in the 1920s, for example in the Polish seizure of Vilna and the Corfu Incident. However, it became a major issue in the 1930s, when the reluctance of Britain and France to take action against the Japanese invasion of Manchuria or the Italian invasion of Abyssinia seriously undermined the League.

Effects of the Great Depression

Economic problems in a country often have major political implications. The Great Depression affected many countries badly, causing mass unemployment, deflation and growing poverty. In some countries, such as the USA, Britain and France, governments had to focus on dealing with the social effects of depression at home and they were less concerned about what was happening in other countries. In Germany, for example, the democratic government proved unable to provide solutions to the challenging social and economic conditions. Hitler emerged as a fascist dictator, and his aggressive nationalism and hatred of the Treaty of Versailles would destroy the chances of peace in Europe.

Increasing nationalism

A major element of the fascism that emerged in this period was a form of aggressive nationalism – the idea that one's own nation is superior to others and, therefore, has the right to dominate others and that one's country is always 'right' and others are not. Hitler, Mussolini, Franco and the military leaders who dominated Japan in the 1930s illustrate this well. Their aggressive nationalism had great popular appeal in their countries. For example, many Germans were attracted to Hitler's idea of gaining Lebensraum and Mussolini appealed to many Italians with his 'Mare nostrum' ('our sea') policies. The Japanese generals stated that it was Japan's right and destiny to take over China and acquire the raw materials it needed for its economy. In these circumstances, it is not surprising that it was impossible to keep the peace.

Figure 3.18: Mussolini addressing a mass rally in Rome.

KEY CONCEPT 3.2

Interpretations

Historians have debated the reasons for the failure of the League of Nations to keep the peace. In addition to the reasons already covered, they have considered the following:

- There were weaknesses in the League's structure. It did not have an effective decision-making process, and it did not have the means to enforce its decisions.
- The initial intentions were too ambitious. For example, it was unrealistic to expect some nations to disarm while other nations (potential aggressors) did not.
- The ideals advocated by Woodrow Wilson were destroyed by the behaviour of self-seeking European leaders, particularly after 1929.
- The First World War released powerful economic, social and political forces that could not be controlled.
- National interests, the personal ambitions of dictators and the political pressures on popularly elected leaders proved more important than fulfilling the terms of the League's Covenant.

CONTINUED

- The refusal of America to join the League and the departure of Germany, Italy and Japan in the 1930s contributed to the League's failure.
- The impact of the Great Depression on the economies of major powers was a further factor.
- Ongoing divisions between Britain and France over their policies towards aggressors played a part.

Defenders of the League point out that its successor, the United Nations, has not done much better in keeping the peace! The debate will continue.

Draw up six headings to help you categorise the causes of the failure of the League of Nations:

- Unable to achieve widespread disarmament
- Absence of major powers
- Reliance on Britain and France
- Effects of Great Depression
- Increasing nationalism
- Other reasons.

As you revise Chapters 2 and 3 of this book, write down examples under each heading. For example, under 'Unable to achieve widespread disarmament' you might include the failed attempt to produce a treaty in 1925 (Section 2.2) the Geneva Protocol (Section 2.4), and the Washington Conference of 1932 (Section 3.1). Taking notes like this will provide you with a wide range of supporting examples if you are considering the weaknesses or failures of the League of Nations.

ACTIVITY 3.18

Organise a class seminar on the reasons why the League of Nations failed to keep the peace in the 1930s.

a First, identify a list of factors which contributed to its failure. The reasons could include weaknesses in its actual structure, unrealistic ambitions, the initial exclusion of Germany and the USSR, the absence of the USA, the roles of Britain and France, the impact of the Depression and the growth of nationalism. What other factors could be considered?

b Each member of the group should be allocated one factor and should prepare a case for arguing that this factor contributed most to the final failure. They should then read out their case in the seminar, allowing five minutes for each factor, plus two minutes for questions.

c Then the group as a whole should rank the factors in order of importance.

Reflection

After your seminar, consider the questions:

- Why did members of the group have a different order of importance?
- What factors influenced their decision making? Were they different?
- To what extent did members of the group show full awareness of the actual situation in the 1930s?
- How much did hindsight influence their decisions?
- Was anyone influenced by their own nationality?

3.3 Why, and with what effects, did Britain and France pursue a policy of appeasement?

The collapse of the League's disarmament talks and the failure of the League to act firmly over Manchuria, together with the withdrawal of the USA from world affairs after 1932, led to increased pressure on Britain and France to provide leadership to maintain peace and offer guidance in international relations.

Impact of economic, military and social considerations on foreign policy

Over Manchuria and Abyssinia, the League of Nations had failed to act effectively against the kind of aggression it had been established to prevent. Failing to take decisive action against aggressive countries and agreeing to their demands is known as **appeasement**. During the 1930s, the policy of appeasement adopted by Britain and France played a crucial role in the League's failure to confront international aggression.

Looking back, it is easy to criticise appeasement as an unwise policy that destroyed the League and made another world war more likely. In July 1940, after the Second World War broke out, a book entitled *Guilty Men* was published in Britain – it was heavily critical of appeasement and the politicians who had supported it. The book argued that determined action by other European powers would have prevented war in 1939. Some historians still hold this view. It is debatable whether Hitler would ever have stopped trying to reverse the Treaty of Versailles and attempting to expand Germany to the east. During the 1930s, however, there seemed compelling reasons to justify appeasement.

> **KEY TERM**
>
> **Appeasement:** A policy of giving in to demands made by aggressive nations rather than confronting these demands.

Britain

Public opinion in Britain was divided on whether to appease Hitler or to oppose his demands. No-one wanted to repeat the horrors of the First World War. Nearly every family had lost a son, father or brother in that conflict. Thousands were still alive who had been permanently injured or gassed. Technological developments made it clear that any future war would be far worse, with aerial bombing of cities possibly causing enormous numbers of civilian casualties. Evidence of this was seen during the Spanish Civil War, where the civilian populations of several cities suffered heavy bombing.

Effects of the Great Depression

Britain was still suffering from the devastating economic effects of the Great Depression. In a period of high unemployment and hunger marches, many people felt the country could not afford the high costs of preparing for war. Given that the public was heavily opposed to war, it was more politically acceptable to spend money in other areas, for example housing, health and job creation. So, British politicians prioritised avoiding war and maintaining the international trade on which the economy depended.

These two priorities help to explain the failure of the League of Nations to take effective action in response to the Japanese invasion of Manchuria in 1931. Under the terms of its Covenant, the League should have imposed economic sanctions against Japan to force it to withdraw its troops. However, Britain and France did not want to lose their extensive trading links with Japan and East Asia. British representatives at the League argued that economic sanctions would be counterproductive – they would negatively affect the economies of the countries which imposed them, while Japan would trade with other nations instead. Britain was also concerned about its overseas possessions, especially Hong Kong and Singapore. There was a risk that Japan would attack these areas if Britain imposed sanctions, leading to war.

Britain, therefore, put its national interests above its commitment to the League of Nations, and without the support of one of its most powerful and influential members the League was powerless to take effective action against Japan. Similarly, Britain was reluctant to take strong action following Italy's invasion of Abyssinia in 1935. Mussolini was seen as a vital ally against the rising power of Hitler's Germany, and, as a result, the League's response was limited to minor and largely ineffective economic sanctions.

In the same way, responding effectively to Hitler's aggressive actions would have had enormous economic repercussions for Britain. Military intervention would have been needed to prevent Hitler's remilitarisation of the Rhineland in 1936 or his Anschluss with Austria in 1938 (see later in this section). Politicians could not justify such expensive action, particularly with the slaughter of 1914–18 still fresh in their minds. Invading Germany simply was not a realistic possibility.

Figure 3.19: The town of Guernica in northern Spain after German and Italian aircraft bombed it in 1937 during the Spanish Civil War. It was the first time that bombers had been used to destroy purely civilian targets. Fear that this might happen to other cities encouraged appeasement.

The Ten-year Rule

The military strategy followed by the British during the 1930s was based primarily on self-defence. At the end of the First World War, Britain had significantly reduced its military capabilities. The British government adopted the 'Ten-year Rule', which was based on the belief that Britain would not be involved in a major war for the next ten years. The Ten-year Rule led to reductions in defence spending, from £766 million in 1919–20 to £189 million in 1921–22, and £102 million in 1931–32. By the time the 'Ten-year Rule' was abandoned in 1932, Britain was suffering from the economic effects of the Great Depression, and politicians felt that it could not devote large expenditure to expanding its armed forces. In addition, MacDonald, the British prime minister from 1929 to 1935, was a pacifist (he had refused to fight in the First World War). So, the British government's priority was to defend Britain and its empire, not to take military action on behalf of the League in other parts of the world.

The Oxford 'King and Country' debate, 1933, and the Peace Ballot, 1934–35

Public opinion in Britain in the early 1930s favoured relying on the League to keep the peace. Over 400 000 British were members of the League of Nations Union, an organisation committed to upholding the Covenant and what it stood for. In 1933, in a debate at Oxford University, seen as a source of Britain's future leaders, the motion (proposal for debate) that 'This House would not fight for King and Country' passed. Many people abroad viewed the result of the debate as a sign of Britain's unwillingness to stand up to aggression. In reality, it was mainly a vote against the horrors of war. Perhaps more revealing was a 'Peace Ballot' signed by millions of Britons in 1934–35, who overwhelmingly voted that Britain should both remain an active member of the League of Nations, and also take action to enforce the League's decisions.

Opinion was clearly divided. While there was obvious support for the League and what it stood for, politicians suspected there might be less enthusiasm for the implications of that support in terms of soldiers' lives and the cost in taxation.

Fascism as a bulwark against Bolshevism and sympathy for Nazi policies

There was some sympathy for Germany over the terms of the Treaty of Versailles, and this sympathy contributed to support for the early stages of appeasement. Some people in Britain saw Hitler's

Germany as a bulwark (protective barrier) against a communist threat and felt that he should be encouraged. This was particularly the case among the wealthier and more conservative classes. Similarly, many conservatives supported Franco's revolt against the Republicans and the left-wing 'Popular Front' in Spain.

British politicians faced a dilemma. People wanted peace and they were supportive of the League of Nations and what it stood for. On the other hand there was little desire for rearmament and its costs, and no desire at all to actually go to war in defence of a far-off country.

Figure 3.20: Poster published before the Peace Ballot. It shows the dilemma facing the British people in 1934.

France

Public opinion on how to respond to the rise of fascism in Europe was even more divided in France than in Britain.

Economic problems

Economic depression had also affected France in the early 1930s and agricultural and industrial production had greatly declined. Unemployment and poverty grew, and frequently changing governments provided no solutions.

Political divisions: the threat of communism and the elections of 1936

Politics became severely polarised (divided into opposite groups) between Right and Left. Many conservatives in France feared communism and this fear led them to sympathise with Germany and its anti-communist policies and to support Italy with its dictatorial approach to government under Mussolini. The Right strongly opposed the defensive pact that France signed with the communist USSR in 1936 (see Section 3.1) and equally strongly supported Franco's Nationalist revolt against the Left in Spain. The Right felt that cutting public spending was the best solution to the Depression. The Left were briefly united after the elections of 1936 in one 'Popular Front' government. Its members argued for radical social and economic change, and, above all, large amounts of public spending to get France out of the depression.

The French Grand Strategy and the Maginot Line

There were also bitter divisions over military policy and strategy. The Right wanted a large professional army with two years of conscription (compulsory service in the army) for all men. The Left did not like the idea of a large or professional army and opposed conscription. There was also disagreement about how much independence the military should have from civilian politicians.

Within the military, there were serious disagreements about whether to focus on defending France or to prepare the armed forces for attacking other countries (which meant more spending on offensive weapons such as tanks and bombers). There were further divisions about how much to give to defending France's empire in North and West Africa and East Asia. Supporters of defending France as the priority managed to get the funding to build a structure that became known as the Maginot Line. This was an immense line of concrete fortresses and complex defensive networks built during the 1930s along the border between France, Belgium and Germany. It was designed to defend France against another German attack like the invasions of 1870 and 1914.

There was, therefore, no consistent policy or strategy on defence matters in France in the 1930s. France had 16 different ministers of war and 22 different prime ministers between 1929 and 1939, so this was hardly surprising.

Figure 3.21: Soldiers in a tunnel that formed part of the Maginot Line, in 1939.

ACTIVITY 3.19

Either on your own or in a small group, put yourself in the position of: first the French prime minister, and then the British prime minister in 1936.

a Draw up a list of reasons justifying the appeasement of Germany and Italy. Create two separate lists, one for France and one for Britain.

b Consider the following questions:

- i To what extent are the prime ministers' reasons different?
- ii To what extent were domestic factors the most important factors in their thinking?
- iii How valid do you think their reasons were?
- iv What options did they have in 1936?

Actions taken to appease Hitler

Many British politicians believed that the Treaty of Versailles had been too harsh on Germany and that Hitler was addressing genuine grievances. They were convinced that Hitler's aggression would cease once the treaty had been destroyed. Hitler had successfully portrayed himself as a man of peace who was simply seeking fairness for Germany. In January 1934, for example, he signed a ten-year non-aggression pact with Poland. The pact was intended to convince the Poles that Germany had no plans to take back the Polish Corridor, but it was also useful in providing Britain with evidence of Hitler's peaceful intentions. Similarly, when the Saar region was returned to Germany following a plebiscite in 1935, Hitler stated that its return ended all remaining grievances between Germany and France. He claimed that the French had nothing to fear from Germany.

Under these circumstances, many politicians in Britain and some politicians in France convinced themselves that Hitler's actions were justifiable and that he wanted peace. It only became impossible to justify Hitler's actions in 1939, when Germany took control over the whole of Czechoslovakia.

The response to German rearmament and the Anglo-German Naval Agreement, 1935

The Stresa Front, the agreement reached between Britain, France and Italy in April 1935 (see Section 3.1), was intended to ensure that there were no further changes to the Paris peace settlement. In particular, it aimed to oppose Hitler's plans for German rearmament, which violated the Treaty of Versailles. The agreement's weaknesses were quickly exposed.

Two months after the establishment of the Stresa Front, Britain signed an agreement with Germany – the Anglo-German Naval Agreement of June 1935. Under the terms of the agreement, the German navy was limited to 35% of the strength of the British navy, which ensured British naval supremacy. However, by signing the agreement, Britain was agreeing to an expansion of the German navy far beyond that permitted by the Treaty of Versailles. This agreement contradicted the Stresa Front's primary purpose. It was a clear act of appeasement by Britain that allowed Germany openly to defy its treaty obligations in an attempt to improve relations between Britain and Germany. Britain's willingness to sign such an agreement with Germany, without consulting its Stresa Front partners, caused great anger in France. From the French perspective, it was an act of betrayal – Britain was putting its own interests before its commitments to European stability and the security of France.

Aware of the widening divisions between Britain and France, Hitler openly embarked on a large-scale rearmament programme. Between 1933 and 1935 he had secretly expanded the German armed forces, but after withdrawing from the Disarmament Conference and the League, he no longer hid this expansion. Conscription was introduced, to expand the German army from the permitted 100 000 men to one million – many more than he needed for defence. The Luftwaffe (the German air force), was created, containing not only fighters for defence, but long-distance bombers for attacking abroad. German shipyards produced new battleships and submarines for the navy.

German rearmament and the naval treaty aroused little concern in Britian. Britain's prime minister between 1929 and 1935, the pacifist MacDonald, strongly supported the League and was reluctant to act in any way that might appear aggressive. To deal with the effects of the Great Depression, British politicians cut all public spending. This included making major cuts to all the armed forces. As the Naval Agreement ensured that British naval dominance over Germany continued, Germany was not seen as a threat.

France was politically divided with frequent changes of government as well as growing divisions between Right and Left. Events in Germany, therefore, had little impact in France, and those who were worried about Hitler's rearmament felt secure behind the growing Maginot Line.

For Mussolini, however, the Anglo-German Naval Agreement was clear evidence of Britain's weakness and unwillingness to confront aggression. He also knew that France was unlikely to go to war without guaranteed British support.

ACTIVITY 3.20

Figure 3.22: A British cartoon of 1935 titled 'The Boy Who Shouldn't Grow Up'. It comments on the Anglo-German Naval Treaty. The caption under the title says: 'John Bull. "There's your new navy suit. Now you must promise me you won't grow out of it." Germany. "Well, at all events I'll promise not to unless you grow out of yours."'

Look at the cartoon in Figure 3.22.

a What point is John Bull on the right (representing Britain) making?

b Why is the sailor on the left (representing France) looking unhappy?

c What is the relevance of the '35%' on the sailor in the middle, representing Germany?

d How perceptive was the cartoonist?

Inaction over the Rhineland

Hitler was increasingly convinced that none of the other major European countries would take serious action against him, so he continued to challenge the Treaty of Versailles. At the Paris Peace Conference, France had insisted that there should be no troops (demilitarisation) in the Rhineland, as Germany had invaded France and Belgium through that area in 1914. Under the terms of the Treaty of Versailles, Germany was not permitted any military presence west of the River Rhine or within 50 kilometres of the river on its German side. It was stated that any violation of this would 'be regarded as committing a hostile act, and as calculated to disturb the peace of the world'. In the Locarno Treaties of 1925, Germany had agreed to keep the Rhineland as a demilitarised area.

In March 1936, Hitler ordered German troops to enter the Rhineland. He justified his action by arguing that the Franco-Soviet Treaty of 1935 posed a serious threat to German security, and that Germany now needed to secure its border with France. Sending troops into the Rhineland was a calculated gamble by Hitler. He knew that France would interpret the remilitarisation of the Rhineland as a clear threat to French security. He also knew that his army was not yet strong enough to challenge any military opposition to this action.

Considering the implications of their presence in the Rhineland, openly violating the Treaty of Versailles, it may seem incredible that the German troops encountered no opposition. In fact, Hitler had ordered his generals to retreat if they met French troops. However, Hitler's great gamble was successful.

Hitler had timed the action well. France was in the middle of a financial crisis, the government increasingly reliant on loans to avoid running out of money. The French government overestimated the number of German troops entering the Rhineland, and the French war minister argued that removing them would require the full mobilisation of the French armed forces – costing 30 million francs a day. Concerned about the forthcoming elections, the French government felt it could not justify such spending.

Although it decided against military action, the French government issued statements heavily criticising Germany's actions. The government also claimed that 'France will place all its forces at the disposal of the League of Nations to oppose a violation of the Treaties'. This statement attempted to test whether Britain would be willing to honour its obligation to oppose a violation of the treaties of Versailles and Locarno. However, Britain had its own reasons for not wanting to take military action in response to Germany's remilitarisation of the Rhineland:

- The British generally could see little harm in German troops occupying German territory. One politician claimed it was simply Germans walking into their own backyard. Many British politicians also saw Hitler's actions as an understandable response to the Franco-Soviet treaty of 1935.
- Even before German troops entered the Rhineland, Britain had expressed willingness to negotiate with Hitler over Germany's right to remilitarise the area. The British government had viewed the Rhineland issue as a possible bargaining tool for developing more effective relations with Germany.
- The new British prime minister, Baldwin (1935–37), argued that Britain lacked the resources to enforce its treaty obligations, as it was still suffering from the effects of the Great Depression.
- Public opinion in Britain was strongly anti-war and members of its **Commonwealth**, including Australia, New Zealand, South Africa and Canada, made it clear that they would not support military action to restore the demilitarisation of the Rhineland.

KEY TERM

Commonwealth: A group of former British colonies, which had become largely independent but retained the British monarch as their head of state. These countries provided many troops to fight with Britain in the First World War.

- British politicians did not respect or trust their French counterparts. One leading member of the Cabinet suggested to Baldwin that 'France will be as selfish and as pig-headed as France has always been' over the Rhineland issue.
- The British government was convinced that the best way of dealing with Hitler was to negotiate with him.

Just a year after introducing conscription, Hitler had overturned another element of the Treaty of Versailles. Also, as well as effectively destroying the Locarno agreements of 1925, Germany's remilitarisation of the Rhineland posed an obvious threat to the security of France. The French government referred the matter to the League of Nations, arguing that the League had an obligation to take collective action, to enforce treaty agreements and ensure the removal of German troops from the Rhineland. However, the League could not respond effectively because Britain refused to support any action that might involve it in a war against Germany. The British government was certain that the best way to deal with the crisis was to negotiate.

From Hitler's perspective, the lack of effective action in response to Germany's remilitarisation of the Rhineland had exposed major weaknesses in the relationship between Britain and France, and the growing distrust between them. His instinct that they would do nothing to prevent his further attempts to undermine the Treaty of Versailles proved correct when Germany secured the Anschluss in March 1938, with no opposition.

ACTIVITY 3.21

Working on your own, consider these questions.

a Identify the reasons why Hitler was able to remilitarise the Rhineland without having to fight for it.

b Place those reasons in order of priority, explaining your reasoning behind (i) the most important and (ii) the least important.

Reflection

Compare your answers with others in your group. What criteria did each of you use to rank these reasons in order of importance? Would you change your criteria when attempting a similar task in future?

Acceptance of the Anschluss

Hitler's next expansionist move was union with Austria, the Anschluss, which the Treaty of Versailles had forbidden. In early 1938, Nazis in Austria started a series of violent demonstrations demanding union with Germany, encouraged and funded by Germany. The Austrian police struggled to maintain order, so Hitler used this as an excuse to invade Austria to protect lives and property. (He successfully used this technique later, too.) On 12 March 1938, German troops crossed the border into Austria. The Austrian government had ordered its forces not to resist the invasion, and German troops were met by crowds of Austrians waving Nazi flags. Hitler himself entered Austria by car and drove in triumph to Vienna, where on 15 March he proclaimed the union of Austria and Germany to cheering crowds.

With its entire western half surrounded by Germany, Czechoslovakia was the country most threatened by the Anschluss. However, on 11 March, Hitler had assured the Czechs that they did not need to fear Germany's intention to take control of Austria. In any case, he knew that Czechoslovakia was too weak to resist Germany without support from the other major European powers. Hitler also knew that Italy would not oppose him. Mussolini had resisted Hitler's earlier attempt at Anschluss in 1934 but was now Hitler's closest

Figure 3.23: Hitler leading a procession in Vienna to celebrate the Anschluss in 1938.

ally following the formation of the Rome–Berlin Axis (see Section 3.1). Mussolini had made it clear that he was no longer interested in Austria. So, serious opposition to the Anschluss could only come from Britain and France.

As before, both Britain and France lacked the political will to take action against Hitler. France was experiencing political turmoil because its entire government had resigned on 10 March after failing to gain support for its economic plans. It was in no position to react decisively to Germany's takeover of Austria, and, besides, it could not have done so without British support. France was not prepared to become involved in a war in central Europe to defend Austria, especially when most Austrians seemed to support the union. So, in another act of appeasement, France took no action against Germany for its latest violation of the Treaty of Versailles.

In May 1937, **Neville Chamberlain** had become British prime minister. Chamberlain supported appeasement and was determined to negotiate with Hitler rather than annoy him. Some politicians opposed Chamberlain's appeasement policy. Anthony Eden had resigned from his post as foreign secretary in February 1938 because of Chamberlain's willingness to negotiate with Mussolini. Similarly, Winston Churchill, Britain's future war leader, argued that the Anschluss posed a major threat to European peace, and that Britain should respond by taking strong and decisive action.

KEY FIGURE

Neville Chamerlain (1869–1940)

Chamberlain became British prime minister in May 1937. He believed firmly in the policy of appeasement, arguing that the best way of dealing with Hitler was by negotiation rather than confrontation. He finally accepted that appeasement had failed and declared war on Germany in 1939. He resigned in May 1940, and died later that year.

However, Chamberlain had the support of large sections of British public opinion, which still opposed any action that might involve Britain in another major war. The Anschluss did not seem to threaten Britain, and most of Austria's population appeared to support it. Most British people thought it foolish to risk going to war with Germany to defend Austrian independence against the wishes of the Austrians. The Anti-Comintern Pact (see Section 3.1) meant that such a war might escalate to include Italy and Japan. Britain was not able to fight so many enemies.

So, Britain and France issued strongly worded condemnations of Germany's takeover of Austria but took no direct action in response to it. As Hitler had predicted, neither government was prepared to use force. Another gamble had succeeded, and Hitler was keen to go further.

The Sudetenland Crisis

Chamberlain's belief in a policy of appeasement was most clearly evident in the Sudetenland Crisis of 1938.

Despite his assurances that Czechoslovakia had nothing to fear from Germany, Hitler clearly intended to take control of the Sudetenland region of Czechoslovakia. His justification was that he was supporting the many German-speaking people living in the region, who were being unfairly treated by the Czech government.

Hitler justified his claims to the Sudetenland as follows:

> I am not asking that Germany be allowed to oppress three and a half million Frenchmen, nor am I asking that three and a half million Englishmen be placed at our mercy. Rather I am simply demanding that the oppression of three and a half million Germans in Czechoslovakia cease and that the inalienable right to self-determination take its place.
>
> **From a speech by Hitler on 12 September, 1938.**

He demanded that the Sudetenland should be allowed to 'return' to Germany, where it rightfully belonged. The German government sent agents into the Sudetenland to create trouble for the Czech government. When the Czech government reacted firmly against those agents, Hitler claimed that the Czechs were using violence against the Germans in Czechoslovakia.

Figure 3.24: The Sudetenland Crisis.

Initial negotiations between the Czechs and the Germans failed to resolve the problem. At first, Hitler asked only for areas where 50% or more of the population was ethnic German, but he later increased his demands to include the whole of the Sudetenland region. The loss of such a strategically important area, containing over 70% of Czechoslovakia's heavy industry, would leave Czechoslovakia defenceless, which the Czech government could not accept.

Czechoslovakia had been established as a country by the Paris peace settlement and Germany's plan to take part of it would unquestionably pose a major threat to peace in Europe. As negotiations broke down, it seemed increasingly likely that the situation would lead to a major European war. Under the terms of the Paris peace settlement, and in line with their commitment to the League of Nations, Britain and France would be required to protect Czechoslovakia against German aggression.

The Munich Conference and its outcome

Again, Hitler achieved German territorial expansion without bloodshed. An international conference at Munich in Germany was called on 30 September 1938 and was attended by the political leaders of Germany, Britain, France and Italy (Hitler, Chamberlain, Daladier and Mussolini respectively). Hitler managed the conference negotiations effectively, and the attendees gave in to his demands. The government of Czechoslovakia was not invited to the conference or consulted about its decisions. Despite the USSR's alliances with France and Czechoslovakia, and its strategic interest in the area, Stalin was not invited to the conference either. Britain and France were responsible for this error, which cost them dearly later.

The Munich Conference reached decisions that were designed to prevent a major European war. It was agreed that Germany should take control of the whole of the Sudetenland, in return for Hitler's guarantee that he had no further territorial ambitions. Other parts of Czechoslovakia were given to Poland and Hungary, in line with the concept of self-determination for ethnic minorities. Czechoslovakia was left defenceless and independent in name only. The Czech government was informed that it must accept the Munich Agreement, or fight Germany alone.

The Munich Conference is the clearest example of appeasement in the 1930s. In a desperate attempt to avoid a major war, Britain and France were effectively giving in to Hitler's demands. Both Britain and France were ignoring their commitment to uphold the Paris peace settlement and France was ignoring its obligations under the terms of its defensive alliance with Czechoslovakia.

Chamberlain was convinced that Hitler's demands were both justified and reasonable, and returned to Britain proudly boasting that the Munich Agreement guaranteed peace in Europe. After all, to many Britons, Czechoslovakia was 'a small country, far away' like Manchuria and Abyssinia.

Figure 3.25: Neville Chamberlain returning to Britain after the Munich Agreement with Hitler in 1938. He was greeted with great enthusiasm as he said that there would be 'peace in our time'. The piece of paper he is holding is Hitler's promise that the Sudetenland would be his last demand, and he would not attack the rest of Czechoslovakia – or anywhere else.

Daladier was less convinced than Chamberlain. He believed that Germany's success in gaining the Sudetenland would lead to further territorial demands by Hitler, posing a threat to countries such as Poland. He agreed to go along with the decisions made at Munich only because he knew that France was neither militarily nor financially prepared for war. He also knew that Britain would not support France militarily. He returned to France anticipating a hostile reception from the French people. Instead he was applauded as the man who had helped to prevent a war. Appeasement had popular support.

The apparent ending of the threat of imminent war was greeted with relief in Britain and France. Elsewhere, too, people saw Chamberlain and Daladier as great statesmen for their efforts in preserving peace. Newspapers in Sweden and Norway campaigned for Chamberlain to be awarded the Nobel Peace Prize. The prime minister of Egypt sent a telegram to Chamberlain thanking him for averting war and describing him as the 'statesman who saved civilization from destruction'.

The outcome of the Munich Conference caused disappointment, anger and concern in the USSR. Like France, the USSR had signed a treaty of mutual assistance with Czechoslovakia, and Stalin felt he should have been involved in decisions over Czechoslovakia's future. In his absence, Britain and France had agreed to allow Germany to take control of Czech territory, greatly weakening a country that formed a defensive barrier between Germany and Russia. From Stalin's perspective, Britain and France had allied with Hitler, rewarding his aggressive actions in a way that threatened the national security of Russia. As Britain and France had failed to defend Czechoslovakia, Stalin concluded that they would not respond if Hitler acted aggressively against Russia. So, after the Munich Conference, Stalin fundamentally changed his foreign policy in the interests of Russia's security. Rather than seeking better relations with Britain and France, which he now considered unreliable allies, Stalin decided to seek negotiations with Hitler. This led directly to the Nazi–Soviet Pact of the following year.

KEY CONCEPT 3.3

Similarity and difference

Compare the policies of France and Britain towards the appeasement of Germany and Italy. Consider:

- the domestic political pressures on the leaders
- the consistency of their policies
- the reasoning behind their policies
- the different strategic interests of the two countries.

What similarities can you see between them? What were the differences? How would you explain these?

The appeasement policies of Britain and France may have seemed logical and popular at the time, but they had catastrophic effects. They undermined the effectiveness of the League of Nations to the extent that Japan and Italy were allowed to succeed in open acts of aggression in Manchuria and Abyssinia. They also allowed Hitler to progressively destroy the Treaty of Versailles – through rearmament, remilitarisation of the Rhineland, the Anschluss and claiming territory that was vital to the viability of Czechoslovakia. By the late 1930s, appeasement had helped to create a situation in which three countries posed a significant risk to international peace. These three countries were all dictatorships committed to territorial expansion and all were in alliance with each other.

ACTIVITY 3.22

SOURCE A

Figure 3.26: A cartoon by an American cartoonist, September 1938. Neville Chamberlain is seated at his typewriter and Adolf Hitler is standing over him, dictating: "The Czech cabinet accepts the British-French plan for the partition of Czechoslovakia." The man on the right asks Hitler: "After the Czechs - what next?"

SOURCE B

A GREAT MEDIATOR

Figure 3.27: A cartoon by a British cartoonist, November 1938. It is titled 'A Great Mediator'. Neville Chamberlain is on the left. John Bull is on the right, representing the British people.

Study the cartoons in Figure 3.26 (Source A) and Figure 3.27 (Source B).

- a What point is the cartoonist in Source A making?
- b What point is the cartoonist in Source B making?
- c What are the main differences between the two?
- d Are both cartoonists making a fair comment?

Responses to Hitler's occupation of Prague

In March 1939, Hitler invaded the rest of Czechoslovakia and led his army into the capital, Prague, on 15 March. He believed that France, Russia and Britain were unlikely to act together to stop him. He was correct. Czechoslovakia was absorbed into Germany. The large Czech army was disbanded, the Czech airfields were taken over by the Luftwaffe (the German air force), and the large Czech arms industry fell into German hands. France, Russia and Britain had lost a valuable potential ally against an aggressive Germany.

The League protested, but it was ignored. Perhaps more importantly, Stalin became more convinced that Britian and France would never stand up to Hitler, and that he needed to take other steps to secure Russia from Germany's eastwards advance. Hitler's promise not to expand further after the Munich Conference had lasted only a few months.

At this point, Britain and France finally accepted that Hitler could only be stopped by force. Public opinion in both countries recognised that appeasement had failed, that rapid rearmament was necessary, and that war was increasingly likely. Britain and France realised that Poland would probably be Hitler's next target. He resented the Polish Corridor which divided East Prussia from the rest of Germany, and the fact that Danzig was not a 'German' port. Both arrangements had been created by the Treaty of Versailles and, therefore, provided him with an excuse for aggression. Britain and France agreed to defend Poland by force, if Germany invaded it. In March 1939 Britain and France signed an agreement known as the 'Polish Guarantee', in which they promised to protect Poland if Germany invaded it. It was hoped that this change in policy from appeasement to **deterrent** would put a stop to Hitler's attempts to expand.

Hitler now had to decide whether or not to risk another war.

KEY TERM

Deterrent: Something which discourages a person from doing something. For example, the possibility of a prison sentence could be a deterrent to committing a crime.

Successes of appeasement

It is possible to argue that the policy of appeasing the dictators Hitler and Mussolini was not as disastrous as later critics believed. Appeasement brought some successes.

War postponed

The possibility of war was postponed, at least temporarily. In Britain and, especially, France, public opinion was divided about the prospect of going to war, and political leaders could not be certain of public support for it. Postponing war provided time for the civilian population to understand why it was necessary to fight, and to prepare for the war.

Although the Munich Agreement of 1938 had prevented an immediate conflict, the prospect of war had an important psychological impact on both people and governments. There was greater awareness of the need to prepare the civilian population for the type of warfare that might come – images of bombed Spanish cities appeared daily in newspapers. Extensive preparations were made between the Munich Conference and the outbreak of war in 1939 for protecting civilians from bombing and ensuring that essential supplies could enter Britain, which depended on imports for food and vital war materials. Both Britain and France prepared for the mass mobilisation of civilians into their armed forces. When war finally broke out in September 1939, people were much better prepared for the hardships to come and to support governments and their drastic preparations for war.

Buying time for rearmament

Although Chamberlain saw Munich as a success and believed that Hitler had been successfully 'appeased', he was under pressure from many politicians in his own government, his political opponents, much of the press and public opinion to rearm, even if not actually to fight. The pressure increased as it became evident that Hitler's ambitions in eastern Europe and Mussolini's ambitions in the Balkans and North Africa were still growing. Both French and British governments and many of the public now recognised the need to increase public spending on weapons: a rearmed Britain, with a rapidly expanding French army, might deter Hitler and Mussolini from further aggression.

As a result the British started a major rearmament programme. Substantial sums were spent on defence. The air force was expanded and decisions were taken to build up a strong fighter defensive force (which later enabled Britain to survive a German air offensive against it in 1940–41). The navy too was expanded, with a focus on defending Britain's trade routes and ensuring vital imports. The army got little funding (which cost the British dearly in 1940). In addition, Britain began to plan for a wartime economy. Mass conscription was organised, and factories planned to make tanks instead of cars.

In France, by the end of 1938 there even greater spending on the armed forces – with the focus on defence. However there were still bitter divisions within the French military about spending priorities (for example on the Maginot Line compared with tanks and the air force) and similar disagreements between politicians and the military. Public opinion remained divided, with general distrust of the political leadership. Unlike the British, the French did not make effective use of time 'bought' by the Munich Agreement to prepare for war.

Gaining popular consent

While preparing for war was never popular in Britain or France, by the end of 1938 there was a growing acceptance that war with Germany might happen. Extensive press coverage of events in Spain, news of Mussolini's use of poison gas against unarmed civilians in Abyssinia, and memories of food rationing and the bombing of civilians in the First World War combined to persuade people of the need to prepare for a war which could affect civilians as much as soldiers. Preparations included making extensive air raid precautions, planning for the mass evacuation of cities and conscription for all able-bodied men. Most people accepted that higher taxation was needed to pay for these preparations. Also, building more warships and aeroplanes and increasing recruitment for the armed services led to a large drop in unemployment, and this helped to gain consent for these measures.

Failure of appeasement

However, appeasement served to encourage the leaders of Germany, Italy and Japan in their ambitions. These leaders saw the willingness of Britain and France to make concessions to Hitler and Mussolini as seen a sign of weakness.

Figure 3.28: A British cartoonist's view of the appeasement of Hitler, 1939. The steps from the bottom right say, in order, 'Rearmament', 'Rhineland fortification', 'Danzig', '?', '??', '!!', '!!!'. The one at the top says 'Boss of the Universe'.

Increased resources of dictators

Japan continued to expand into China and gain territory and resources there. German rearmament expanded rapidly. For example, the Germans took considerable care to develop a synthetic petrol industry as Germany had no oil of its own and had to import all it needed. (The successful prevention of imports into Germany in the First World War had been a major factor in Germany's defeat.) The years 1938–39 saw a large increase in the German air force and also in its submarine fleet. In 1938, the German army was ordered to prepare for the invasion of Poland and for further expansion to the east. After 1938, the German economy became entirely focused on the needs of the military and preparation for war. Mussolini consolidated his hold on Abyssinia and started to plan expansion in the Balkans and in North Africa. His generals were ordered to prepare for the possible invasion of Albania.

Increased morale of dictators

Success in Abyssinia, Austria and the Sudetenland increased the popularity of the dictators at home and encouraged them to proceed. The appeasers failed to understand until too late that concessions only encouraged the dictators to demand more.

Growing opposition to the policy

When the French prime minister, Daladier, returned to France after agreeing to the Munich settlement, he was greeted by enthusiastic crowds delighted that war with Germany had been avoided. A public opinion poll taken later in 1938 indicated that while 57% of the population supported what he had done, 37% opposed the concessions made to Hitler. Significantly, 70% said that any further aggression by Hitler or Mussolini should be resisted.

However, bitter divisions remained in France over policy towards Germany. There was a strong fascist party which favoured allying with Germany and supporting Hitler's anti-communist aims. There was also a growing communist movement, which adopted an inconsistent policy towards appeasement as it took its orders from Stalin, whose own policies changed between 1937 and 1939. While there was opposition, it was not a major factor in French politics in the period.

Britain too remained divided on the issue of appeasement. Like Daladier, Chamberlain was greeted by enthusiastic crowds on his return from Munich and received thousands of letters supporting his decision. Much of the enthusiasm was because war had been avoided, rather than because people supported the concessions agreed at Munich. Opinion polls revealed almost identical results to France, although more people supported resisting further aggression by Hitler. However, Munich was a turning point for many in Britain. After the Munich Conference, opposition to further appeasement grew and support for rearmament became stronger. The government and many of its supporters in Parliament remained supportive of appeasement until at least March 1939, as did as much of the popular press. But the opposition party (the Labour Party), and some of the popular press started to demand more rearmament and to insist that the government should refuse to allow further aggression by Hitler or Mussolini.

Reasons for the failure of appeasement

The debate on responsibility for the failure of appeasement started in March 1939, when the German army marched into the Czech capital, Prague, and continues amongst historians to this day. Amongst the reasons considered are:

- The desire for expansion by Hitler, Mussolini and the Japanese military was too strong to be stopped except by force. That force was not available.
- The British and French failed to realise exactly what Hitler and (to a lesser extent) Mussolini intended to do. Until March 1939, Chamberlain felt that Hitler was a reasonable man and he could negotiate with him.
- Britain and France were liberal democracies. Political power depended on winning elections, and public opinion was divided about using force against aggressors until early 1939.
- There were memories of the slaughter and chaos caused by the First World War. Many people knew that new and terrifying weapons were being developed, including bomber aircraft, tanks and poison gas. The German bombing of Guernica and the Italians' use of poison gas and tanks in Abyssinia showed clearly what could happen to civilians in a modern war. Such a catastrophe should be prevented at all costs.
- Two major powers, the USA and Russia, remained largely apart from the issue, seeing their own economic and ideological interests as a priority. These countries later regretted not acting.

ACTIVITY 3.23

The debate on the merits or otherwise of appeasement started after the Munich Conference and continues to this day.

Consider the proposition: 'Appeasement failed, and the politicians who supported it deserve the strongest condemnation'.

Working in two teams, copy and complete this table with a list of factors which might be used to support this proposition, and a list of factors which could be used to oppose it.

Before you start, think carefully about your definition of 'failure' in this context. Try to put yourselves in the position of democratically elected politicians in the late 1930s. A lot of time and money had been spent in the previous 20 years in building war memorials to the millions of people who died in the First World War. Huge sums of money were still being spent on helping people who had been widowed, wounded or gassed in that war. War debts still had not been paid. Take these factors into account as you create your lists.

For the proposition	Against the proposition

3.4 Why did war break out in 1939?

By the middle of 1939 it was clear that appeasement had almost certainly failed. Hitler continued his expansionist policies, developing his network of alliances, while countries such as Britain and France continued to prepare for war.

Aims and impact of Hitler's expansionist policies

There has been much debate about exactly what Hitler's foreign policy objectives were. In his book *Mein Kampf* he wrote of his hatred of Jews, communists and the Treaty of Versailles. These feelings influenced his foreign policy. Hitler wanted Germany to expand to the east, opening up Lebensraum, or 'living room', for the German people. His speeches during his rise to power between 1929 and 1933 were cautious, to avoid putting off moderate voters who opposed war. However, once Hitler was firmly in power by the end of 1934, with all opposition inside Germany brutally destroyed, he was able to put the ideas expressed in *Mein Kampf* into practice.

Underlying aims of Hitler in foreign policy

Some historians argue that Hitler did not plan a major war, but just took opportunities to expand Germany when they arose. Others suggest that from the moment he became chancellor in 1933, Hitler planned for a possible war to expand to the east, with the enthusiastic support of General Blomberg, the war minister. From that time, German generals were ordered to plan not just to defend Germany but for an offensive war in the east. Certainly by 1935 Hitler had overcome the immediate problem of mass unemployment in Germany and ordered that the German economy should focus on planning for war.

Hitler's tactics and policies between 1933 and 1939 were inconsistent. Sometimes he was prepared to cooperate with France and Britain; at other times he saw them as potential enemies. Sometimes he was prepared to cooperate and co-exist with Russia; at other times he saw Russia as a country to be destroyed along with communism. There is evidence, however, that Hitler had broad long-term objectives, namely:

- to rearm Germany to give it offensive capability
- to prepare the German economy for war
- to overturn the Treaty of Versailles and its implications for Germany
- to expand to the east, the policy of Lebensraum
- to destroy communism and the Jewish people.

He intended to take every opportunity that arose to achieve these objectives.

Rearmament and the Anglo-German Naval Agreement, 1935

Soon after he became chancellor in 1933, Hitler secretly ordered the war minister to increase the size of the army and air force, in breach of the Treaty of Versailles. He then withdrew Germany from the Disarmament Conference and the League of Nations. He kept his more specific plans secret until 1935 when he felt more secure in his position and was confident that the German army fully supported him.

In June 1935, Hitler signed the Anglo-German Naval Agreement. Britain's willingness to sign the agreement suggested to him that Britain would not oppose Germany's rearmament or expansion eastwards unless such actions directly threatened Britain or its overseas empire. The agreement limited the German navy to 35% of the size of the British navy, but it allowed the Germans to build up a submarine fleet (something the British were later to regret). The agreement was a clear breach of the Versailles Treaty and also caused a widening rift between Britain and France. Both factors encouraged Hitler to proceed with his other ambitions.

Remilitarisation of the Rhineland, 1936

Hitler's next step towards preparing Germany for war was to send German troops to remilitarise the Rhineland in March 1936. He justified his action, and rearmament in general, by arguing that he was righting the 'wrongs' of the Treaty of Versailles. Hitler correctly predicted that Britain and France would not go to war in defence of the Treaty of Versailles and would not block his aim of expanding Germany's armed forces. Remilitarisation was a gamble on Hitler's part, and it paid off. His generals warned him of the risks, and he proved them wrong. Germany successfully regained full control over the Rhineland, without any fighting.

Britain remained relatively unconcerned about Hitler's actions, but the long-term implications of German rearmament and the remilitarisation of the Rhineland worried France and the USSR. French concerns about security increased, as German troops could be positioned on the French border in the Rhineland. In the USSR, Stalin worried that the rapid expansion of Germany's armed forces would lead to a German attack against Poland. Such an attack could affect the USSR's claims to parts of Poland and could threaten Russia itself. However, neither France nor the USSR felt strong enough to confront Hitler without the guarantee of British support.

Hitler's confidence in his own judgement grew, as did his popularity with the German people. His success in remilitarising the Rhineland was a crucial step forward to achieving his expansionist ambitions.

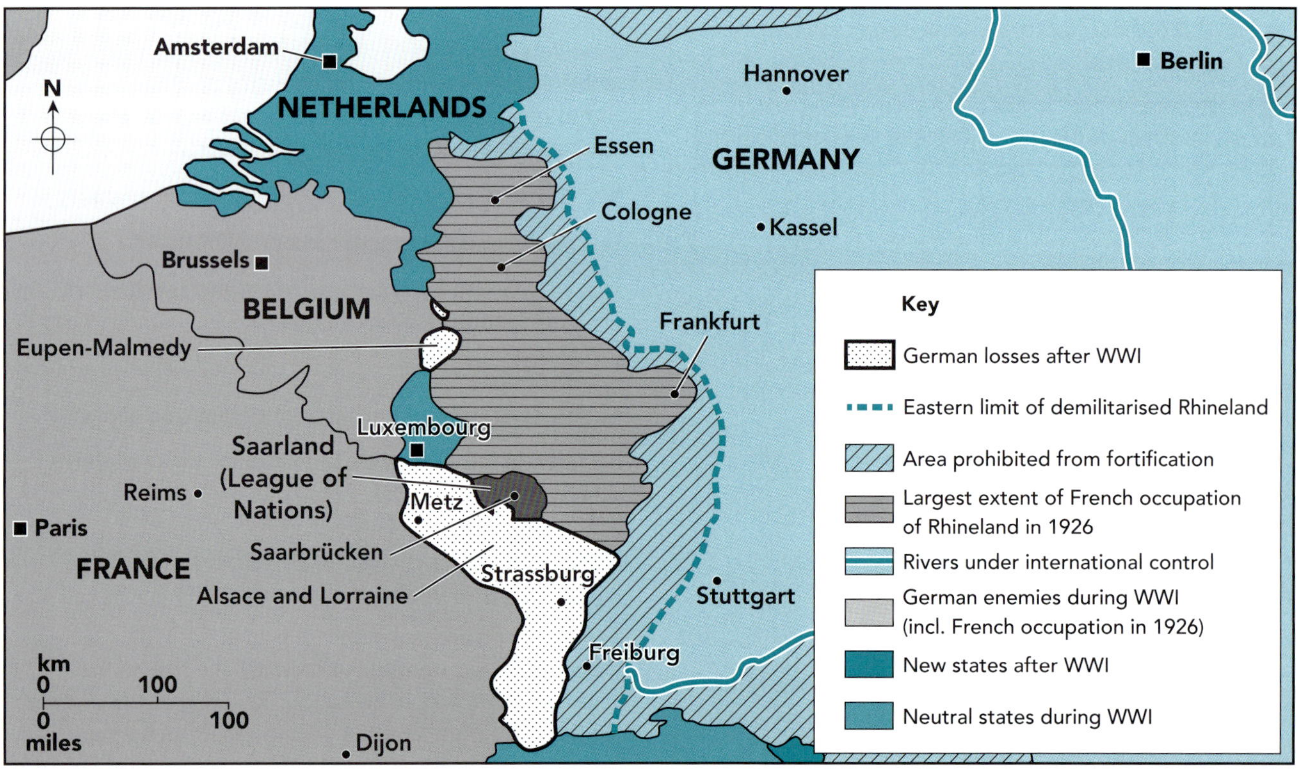

Figure 3.29: Map showing the development of the Rhineland issue and its strategic importance.

ACTIVITY 3.24

Read the following two sources carefully and then answer the questions.

SOURCE A

> The forty-eight hours after the march into the Rhineland were the most nerve-racking of my life. If the French had marched into the Rhineland, we would have had to withdraw with our tails between our legs, for the military resources at our disposal would have been wholly inadequate for even moderate resistance.
>
> **From comments by Adolf Hitler on the remilitarisation of the Rhineland.**

SOURCE B

> Goering was visibly terrified by Hitler's decision to remilitarise the Rhineland. He gave me to understand that Hitler had taken this extremely risky step by his own decision, against the advice of his own generals.
>
> **From comments by Józef Lipski (Polish Ambassador to Germany) on his meeting with Hermann Goering (a senior member of Hitler's Nazi government) in 1936.**

a What do these two sources suggest about Hitler's leadership style?

b Why would Goering have been worried about Hitler's decision to remilitarise the Rhineland?

c Which European country would Hitler have thought most likely to resist Germany's remilitarisation of the Rhineland, and why?

d In fact, no country took any action in response to Germany's remilitarisation of the Rhineland. Why do you think this was? (Look back to Section 3.3.)

Anschluss, 1938

Hitler's attentions now turned to Austria. Although forbidden in the terms of the treaties of Versailles and Saint-Germain, Anschluss (union with Austria) was always one of Hitler's main foreign policy aims. Born in Austria himself, he believed that Anschluss would unite more German-speaking people, provide Germany with Austria's resources and undermine the peace treaties. Again he gambled that there would be no intervention when he invaded Austria in March 1938, and again he was right.

With the success of the Anschluss Hitler gained access to valuable resources such as iron ore, added 7 million people to Germany's population and increased the size of his army by 100 000 men. Germany's strategic position within Europe was greatly strengthened, posing an obvious threat to other countries – especially Czechoslovakia, which was now surrounded on three sides by Nazi territory. Hitler achieved these gains unopposed – again his instinct had proved correct.

Hitler's territorial gains were hugely popular within Germany and his position as dictator was now secure. He had ensured the loyalty of the armed forces and created a terrifying police state to suppress opposition. Ready for his next move, Hitler continued to expand east.

ACTIVITY 3.25

Either in pairs or in a group, consider the following questions:

a Explain why Hitler was so anxious to unite with Austria.

b Explain why Hitler's annexation of Austria received so little opposition.

For both questions, try to identify at least three clear reasons, which you can support with relevant detail. Assess which you think was the most important reason, and why it is the most important.

ACTIVITY 3.26

J'Y SUIS, J'Y RESTE

Mr. Chamberlain. "I shall wait till it clears a bit before I get down."

Figure 3.30: A British cartoon of September 1938. The French words mean 'I am here and I am staying here'. Beneath this it says: '*Mr Chamberlain*. "I shall wait till it clears a bit before I get down."'

Study the cartoon in Figure 3.30.

a What point is the cartoonist making?

b Explain the reference to 'Dangerous Commitments'.

c Look at the date. Do you see the cartoon as critical or supportive of Chamberlain?

Sudetenland, 1938

With the peaceful acquisition of the Sudetenland in 1938, together with its 3.5 million people, strategic advantages and important resources, Hitler's power and confidence continued to grow. His successful diplomacy at Munich convinced him that Chamberlain would not cooperate with France to oppose him in the future. He noted the divisions between potential enemies such as France, Britain and Russia. These divisions convinced him that he could escape a challenge, if he seized what was left of Czechoslovakia.

Czechoslovakia, 1939

Following the methods used in Austria and the Sudetenland, Hitler encouraged riots in Slovakia to damage the Czech government in Prague. Using these riots as a pretext, the German army moved into the rest of Czechoslovakia in March 1939 to 'restore order'. Democracy was destroyed immediately, and a brutal dictatorship imposed. Again Hitler had succeeded in his aims without starting a war. Although there was international protest, there was no action against him.

Hitler was now convinced that Britain and France would never declare war against Germany whatever he did in the east. This time, however, his instincts were wrong. He had justified his earlier actions by claiming that he was correcting the unfair terms of the Treaty of Versailles, but acquiring other parts of Czechoslovakia was different. He had seized territory over which Germany could have no justifiable claim and he had broken his promises from Munich the previous year. Hitler could no longer claim that he had only peaceful intentions. Britain and France now recognised that Hitler was not to be appeased – he would proceed with territorial expansion unless he was stopped. Therefore, they signed the 'Polish Guarantee', in which they agreed to protect Poland if Germany invaded it.

KEY CONCEPT 3.4

Change and continuity

Historians analyse the reasons why changes occur, particularly when these changes are sudden and very different from what had gone before.

Chamberlain had always followed an appeasement policy, believing that this was the best way to avoid Britain's involvement in another major war. As late as 15 March 1939, when German troops entered Czechoslovakia, Chamberlain was still claiming that Hitler had not broken the promises he made at Munich.

By 17 March 1939, Chamberlain's attitude had changed. He was speaking critically of Hitler and making it clear that Britain would resist any future German aggression.

How can we explain this sudden change?

Figure 3.31: A photograph of German troops marching into Prague.

Figure 3.32: A British cartoonist's view of the German invasion of Czechoslovakia, March 1939.

British rearmament in response to Germany's expansionism

Reductions in defence spending in line with the Ten-year Rule (see Section 3.3) meant that in the 1930s Britain was militarily ill-prepared to fight a major war. As international tensions increased following Japan's invasion of Manchuria, Britain abandoned the 'Ten-year Rule' in 1932. Military commanders were worried that, if war broke out, Britain would be unable to defend its empire, its trade and even Britain itself. The government began to think it might be time to rearm, even though the idea was politically unpopular. By 1934, military thinking was that Britain might be involved in a major war within five years, although Hitler's Germany was not seen as the most immediate threat. At that time, the priorities were first to defend British interests in East Asia against Japanese expansionism, and second to protect British-owned India.

By the later 1930s, Germany began to be seen as a possible long-term threat to British security. The military wanted more money to rearm, but with the economic problems caused by the Great Depression the government felt it could not afford such expenditure. Until 1935, the British prime minister, MacDonald, remained opposed to increased military spending, and in fact he cut it drastically along with all other areas of public spending.

Events in Europe and East Asia in 1936 forced the British to rethink. The military argued that war against Germany, Italy and Japan was now extremely likely and warned that Britain could not win. The new prime minister, Baldwin, had been cautious about rearmament to win the election of 1935, but he was able to change policy without endangering his position. The government decided to considerably increase its military spending, especially on the navy and air force, but also to continue with its appeasement policy, in the hope that Hitler could be deterred from further aggression or that Germany's economic problems would force him to abandon his aggressive foreign policy.

Development of aircraft

From 1936, Britain began to develop its defence capabilities. Priority was given to the air force and navy, which were seen as vital to Britain's national defence. The air force had relied on First World War biplanes until 1935. It was now provided with new modern fighter planes, mainly Spitfires and Hurricanes, which could defend Britain against bombing attacks. Less was spent on bombers, seen more as offensive weapons. There was also substantial investment in early-warning radar systems, designed to warn when enemy bombers approached.

Preparation for air raids

In the years 1936 to 1939, Britain also made good progress in preparing for war on the '**Home Front**'. Preparations were made to deal with air raids, in view of the impact that bombs had made on cities such as Guernica, Madrid and Barcelona in the Spanish Civil War. Current military thinking was that the 'bomber would always get through', destroying cities and causing mass casualties. Over 8 million cardboard coffins were ordered. Plans were laid to evacuate children from cities into the safety of the countryside. Air raid shelters were built, and many men were trained in firefighting and in how to deal with the situation when cities were bombed. Plans were also drawn up for conscription and food rationing.

> **KEY TERM**
>
> **Home Front:** The activities of civilians in Britain during wartime, in contrast to overseas 'fronts' (for example, the British army went overseas to the 'Western Front' in France in 1914–18).

Targets and progress by 1939

Although no specific targets were set for rearming Britain's military forces, there were two main priorities, both defensive ones: one for the navy and one for the air force. As it became more clear that Germany and Japan were greatly increasing their naval resources, by 1939, Britain was committed to expanding its navy substantially, to ensure that the navy was powerful enough to defend Britain and its empire, as well as Britain's extensive trade routes. In 1939, Britain imported much of its food and also essentials like oil. The navy was provided with new battleships and aircraft carriers, while some of its other ships were modernised. Smaller warships that were suitable for defending oil tankers and merchant ships carrying war materials and food supplies into Britain were constructed, as German submarines had sunk large numbers of British merchant ships in the 1914–18 war. When the war started, Britain had developed the means of protecting vital imports into Britain.

The air force was greatly expanded after the Munich Conference. New fighters were built (over 800 were available when war broke out, which proved decisive in defending Britain against invasion in 1940), while plans were laid for a new bomber force capable of undertaking offensive operations in Europe. The air force also ensured that there was a good supply of trained pilots ready to replace those lost in action, and also ready for the expansion of the air force if war broke out. A sophisticated radar system was developed, covering the approaches to Britain, which provided advance warning of incoming bombers. The system was also to prove vital in defending Britain in 1940.

Less was spent on the army because of the enormous expenditure involved in developing the air force and the navy. The government saw sending armed forces to fight in Europe as a last resort. The army was promised modern weapons and tanks, but these took time to be manufactured, and only limited progress had been made by the outbreak of war in 1939, leaving the British army too poorly equipped to face a larger and modernised German army.

In response to the imminent threat of war posed by Hitler's claims over the Sudetenland region of Czechoslovakia, a British Expeditionary Force (BEF) was established in 1938. If war broke out, the BEF would be stationed in France to prevent Germany from threatening Britain by gaining access to the French ports. The BEF proved to be a small and poorly equipped force. Government subsidies were provided to encourage many privately owned factories to prepare to produce military equipment in the time of war. Between 1938 and 1939, the production of anti-aircraft guns increased four-fold, and 20 new radar stations, designed to spot incoming bombers, were built around Britain's coastline.

The primary purpose of the rearmament programme was the defence of Britain rather than to fight a war in Europe, which Britain still hoped to avoid by pursuing a policy of appeasement. In reality, Britain was ill-prepared to launch an attack on Hitler's Germany. On the day war broke out, the British army was composed of only 897 000 men. The French army numbered 5 million, and during the Second World War over 13 million soldiers served in the German army. Britain had spent £350 million on armaments in 1937 to 1938, but Germany had spent £1600 million. By the end of 1938, Britain had fewer than 1000 modern aircraft – Germany had 2800.

Development of German alliances

Germany and its allies had lost the First World War partly because they had to fight on too many fronts. In 1917, for example, they were fighting in France and Belgium in the west, in Italy in the south and in Russia in the east. They lacked the resources to be successful in all three. Hitler was determined not to repeat this situation and to ensure that, if he had to fight, he would face only one enemy at a time.

The Anti-Comintern Pact

In 1936, Hitler had signed the Anti-Comintern Pact with Japan, with Italy joining the pact the following year. Although officially the agreement aimed to fight against communism, Hitler also saw the pact as a means to expand to the east and take over parts of Russia. After the takeover of Czechoslovakia in March 1939, Hitler accelerated his planning for his invasion of Poland and, ultimately, expansion into Russia. He wanted the wheatfields of Ukraine and the oil of the Caucasus. Germany had to import wheat and had no oil wells of its own. Hitler's rapidly expanding mechanised army needed petrol for its tanks, and his growing air force also needed fuel.

Hitler now wanted to be sure of support in case Britain and France fulfilled their promise to support Poland. The Anti-Comintern Pact gave him some security, but he wanted to make sure that there was no threat from the south.

The Pact of Steel

In May 1939 Hitler sent his foreign minister, Ribbentrop, to develop the vague Rome–Berlin Axis into a formal military and political alliance. This 'Pact of Steel' between Germany and Italy agreed that, in the event of war, the two countries would assist each other with their armed forces. Neither country would make peace without the other.

Hitler and Mussolini did not trust each other, but the pact suited the ambitions of both dictators in the spring of 1939. Hitler was now secure from possible threats from the south. Mussolini felt he would be free to expand his empire into the Balkans, East and North Africa, making the Mediterranean the 'Italian sea' he dreamed of. Hitler and Mussolini did not have common interests, but they had common potential enemies: Britain and France. Ultimately the pact turned out to be an unwise move for both men. Mussolini had originally wanted to call it the 'Pact of Blood', which might have been a better title.

Figure 3.33: Hitler and Mussolini – the two fascist dictators who entered into the Pact of Steel in May 1939.

The Nazi–Soviet Pact

Convinced that Britain and France would not defend Poland, and having successfully negotiated the Pact of Steel, Hitler continued with his advance eastwards, towards Poland. The main obstacle to Hitler's plans in the east was the USSR. The USSR had its own historic claims to parts of Poland, so Stalin was likely to resist any German attempt to take possession of it.

To the astonishment of the rest of Europe, Germany and the USSR signed a treaty of friendship and non-aggression on 24 August 1939, following secret negotiations conducted by their respective foreign ministers, Ribbentrop and Molotov. Many people found it hard to believe that Stalin would sign an agreement with Hitler. Stalin feared Germany under its fascist dictator, while Hitler had spent his political career attacking communism. In the Spanish Civil War, the Russians had sent money and arms to help the Republic while the Germans supported General Franco. More recently, Hitler's aggressive intentions clearly threatened the security of the USSR. It was equally surprising that Hitler would enter an agreement with a country whose political philosophy he detested, and which was an obvious target in pursuit of his policy of Lebensraum.

Officially, the Nazi–Soviet Pact (sometimes referred to as the Molotov–Ribbentrop Pact) was an economic agreement extending trading links between Germany and Russia, together with a promise not to attack each other. However, it contained a secret agreement allowing Germany to attack Poland without Russian interference.

Figure 3.34: The Nazi–Soviet Pact agreed. The foreign ministers of the USSR and Germany: Molotov is on the left, shaking hands with Ribbentrop on the right.

In exchange, Hitler agreed that the USSR could invade the eastern parts of Poland and invade and take over the independent countries of Finland, Estonia, Latvia and Lithuania. The two dictators, therefore, agreed to destroy five independent sovereign nations.

It is unlikely that Hitler intended to honour his promise not to attack the USSR, and Stalin probably knew this. In fact, Stalin had long been convinced that Hitler's ultimate intention was to attack the USSR. There were logical reasons for Stalin's decision to sign the pact. His attempts to form an alliance with Britain and France in the interests of the USSR's national security had failed. Also, the decision of Britain and France not to involve the USSR in the Munich Conference and their policy of appeasing Hitler had convinced Stalin that they would do nothing to oppose any German attack on the USSR, and they might even welcome it. Meanwhile, Russian territory in East Asia was coming under threat, Japanese forces having attacked it near Manchuria in May 1939. The USSR might be facing war on two fronts against the combined power of Germany, Italy and Japan, allies in the Anti-Comintern Pact.

Stalin reasoned that signing an agreement would at least delay any possible German attack on the USSR, giving him time to build up his armed forces in preparation for it. In his rise to power, Stalin had carried out a series of **purges** to ensure his dictatorship, including executing the majority of the senior officers in the Soviet army, navy and air force. As a result, the armed forces were not well prepared to go to war. The pact also gave him a defensive barrier against Hitler. Stalin informed one of his senior officials: 'Of course, it's all a game to see who can fool whom. I know what Hitler's up to. He thinks he's outsmarted me, but actually it is I who have tricked him.'

Stalin was wrong. It seems that he genuinely believed that Hitler would not attack Russia in the future and continued to believe that until the day that Hitler invaded Russia in 1941. Like Chamberlain, Stalin made the mistake of believing Hitler's promises and underestimating him.

KEY TERM

Purges: The term given to Stalin's elimination of his opponents. To prevent any opposition, hundreds of thousands of potential opponents were murdered and millions sent to slave camps in Siberia to be worked to death. The victims included most of the senior officers in the army, navy and air force.

ACTIVITY 3.27

SOURCE A

Figure 3.35: Hitler stabs Stalin in the back and says: 'Forgive me Comrade, but it seemed such a good opportunity!'

SOURCE B

Figure 3.36: Hitler and Stalin shake hands while standing on a map of Poland, each holding a gun behind their back.

Study the two British cartoons in Figure 3.35 (Source A) and Figure 3.36 (Source B) about the Nazi–Soviet Pact.

a Which of the two cartoons gives the most accurate picture of the relationship between Hitler and Stalin in August 1939?

b The background of Source A shows oil wells and wheatfields. What is the relevance of this?

c Explain the reference to the 'good opportunity' in Source A.

The signing of the Nazi–Soviet Pact was equally helpful to Hitler. It guaranteed that the USSR would not interfere with his plans for an invasion of western Poland. Hitler remained convinced that Poland could expect no help from Britain and France, who would continue to be committed to the policy of appeasement. If they did support Poland, at least he would not have to fight the Russians as well. The Russians also provided Germany with important raw materials as part of the pact (Germany did not offer much in return). Hitler reasoned that once Poland had been taken, there would be nothing to prevent him invading the USSR. He would be in a much better strategic position to do so.

ACTIVITY 3.28

Consider the question 'Who gained most from the Nazi–Soviet Non-Aggression Pact?'

You will need to do a little research on the early events of the Second World War in Europe between 1939 and 1941, up to the German invasion of Russia in 1941. Did the short-term gains outweigh the longer-term gains? Draw up two lists – one identifying the benefits that the Pact brought to Hitler, and one looking at the benefits that it brought to Stalin, both then and later.

The rest of Europe understood that the Nazi–Soviet Pact was a treaty of convenience between two dictators who neither liked nor trusted each other. However, the implications of it were clear. An alliance between Britain, France and Russia to discourage Hitler from further aggression was no longer possible. Appeasement had been based on the belief that Hitler's demands were reasonable and that the best approach was to negotiate with him. However, Hitler had ignored the promises he made at the Munich Conference by taking control of the whole of Czechoslovakia. Now, the security of Poland was clearly under the threat of German aggression. The prospect of a full-scale European war seemed greater than ever.

The long- and short-term motives of the participants

The long-term motives for the three pacts made by, and between, Germany, the USSR, Italy and Japan in the years just before the outbreak of war were similar in many respects. All four nations had aggressive and expansionist ambitions. Germany wished to expand to its east, regain territory lost by the terms of the Treaty of Versailles and acquire the wheat and oil of Ukraine and Romania. The USSR hoped to regain territory it had lost in Finland, Poland and the Baltic states as a result of the First World War and the collapse of the tsarist empire. Italy wanted to expand into the Balkans and add to its empire in North and East Africa. There was also an element that the three countries wished to export their ideologies (Germany and Italy wanted to export fascism, while the USSR wanted to spread communism), but this was never the dominant motive. Japan simply wanted to take over territory which contained the raw materials its military rulers felt it needed. All four nations shared this aggressive nationalism.

The short-term motives varied according to each country's specific aims. Hitler had little respect for Mussolini and did not see him as a reliable ally, but he needed to ensure support to the south of Germany in case Germany became involved in a war with Britain and France as well as the USSR. Hitler viewed the Nazi–Soviet Pact as a temporary measure to enable him to acquire parts of Poland and secure his eastern flank, if Britain and France supported the Poles. He had no intention of stopping his march eastward or abandoning his goal of destroying communism. Stalin viewed the pact with Germany in much the same light. Having shot many of his military commanders in his purges, he needed time to build up his forces again. He still intended to retake Finland and the Baltic States. Mussolini, always worried that Germany might become the dominant partner in their pact, would ally with anyone who might help him against France and Britain. The Japanese leadership joined the Anti-Comintern Pact partly to stop communist influence spreading south from Russia into China and partly to gain allies against the British and French, both colonial powers in East Asia who might prevent Japanese expansion into Indo-China, Burma and Malaya (Vietnam, Laos, Cambodia, Myanmar, and Malaysia). The pacts were largely short-term measures designed to deal with the immediate problems facing aggressive and nationalist nations.

The attack on Poland, 1939

With Soviet neutrality now assured, there seemed to be nothing to prevent Hitler from carrying out his planned invasion of Poland.

German–Polish issues: Danzig and the Polish Corridor

Hitler had relentlessly attacked the terms of the Versailles Treaty which concerned Danzig and the Polish corridor (see Section 2.2). He continued to see the loss of the important shipbuilding city of Danzig and the separation of East Prussia from the rest of Germany as insults to Germany. Hitler used the fact that many German-speakers who saw themselves as German had been forced to live in Poland as an excuse for his aggression towards Poland. In 1937, the British foreign secretary had indicated that the British would not object to some 'revisionism of the Danzig question, provided it did not lead to any unpleasant circumstances'. Based on this statement, together with the security offered by the Nazi–Soviet Pact, Hitler took the decision to go to war with Poland.

The day after the Nazi–Soviet Pact was signed on 23 August 1939, Hitler ordered his generals to prepare for the invasion of Poland 'within days'. He also made a series of demands to Poland about its borders, Danzig and the Polish Corridor, which he knew would be unacceptable to the Poles. Despite some pressure from the British and the French, the Poles rejected those demands. Rejecting them was the only way that Poland could remain an independent nation.

Disagreement between Hitler and the German High Command

There was no political opposition in Germany to Hitler's domestic or foreign policy: within months of getting into power he had murdered his political opponents. The only possible brake on his ambitions came from the German military. Hitler had fought as a corporal in the First World War, but many of his senior commanders had been involved at a higher level and were better aware of the implications of fighting a major war over a long time.

Hitler's generals (the military High Command) urged him at least to delay the invasion, warning him that if Britain and France supported Poland he could face defeat. The generals argued that the German army was not ready to fight in both the east against the Poles and the west against Britain and France if they supported Poland. There were few German defences in the west against a well-led French army. The German navy was seriously inferior to the British navy. The German air force was well led and experienced, but its planes were becoming obsolete and there were problems in supplying and servicing them. German industry was not ready to support a long-term war because conscription and high demand had led to severe labour shortages. There was no secure supply of oil and military transport depended heavily on horses. German agriculture was inefficient, so food supply could be an issue. Hitler's generals pointed out that Germany was well prepared for a short and limited war in the summer of 1939, but not for a longer war against major powers. They wanted to wait until at least 1942 to prepare for a possible conflict with Britain and France.

Hitler dismissed their concerns. He remained convinced that Chamberlain and Daladier were weak and would avoid war. In Hitler's opinion, Britain's guarantee of support for Poland was a bluff. He also believed that a German offensive would quickly achieve a decisive victory in Poland before Britain and France could react.

The end of appeasement and the Anglo-French guarantee to Poland, March 1939

On 25 August the British signed the Anglo-Polish Treaty with the Poles, promising military assistance in the event of aggression. This treaty reinforced the earlier treaty signed in response to Hitler's invasion of Czechoslovakia in March 1939. The French reluctantly did the same. Hitler then demanded that Britain agree to his demands for Danzig and the Polish Corridor, but the British refused. Their refusal placed Hitler in a dilemma. If he did not act, he would lose face in Germany and internationally, and possibly fuel the growth of opposition in Germany. If he acted, he risked a war with Britain and France that he might not win. Such a war could be catastrophic for himself and Germany. Again he gambled. He believed the British and French appeasers would not fight. On 28 August he ordered the German army to invade Poland on 1 September 1939.

War breaks out

On 31 August 1939, Nazi soldiers wearing Polish uniforms staged a fake 'invasion' of Germany, an 'unforgivable act of aggression' that Hitler used as justification for the German attack on Poland. On 1 September 1939, the German army marched into Poland, with German aircraft bombing its airfields and cities. At 8 a.m. on the same day, the Polish government requested the promised military support from Britain and France. Still hopeful that Hitler could be persuaded to back down, and militarily unprepared for the speed of Germany's offensive, Britain and France were in no position to take immediate action. However, the British government issued an ultimatum to the German foreign minister, Ribbentrop, threatening war unless Germany withdrew from Poland. Germany refused, so Britain and France declared war on Germany on 3 September 1939.

Hitler's instincts had been wrong. The invasion of Poland proved to be a gamble too far. On the day war was declared, Britain passed the National Service (Armed Forces) Act, which made all men between the ages of 18 and 41 liable for conscription. France fully mobilised its forces. By the end of 1939, over 1.5 million men had been conscripted into the British armed forces. In support of Germany, Stalin sent Soviet military forces to the Soviet–Polish border. Stalin negotiated a ceasefire agreement with Japan, preventing further Japanese inroads into Soviet territory near Manchuria. He then ordered an invasion of eastern Poland on 17 September 1939, advancing up to the line agreed in the Nazi–Soviet Pact. Hitler and Stalin destroyed Poland as a nation.

Twenty-one years after the conclusion of the 'war to end all wars', the world was at war again.

LATEST PRICES

LATE NIGHT FINAL

Evening Standard

GERMANS INVADE AND BOMB POLAND BRITAIN MOBILISES

Warsaw, Cracow, Nine Other Towns Bombed: Danzig is "Annexed"

FRANCE DECLARES "STATE OF SIEGE"

GERMANY INVADED POLAND TO-DAY. COMPLETE MOBILISATION HAS BEEN ORDERED IN BRITAIN.

Orders in Council for the complete mobilisation of the Navy, Army and Air Force were signed by the King at a Privy Council today. The King also approved other Orders in Council dealing with the emergency.

Warsaw has been bombed. Other German aircraft raided Kursk, Gdynia, Thorn, Bialystock, Grodno, Dihiva and Bydgoszoz. A few hours later, Cracow, Katowice and Czenstowice were bombed.

THE EVENING STANDARD LEARNS THAT THE POLISH AMBASSADOR SAW LORD HALIFAX TO-DAY. HE INFORMED THE FOREIGN SECRETARY OF THE GERMAN ATTACK UPON POLAND, WHICH HE SAID CONSTITUTED A CASE OF DIRECT AGGRESSION, AND HE INVOKED THE ANGLO-POLISH TREATY.

French aid has also been invoked.

The French Cabinet met for an hour and 35 minutes. They decided to call Parliament immediately, to order general mobilisation of Army, Navy and Air Force beginning to-morrow, and to proclaim a "state of siege."

The Germans attacked without having delivered any ultimatum.

Attack On Both Sides

They are striking at the "Corridor" both from the East and the West—from the East at the town of Dzialdowo, on the East Prussian frontier, and from the West at Chojnice, about 60 miles from Danzig.

Dzialdowo is about 80 miles north-west of Warsaw.

(Continued on PAGE FOUR)

Air Raid Warning System In Force

'BRITAIN WILL FULFIL HER OBLIGATIONS'

Parliament Meeting To-night

Figure 3.37: A British newspaper announces the German invasion of Poland, which started the Second World War.

Hitler's intentions

In his book *Mein Kampf*, written in prison in the 1920s, Hitler described his long-term ambitions for Germany and what he would do when he and his Nazi Party were in power. There was no clear order of priority evident in the book, but his intentions included:

- destroying the Versailles Treaty
- restoring a German empire
- expanding Germany to the east, to gain Lebensraum or 'living room'
- acquiring the oil and wheat that Germany needed
- eliminating the Jewish people and communism
- creating a 'master race' – the 'Aryan' people who would dominate Europe.

By September 1939, these intentions were evident in both his domestic and foreign policies; and Germany's actions towards Poland after the invasion of 1939 showed clearly that Hitler was still pursuing these early ambitions.

KEY CONCEPT 3.5

Interpretations

The debate on Hitler's intentions

Historians disagree about the long-term motives and ambitions of Hitler's foreign policy.

In the period immediately after the Second World War, some historians argued that Hitler had always intended for Germany to become involved in a major war. They claimed that his long-term aim had consistently been the conquest of the USSR; that acquiring Poland was just the first step towards attacking the USSR; and that sooner or later this policy was bound to lead to a war against the other major European powers. Evidence for this theory comes from Hitler's own words in *Mein Kampf*, written long before he rose to power in Germany, in which he stated that the German population was too large for its boundaries and proposed Lebensraum as a solution. It is also known that Hitler explained his expansionist ideas to key army personnel at a meeting in 1937; this is recorded in the Hossbach Memorandum, a summary of the meeting made by Colonel Friedrich Hossbach, who attended it.

Other historians argue that Hitler intended to fight a major European war to remove the shame attached to Germany's defeat in 1918. One historian claimed that 'The only antidote to defeat in one war is victory in the next.' Another agreed, writing that 'Hitler had never doubted, and had said so on innumerable occasions, that Germany's future could only be determined through war.' In 1989, a leading German historian argued that Hitler always worked for 'the establishment of a greater Germany than had ever existed before. The way to this greater Germany was a war of conquest fought mainly at the expense of Soviet Russia.'

Some historians challenge this theory, arguing that Hitler had never intended a major war. They suggest that Hitler was an opportunist, taking advantage of situations as they occurred, and that his foreign policy was not based on a step-by-step plan of conquest. They claim that such a long-term plan would have been impossible because Hitler could not have predicted how Britain and France would react to developments such as rearmament and the occupation of the Rhineland. As evidence to support this view, they cite Hitler's own concerns that, in 1936, German soldiers might be forced to withdraw from the Rhineland if they met resistance from other European countries. They suggest that the idea of Lebensraum was only a propaganda tool to gain further support for the Nazi Party and was never intended as a plan for aggressive action.

Another historian suggests that Hitler never intended or wanted a world war and, least of all, a war against Britain and France. Such a war would make it much harder for Hitler to defeat the USSR by forcing Germany to fight on two fronts, against the USSR in the east and against Britain and France in the west. The weak British response to Hitler's aggression between 1933 and early 1939 had convinced him that Britain and France would not interfere with his plans to attack Poland, leaving the way open for a German attack on the USSR. He had every reason to believe that Britain and France would do nothing to support Stalin's communist regime. This view leads to the conclusion that, like the world war that preceded it, the Second World War was largely the responsibility of Germany, and above all Hitler, but that other countries must take responsibility, too.

Debate will continue, both on Hitler's intentions and on responsibility for the Second World War.

- Hold a class debate on the proposition 'Hitler, and Hitler alone, must take the blame for the outbreak of the Second World War'.
- One side should focus on the factors which can be seen purely as Hitler's responsibility (for example he personally gave the order to attack Poland).
- The other side should argue that other people/factors are at least partly responsible (consider for example the German people who helped elect Hitler; the German army; Mussolini and Stalin; the League of Nations; Britain and France).

Practice questions

Source-based question

Read the sources and then answer **both** parts of the question.

SOURCE A

I write to inform you, very confidentially, of the government's present position regarding the Abyssinian issue. Public opinion is greatly hardening against Italy. The people regard the League of Nations as an instrument of collective security, and are determined to stick with the League's Covenant, yet are anxious to keep out of war. These points are self-contradictory, but at present the country believes that they can be reconciled. It is essential that we are seen to support the League. It must be the League, and not the British government, which is seen to declare sanctions against Italy impracticable. The blame should be placed on League members who will not play their full part or non-members whose absence would make the application of sanctions futile. Treat this letter as entirely between you and me.

From a confidential letter by Samuel Hoare (British foreign secretary), to the British ambassador in Paris, 24 August 1935.

SOURCE B

In conformity with its obligations, the League stands, and my country stands with it, for the collective maintenance of the Covenant in its entirety, and particularly for collective resistance to all acts of unprovoked aggression. The attitude of the British nation in the last few weeks has clearly demonstrated the fact that this is no variable and unreliable sentiment, but a principle of international conduct to which they and their government hold with firm, enduring and universal persistence. The British people have clung to their ideal of collective security and are not prepared to abandon it. Britain will be second to none in its intention to fulfil, within measure of its capacity, the obligations which the Covenant

CONTINUED

lays upon it. However, the lack of agreement within the League itself has created uncertainty.

From a speech by Samuel Hoare (British foreign secretary) to the League of Nations Assembly in Geneva, 11 September 1935.

SOURCE C

There is no sign of any weakening in overwhelming support for the Covenant, nor any sign that members of the League would be unwilling to shoulder their obligations should the situation demand it. The only nation which has shown a marked lack of enthusiasm for effective action against Italy is France. The French are concerned about Germany and cannot bring themselves to take any step which could weaken a united front against the German peril. Britain's view that the failure of the League to act firmly against Italy at this time would fatally weaken it in any future crisis does not appeal with equal force to the French. French support of the League does not rest on a conception of international law. They regard it mainly as an instrument of French policy, to be used when it is convenient to France. Their aim is not to antagonise Italy while keeping the League alive for another crisis when it may be of value to them.

From a telegram to the British government from the British Minister for League of Nations' Affairs in Geneva, September 1935.

SOURCE D

Mr Baldwin assured us that Britain held faithfully to all its pledges with regard to the League. However, he said that taking action against Italy raised extremely difficult questions. He explained the great gravity of the European situation, including the danger that Mussolini might make a 'mad dog' attack on the British fleet. Though this would, in the long run, lead to the defeat of Italy, the war might last a long time and produce both losses and serious diplomatic complications.

CONTINUED

He added that Britain could not rely on effective support from any other member of the League. With the exception of Britain (and its own preparations had fallen far into arrears) none of the members of the League seemed in a position to take decisive action against Italy. As to France, the whole French nation had a horror of war and could hardly be mobilised by any provocation short of actual invasion.

From a report by a League of Nations delegation following a meeting with Stanley Baldwin, the British prime minister, December 1935.

1 a Read Sources **C** and **D**.

Compare Sources C and D as evidence of League of Nations members' views on action against Italy in 1935. **[15 marks]**

b Read **all** of the sources.

'In 1935 the British government was willing to support the League of Nations over Abyssinia.' How far do Sources A to D support this view? **[25 marks]**

Essay-based questions

Answer **both** questions. Answer **both** parts of each question.

2 a Explain why Germany became involved in the Spanish Civil War. **[10 marks]**

b 'By the end of 1938, Hitler had completely destroyed the Treaty of Versailles.' How far do you agree? **[20 marks]**

3 a Explain why Stalin was prepared to sign the Nazi–Soviet Pact. **[10 marks]**

b 'A foolish and pointless gesture.' How far do you agree with this assessment of Britain's guarantee to support Poland in 1939? **[20 marks]**

Improve this answer

1 a Read Sources **C** and **D.**

Compare Sources C and D as evidence of the League of Nations members' views on action against Italy in 1935. **[15 marks]**

The two sources agree in two main respects, that Britain is determined to support the League of Nations in not only condemning Italy's actions over Abyssinia, but also in taking firm action against Italy. 'Britain's view that the failure of the League to act firmly ... would fatally weaken it' shows that determination in Source C. Source D says that the British prime minister, Baldwin, assured the League delegation that 'Britain held faithfully to all its pledges with regard to the League.' The delegates clearly assumed that this meant he was prepared to act firmly. The other area of agreement is that France was not at all keen on taking any action against Italy, although for different reasons. Source C suggests that France had a 'marked lack of enthusiasm' for any move against Italy and Source D suggested that France would only act if it was actually invaded, such was the French people's horror of war.

The principal differences between the two sources are that Source C suggests that there is strong support in the League in Geneva for the whole idea behind the Covenant, as well as action against Italy, while Source D says that 'Britain could not rely on any effective support' from the League. Also, Source C suggests that members of the League would also be prepared to support military action as well, while Source D says that 'none of the members of the League seemed in a position to take decisive action against Italy'. These are definitely contrasting views.

Source C is a report from the British minister in Geneva, responsible for reporting what was happening at the League's meetings at the time. He would have no reason for not reporting events and opinions exactly as he found them, and in carrying out the wishes of the government in London. It is likely to be an accurate report. Source D is a report from a League delegation in London, back to the League in Geneva. While they would have no reason to do anything other than report back what Baldwin told them, they may not have been in a position to question him about why his views seemed to differ from what they knew might be the case back in Geneva.

Remember that the key to the best performance in this type of question lies in:

- Making a **developed** comparison between the two sources, explaining what the similarities and differences are. You must show evidence of sound understanding of both sources.
- Your explanations of the similarities and differences should demonstrate both good contextual knowledge and good source evaluation.

Both similarities and differences are well covered and competently explained and there is every indication in the response that both sources are fully understood. There are relevant and perceptive quotes, which are used to support valid points. It would improve the response a little to suggest whether the similarities are greater than the differences (or the other way round) and why. Doing this would turn the response into the really 'developed' comparison needed to meet the requirements of the first bullet point.

Most improvement could be made by addressing the second bullet point – demonstrating greater evidence of contextual knowledge and source evaluation. Why do you think that Baldwin and the British minister in Geneva had differing views on the support that other members of the League might provide? What might be happening in Britain which leads Baldwin to pass on the opinions he did to the League delegation? You need to show that you have thought carefully about evaluating the sources and not just taken them at face value.

Now write your own answer to the question, taking into account the suggestions for improvement.

Improve this answer

2 a Explain why Germany become involved in the Spanish Civil War. **[10 marks]**

There are three main reasons why Germany became involved in the Spanish Civil War in 1936. Hitler was very anxious to try out new weapons that had been developed for his army and air force and he could use them in Spain without having to fight another major power such as France. He was also anxious to support another fascist dictator, Franco, as he could gain another ally if he had to go to war with Britain and France. Hitler also disliked the League of Nations, having left it at the end of the Disarmament Conference in 1933, and the League was trying to prevent any foreign power from becoming involved in a civil war, seeing it as an internal event which other nations should not get involved in. These are the reasons why Germany became involved in the Spanish Civil War.

A quick look at the advice in Chapter 4 or a generic mark scheme for a question like this would help you see what is good in this response and how it could be improved. The best responses for a question of this type would:

- link factors to reach a reasoned conclusion
- be well focused and explain a range of factors supported by relevant information
- demonstrate a clear understanding of the connections between causes.

Study the response to question **2 a**. Is there a conclusion here? Of the three reasons given, which reason is the most important and why? Demonstrate in your response some evidence that you have thought about the question and not just remembered some facts.

The answer shows some focus – the three points are all correct and relevant. But are these points backed up with some relevant information? What facts could be included to back up the point about the air force? Why might there be tension between Germany and France and Britain? You can't include every possible fact in the time available, but should his support for Italy be mentioned? Hitler was anxious to support Italy as he knew that Italy might try to stop him taking over Austria.

Is there evidence of connection between the causes? Were they all quite separate – or part of a broader plan on Hitler's part?

Now write your own answer to the question, bearing in mind the suggestions for improvement.

SELF-EVALUATION CHECKLIST

After working through this chapter, complete the table.

You should be able to:	Needs more work	Almost there	Ready to move on
explain the ways that the Great Depression impacted political ideologies and agendas in Germany, Japan, Italy, and the USA			
analyse the reasons for the World Disarmament Conference			
identify the factors that shaped the relationships between the major powers in the 1930s			
explain the League's response to crises in Manchuria and Abyssinia			
discuss the ways that the major powers' attitudes toward the League changed			
describe the League's responses to the Spanish Civil War			
analyse the reasons for the failure of the League of Nations			
describe the ways that economic, military, and social concerns shaped foreign policies			
identify the actions taken to appease Hitler			
analyse the successes and failures of appeasement			
explain the goals of Hitler's expansionist policies and their impacts			
describe the ways that Britain rearmed in response to German expansionism			
identify important German alliances and the motivations of the participants			
discuss the motivations for and outcome of the attack on Poland.			

› Chapter 4

Preparing for assessment

The information in this section is based on the Cambridge International Education syllabus. You should always refer to the appropriate syllabus document for the year of examination to confirm the details and for more information. The syllabus document is available on the website: www.cambridgeinternational.org.

Introduction

As we saw in the Getting started with Cambridge International AS Level History section of this book, to achieve success in Cambridge International AS Level History you need to develop skills that enable you to analyse and interpret your historical knowledge in depth. The methods of assessment reflect this requirement. This chapter focuses on those skills and helps you prepare for assessment.

4.1 Overview of assessment and assessment objectives

For the Cambridge International AS Level History (9489/9982) assessment, you will take two papers:

- Paper 1: Historical Sources (1 hour 15 minutes) This paper is worth 40% of the AS Level. You will be asked to answer one two-part question based on historical sources.
- Paper 2: Outline Study (1 hour 45 minutes) This paper is worth 60% of the AS Level. You will be asked to answer two two-part questions.

There are three assessment objectives (AOs) which are used in AS Level History. These objectives describe the skills that are assessed in the course. Table 4.1 lists the AOs and the proportion of marks which are allocated to each one.

Marks are allocated between the two papers as follows:

- Paper 1: AO1 – 25% of the marks. AO3 – 75% of the marks.
- Paper 2: AO1 – 50% of the marks. AO2 – 50% of the marks.

These allocations show us that while learning knowledge and using it appropriately (AO1) is important, you cannot be successful in your course without being able to show the higher-level analysis and evaluation skills of AO2 and AO3.

4.2 Understanding what a question is asking you to do

Broadly, there are two main types of question: source-based questions and essay-based questions.

There are certain key words that appear in many AS Level History questions. These 'command words' are the instructions that specify what you need to do. They make it clear what is expected from a response in terms of skills, knowledge and understanding.

We will discuss the two main types of question separately, considering the command words that they might contain.

Assessment objective	Description	Percentage of total marks
AO1 Historical knowledge	Recall, select and use appropriate historical knowledge.	40%
AO2 Historical explanation, analysis and judgement	Identify, explain and analyse the past using historical concepts: • cause and consequence • change and continuity • significance. Explain and analyse connections between different aspects of the past. Reach a judgement.	30%
AO3 Historical sources	Understand, analyse, evaluate and interpret a range of historical sources in context.	30%

Table 4.1: Assessment objectives from the Cambridge International AS Level History syllabuses (9489/9982) for examination from 2027.

Source-based questions

You were introduced to the concept of source analysis in the Getting started with Cambridge International AS Level History section. You are going to look at historical sources in more detail now that you have the necessary topic knowledge from studying Chapters 1–3.

Dealing with sources

How you understand, analyse, evaluate and manage different types of sources is vital to success in assessments at AS Level. You must take time to reflect critically when you look at sources, and not just accept them at face value. This means that you must:

- Show that you have fully grasped what the source is saying. Try highlighting the key points. Remember that the key point can often be in the last sentence.
- Evaluate the sources clearly and weigh up their value individually and as a set of evidence. You can do this by demonstrating that you have thought about each source's provenance (background) and reliability. You must not just accept what the source is saying. Think about what the author might have left out. You need to test a source's reliability by:
    - comparing what it says with what other sources say and with your own subject knowledge
    - looking carefully at who created it, when, why and for what purpose or audience
    - establishing if there are any reasons to doubt the reliability of the source.

  Always include as much contextual knowledge as you can to develop a point – particularly when commenting on the accuracy/validity of a source by linking it to its historical context.
- Interpret. What can be learned from the source, taking into account your judgement on how reliable the source is?
- Remain objective. Always look at a source objectively and with an open mind.
- Never make assumptions. For example, do not assume that a source must be biased because it was written by a certain person from a certain place at a certain time. These points might establish a motive for bias, but they do not necessarily prove that a text is biased.
- Never make sweeping or unsupported assertions. A statement such as '*Source A is biased* ...' must be accompanied by evidence that you know exactly what bias is, as well as evidence and examples to demonstrate in what way it is biased, together with reasons to explain why it is biased.
- Compare sources. If you are asked to compare two sources, make sure you analyse both sources carefully before you start to write your answer. Draw up a simple plan.
- Draw conclusions. What can you learn from your analysis of the sources? How does it enhance your knowledge and understanding of a topic or event?

To analyse a source effectively, you need to consider certain questions:

- Who wrote/spoke/produced the source?
- When was it written/produced?
- What is the context?
- What does the source say / what is its message?
- Who was the intended audience?
- Why was it written/produced?
- What was the author's motive?
- How does it compare with other sources?
- How reliable is it likely to be?

It may be that one or two of those questions are more important when considering a specific source or answering a specific question, but the general principles are the same for all sources. After you practise thinking about these questions for a number of different types of sources, you will find yourself naturally asking the right questions when you look at a source.

Understanding, analysing and evaluating a text source

As you will have seen in Chapters 1–3 there are many different types of text sources, from private diaries to journalists' articles in newspapers to memoirs written by actual participants some years after the events. All these sources need careful evaluation.

Let's look at an example and see how it works in practice. The following source is an extract from a speech by Francisco Franco from 17 July 1936.

> Spaniards! The situation in Spain grows more critical every day. Anarchy reigns in most of the countryside and towns, while the government fails to impose law and order. Murderers use pistols and machine guns to settle their differences and to kill innocent people. Revolutionary strikes paralyse the nation, destroying its wealth and creating hunger, forcing working men to the point of desperation. Serious crimes are committed, yet the government refuses to allow the armed forces to defend public order.
>
> **From a speech by Francisco Franco, 17 July 1936.**

- **Who wrote (spoke) this speech?** Francisco Franco, a general in the Spanish army.
- **When was it written?** On 17 July 1936.
- **What is the context?** Spain was in turmoil and its elected government was unable to provide solutions to the country's social and economic problems, or even maintain public order. On 17 July 1936, the date on which Franco made this speech, a group of army generals, working in collaboration with the right-wing Falange, began a revolt. Franco was flown in from the Canary Islands to assume leadership of the revolt.
- **What does the speech say?** The main point is that Spain had descended into anarchy and was facing the prospect of revolution. The democratically elected government had lost control, and no longer had the power or authority to govern the country. By implication, the army needed to take control in order to restore order and prevent further violence and catastrophic strikes.
- **Who was the intended audience?** The people of Spain.
- **Why was it written? What was the author's motive?** To encourage support for, and reduce opposition to, the army's attempt to take control of Spain.
- **How does it compare with other sources?** There was clearly considerable opposition to the army's attempt to take control of Spain – as evidenced by the fact that the Spanish Civil War lasted so long. Spain was divided into those who supported the army's revolt and those who strongly opposed it. Sources reflect this division.
- **How reliable is it likely to be?** It is a very one-sided speech that seeks to justify a military takeover of Spain in defiance of the country's constitution and against the wishes of many Spaniards.

So, overall, do you think that this is a very important source which tells us a great deal – or considering what Franco is saying and when he is saying it, is it a predictable piece of propaganda?

Understanding, analysing and evaluating a visual source

Many of the sources you will encounter are texts, but you will also be required to use visual sources. Visual sources may be cartoons, posters or photographs. You will analyse and evaluate visual sources in much the same way as text sources, so do not worry. However, it is a good idea to practise working with visual sources, so that you are comfortable with using them.

Let's look at some examples and see how they work in practice.

Cartoons

Cartoons can be difficult to analyse. In most cases they are drawn and published for one or more of three reasons:

- to amuse and entertain
- to celebrate
- to criticise and send a message.

To achieve these aims, cartoons might use symbolism and a subtle form of humour that people at the time might have understood, but which is less obvious to us.

Look at the cartoon in Figure 4.1 (see next page). Hitler (left) and Stalin (right) are drawn as clearly recognisable figures. They look smug and pleased with themselves. They are greeting each other with exaggerated politeness (removing caps, bowing, hands on hearts), but their words imply mutual dislike. Hitler greets Stalin with the words 'The scum of the earth, I believe', while Stalin says 'The bloody assassin of the workers, I presume'. Both carry guns, symbols of their warlike and aggressive tendencies. They are shown as meeting over the body of a soldier, representing Poland. Debris and rubble show the destruction of war and the aggressive nature of Germany's invasion of Poland. The background could be interpreted as smoke rising from bombs, or as storm clouds gathering to represent future conflicts.

Figure 4.1: This cartoon was published in a British newspaper on 29 September 1939. The image text reads: [Hitler] 'The scum of the Earth, I believe?' [Stalin] 'The bloody assassin of the workers, I presume?'

- **Who produced the source?** The cartoonist and the British newspaper which published the cartoon. The easily recognisable signature at the bottom right tells us that the cartoonist was David Low, who worked in Britain and was well known for his politically inspired cartoons.
- **When was it published?** 29 September 1939.
- **What is the context?** Germany's invasion of Poland, which started on 1 September 1939 and finally led to the end of appeasement. Britain and France declared war on Germany on 3 September 1939. However, it took time for these countries to mobilise their troops and they were able to offer little support to Poland, which fell by 29 September 1939. As agreed in the Nazi–Soviet Pact, Germany and the USSR divided the spoils between them.
- **What does the source say / what is its message?** Hitler and Stalin are portrayed as dishonest, evil, selfish and aggressive. Their plan to conquer Poland and divide the spoils between them has been successful. They are proud of what they have achieved and show no remorse. The Nazi–Soviet

Pact is depicted as a treaty between enemies who are prepared to ignore their mutual hatred in order to further their desire for territorial conquest. The policy of appeasement had clearly failed. It had not stopped Hitler from continuing with an aggressive foreign policy, leading to the destruction of Poland. It is likely that Hitler will continue to seek further conquests.

- **Who was the intended audience?** The cartoon was published in a British newspaper and was intended for a British audience – an audience that was now involved in a war against Hitler's Germany.
- **Why was it produced? What were the motives of the cartoonist and the editors of the newspaper?** Britain's declaration of war on Germany obviously caused great concern to the British people. Fear of involvement in another major war had been a key reason why British public opinion had largely supported Britain's appeasement policy during the 1930s. Some people thought it was not wise for Britain to go to war to defend a country situated far away in central Europe. The cartoon was intended to address these concerns by stressing that Britain's decision to declare war on Germany was justified – the British people were involved in a just and honourable war against evil and unprovoked aggression.
- **How does it compare with other sources?** The message is very clear and the images of the two dictators are good evidence of the opinion that the cartoonist holds of the two men and what they have done. (You would have to study other sources to be able to make comparisons.)
- **How reliable is it likely to be?** A Russian or a German might challenge the portrayal of their leader, but, because of the context (the fact that Poland had just been destroyed), it is a fair reflection of what many outside of Russia and Germany felt at the time.

When you study a cartoon like this, you need to reflect carefully on how far your own subject knowledge supports or challenges the views represented.

Posters

Posters are created with a specific intention. They aim to convey a message – for example to encourage people to join the army, or to vote for a candidate in an election. They do not give us a balanced view of a situation, but they can give a very clear idea of what might have inspired and motivated people at the time.

Figure 4.2: Republican poster published c.1937. The poster shows Republican supporters fighting a defensive battle against Franco's Nationalist forces during the Spanish Civil War. The caption reads 'They shall not pass'.

Look at the poster in Figure 4.2. What can this source tell us?

- **Who produced the source?** The Republican side in the Spanish Civil War.
- **When was it produced?** During the Spanish Civil War, c.1937.
- **What is the context?** In 1936, a group of army generals, in collaboration with the right-wing Falange Party, began a revolt designed to remove the democratically elected government of Spain and take control of the country. They were known as the Nationalists and led by General Franco. They were opposed by the Republicans in a civil war which lasted until Franco finally gained victory in 1939. Those who fought on the Republican side were mainly civilian volunteers, supported by foreigners who had gone to Spain after joining the International Brigades.

- **What is the message of the poster?** The Republicans are fighting a determined war against the military Nationalist forces of General Franco. The Republican fighters are totally committed to the task of preventing Spain falling under military control. They are well organised (for example, they all appear to be wearing similar uniforms), and, therefore, have every chance of winning the war.
- **Who was the intended audience?** The people of Spain. It is possible that the poster was also distributed in other countries.
- **What were the motives for producing the poster?** To encourage more people to join the Republican fighters in the war against the Nationalists.
- **How does it compare with other sources?** It is likely to be less balanced than other sources, but it can give a clear idea of the sense of strength and determination that the Republicans wanted to demonstrate.
- **How reliable is it likely to be?** Posters are designed to influence and inspire. They can give a good picture of one side of an issue.

  Unlike the professional soldiers under Franco's command, the Republicans were largely armed workers who lacked military experience, organisation and discipline. Moreover, while Franco had maintained the unity of the various right-wing groups that made up the Nationalists (for example, the army, the Church, monarchists, Falangists), the Republicans were far less unified, comprising various left-wing groups with their own, often contradictory, aims (for example, communists, socialists, anarchists). A considerable amount of evidence suggests that, in reality, Republican fighters were not as well-organised and well-equipped as the poster implies.

Posters can be very useful in gaining understanding of issues and what motivated people at the time.

Photographs

Posters and cartoons are drawn or painted. Photographs are different from posters and cartoons because they can generally only visualise a scene that existed at a specific place and at a specific time – a scene that a camera captured. Photos can add to our understanding of issues and the grasp of specific events.

What does the image in Figure 4.3 tell us?

- **Who produced the source?** A press photographer covering the Spanish Civil War.
- **When was the photograph taken?** Approximately 1937, but, as with the poster, the exact date is uncertain.
- **What is the context?** The Spanish Civil War. The context is the same as for the poster.
- **What does the source show?** Like the soldiers in the poster in Figure 4.2, the Republican supporters in this photograph are fighting with courage and dedication for a cause they obviously believe in strongly. However, the impression given here is very different from that of the poster. There are fewer Republican fighters here than those shown in the poster. They seem less well organised (they are not all wearing similar uniforms, and some are clearly in civilian clothing). They also seem less well equipped (they are firing different types of weapons, including handguns which would be relatively inefficient in such a battle).
- **Who was the intended audience?** Readers of the newspaper(s) in which the photograph was published.
- **Why was it produced? What were the motives of the photographer?** The press photographer would make money by selling pictures of the war to newspapers. The photograph would be used to illustrate written coverage of the Spanish Civil War. To speculate further about motives, we would need to know something about the photographer, such as his nationality and whether there were reasons to suspect that he favoured either the Republicans or the Nationalists in the Spanish Civil War.
- **How does it compare with other sources?** This photograph fits more logically than the poster with the mass of evidence about the nature of the Republican resistance to Franco's forces in the Spanish Civil War. However, we need to remember that it is simply a single photograph of one particular incident in the war, which may or may not be typical. You might compare the photograph with other sources (such as the poster in Figure 4.2) to make some judgements about the numbers of fighters, the equipment and the tactics of the Republican forces.

- **How reliable is it likely to be?** Photos always need to be treated with caution before accepting them as evidence. They can be carefully stage managed and altered. You might think about what the photograph appears to show (men getting ready for combat) and then consider whether the photographer would really have stood up alongside them, perhaps on the other side of the wall, and perhaps higher than the armed men, in order to take a photograph. If this does not seem likely, what other explanations might there be for this image?

Like all sources, photographs can be of tremendous value to a historian, but they need to be used with care. Photographs can easily be stage-managed. For example, there is a well-known photograph of Hitler being enthusiastically welcomed into Vienna by large numbers of Austrians following Anschluss in 1938. The impression is that the Austrian people were delighted that their country had been united with Germany. Can we be certain, however, that their delight was genuine? Could they have been acting in response to guns trained on them by German soldiers strategically positioned out of camera shot? We should also remember that photographs can easily be altered to give a totally different impression to that originally intended.

Figure 4.3: Republican fighters defending an unidentified road against Nationalist forces during the Spanish Civil War (photo taken by an unknown press photographer in c.1937).

Comparing two sources

Very often, two sources will offer contradictory views. Whenever you compare two or more sources, you should draw attention to the similarities and what they have in common. You should also draw attention to the differences and points where they disagree.

At AS Level, you are expected to do much more than just give a summary of the two sources. You must show that you have reviewed the content of the sources and that you fully understand them and can use your knowledge and understanding of them to answer the question. Make sure you demonstrate your full grasp of the points made in each source and establish very clearly what the main similarities and differences are. Quote briefly from each source to evidence your points – no more than five or six words is usually fine. Take care to explain clearly **why** there are similarities and differences as well. That explanation is important. Do demonstrate contextual knowledge and show that you are fully aware of the sources' provenance. When evaluating each source do not just make a vague comment, comment quite specifically on each source.

Let's look at an example and see how it works in practice. Study Source A and Source B on whether the USA should join the proposed League of Nations.

SOURCE A

The Republicans are trying to defeat the plan for a League of Nations, which, if organised, will reduce military armament among all the great powers, and make war almost, if not completely, impossible. If the Senate destroys the League of Nations, then the USA must begin at once to arm on a greater scale than any other nation in the world, because we must be strong enough to beat all comers. This means a navy in the Atlantic big enough to overcome the combined navies of at least three European powers. It means a navy in the Pacific bigger than Japan. It means the greatest standing army we have ever had. If we want to promote human slaughter and increase taxation, we should defeat the League of Nations. If we must abandon the glorious ideas of peace for which this nation has always stood, we must do so with full knowledge that the alternative is wholesale preparation for war.

From a public speech by Senator William G. McAdoo (Democrat), 1919.

SOURCE B

Can any American be willing to merge our nationality into internationality? We do not mean to live within and for ourselves alone, but we do mean to hold our ideals safe from foreign interference. Americans will not fail civilization in the advancement of peace. We are willing to give, but we resent demand. We desire a world relationship which will maintain peace through justice rather than force, yet still hold us free from menacing involvement. It is better to be the free agents of international justice than to be shackled by a written compact which surrenders our freedom of action and gives the League the right to proclaim America's duty to the world. No surrender of rights to a world council should ever summon Americans to war. There is sanctity in that right which we will not surrender.

From a public speech by Senator Warren G. Harding (Republican), 1919.

In order to look at the similarities and differences between the two sources, you will first need to analyse them. You might want to think about these questions:

- **Who made these speeches?** Two American Senators, William McAdoo and Warren Harding.
- **When were these speeches made?** Both in 1919.
- **What is the context?** Democratic President Woodrow Wilson returned to the USA in 1919 with details of the proposals, agreed at the Paris Peace Conference, for the establishment of a League of Nations. He actively sought political and public support for these proposals. In 1919, the US Senate was split largely along party lines. Most Democrats supported Wilson's proposals – they favoured internationalism, which meant that the USA would work closely with other nations to develop a League of Nations which would reduce the risk of future wars. However, the Republicans now held a majority in the Senate and most Republicans supported isolationism – they argued that membership of the League would undermine American independence, and force the USA to become involved in wars in support of the League's decisions. As a presidential election was due in 1920, both Democrats and Republicans tried to sway public opinion to support their contrasting views. These speeches were made during the heated debate which then took place, both

within the Senate and across the country, regarding whether the USA should become a member of the League of Nations.

- **What do the sources say?** The two sources present different views on the debate which took place in the USA during 1919 regarding whether or not the country should join the proposed League of Nations. The sources are both extracts from speeches. Source A argues that the USA should join, while Source B argues that it would be against American interests to do so.
- **Who was the intended audience?** Since these were both public speeches, the Senators were addressing the American people.
- **What were the authors' motives?** To sway American public opinion on the issue of whether or not the USA should become a member of the League of Nations.
- **How do the sources compare?** Speeches can give us very useful information about the issues and the way politicians wanted their listeners to understand them. You might compare the way two different speakers, speeches made at different points in time, or speeches to different audiences discuss the same issue. In this case, consider the points of similarity between the provenances of the speeches, and the contents of the speeches. Then identify the differences and think about what might lie behind these differences.
- **How reliable are the sources likely to be?** These were politically motivated speeches, reflecting the personal views of the speakers and the parties they represented. Political speeches always need to be treated with caution before accepting them as evidence. They are always written very carefully, with a good understanding of the audiences who would hear them. They are always written to persuade, but saying this alone does not provide a very deep insight into the specifics of the situation. Consider what you know about the two speakers: were they equally well-known and influential? Consider what you know about the debates that were important at the time: do these speeches represent typical statements of the main positions in the debate? Consider the feelings of most Americans at this time: which speech better strikes a tone that would be likely to arouse the sympathies of the audience?

So, how do you organise these ideas and use them to answer the question?

A good way of comparing the views contained in these two sources is to make some brief notes on the key points, focusing strictly on the issue of whether or not the USA should join the League of Nations. For example, Source A argues that:

- The League of Nations would lead to disarmament and make future wars 'almost, if not completely, impossible'.
- If the USA did not join the League, it would need to increase its armed forces in order to protect its interests and ensure its national security.
- Enhancing the USA's armed forces would require an increase in taxation.
- Joining the League was the best way to ensure future peace – not becoming a member of the League would lead to the USA's involvement in wars.

McAdoo, a Democratic Senator, is heavily critical of the Republican Party's attempts to defeat the proposals for US membership of the League of Nations.

And Source B shows that:

- Harding supports the basic aim of the League (maintaining 'peace through justice rather than force'), but argues that membership of the League would undermine the USA's independence.
- Membership of the League would lead to foreign interference in American affairs.
- Joining the League could also lead to the USA's involvement in wars in support of decisions made by the League.
- The USA should be free to make its own decisions on issues such as whether or not to go to war – it should not be forced to do so because of its commitments to a League of Nations.

Harding was a Republican Senator who strongly opposed Wilson's vision of a League of Nations and was later victorious in the presidential election of 1920.

From this plan it is easy to see where the authors agree and disagree. They both want international peace and the avoidance of the USA's involvement in any future war. However, they disagree about the best way to achieve these aims, and the possible implications if the USA decided to become a member of the League of Nations.

Source-based questions in assessment

Now that we have looked at different types of sources and the key source analysis skill of comparing sources, let's look at types of question that you might meet in assessment.

Source-based questions test your ability to:

- understand a question and its requirements
- understand the content of a source in its historical setting
- consider how we need to understand a source's meaning in relation to who produced it, and what the writer of the source was trying to achieve
- analyse and evaluate source content and the sources themselves
- reach a focused and balanced judgement based on evidence
- communicate your argument in a clear and effective manner.

TIP

When answering, remember:

- You do not need to provide a summary of the sources, or copy out large parts of them. However, you might need to quote just a phrase or two to back up your points.
- Evaluate the sources. You must show clearly that you have really thought about their provenance and validity.
- Include relevant contextual knowledge.

Consider the source-based question provided in Chapter 3. It contains four sources on the League of Nations' response to the Italian invasion of Abyssinia. Then, it asks two questions:

1 a Read Sources **C** and **D**.

Compare Sources C and D as evidence of League of Nations members' views on action against Italy in 1935. **[15 marks]**

b Read **all** of the sources.

'In 1935 the British government was willing to support the League of Nations over Abyssinia.' How far do Sources A to D support this view? **[25 marks]**

First of all, you must study the sources carefully.

SOURCE A

I write to inform you, very confidentially, of the government's present position regarding the Abyssinian issue. Public opinion is greatly hardening against Italy. The people regard the League of Nations as an instrument of collective security, and are determined to stick with the League's Covenant, yet are anxious to keep out of war. These points are self-contradictory, but at present the country believes that they can be reconciled. It is essential that we are seen to support the League. It must be the League, and not the British government, which is seen to declare sanctions against Italy impracticable. The blame should be placed on League members who will not play their full part or non-members whose absence would make the application of sanctions futile. Treat this letter as entirely between you and me.

From a confidential letter by Samuel Hoare (British Foreign Secretary), to the British Ambassador in Paris, 24 August 1935.

SOURCE B

In conformity with its obligations, the League stands, and my country stands with it, for the collective maintenance of the Covenant in its entirety, and particularly for collective resistance to all acts of unprovoked aggression. The attitude of the British nation in the last few weeks has clearly demonstrated the fact that this is no variable and unreliable sentiment, but a principle of international conduct to which they and their government hold with firm, enduring and universal persistence. The British people have clung to their ideal of collective security and are not prepared to abandon it. Britain will be second to none in its intention to fulfil, within measure of its capacity, the obligations which the Covenant lays upon it. However, the lack of agreement within the League itself has created uncertainty.

From a speech by Samuel Hoare (British Foreign Secretary) to the League of Nations Assembly in Geneva, 11 September 1935.

SOURCE C

There is no sign of any weakening in overwhelming support for the Covenant, nor any sign that members of the League would be unwilling to shoulder their obligations should the situation demand it. The only nation which has shown a marked lack of enthusiasm for effective action against Italy is France. The French are concerned about Germany and cannot bring themselves to take any step which could weaken a united front against the German peril. Britain's view that the failure of the League to act firmly against Italy at this time would fatally weaken it in any future crisis does not appeal with equal force to the French. French support of the League does not rest on a conception of international law. They regard it mainly as an instrument of French policy, to be used when it is convenient to France. Their aim is not to antagonise Italy while keeping the League alive for another crisis when it may be of value to them.

From a telegram to the British government from the British Minister for League of Nations' Affairs in Geneva, September 1935.

SOURCE D

Mr Baldwin assured us that Britain held faithfully to all its pledges with regard to the League. However, he said that taking action against Italy raised extremely difficult questions. He explained the great gravity of the European situation, including the danger that Mussolini might make a 'mad dog' attack on the British fleet. Though this would, in the long run, lead to the defeat of Italy, the war might last a long time and produce both losses and serious diplomatic complications. He added that Britain could not rely on effective support from any other member of the League. With the exception of Britain (and its own preparations had fallen far into arrears) none of the members of the League seemed in a position to take decisive action against Italy. As to France, the whole French nation had a horror of war and could hardly be mobilised by any provocation short of actual invasion.

From a report by a League of Nations delegation following a meeting with Stanley Baldwin, the British Prime Minister, December 1935.

Look at how you might answer these questions.

You will see that the part **a** question requires you to compare two sources.

Here is some advice on answering part **a**.

1 a Read Sources **C** and **D**.

Compare Sources C and D as evidence of League of Nations members' views on action against Italy in 1935. **[15 marks]**

A response to this question should include:

- Evidence that you have really understood the points made in both sources and grasped their overall argument.

  For example, *Source C suggests that Britain and most other nations are supportive of firm action against Italy, but France is against it. Source D shows Britain is not keen on the idea of action against Italy, and is more sympathetic to France's views.*

- Evidence that you have identified areas of both difference and similarity between the two sources. A good response will comment on whether there are more similarities than differences, and why. The answer should provide a clearly developed explanation of both similarities and differences, making careful use of both sources.

  For example, *Both sources are critical of Italy and dislike what it has done to Abyssinia, but they differ over Britain's attitude towards France and also over the attitudes of other members towards taking action against Italy. The differences are more evident than the similarities.*

- Contextual awareness, showing that you have background knowledge on the topic.

  For example, mention could be made of the growing threat of Germany by 1935 and the need for Baldwin to keep Italy as a possible ally against Germany, as referred to in Source D.

- Evaluation of both sources and consideration of their validity and provenance. Which would you trust more and why?

  For example, *Arguably C is the most reliable as the Minister is actually in Geneva at the time and his primary role is to report accurately to London what is going on at the League of Nations. He has no reason to do anything other than provide accurate evidence. Baldwin in Source D is possibly misrepresenting the information in Source C as he is under strong domestic pressure in 1935 to avoid going to war or antagonising Italy.*

- Look at the dates of the sources and reflect on what has been happening of relevance when the sources were written. Think about the authors of the sources.

    For example, *Both authors are writing at the time of the crisis, but have very different roles – and they have different responsibilities as well.*

Have a look at the other part **a** source questions at the end of Chapters 1 and 2. You will see that although the wording may differ, the questions are looking for similar skills.

TIP

When a question asks you to compare two sources, make sure you use only the two sources mentioned.

The part **b** question asks you to consider four sources together. Here is some advice on answering this type of question where information from a number of sources needs to be evaluated.

1 b Read **all** of the sources.

'In 1935 the British government was willing to support the League of Nations over Abyssinia.' How far do Sources A to D support this view? **[25 marks]**

A response to this question should include:

- A clear answer to the question. Set out your judgement at the beginning of your response and be firm and specific. You need to make it clear how far the sources do, or do not, support the view – do not just give a vague 'to some extent'.

    For example, *There is ample evidence in the sources that despite the appearance of full support, Britain was actually extremely reluctant to support the League wholeheartedly. Britain had specific reasons for not wishing to provoke Italy, not the least of which was the desire to remain in alliance with France, but the sources show that of equal concern was that Britain should appear to be fully in support of the League to the rest of the world.*

- A balanced argument to support your judgement, demonstrating source analysis skills. A balanced argument is one that considers several different points of view. The supporting paragraphs after your judgement are a good place to do this. Always carefully study the sources while considering what the question is actually asking. Make it clear that you have understood all four sources (not just the two specified in the first question!) and grasped their overall arguments. You must use all four sources in your answer.

A good way of structuring a response to this type of question is to start by discussing the sources which **support** the view, and then follow with the sources which **oppose**. You must identify the key points showing agreement and disagreement. Some sources will fully support or oppose the view, others may be divided on the issue. You need to include evidence that shows the extent to which each source supports it. Do not just copy out parts of the sources in your answer but do quote short phrases to back up points that you make.

For example, *The sources provide different insights into Britain's attitude to the situation in Abyssinia. It is clear that the sources intended to be made public, or with the potential to have an impact on British foreign relations, suggest that Britain was concerned with being seen to be willing to support the League. Sources B and D express this view most clearly. Source D adds some new information about British reasons for wishing to avoid antagonising Italy.*

The sources drawn from private communications between British officials show that Britain's position was less decisively pro-League in reality. Sources A and C privately urge more caution. Source A shows the British government keen to satisfy public opinion, but avoid war and therefore (privately) intent on not being seen to be responsible for not holding Italy to account. Source C presents a British analysis of French official attitudes and it implies that supporting the French was also a British priority. It also agrees with Source D's analysis of French determination to avoid war.

TIP

You do not have time to spend on 'background' or 'setting the scene'. Keep to the point and show clearly that you fully understand all the sources as well as the question.

- Evaluation of the context, validity and provenance of the sources. Make sure that you evaluate all the sources in context and consider their validity and provenance. Have you considered the nature, origin and purpose of each source? Is the date of the source important?

  Use your own ideas on the provenance of the sources, and your own contextual awareness, to support your argument. You need to show that you have background historical knowledge and understanding and that you are not just relying on the sources for information.

  For example, *The sources provide small clues at the kinds of concerns the British had at the time – the position of the British fleet, references to French concerns about Germany, references to war, for example. These sources are all valid as evidence of the British government's position, but they are valid for different things. Source A shows what the British government wanted the French government to know about the difficult position they felt they were in, balancing the need to satisfy public opinion with the need to support the League. Source B is valid evidence of the British government's official statement of its position, but not very valuable as an indication of the complex realities. Source C is valid as an indication of what the British government was telling its officials at the League, so that they understood how they should interact with other League members. Source D is valid as a summary of the British prime minister's more guarded justification for relative inaction by December 1935.*

- A good way to end your response. It is important to suggest whether you think the weight of the evidence supports the view or not – and why. You also need to show that you have thought about the 'extent' to which the sources agree or disagree with the view and made up your own mind about it.

  For example, *The sources show that Britain wanted to appear to be ready to provide full support to the League, but they also show that Britain's position was more complex than that. Overall, the weight of the evidence suggests that Britain supported the League in public, but was ultimately unwilling to support the League fully.*

As with part **a**, have a look at the other part **b** source questions in the Practice question sections at the end of Chapter 1 and Chapter 2. Although the wording of each question is slightly different, all these questions ask you to consider how far the four sources support a view, so what you are being asked to do is the same.

Essay-based questions

You were introduced to essay-writing skills in the Getting started with Cambridge International AS Level History section of this book. Now you will see how to apply the earlier information to some specific examples.

In this book, you have met the following examples:

Chapter 1:

1 a Explain why Japan was victorious in the Russo-Japanese War of 1904–05. **[10 marks]**

  b To what extent was the adoption of western technology the main reason for Japanese modernisation during the 19th century? **[20 marks]**

2 a Explain why the USA entered the First World War in 1917. **[10 marks]**

  b 'Victory in the war against Spain (1898) was the main reason for the USA's emergence as an imperial power.' How far do you agree? **[20 marks]**

Chapter 2:

1 a Explain why the Dawes Plan was developed in 1924. **[10 marks]**

  b 'The Locarno Treaties of 1925 greatly reduced tension between European nations.' How far do you agree? **[20 marks]**

2 a Explain why France occupied the Ruhr region of Germany in 1923. **[10 marks]**

  b 'The structure of the League was the main reason for its weakness in the 1920s.' How far do you agree? **[20 marks]**

Chapter 3:

1 a Explain why Germany became involved in the Spanish Civil War. **[10 marks]**

  b 'By the end of 1938, Hitler had completely destroyed the Treaty of Versailles.' How far do you agree? **[20 marks]**

2 a Explain why Stalin was prepared to sign the Nazi–Soviet Pact. **[10 marks]**

b 'A foolish and pointless gesture.' How far do you agree with this assessment of Britain's guarantee to support Poland in 1939? **[20 marks]**

You will see that in fact each numbered question contains two separate question types. Each question type needs to be approached slightly differently, so we will discuss each question type in turn.

Questions that highlight knowledge and understanding

These questions may ask you to show your knowledge and understanding by explaining why something happened.

Let's look at an example:

a Explain why Britain pursued a policy of appeasement towards Nazi Germany during the 1930s. **[10 marks]**

A good-quality answer to this type of question will:

- Be entirely focused on this question. It should only discuss the reasons why Britain pursued a policy of appeasement towards Nazi Germany in the 1930s. No reference to other important factors is expected.
- Identify three or four relevant points and develop them with supporting detail. It is a good idea to add them in order of importance.

  For example,

  - *British politicians feared another major war with Germany, and British public opinion was overwhelmingly pacifist.*
  - *Britain knew that the USA would not be willing to get involved in a conflict in Europe, and the USSR was not a trusted ally at this time.*
  - *British armed forces were not large or well-equipped, and the effects of the Great Depression meant that the British economy could not cope with the cost of rearmament.*
  - *Many British politicians thought that Hitler could be reasoned with, and that once his primary concerns had been addressed, his foreign policy would become less aggressive.*

- Indicate which of those points you feel are the most important, and why. This is vital in an 'explain why' type of question to demonstrate that you have thought about the relative importance of the points you are writing about.

  For example, *The most important reason why Britain followed a policy of appeasement was that there was a strong desire to avoid war, at almost any cost. Politicians and the general public were united in their pacifism and this attitude underpinned all of the other factors.*

- Be written in as clear English as possible.

This type of question is testing understanding as well as knowledge. It is not enough just to remember one relevant point. It is also very important to show that you understand its significance in context.

In addition, the question is assessing your ability to select and apply your in-depth knowledge effectively and your ability to explain something clearly.

TIP

When answering, remember:

- Explain why.
- Answer the question that was asked. Do not spend time on other factors.
- Do not just list facts which might or might not be linked to the question.
- Make specific points and back them up with relevant and accurate detail.

Questions that highlight analysis and evaluation

There are many forms of question that ask you to show analysis and evaluation. These include questions that ask you to what extent / how far something was the case, or how important/significant something was. You might also be asked (for example) how effective or successful something was, or how far you agree with a view. All these questions are assessing your skills of analysis and evaluation.

Let's look at an example and see how it works in practice:

b How far do you agree with the view that Japan's motives for invading Manchuria in 1931 were economic rather than political? **[20 marks]**

- Your answer should contain a clear judgement or argument.

- Your answer should be entirely focused on this question. The question is not asking how successful the invasion was. It is asking whether you think economic factors were more important than political factors in explaining why Japanese troops took possession of Manchuria in 1931. Be careful not to write a narrative history of the invasion itself or spend time on the background history of relations between China and Japan unless you can show how such an account is directly linked to the question set.
- Demonstrate that you have thought about causative factors in general. You need to demonstrate an understanding of Japan's economic and political circumstances in 1931, and how they impacted on its foreign policy. For example, the growing unpopularity of Japan's democratically elected government, and the country's desperate need for new sources of raw materials at a time when it was facing major economic problems.
- Be balanced: show that you have considered the ways in which both economic and political factors can be used to explain why Japan invaded Manchuria.
- Demonstrate that you have thought about a wide range of issues, weighed them all up and reached your own conclusion.
- Offer knowledge and understanding by backing up the various points you make with accurate and relevant detail.

TIP

Tips for answering questions that ask 'How far do you agree?'

How far do you agree with the view that Japan's motives for invading Manchuria in 1931 were economic rather than political?

Try thinking about this in terms of a scale, with 'I completely agree because …' at one end, and 'I completely disagree because …' at the other, with 'I somewhat agree' and 'I somewhat disagree' in between:

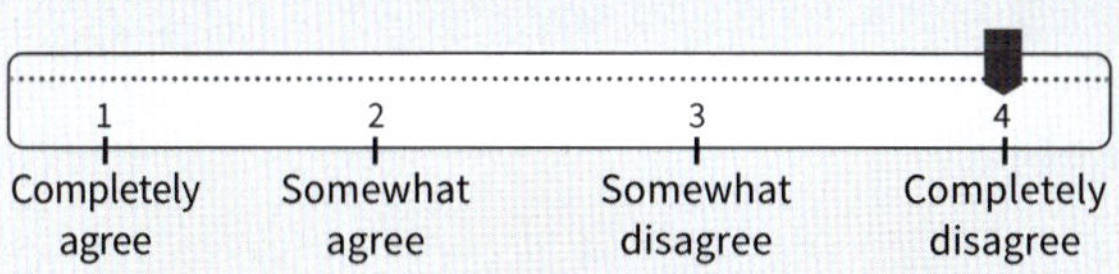

CONTINUED

Depending on where you are on the scale, your responses could begin with an opening section similar to one of these:

1. Economic factors were the principal motivations for Japan's invasion of Manchuria in 1931. This can be evidenced by … While there were other causative factors, such as … and …, they did not play nearly such an important part as the economic factors.
2. While political factors did play an important role in Japan's motivations for invading Manchuria in 1931, for the following reasons …, it was the economic factors that were more important. Economic factors were more important because …
3. Economic factors cannot be seen to have played anything other than a minor role in Japan's motivations for invading Manchuria in 1931. The principal causes were political, which can be seen by the growing unpopularity of Japan's democratically elected government, and the country's desperate need for new sources of raw materials …
4. Economic factors did not play a significant role as motivation for Japan's invasion of Manchuria in 1931. Much more important were … and … as it was these two factors which …

Opening sections like these demonstrate thinking about the relative importance of causes and not just trying to remember what all the causes were. Such opening sections show analytical skills and understanding, not just knowledge. Remember that all three are being assessed at AS Level.

Let's look at some other examples of questions that highlight analysis and evaluation.

A question might ask you to consider how effective someone or something was. If you were analysing the effectiveness of the League of Nations in the 1920s, a good response would:

- Be entirely focused on the League's effectiveness during the 1920s. The question is not asking about how the League came to be established, or why it failed to maintain international peace and security in the 1930s. It needs to be just about how effective it was during the 1920s, on a scale from very effective to very ineffective.
- Demonstrate evidence of thinking about how effectiveness might be shown in the very challenging circumstances confronting the League in the 1920s. Did the League maintain international peace? Did it uphold the Paris peace settlement, facilitating peaceful resolutions to border disputes and encouraging international disarmament? Did it have the support of all the major powers? It is important to show that you are thinking analytically.
- Demonstrate knowledge and understanding by identifying the League's aims and the various ways in which the League influenced international relations during the 1920s.
- Show analytical ability by weighing up the League's stated aims, commenting on the extent to which you consider its actions during the 1920s to be effective or not. The focus should be on the effectiveness of each action, but there should also be comment on the overall effectiveness.

Similarly, a question might ask how successful something was at achieving its aim. For such a question, you would use a similar approach as when analysing how effective something was. For example, if assessing the success of attempts to improve international relations during the 1920s, you should consider whether success means easing tensions between France and Germany? Reducing the Western Powers' concerns regarding Japanese intentions in the Far East? Establishing an organisation designed to prevent future wars? Such a question requires an examination of evidence for the impact which the various attempts to improve international relations had aimed for – specific examples being the conferences in Genoa (1922) and Locarno (1925). A good response will come to a firm judgement based on the evidence. Avoid vague responses such as 'It had some effect'. Argue your case strongly.

Another question might ask 'how far' or 'to what extent' something was the case. This type of question is also assessing your analytical skills. You would have to give a firm judgement on the issue of extent. So if you are analysing the extent to which the Berlin Conference can be considered a success, you should also provide evidence that you have analysed the negative outcomes of the conference or the problems it did not solve, then you should come to a conclusion based on the evidence.

Whatever the wording of the question, remember that you need to show strong evidence of analysis and evaluation as well as knowledge and understanding.

TIP

Plan your answer before you start to write. You could set out plans for the longer essay-based questions, such as 'To what extent ...', in columns headed 'case for' and 'case against' – or as a mind-map, which has a focus on thinking out an answer. A plain list of facts will not be much help as a plan. Use the plan to clarify your ideas on what the question is asking.

Structuring an answer

Consider the following practice question:

b 'Imperial tensions brought European powers closer to war before 1914.' How far do you agree? **[20 marks]**

Different students will take different approaches to this type of question, and you will find your own preferred approach. While you are developing your techniques, you might find the structure presented in Table 4.2 helpful. Even if you choose to organise your essay differently, it is important to note the strengths of this one and apply the same principles in your own writing.

Paragraph	Content
1	This needs to contain a clear answer to the question. Did imperial tensions bring European colonial powers closer to war or not? An answer might be, for example: *Although European powers went to war in 1914 and imperial affairs were certainly a cause of some tension before 1914, it would not be true to say that imperial tensions ever really threatened to lead to war. Evidence in support of this view includes:* *(a) …* *(b) …* *(c) …* This paragraph does not need to contain much detail, just broad reasons. The paragraph should demonstrate that you are focusing on the question and thinking analytically. Mention briefly possible points 'against' – (d) and (e) – to develop later and show the required analysis and balance. Avoid vague introductions or trying to 'set the scene'.
2	In this paragraph you could take point (a) and develop it in detail. Make sure that the objective of the paragraph is made clear from the start, for example: *The principal reason for suggesting that imperial tensions did not bring European powers close to war was …* Then include three or four accurate and relevant facts to back up your point: the evidence. This section might also explain why you feel this particular issue was the most important point, highlighting an analytical approach.
3	You could develop point (b) here in a similar way. Again, take care to ensure that the objective of the paragraph is made clear: that you are relating what you write very obviously to your answer that imperial tensions did not bring Europe close to war. There is often a tendency to forget the purpose of the paragraph and simply list the facts. A list of facts often leaves the reader asking, 'So … ?'
4	Make the objective clear and add as much commentary as you can to explain why this point is less important than (a).
5	This is a good place to develop the case 'against' the view in points (d) and (e), to demonstrate the balance required in this type of response. There is nothing wrong with strong arguments, however, and if you feel there is no case 'against', say so and why. It might still be a good idea to start this paragraph with, for example: *Those who support the view that European powers came close to war because of imperial disagreements might argue that …* and bring out a possible defence of this view, however weak you might think it is.
6	If you have developed your response, your final paragraph can be quite brief. Avoid repetition and do not just summarise previous points but make it clear why you have reached your conclusion. The best final paragraphs contain either a definitive judgement (avoid a vague 'to some extent … ' and make sure your judgement doesn't conflict with the initial one – do not change your mind!) or a final clinching argument (the main reason why you have come to that conclusion) which reinforces your opening views.

Table 4.2: An example answer structure for a question that highlights analysis and evaluation.

TIP

- Make sure you that you answer the question in your introduction. Writing an introduction means that if you run out of time, you will still have answered the question. Otherwise you may find that you have to stop writing when you have only presented the case 'for' and 'against' the view, without demonstrating analysis or judgement.
- Avoid getting into a situation where you present a long and detailed 'for' the view in the question and a briefer and undeveloped case 'against' the view – and then briefly conclude that the case 'against' is stronger, even though all the facts presented point the other way. This would mean that you cannot provide enough analysis to fully answer the question.

4.3 Revision techniques

Too often, students think that the purpose of revision is to get information into their brain in preparation for an assessment. It is seen as a process where facts are learned. However, if you have followed the course appropriately and made sensibly laid-out notes as you have gone along, all the information you need is already there. The key purpose of revision is not to gain new information, but to ensure that you can retrieve the knowledge you have learned when it is required.

Revision needs to be an ongoing process throughout the course, not just in the days or weeks before an exam. The focus of your revision should be identifying the key points, on, for example, why there was dissatisfaction with the peace treaties of 1919. Making good notes as you study the course content will help you do this (see the Getting started with Cambridge International AS Level History section).

Quality revision and plenty of practice in attempting questions under timed conditions are essential. If you feel you have not practised enough at school, you could ask your teacher to provide some questions so you can practise on your own under timed conditions.

4.4 Assessment preparation

This section offers a few general points about how you could approach an assessment. Some might seem obvious, but it is worth remembering that, under pressure, we are all capable of making mistakes. It is useful to be aware of potential pitfalls.

The syllabus includes details of what you need to know during your course and for assessment. You should be aware of:

- What topics the questions can be about. This will be covered during your course.
- What form the questions can take. Your teacher can help you understand the types of task you are likely to face, and the syllabus will give details of wording.
- How long you will have to answer a question paper.
- Which parts of a question paper you can ignore. Some papers might have separate sections for those who have studied Modern Europe and for those who have studied US History.
- The equipment you will need for writing and what you may or may not bring into an exam room. There are very strict rules on mobile phones, for example, and smart watches. Check if you are allowed to bring water in.

Rubric

All question papers contain rubric. This provides you with essential information about how long a timed assessment will last, how many questions you must answer and from what sections, and so on. Students can make rubric errors by attempting too many questions, for example, or questions from inappropriate sections of a paper. These basic errors can really damage your chances of success.

Timing

It is a good idea to work out in advance how long you have to complete each question or part of a question. Make a note of it and make every effort to keep to that timing.

Practising answering questions under timed conditions is something you can do on your own as part of your revision. Take care not to make the mistake of spending too much time on a question which you know a great deal about and leave yourself insufficient time for a question which might carry twice as many marks.

If you run out of time, you will not be able to answer all the questions fully. If you have spent too long on your first question with its two parts, it might be a good idea to attempt the second part of the next question if it carries more marks.

Planning

There is nearly always the temptation in an exam to just get started rather than spending time on planning. Without planning, however, there is a risk that you will include irrelevant information, or not fully explain the relevance of information. So, make a plan before you start to write!

How much should I write?

There is no requirement to write a specific number of words in a response, nor to fill a certain number of pages. Aim to keep your focus on writing a relevant response to the question set and making sure that you are aware of the assessment criteria for the type of question you are dealing with. Do not worry if another student seems to be writing more than you are.

What can I use to help me prepare for assessment?

Exam boards provide materials to help students and their teachers prepare for assessment. It is important to make full use of these materials. They include:

- the syllabus
- past papers
- mark schemes for those papers
- examiner reports on students' performance in examinations
- the assessment objectives for papers.

The syllabus

The syllabus provides:

- details of the options to be studied at AS Level
- how many options have to be taken
- how long each examination is
- what proportion of the overall marks are allocated to each paper
- the assessment objectives and the relationship between them and the different papers you take
- details of each of the papers
- the Key questions (these indicate broad areas of history for study; all questions will be based on the Key questions)
- key content.

Past papers

Past papers are helpful in two ways. First, past papers show you the types of question that have been set in the past. You can see how marks were allocated and calculate how much time you should spend on similar questions or sub-questions. Be careful, however – syllabuses are updated regularly so you may see past paper questions on subject content which is no longer included in the syllabus, or there may have been other changes. Always refer carefully to the syllabus for your year of examination.

Second, past papers help you to revise and practise. The same questions will not be asked again, but you can see the type of question that could be asked, and check whether you have the knowledge and understanding to answer a similar question. Planning an answer to a past question will encourage you to think about that topic and consider the points that you might make when answering such a question.

Mark schemes

Mark schemes accompany the question papers and make it clear how your work will be assessed. They are usually in two parts, a generic one and one for each question set:

- A **generic mark scheme** will help you to understand how answers are marked and what needs to be included in a good answer. It specifies the elements that make up high-quality work, such as developed analysis, balance or source analysis/evaluation.
- An **indicative content mark scheme** will give you a good idea of the sort of answer that is expected. Remember that there is never a 'right' answer to a question in History at this level.

For example, for a question asking you to compare two sources, you can see the sort of similarities and differences in the two sources that you should discuss, the sort of contextual knowledge that you might include in your answer, as well as comments on the provenance of the sources. You can also see how you can develop points from the sources to support your answer.

For an essay-based question you can see the level of explanation needed and the sort of points you might make. The mark scheme will give you a clear idea of the depth you will need to write a good answer and the sort of arguments that you might develop. You do not have to mention every point or fact in the mark scheme.

In summary, mark schemes help you to see what a good-quality answer looks like. You can use this knowledge to reflect on your own work and consider how it might be improved.

Examiner reports

After every examination, a detailed report is written on how students performed. These can be helpful as they highlight both the stronger answers (so, note those answers' strengths!) and the weaker answers (so, do not repeat those answers' weaknesses!). It is worth looking at several examiner reports for both source-based and essay-based papers. You will see what types of answer have performed well.

Common errors (and how to avoid them!)

When preparing for assessment, try to avoid the following errors – they are more common than you might think.

- **Poor time management.** Do not spend too long on the first part of a question, leaving yourself too little time to answer the second part. So, practise writing answers under timed conditions.
- **Lack of planning.** Clear planning will help you to make sure that your answer is focused on the question being asked.

> **TIP**
>
> You might like to write a little mind-map or similar, to help you pause and think about your topic before starting to write. Have a think about what style of plan works best for you.

- **Long introductions to essay-based questions asking you how far you agree with a view (or similar).** Such introductions are not necessary and waste a lot of time. So, avoid these – get on and answer the question.
- **Supporting paragraphs which contain a lot of detail but no clear point.** If you provide facts that are relevant and accurate, but it is not clear what point you are making, you are likely to demonstrate your historical knowledge well, but not your skills in historical explanation, analysis and judgement. So, make sure the purpose of a paragraph is clear. Link it carefully back to the argument being made.
- **An implicit answer.** This means that the answer to the question is hinted at but not clearly stated. This weakness is especially common in essay-based questions which ask students how far they agree with a view. Students sometimes provide a list of factors 'for' the view and a list of factors 'against' the view – but they do not actually answer the question. The facts might point to a conclusion, but the response never actually provides one. So, answer the question.
- **Lack of awareness of what the command words require.** So, explain or compare when you are asked to – do not just describe.
- **Writing the answer to a question you wished you had got, not the one you did get.** You may have done a brilliant essay on the League's failure to achieve its aims some months ago, but the question set is specifically about the League's failure to achieve disarmament. So, don't write a general answer about the topic, write a specific response to this exact question!
- **Too little time spent reading the sources.** Often key points which just happen to be towards the end of the last source never get mentioned. So, spend enough time reading all the sources very carefully (highlighting key points, etc.). And make sure you double-check the last source!

Careful preparation is the key to success in assessment. We hope this guidance will help you to achieve to the best of your abilities.

Glossary

Advocate: To argue strongly for something; an advocate is someone who argues strongly for something.

Alliance system: A formal agreement between two or more states for mutual support in case of war.

Allies, the: The term that the British Empire, the French, the Russians, and later the Americans used to describe their own military alliance during the First World War. Because of the Triple Entente, signed in 1904–07, these countries were also known as the Entente powers.

Annex: To take possession of a territory, usually by force or without permission.

Antisemitism: Hostility towards, and discrimination against, Jewish people.

Appeasement: A policy of giving in to demands made by aggressive nations rather than confronting these demands.

Arbitrary: Not based on a system (this means that if something is seen as arbitrary it is often believed to be unfair).

Arbitration: The settling of a dispute between two parties by an impartial third party.

Armistice: An agreement between all sides in a war to stop fighting for a certain time (also known as a truce).

Assimilation: The process of becoming similar to others by taking in and using their customs and culture.

Balance of payments: The difference between the money coming into a country and the money going out of it. An adverse balance of payments occurs when a country pays out more money to import goods and services than it brings in by exporting goods and services.

Boer: People of southern Africa who trace their ancestry back to Dutch, German and French settlers who moved to the area in the late 17th century. The Boers' present-day descendants are the Afrikaners.

Bolshevik Party: A communist party led by Lenin, which seized power in Russia in the second Russian Revolution in October 1917.

Budget deficit: When a government is paying more money to run the country than it is receiving in taxes.

Bureaucratic: Describes the way a government runs using state officials, systems and rules to make important decisions, rather than based on decisions by elected representatives.

Capitalism: An economic and political system in which individuals, rather than the state, own businesses to make a profit.

Central Powers: The term used by the Allies to describe the military alliance of Germany, Austria-Hungary, Bulgaria and the Turkish Empire during the First World War. Because of the Triple Alliance, signed in 1882, these countries were also known as the Triple Alliance powers.

Charter: A written grant by a superior power, by which a body such as a company is founded and/or has its rights defined.

Civil war: A war between people, groups or armies from the same country.

Collective security: The idea that if any member state of the League of Nations was threatened, all the other member states would work together to defend it.

Colonies: Areas under the direct or indirect control of another country, acquired by colonisation processes.

Comintern: An organisation created by Lenin in 1919 with the aim of spreading communism and starting a worldwide anti-capitalist revolution. The term is short for Communist International.

Commonwealth: A group of former British colonies, which had become largely independent but retained the British monarch as their head of state. These countries provided many troops to fight with Britain in the First World War.

Communist: Supporting (or someone who supports) communism, a system of social, political and economic organisation in which all property is owned by the community and each person contributes according to their abilities and receives whatever they need.

Concentration camps: Places where prisoners or members of persecuted minorities are imprisoned in a small area, and with inadequate facilities.

Concession: Something that is allowed or given up to one party in a dispute to get their agreement in other areas. To give something up in this way is to concede it.

Conciliation: Trying to reach a peaceful settlement to a dispute and reduce tension.

Congress: A congress is a formal meeting between delegates. In the context of US politics, 'Congress' refers to two institutions which, together, form the law-making branch of the federal (national) government. Congress meets in the Capitol building in Washington DC. The two institutions (the Senate and the House of Representatives), which occupy one end each of the Capitol building, have slightly different roles. The Senate takes more responsibility for American foreign policy.

Consensus: General agreement between people.

Constitution: The set of rules according to which a country or organisation is run.

Constitutional monarchy: A system in which a country is ruled by a king or queen; however the ruler's powers are limited by a set of rules known as a constitution, and most power lies with democratically elected ministers who are accountable to an elected parliament.

Consul: An official appointed by a state to live in a foreign country to protect the state's citizens' interests there.

Consumerism: Where the focus of the economy is on the interests of consumers (ordinary citizens), that is, on producing things which improve the quality of life of individuals, as opposed to producing things like tanks or battleships.

Council of Ambassadors: An intergovernmental agency founded in 1920 with the task of implementing the terms of the Paris peace settlement and mediating territorial disputes between European states. Chaired by the French foreign minister, the other nations represented were Britain, Italy and Japan. Because of its decision not to ratify the Paris peace settlement, the USA had observer status only (it could oversee the rulings of the Council of Ambassadors but had no power to change them).

Covenant: A written, formal and binding agreement.

Deflation: Falling prices caused by a drop in demand. This leads to falling wages and unemployment, which, in turn, further reduces demand as fewer people can afford to buy goods.

Democracy: A system of government where the whole population have some political power. People govern themselves, usually through representatives who are chosen periodically in elections.

Democrats and Republicans: The two major political parties in the USA are the Republican and Democratic (or Democrat) Parties.

Deterrent: Something which discourages a person from doing something. For example, the possibility of a prison sentence could be a deterrent to committing a crime.

Dictator: A leader of a country who has no limits to their power.

Disarmament: Reducing the size of armies, navies and air forces, as well as certain military resources such as submarines and tanks.

Economic depression: A situation when demand for goods and services drop, investment declines, prices fall and unemployment rises.

Economic sanctions: Refusing to trade with a nation, hoping that such economic pressure will force the nation to act differently.

Egalitarianism: Belief in the principle that all people are equal and deserve equal rights and opportunities.

Entente: Less formal than a treaty, an entente is a friendly understanding or informal agreement between states.

Ethnic: Relating to a group of people who share a common history and culture.

Expansionism: The policy of expanding the size of the territories under a country's control.

Fascist: Supporting (or someone who supports) fascism, a political philosophy which believes in state control over all aspects of society and the economy and is heavily nationalistic. In a fascist state, power is held by a small elite, usually under the direction of a dictator, and political opposition is banned. A fascist government maintains power through control of the country's armed forces.

Federation: A group of states which have independence over their own internal affairs but are organised and controlled by a single central government.

Feudalism: The main form of social, political and economic organisation in the medieval and early modern world. Land and power was distributed to the nobility by the monarch, and taxes and military service were provided to the monarch by the lower classes in society.

General strike: A national strike, or refusal to work, by all the workers in major industries, such as transport, energy and manufacturing, in a country on the same day.

Genocide: The deliberate and systematic destruction of an ethnic, racial, religious or national group.

Gold standard: A monetary system where a country's currency or paper money has a value directly linked to gold.

Great Depression: The period between c.1929 and c.1936 when many national economies collapsed. There was rapid deflation, mass unemployment and serious poverty in almost every developed nation.

Great power: The term 'great power' was first used in the early 1800s to describe the five most powerful countries in Europe: the Austrian Empire, France, Great Britain, Prussia and Russia.

Home Front: The activities of civilians in Britain during wartime, in contrast to overseas 'fronts' (for example, the British army went overseas to the 'Western Front' in France in 1914–18).

Imperialism: The policy of extending a nation's power by gaining political and economic control over more territory. This is sometimes referred to as colonialism and the territories taken under control are known as colonies.

Indigenous: Relating to the people who lived in a place long before the arrival of colonists.

Industrialisation: The process of economic change a country undergoes as agriculture becomes less important and manufacturing industries become larger and more important.

Inflation: A process that leads to an increase in the price of goods and services. It drives down the value of income and savings, discouraging investment and causing demands for increased wages. This loss of value in turn leads to higher prices, an inflationary spiral that can result in increased unemployment.

International Red Cross: An organisation founded in Geneva, Switzerland, in 1863 with the aim of easing the suffering of people affected by war and armed conflict across the world. The International Committee of the Red Cross has been awarded the Nobel Prize on three occasions, in 1917, 1944 and 1963.

International relations: The relationships between countries.

Isolationism: The policy of keeping one's country separate from the affairs of other nations, by avoiding alliances and international commitments.

Latin America: The parts of North, South, and Central America south of the United States, where Spanish, Portuguese or French are spoken by many people.

League of Nations: An international organisation, of which every country in the world could be a member, designed to provide solutions to problems and disputes between nations.

Lease: An agreement by which land is given, for a specific period of time, in return for payment.

Lebensraum: Literally 'living room'. Hitler dreamed of the German people expanding eastwards and dominating much of east and central Europe. He wanted the farmland and the natural resources in those regions, such as coal, iron ore and oil.

Left-wing: Supporting the political 'left'; believing that all parts of society should share wealth and power.

Legitimate government: A government that is accepted both by the people of the country and also by other nations as having a right to rule that country.

Legitimate: Allowed or accepted by laws or rules.

Liberal: Believing (or someone who believes) that government should allow as much personal and economic freedom as possible.

Liberal democracy: Where a government is elected and implements liberal principles such as the rule of law, protection for individual rights and liberties and freedom of speech.

Mandates: Overseas territories taken from the defeated countries at the end of the First World War. Responsibility for these territories was passed to other countries, which would administer them on behalf of the League of Nations.

Memorandum: A short report, written specially for a person or group of people, containing information on a particular subject.

Mercantilism: An economic policy based on the belief that there was only a limited amount of wealth in the world. European nations aimed to increase their share of that wealth at the expense of their rivals. This situation encouraged the acquisition of colonies and led to frequent wars.

Militarism: The belief that a country should use force and its military to achieve its foreign policy goals.

Nationalism: A sense of belonging to a nation and supporting its interests above those of other nations. Also the belief that your country is superior ethnically, culturally, politically and historically to all other countries.

Nationalist: Someone who strongly identifies with their nation and supports its interests, even where this may harm the interests of other nations.

Naval race: An arms race in which two or more countries build warships to maintain an advantage over their rivals.

Neutrality: Staying out of a conflict; not supporting either side in a war. Countries which do this are known as neutral countries.

Pacifist: Someone who opposes war or violence as a means of settling disputes.

Pact: A formal agreement. It could mean a treaty between two or more countries, as in the case of the Rapallo Pact, or an agreement to recommend a course of action, as in the case of the Hoare–Laval pact.

Parliament: The organisation within a government that makes laws.

Passive resistance: Taking an action which does not involve any violence to prevent your opponents achieving their objectives: for example, refusing to work or sitting down and blocking a road.

Patriotism: Love for and pride in your country.

Plebiscite: A referendum (vote) in which local people express their opinion for or against a proposal relating to a constitutional issue.

Political extremism: When people are attracted to radical political ideas such as fascism on the 'Right' or communism on the 'Left', rather than to liberal democracy.

Popular Front: A government made up of an alliance of many different left-wing groups and parties, such as communists, socialists and radical liberals.

Possessions: In the context of imperialism, areas under the control of another country, acquired by any means, including colonisation, conquest, purchase or lease (an agreement by which a land is given, for a specific time, in return for payment).

Private enterprise: Businesses owned and managed by individuals, free of government restrictions.

Progressive: Supporting (or someone who supports) social reform.

Propaganda: Communication designed to influence an audience to support a specific action or political agenda. It does so by spreading ideas, information or rumours in ways that appeal to people's beliefs and feelings.

Protectionism: The placing of high tariffs on imports to protect domestic industries from foreign competition. Protectionism is the opposite of free trade.

Protectorate: A territory under indirect rule, that is, under the protection but not direct control of another country. Local rulers retained control over internal affairs and the colonial power controlled defence and foreign relations.

Protocol: A written proposal which, if agreed by all nations, would become a binding agreement.

Purges: The term given to Stalin's elimination of his opponents. To prevent any opposition, hundreds of thousands of potential opponents were murdered and millions sent to slave camps in Siberia to be worked to death. The victims included most of the senior officers in the army, navy and air force.

Putsch: An attempt to overthrow a government using violence.

Racism: A belief in the superiority of one race over another, based on prejudice and leading to discrimination.

Radical: Supporting (or someone who supports) drastic or complete change.

Ratify: To give formal acceptance to something.

Reparations: Money that one country has to pay another as compensation for war damage.

Reservations: Areas of land set aside for members of an indigenous group.

Revisionist: Wishing to change something, or someone who wishes to change something.

Right-wing: Describing people or groups, often strong nationalists, whose political beliefs are based on an ordered society that values tradition and discipline. They usually oppose socialism and communism, believing that social inequality is natural and desirable, and because both pose a threat to private property.

Scorched earth: A battle tactic in which an army deliberately burns crops and property in an area to deny the enemy food and shelter.

Scramble for Africa: The phrase 'Scramble for Africa' was first used in the British newspaper *The Times*, in 1884. Since then, it has been used by historians to describe the way European powers competed to gain control of territory in Africa, between approximately 1870 and 1914.

Self-determination: The principle that people of common nationality should have the right to form their own nations and govern themselves.

Slav: A member of a group of peoples in central and eastern Europe speaking Slavic languages.

Socialism: An economic and political philosophy that pursues social ownership of the means of production (for example, factories), as opposed to private ownership.

Socialist: Supporting (or someone who supports) socialism – an economic and political philosophy that pursues social ownership of the means of production (for example, factories), as opposed to private ownership.

Sovereignty: The right to supreme power or authority.

Sphere of influence: An area in which a country has the power to affect events and developments, despite it being outside the country's direct control.

Stock market: A place where shares are bought and sold. Companies sell shares to raise the money (capital) required to establish their factories and businesses. People buy shares in a company as an investment to gain from its subsequent profits.

Stormtroopers: Nazi gangs that specifically used violence against Hitler's opponents.

Successor states: Newly formed states whose territory and population were previously under the sovereignty of another state.

Tariff: A tax imposed on specific goods imported from specific countries, usually used to make those goods more expensive than the locally produced alternatives.

Third Reich: The term used by Hitler that linked the present with Germany's past glories. The First Reich (empire) was the Holy Roman Empire (962–1806). The Second Reich followed the unification of Germany in 1871 and lasted until 1918.

Totalitarian: A system of government that is centralised and dictatorial and requires complete obedience to the state.

Trade union: An organisation formed with the aim of improving the treatment of workers in a specific field of work.

Triple Entente: The name given to Britain, France and the Russian Empire – the countries that signed ententes in 1904 and 1907.

Ultimatum: A final demand that, if rejected, will lead to serious consequences such as war.

Unanimous: Agreed by everyone.

Unification: A process of becoming unified or made whole. In the case of Germany, the process by which the various German states were formed into the country of Germany during the 19th century.

Unviable: Unlikely to work; having no chance of success. (Something that can work is known as 'viable'.)

Violating/violation: Breaking or acting against something, for example a law, agreement (such as a treaty), or something that should be treated with respect.

Western powers: A term used to refer to the European countries with the most powerful economies, armies and navies, and the USA.

Westernisation: The process of becoming more like a country in the so-called Western world (usually including the countries in western Europe, North America and Australasia).

Working-class: Belonging to the working class, a group in society consisting of people who work, often in jobs involving physical labour, and who earn or possess little money compared to other social classes.

Acknowledgements

The authors and publishers acknowledge the following sources of copyright material and are grateful for the permissions granted. While every effort has been made, it has not always been possible to identify the sources of all the material used, or to trace all copyright holders. If any omissions are brought to our notice, we will be happy to include the appropriate acknowledgements on reprinting.

Thanks to the following for permission to reproduce images:

Cover Leemage/Corbis via Getty Images; *Inside* **Chapter 1** Universal History Archive/GI; London Stereoscopic Company/GI; Fig. 1.6 Simplicissimus (3 May 1904), vol. ix, no. 6, p. 58, drawing by Wilhelm Schulz; Duncan1890/GI; De Agostini Picture Library/GI; Stock Montage/GI; Universal History Archive/GI; Paul Popper/Popperfoto via Getty Images; Print Collector/GI; Hulton Archive/GI; Universal History Archive/GI; DEA Picture Library/GI; Jon Bower/ Alamy Stock Photo; Fig. 1.18 source unconfirmed; Foto search/GI; Heritage Images/GI; Universal History Archive/ GI; Chronicle/Alamy Stock Photo; Print Collector/GI; Signal Photos/Alamy Stock Photo; Punch Cartoon Library/ TopFoto; Universal History Archive/GI; Universal Images Group/GI; Leemage/GI; Hulton Archive/GI; Bettmann/GI x2; Interim Archives/GI; Bettmann/GI x2; Hulton Archive/GI; Bettmann/GI; Heritage Images/GI; **Chapter 2** Harold Cunningham/GI; Historical/GI; Hulton Archive/GI; Bettmann/GI; Fig. 2.4 by Burt Randolph Thomas, The Detroit News in Review of Reviews, Vol. 59, No. 6, pp. 570 (via Wikimedia Commons); Chronicle/Alamy Stock Photo; Walter Sanders/GI; Hulton Archive/GI x2; Granger- Historical Picture Archive/Alamy Stock Photo; Punch Cartoon Library/ Topfoto x2; Universal Images Group/GI; Bettmann/GI x2; Archive Photos/GI; Apic/GI; Universal Images Group/ GI; Chronicle/Alamy Stock Photo x2; Three Lions/GI; Chronicle of World History/Alamy Stock Photo; Culture Club/GI; Bettmann/GI; Culture Club/GI; Album/Alamy Stock Photo; Hulton Deutsch/GI; AFP/GI; Fig. 2.29 from The Digs (photo archive of the Pittsburgh Post Gazette); Granger- Historical Picture Archive/Alamy Stock Photo; **Chapter 3** Historical/GI; Bettmann/GI; Wikimedia Commons; Hulton Archive/GI; Fig 3.2 Library of Congress LC-USZ62-39035; Sueddeutsche Zeitung Photo/Alamy Stock Photo; Granger- Historical Picture Archive/Alamy Stock Photo; Wikimedia Commons; Digital Commons; Henry Guttmann Collection/GI; Punch Cartoon Library/ Topfoto; Granger- Historical Picture Archive/Alamy Stock Photo; Art Media/Print Collector/GI; Hulton Archive/ GI; Universal History Archive/GI; Album/Alamy; Keystone-France/GI; Keystone/GI; Universal History Archive/GI; Fig. 3.20 © Northern Friends' Peace Board; Keystone-France/GI; Chronicle/Alamy Stock Photo; Hulton Deutsch/GI; Fox Photos/GI; Bettmann/GI; Fig 3.26 by McCutcheon, Chicago Tribune; Granger- Historical Picture Archive/Alamy Stock Photo; Punch Cartoon Library/Topfoto; Three Lions/GI; Fig. 3.32 'Extinguished' cartoon by Strube reproduced with the permission of Mirrorpix, image courtesy of the British Cartoon Archive; Ullstein Bild Dtl/GI; CBW/Alamy Stock Photo; Figure 3.35 by Leslie Gilbert Illingworth, used by permission of Llyfrgell Genedlaethol Cymru / The National Library of Wales and dmg media licensing; Album/Alamy Stock Photo; Hulton Archive/GI; **Chapter 4** Chris Ryan/GI; Universal History Archive/GI; STF/GI

Cartoons by David Low in Figures 2.26, 2.27, 3.5, 3.6, 3.10, 3.28, 4.1 are reproduced with permission of dmg media licensing, images courtesy of the British Cartoon Archive

GI = Getty Images

Index